POETS OF THE YOUNGER GENERATION

· RICHARD · HOVEY ·

POETS OF THE YOUNGER GENERATION

BY

WILLIAM ARCHER

WITH THIRTY-THREE FULL-PAGE
PORTRAITS FROM WOODCUTS BY
ROBERT BRYDEN

AMS PRESS
NEW YORK

Reprinted from the edition of London and New York, 1902
First AMS EDITION published 1970
Manufactured in the United States of America

International Standard Book Number: 0-404-00367-2

Library of Congress Card Catalog Number: 76-120572

AMS PRESS, INC.
NEW YORK, N.Y. 10003

PREFATORY NOTE

*This book was ready for the press in the autumn of 1899,
when the outbreak of the war in South Africa led to the
postponement of publication. Two years—and such years
—are a long time. There is nothing in the book that I
do not believe to-day, as I did two years ago; but there
are many things which, were I writing to-day, I should
express differently. For instance, several poets who in
1898–99 were "still more or less on probation," are now
on probation no longer, and the tone of advocacy which I
have here and there adopted may perhaps seem uncalled
for. It is not my fault, however, that the great critic,
Time, has in these cases been beforehand with me. I
tried to anticipate his judgment; he has turned the tables
and anticipated mine.*

*A few additions have been made to the text in the
interim; but the book stands substantially as I wrote it in
1898–99.*

*Mr. E. C. Stedman's Anthology of American Poetry,
with its 580 names, for the most part of living writers,
has shown me how superficial has been my survey
of the transatlantic field. But it has also shown me the
hopelessness of attempting to do more than cull a flower
here and there in so vast and luxuriant a prairie.*

v

PREFATORY NOTE

The title I originally had in mind was Living Poets of the Younger Generation; *but while the book lay in manuscript, the death of that very able writer, Mr. Richard Hovey, made a melancholy gap in my list of "living" poets. Death having, so to speak, called him out of the rank, I have made Mr. Hovey's portrait the frontispiece of this volume. A fortuitous ground of selection was the only one possible in a book in which any attempt at comparing values, or establishing an order of merit, is deliberately abjured.*

W. A.

August 1, 1901.

CONTENTS AND
LIST OF WOODCUTS

CONTENTS AND LIST OF WOODCUTS

POETS OF THE YOUNGER GENERATION

INTRODUCTION

APPRECIATION is the end and aim of the following pages. The verb " to appreciate " is used, rightly or wrongly, in two senses ; it sometimes means to realise, at other times to enhance, the value of a thing. I use the word in both significations. While attempting to define, to appraise, the talent of individual poets, I hope to enhance the reader's estimate of the value of contemporary poetry as a whole. Some readers, of course, may already have formed a higher estimate than mine of the body of work which is here reviewed : but the general tendency among cultivated people is, I think, to assume that English poetry has of late entered on a (temporary or permanent) period of decadence. Criticism has made great play with the supercilious catch-word " minor poet." No one denies, of course, that there are greater and lesser lights in the firmament of song ; but I do most strenuously deny that the lesser lights, if they be stars at all and not mere factitious fireworks, deserve to be spoken of with contempt. Now a shade of contempt has certainly attached of late years to the term " minor poet," which has given it a depressing and sterilising effect. It is this effect that I would fain counteract in some degree, by ignoring an invidious and inessential distinction. The valid distinction, the only one that really matters, is between true poets and poets falsely so-called. All the writers dealt with in the ensuing pages are, in my estimation, true poets, however small may be the bulk of their work, however unequal its merit; for a poet should be judged by his best work, not by his worst. I do not for a moment doubt that some of the writers whom I discuss will be reckoned by posterity among the major poets of our time; others, very probably, will take minor rank. I leave the distinction to posterity; it does not at present concern me. Only this I know, that the surest way to check the growth of a rising talent is to affix to its possessor the sneering label of " minor poet."

It is impossible in such a book as this to adopt any principle of inclusion and exclusion that shall not give offence, probably in many quarters. It may perhaps obviate some misunderstanding if I explain the sense in which I employ on the title-page the phrase " of the Younger Generation." My rule has been to include only poets born since 1850— poets, that is to say, who have lived entirely within the half century which has just come to an end. But I have not looked very closely into birth certificates. My choice has been ultimately guided by another consideration more essential than the mere accident of age. I have dealt only with those poets who still seemed to be more or less on probation— whose position was still in some degree a matter of doubt. This principle excluded not only the great poets of the older generation, Mr. Swinburne and Mr. Meredith, but such admirable writers as Mr. W. E. Henley, Mr. Robert Bridges, and Mr. Austin Dobson, whose uncontested genius needs no further vindication.

I am far from assuming that my list includes all those poets who, in point of age and position, might justly have claimed a place in it. The output of verse, as all reviewers know, is so huge, that very probably the work of more than one poet whom I would willingly have included lies buried in the mass, and has never happened to come within my ken. Other writers, again, I have regretfully omitted for no better reason than that their work does not happen to chime with my idiosyncrasy. Intellectually, I can recognise its merit ; but it does not touch my emotions : it leaves me cold. I could name several writers whose work I have read and re-read, while preparing this book, in the hope that my mere formal approval would kindle at some point or other into vital admiration ; but no amount of mental friction has generated the electric spark. I am quite willing to believe that in some of these cases the fault, the limitation, is on my side ; but this belief has not induced me to affect a warmth I do not feel. The one merit I claim for my criticism is sincerity. The things I praise are the things I genuinely and spontaneously enjoy ; and I could not if I would simulate such enjoyment. Every one, I presume, is subject to these personal limitations of taste ; at any rate, when I find a man who professes to enjoy everything in literature, I am apt to doubt whether he really enjoys anything. And enjoyment is to my thinking the essence, the soul, of poetical criticism. Familiarity with critical canons, power of logical analysis, breadth of philosophic intelligence, will be of no avail if the critic lack that emotional sensibility to which poetry (not in its emotional passages alone) makes its peculiar, its specific appeal.

The expression and justification of enjoyment being, then, the highest function of criticism—or at any rate the main purpose of this book—I have included only those poets whose work, or some substantial portion of it, gives me genuine pleasure. At the same time I have by no means refrained from criticism in the narrower sense of the word. What I have attempted in each case has been the definition or delimitation of a talent. Every poet, even the greatest, has done less mature and more mature, less successful and more successful, work. My effort has been to encourage readers to seek for and cling to what is noble, rare and permanent in a poet's work, not to persuade them, against all precedent and common sense, that any poet is infallible and evenly inspired throughout the whole mass of his production.

One somewhat inconvenient restriction I felt it necessary to impose upon myself from the outset. It would have been impertinent and essentially uncritical on my part to attempt to marshal the writers with whom I dealt in any order of merit, to range them in an ascending or descending scale. And as an imperfect and casual marshalling would have been as invidious as an exhaustive one, I found myself compelled to forswear all comparison whatsoever between the poets on my list. The essays are ranged in alphabetical order, and each writer is treated as though he or she were the only poet of the younger generation in England or America. This self-denying ordinance has cost me not a little trouble. Innumerable are the times when I have checked myself on the verge of slipping into the comparative mood. In some cases I have had to renounce what seemed to me a desirable elucidation or apt illustration, because it would have involved a parallel or contrast between two of the poets in question. Even where such confrontation would apparently have redounded to the honour of both, I have regarded it as the thin end of the wedge and have resolutely foregone it. Perhaps I have carried this scruple to the point of pedantry. I merely note it as one of the conditions which, rightly or wrongly, I felt to be imposed on me.

It follows from this that I could attempt no grouping in schools, or tracing of general tendencies. Regarding each poet as an isolated phenomenon, related only to the literature of the past, I have had to confine myself almost entirely to æsthetic criticism, the somewhat schoolmasterish testing of methods and results by standards generalised from the practice, as I understood it, of our classic writers. The poet's philosophy I have in every case accepted without cavil, trying to define it no doubt, and remonstrating when it seemed to me obscure (for lucidity, after all, is a technical quality like another), but neither examining into its merits, nor attempting to place it in relation to the intellectual currents of the time. For such an attempt, indeed, my knowledge would probably not have sufficed ; wherefore I had the less difficulty in renouncing it. As for grouping the poets in schools, that, too, was a task I readily pretermitted ; for the main characteristic of almost all the men and women of whom I treat seems to me to be their marked individuality, their total dissimilarity one from another. Here and there, two, or perhaps three, might have been bracketed together ; but from the point of view of a contemporary, the only perspective as yet attainable, it seems to me that the majority of the writers here dealt with defy co-ordination, and stand alone. If the reader will simply glance through the extracts I have been permitted to make, I think he will feel that whatever be the absolute power of this body of work, its variety could scarcely have been surpassed at any period of our literature.

If philosophical criticism was impossible to me, psychological criticism was almost equally out of the question. In very few cases had I any data to go upon, except those afforded by the poems themselves. " The most important data of all ! " it may be said, truly enough ; and I have of course tried to throw into relief such character-traits as I found imprinted on the work before me. But psychological criticism, to be of much value, must consist in the harmonisation of the talent and temperament revealed in the work of art, with family and personal history, or at least with non-artistic manifestations of idiosyncrasy and opinion. It must consist in the synthesis of external and internal data, the tracing of effects in art to causes in character and environment. It implies, in a word, a certain amount of biographical information, proceeding either from books or from personal knowledge. Now, in most cases, no such knowledge was available to me, and in no case did I regard it as my business to go in search of it, or to make use of such chance rumours as happened to have reached my ears. It would be possible, no doubt, for a writer of extraordinary tact and skill to go over exactly the ground I have covered and produce a gallery of critical character-sketches, instead of the series of talent-definitions here presented. Such a work would, under present conditions, be one of extreme delicacy ; and I, for my part, felt no impulse to attempt it. There is a time for everything, and, in the case of most of the poets here dealt with, the time for psychological criticism, in the full sense of the word, has not yet come. When it does come, I hope the critics who take the task in hand may not find my preliminary studies of talent quite unhelpful towards the ultimate co-ordination of talent and character.

It may not be quite superfluous to mention that many of the poets here treated of are personally unknown to me, while with none have I more than the merest passing acquaintance. Whatever the errors of my criticism, they are in no case due to clique-enthusiasm.

Only one of the ensuing essays—that on Mr. A. E. Housman, reprinted by permission from the *Fortnightly Review*—has already appeared in anything like its present shape. In other papers I have embodied occasional passages and phrases from articles in the *Daily Chronicle*, the *Pall Mall Gazette*, the *Westminster Gazette*, the *Sketch*, and the *Pall Mall Magazine*. But to all intents and purposes the book is entirely new.

Mr. John M. Robertson, in his very able *New Essays towards a Critical Method* (1897), advances a plea for scientific criticism which puts to shame the irresponsible dilettantism of the following pages. I have already explained why, even had I possessed Mr. Robertson's intellectual machinery, I could scarcely have applied it to advantage in dealing with the productions of living men and women whose work is, by hypothesis, far from complete, and whose personal history is not yet before the public. One of Mr. Robertson's suggestions, however, which he puts forward as a far-off ideal, seems to me perfectly practicable even in the " ignorant present." It amounts to this, that the critic should give the reader and the person criticised an opportunity of checking his individual judgments, and estimating their value, by a reference to his general culture and habit of mind; so that (for example) an author whom he condemns in the present may know what authors of the past fall under a similar ban, and may possibly take comfort from the company in which he finds himself. But I will let Mr. Robertson himself expound his proposals. He writes :

The perfect scientific critic, the critic of the future perhaps, might be conceived as prefacing his every judgment—or the body of his judgments—with a confession of faith, bias, temperament, and training. As thus: "I have a leaning towards what is called 'exact' [or religious or mystical] thought, with [or without] a tenderness for certain forms of arbitrary [or spiritual] sentiment which prevail among many people I know and like. I value poetry as a stimulus to sympathy and moral zeal [or, as the beautiful expression of any species of feeling], caring little [or much] for cadence and phrase as such; accordingly I value Browning and Dante and Hugo above Heine and Musset and Tennyson * [or vice versâ]. . . . I am reverent [or irreverent] of august tradition and social propriety; and I have little taste [or, I care above all things] in imaginative literature, for those forms called realistic, as aiming at a close fidelity to everyday fact [or, for those exercises of invention which carry me most completely out of my normal relation to my

---

* If this were other than a mere formula, in which the particular names used are of no importance, one could not but wonder to find Dante figuring among the scorners of "cadence and phrase."—W. A.

surroundings]. I am a Unitarian [*or* a Baptist, *or* a Catholic, *or* an Agnostic], having been brought up in that persuasion [*or* having come to that way of thinking in mature life]. In politics I am ——. My main physical diathesis is ——. Finally, I am —— years of age in this year ——."

This is more than a merely sportive suggestion on Mr. Robertson's part. The day may very well come when every critic will be called upon to fill up some such schedule of temperament and qualification, in order that readers may know clearly through what medium they are invited to contemplate any given work of art.* Nowadays we are far enough from any such ideal. We do not even demand to know the name of a critic, so as to correlate one judgment with another; much less do we make any formal inquiry into his culture, his temperament, his prejudices. Yet it is only by such vague knowledge on these points as we can glean from the internal evidence his work affords, that we are able to attach anything like their true value to the simplest terms he employs. Engine-drivers are examined (at least we hope so) lest perchance they should prove to be colour-blind; but we apply no such tests to critics, though they are called upon to make infinitely subtler discriminations than the mere distinguishing of a red light from a green.

There is all the more likelihood, however, of Mr. Robertson's suggestion finding acceptance, since it is eminently comfortable to the egotist within us. Without inquiring whether I am fulfilling a duty or yielding to a temptation, I propose to give the reader some such material for checking the judgments contained in the following pages as Mr. Robertson's scientific ideal demands. Poetry being the sole question at issue, I shall confine my con-

---

* It might perhaps be desirable, for the guidance of the persons criticised, that a statement of the critic's athletic record, his chest-measurement and his fighting weight should be included.

fidences to such matters as seem to bear directly or indirectly upon my qualifications as a critic of poetry.

In the first place, I am a pure-bred Scotchman. There is some vague family legend of an ancestor of my father's having come from England with Oliver Cromwell and settled in Glasgow; but I never could discover any evidence for it. The only thing that speaks in its favour is that my name, common in England, is uncommon in Scotland. My maternal grandfather and grandmother both came of families that seem to have dwelt from time immemorial in and about Perth, at the gateway of the Highlands. This being so, it appears very improbable that there should not be some Keltic admixture in my blood; but I cannot absolutely lay my finger on any " Mac " among my forbears. Both my parents belong to families of a deeply religious cast of mind, ultra-orthodox in dogma, heterodox, and even vehemently dissenting, on questions of church government. I can trace some way back in my mother's family a strain of good, sound, orthodox literary culture and taste; of specially poetical faculty, little or none. It may perhaps be worth mentioning that one of my great-grandfathers or great-grand-uncles printed, and I believe edited, an edition of the poets, much esteemed in its day.

The earliest symptom I can find in myself that can possibly be taken as showing any marked relation to the poetic side of life, is an extreme susceptibility (very clearly inherited from my father) to simple, pathetic music. It is related that, even in my infancy, one special tune—the *Adeste Fideles*—if so much as hummed in my neighbourhood, would always make me howl lustily; and indeed to this day it seems to me infinitely pathetic. I have carried through life, without any sort of musical gift, and with a very imperfect apprehension of tonality, harmony, and the refinements and complexities of musical expression, this keen sensibility to the emotional effect of certain lovely rhythms and simple curves of notes. I am not sure that *Lascia ch'io pianga, Che farò senza Euridice,* and the cantabile in Chopin's Funeral March do not seem to me the very divinest utterances of the human spirit, before which all the achievements of all the poets fade and grow dim. But it is all one to me (or very nearly so) whether they are reeled off on a barrel-organ or performed by the greatest singers, the finest orchestra. Nay, my own performances of them, in the silent chamber-concerts of memory, are enough to bring the tears to my eyes.

I cannot remember that the poetry I learned at school interested or pleased me particularly—-" On Linden, when the sun was low," " Fitz-James was brave, yet to his heart," " The Assyrian came down like the wolf on the fold," and so forth. At about the normal age, fourteen to fifteen, I was seized with the normal attack of Byronism, knew by heart " The Isles of Greece," " Then rose from sea to sky the wild farewell,"

> Slow sinks, more lovely ere his race be run,
> Along Morea's hills the setting sun,

with other gems, and bought and read devoutly Moore's life of my hero. The first composition of mine that ever found its way into print was some sort of rhapsody (in prose) on Byron at Missolonghi. The attack passed off in six months or so, and I am not aware that it left behind any permanent ill effects. About the same time I read the greater part of *The Faery Queen*, with a certain pleasure, but without any real appreciation. It was from Wordsworth, whom I read for a college essay, that I learned the true meaning of the word poetry. I did not win the prize, but I won what was much more valuable—a perception, as yet vague and uncertain enough, of the distinction between fustian and style. Let me not be understood to imply in this phrase anything like wholesale disrespect for Byron. He is undoubtedly one of the most striking figures in the marvellous romance of English literature : a great man of letters always, a great poet sometimes, but a great artist only by chance, if, indeed, that be not a contradiction in terms. We return to Byron occasionally, with amusement, refreshment, admiration ; Wordsworth we have always with us.

Coleridge, of course, came to me in the train of Wordsworth, and *The Ancient Mariner* seemed to me at seventeen, what it seems to me now, the most magical of poems, an inspiration and a miracle. But my feeling for the more intimate refinements of the art was still very backward. Tennyson I read with pleasure, but cared principally for *Locksley Hall, The Dream of Fair Women, Come into the Garden, Maud*, and such sugar-plums, exquisite though they be. Keats had as yet taken no hold on me. Milton I could not read.

The Scotch school and college course in my day was carefully devised so as to prevent even a moderately intelligent boy from coming into anything like vital relation with classical literature. In Greek I read portions of the *Iliad*, six books of the *Odyssey*, and a tragedy or two—all purely as a task. In Latin I acquired some real relish for Horace, but such imperfect appreciation as I have of Catullus and Virgil has come to me since my college days. Of Lucretius I know only one or two hackneyed scraps ; of Juvenal some longer fragments. Here endeth the tale of my communion with the poets of antiquity.

Shakespeare the dramatist I came to know, in a general way, pretty early, both on the stage and off ; but my appreciation of Shakespeare the poet came only with maturity, and has grown with each succeeding year. To know Chaucer was to love him at once and for ever, sweetest of singers and of spirits. Matthew Arnold has somewhere demonstrated that Chaucer is not a poet of the very first order, not quite

the peer of Dante or of Shakespeare. Of course he is right;
but why talk about it? Why make criticism an affair of the
foot-rule? Whatever other poets there have been or may
yet be, so long as English is English lovers of poetry will
always say Amen to that line of old Dunbar's:

> The noble Chaucer, of makars flower.

But the test of a mature sense of poetical values is, to my
thinking, a genuine appreciation of Milton. With me it
came late. I spent my twentieth year idling in Australia,
and being somewhat hard up for literature, I set myself to
read *Paradise Lost* from beginning to end, at the rate of a
book a day. I accomplished the task, but it bored me
unspeakably, and I used to take an unholy revenge in
chuckling between-whiles over Taine's analysis of the poem.
I did not return to it for seven or eight years, until one day
I found myself starting on a railway journey with nothing to
read, and paid a shilling at the station bookstall for a pocket
Paradise Lost. That was to me an ever memorable journey;
the poem became my bedside book for months; and ever
since, when I have ten minutes to spare for pure pleasure, I
open *Paradise Lost* almost at random. Its story may very
probably merit Taine's strictures. I neither know nor care.
For me it has no story. It is simply an inexhaustible mine
of the pure gold of poetry.

Except in the case of a few college exercises, my own
metrical efforts have been almost entirely confined to comic,
or at any rate journalistic, verse. They have given me more
or less insight into the methods, the mental processes, of
verse-making; but I never attained even the fluency of the
practised newspaper rhymester. Greek and Latin verses
were undreamt of in the Scottish curriculum of my day.
Practically, we knew not what quantity meant.

Having traced, in something like their order, the poetical
influences of my boyhood, I will now give a sketch-map of

the main grooves into which my mature predilections have
settled. As I survey the wide expanse of English non-
dramatic verse, three figures seem to me to stand pre-
eminent, the summits or landmarks of the scene. They are
Chaucer, Milton, Keats. Other poets have surpassed them
in this way and in that : in their divination and realisation
of the highest potentialities of beauty in language, they are
unsurpassed and unsurpassable. If they were the only
poets in our tongue, English would still rank second to none
among the idioms of poetry. In Elizabethan and Jacobean
non-dramatic verse I am by no means well read ; but I take
unbounded delight in the lyric poets of the seventeenth
century, from Herrick and Crashaw and Campion down-
wards. What an age was that in which (say) Sir Henry
Wotton could hold an almost unregarded place—the man
who wrote :

> You meaner beauties of the night,
>   That poorly satisfy our eyes
> More by your number than your light,
>   You common people of the skies ;
>   What are you, when the moon shall rise ?
>
> You curious chanters of the wood,
>   That warble forth Dame Nature's lays,
> Thinking your passion understood
>   By your weak accents ; what's your praise
>   When Philomel her voice shall raise ?
>
> You violets that first appear,
>   By your pure purple mantles known
> Like the proud virgins of the year,
>   As if the spring were all your own ;
>   What are you, when the rose is blown ?

The author of this glorious lyric was himself one of the
" meaner beauties of the night." In Mr. Saintsbury's
Elizabethan Literature he is dismissed in one line ; in
Mr. Gosse's *Jacobean Poets* he is not mentioned (at any rate
not indexed) at all. I do not impugn these gentlemen's

sense of proportion ; on the contrary, I believe it to be in this instance quite just. But what a testimony to the wealth of the age !

For the eighteenth century and its great precursor, Dryden, I have a true esteem, a warm affection. Where I find high literary power in verse, I am quite willing to enjoy it without inquiring too curiously into its imaginative quality, or troubling overmuch as to whether or no it deserves the name of poetry. If our definition of poetry has no room for the following lines (from *Don Sebastian*), then I think it needs enlargement ;

> Death may be call'd in vain, and cannot come ;
> Tyrants can tie him up from your relief,
> Nor has a Christian privilege to die.
> Alas ! thou art too young in thy new faith ;
> Brutus and Cato might discharge their souls,
> And give 'em furloughs for another world ;
> *But we, like sentries, are oblig'd to stand*
> *In starless nights, and wait the appointed hour.*

The many prosaic associations of the ten-syllable couplet ought not to blind us to the splendid flashes of true poetry in Pope, in Goldsmith, aye, even in Johnson ; nor can I understand how any one can suppose the torch of imagination to have been extinguished in the age of Collins and Gray. The feeling that literary power is in itself admirable and delightful, even if it have not the supreme charm of poetry, enables me to read Cowper and Crabbe with great pleasure. Perhaps it is the same feeling that leads me to differ from those critics who, taking Carlyle's cue, apologise for Burns as a poor, stunted, incomplete creature—a view which even Mr. J. M. Robertson in the main accepts. It seems to me that in his songs (to which Mr. Robertson applies a quite inapplicable standard of formal perfection) Burns often touched the very summit of lyric charm, while in his other verse, except, of course, in a few manifest failures, he showed himself a superb literary craftsman, whom no amount of "culture" or "leisure" could possibly have improved. I say then, with Mr. Henley, that in Burns "the poor-living, lewd, grimy, free-spoken, ribald, old Scots peasant-world came to a full, brilliant, even majestic close."

My attitude towards the Lake Poets and their satirist has already been sufficiently indicated. Blake I read with pleasure, but he does not take strong hold on me. Scott, one of the greatest of great men, seems to me very nearly a great poet when he draws his inspiration direct from those border ballads, which, by the way, contain some of the purest poetic treasures of the language.

Now comes the point at which the critic has doubtless been lying in wait for me. "Then they said unto him 'Say now Shibboleth'; and he said 'Sibboleth.' . . . Then they took him and slew him at the passages of Jordan." In English criticism Shibboleth is spelt "Shelley," and he who pronounces the word without a genuflexion is slain "right there"—in the esteem of an influential school of critics. Well, I genuflect, with a difference. I think Shelley was one of the rarest poetic spirits the world ever saw—a prince of song, who, but for a capful of wind in the Gulf of Genoa, might have become an almost peerless king. His figure is one of the most sympathetic, his story quite the most tragic and haunting, in the aforesaid romance of English literature. But though he lived four years longer than Keats, and wrote so much more, I cannot but regard him as the more unful-filled, the more problematic, genius of the two. Shelley resembles a glorious statue roughly blocked-out, Keats a finished masterpiece, sadly truncated indeed, but with the vine-wreathed head complete and godlike. Shelley's genius never really clarified, or only for brief intervals. To the last—even in *Adonaïs*—his thought was more obviously conditioned by his rhyme than it ought to be in verse of classical perfection. His three or four great lyrics, and some of his small ones, apart, his work produces on me very much the effect of "absolute music"—charming for a little while, unsatisfying in the long run. To my unmusical soul, a classical concert is delightful for ten minutes ; after that my attention begins to wander, and presently I find myself suffering the inverse tantalisation of one who is seated at a gorgeous banquet for which he has no appetite. In precisely the same way does the greater part of Shelley's poetry affect me. *Prometheus Unbound*, for instance, I regard as probably the greatest symphony in literature ; but alas ! I have no soul for symphonies.

It is absurd to attempt, in this summary way, to define my attitude towards so complex a phenomenon as Shelley. I have probably made myself out a greater barbarian than I am. But the fact remains, and the murder will out, that I am of the Keats-Tennyson, not of the Shelley-Browning, faction. With regard to Browning, indeed, I am heretical to the point of paradox. The accepted view, I take it, is that Browning was perhaps not very strong in poetry pure and simple, absolute poetry, but that he was a profound thinker, and the only dramatist since Shakespeare. My view is that he was not a dramatist at all, failing in the primary essentials of dramatic construction and expression ; that he was an inefficient thinker, greatly inferior in specula-tive power and consistency to the intellectually-despised Tennyson ; and that he has produced some of the noblest and most thrilling absolute poetry in the language. Were I writing a study of Browning, I should of course have to qualify in some measure these too sweeping statements. For the present, my object is simply to enable readers of the following pages to check, and if need be discount, my judgments, in the light of what they may think my errors of general theory ; and to that end I am at no pains to smooth away rough edges or harsh outlines.

Matthew Arnold I delight in. My love for Rossetti is greater than, according to the strict letter of my critical prin-

ciples, it ought to be. Mrs. Browning I regard as a woman
of immense genius, to some extent marred by an unfortunate
method. For Christina Rossetti I have the very highest
regard. William Morris I read with admiration and pleasure
—when I have time. And it is one of my pet beliefs that
justice has never been done to Robert Louis Stevenson's
merit as a poet. His vein was a somewhat narrow one,
but it yielded pure gold, on which he stamped unmistakably
his own image and superscription.

In American poetry the three chief figures, to my thinking, are Poe, Whitman, and Emerson. The element of the
factitious in Poe's verse renders him very hard to " place,"
but his genius is not to be contested. He has recently
found a powerful champion in Mr. Robertson, whose
vindication of him (in the book above cited) is a masterly
piece of criticism. For Whitman I have a sincere affection,
though far on this side of idolatry. Emerson, in spite of
his occasional helplessness of form, seems to me a true
poet, subtle and searching in thought, individual, if not
always harmonious, in utterance.

Dante I read and re-read, but otherwise know scarcely
anything of Italian poetry. Of French non-dramatic verse
I am, alas ! almost equally ignorant. I have never succeeded
in attuning my ear to French prosody. Not that I am
incapable of enjoying the delicate harmonies of Racine, the
movement and colour of Victor Hugo's alexandrines.
Even lyric poets—Ronsard, Hugo, Musset, Baudelaire,
Verlaine—I read and ignorantly admire. But the feeling
that I do not understand the principles of their versification,
that I cannot with any certainty distinguish between good
verse and bad, prevents the finest work from taking real
hold on my mind. The result is that French poetry is not
a living factor in my intellectual life. I approach it rarely,
and then for some definite purpose. I do not return to
it instinctively and for pure pleasure.

With German poetry the case is different. Here, the metrical system being practically the same as our own, I can enjoy and feel sure that I know what I am enjoying. Heine is a pure delight to me; for Schiller and Goethe, colossal figures in the world of art, I have the warmest admiration. At the same time I am not sure that the superior homogeneity of their language does not give German poets a superficial advantage, which becomes in a higher sense a disadvantage. For the *Lied*, the simple folk-song, either in its primitive simplicity or developed and glorified with subtle art, German is an incomparable medium—witness the divine *Lieder* in *Faust* and Heine's " Diamanten und Perlen " of song. The *Lied*, I take it, is the characteristic contribution of Germany to the world's poetry. But apart from the glorified folk-song, is it possible, I wonder, to discern in German poetry any quality equivalent to that supreme gift of style in which lies the true greatness of our greatest singers? I ask the question, not rhetorically, to point a negation, but sincerely, to express an unresolved doubt. Is there anything like the heaven-wide difference between the best and the worst German blank verse (for example) that there is between Milton's blank verse and Byron's? I fully recognise, of course, the wonderful suavity and dignity of such a masterpiece as Goethe's *Iphigenie;* but does it not lie rather in the general spirit and structure of the poem than in the diction and versification, beautiful though these undoubtedly are? I have a lurking suspicion, in fact, that German poets work in a softer medium than their English brethren. Their exceedingly copious and yet homogeneous language has no lurking pitfalls for them, but at the same time deprives them of the glory of pitfalls successfully avoided, difficulties brilliantly overcome. They are neither stimulated nor depressed by such majestic models as are at once the joy and the despair of the English artist. Perhaps—who knows?—the fact that their second-rate craftsmen can

18

translate Shakespeare so admirably has something to do with the equally evident fact (as it seems to me) that the supreme felicities of Shakespeare's style are unequalled even by their greatest poets.

This brings me to the last point in my confession of faith. Having sketched the growth of my taste for poetry, outlined my knowledge and my ignorance, and made a clean breast of my preferences and prejudices, it is time that I should try to state in general terms what I understand by the word poetry. A hopeless task, yet it must be attempted. Though I cannot define the indefinable, I can let the reader see in what sense I would define it if I could.

Wordsworth has given a poet's definition of poetry : "The breath and finer spirit of all knowledge." Coleridge has tried to sum it up in an epigram : " The best words in the best order "—which, however, fails to differentiate it from the best prose. Poe, to my thinking, came as near the mark as it was possible to come in five words, when he called poetry " The rhythmical creation of beauty." Oliver Wendell Holmes, with his usual winning fancifulness, wrote : " There are words that have loved each other since the birth of the language, and when they meet that is poetry." This goes to the heart of the matter : the sense of predestination which it carries with it is one unfailing mark of fine poetry. When words are rightly wedded, we feel that the poet was but the officiating priest—the marriage was made in heaven.

The same thought, however, may be stated rather more comprehensively. The essence of poetry, to my mind, is its magical, its miraculous quality. When we feel that the artist has done something which could not possibly have been accomplished by the highest intelligence, culture and industry—when his words seem to have flown together, not at the bidding of his mere reason, but in obedience to some incommunicable spell—then " This," we say, " is poetry." What is a miracle? We define it as a phenomenon not referable to any general law or reproducible by any process explicable to the reason, but appearing to depend on some mystic effluence from a particular personality, human or divine. But true poetry is precisely such a phenomenon. It may be the simplest thing in the world, yet not all the world can compass it save one particular man; and he cannot tell you how he does it, or, for all the wealth in the world, teach any one else the secret. Take, for instance, such a mere versicle as this:

"FRATER AVE ATQUE VALE."

Row us out from Desenzano, to your Sirmione row!
So they rowed, and there we landed—" O venusta Sirmio!"
There to me through all the groves of olive in the summer glow,
There beneath the Roman ruin where the purple flowers grow,
Came that "Ave atque Vale" of the Poet's hopeless woe,
Tenderest of Roman poets nineteen hundred years ago,
"Frater Ave atque Vale"—as we wandered to and fro,
Gazing at the Lydian laughter of the Garda Lake below
Sweet Catullus's all-but-island, olive-silvery Sirmio.

There is here no thought, no wit, no wisdom, no passion, no drama, nothing that can even be called description. There is not a word, except the two or three words of Latin, which a child of seven would not understand. All the writer says is, "We rowed to a certain place and a certain Latin phrase ran in my head." But because the writer happens to be Tennyson, he creates out of this nothing an ineffably beautiful, immortal something, an "unearned increment" of beauty to the English tongue, a miracle—in short, a poem. And, Tennyson dead, all the king's horses and all the king's men cannot work just such a miracle over again. Other poets (thank heaven!) can work other miracles, and rhymesters can produce echoes of this particular miracle which may be clever enough in their way, but are at once dismissed as worthless, simply because there is nothing miraculous about them. Tennyson's lines are not in the least clever. So far as their substance is concerned, they might have been written by a man of the scantiest intelligence. They are magical, that is all ; and the abracadabra which summoned them out of nothingness passed away with the magician,

> When that which drew from out the boundless deep
> Turned again home.

Moreover, Tennyson had two brothers, constituted like himself, educated like himself, and devoted like himself to the poet's craft. There is nothing to show that their intelligence, their general brain-power, was notably inferior to his ; at all events, any difference there may have been was as nothing in comparison with the gulf that separates his poetry from theirs. And why? There is only one possible answer—because Nature (or if you prefer the older mythology, the Muses) whispered to Alfred in his cradle some word of magic might, which Charles and Frederick only half heard, or misheard, or heard not at all.

It may be objected that this theory, or rather this apologue, for it is no more, breaks down on the question of imitation. The poetic miracle, it may be said, is notoriously imitable ; was it not Tennyson himself who wrote

> All may grow the flower now,
> For all have got the seed ?

Yes—but who has grown the flower? Where is the second Tennyson who has equalled by imitating him? or who has won anything more than a spurious and transient reputation, among people incapable of distinguishing the paste from the diamond, the mock-miracle from the real one? There is of course an imitable element—even a large element— in all poetry ; but it is precisely the inimitable final touch, crowning and consecrating the whole, that constitutes the miracle and proclaims the poet. The greatest poets have imitated the imitable element in others, but they have made the work their own by adding to it their own inimitable somewhat, transmuting it by their own spell. Up to a certain point, Pharaoh's magicians imitated the miracles of Moses; but it was his inimitable masterpieces that proved his divine calling and election.

It is no new idea—it is as old as the first babbling of criticism round the primeval camp-fire—to insist on this magical quality as the true differentia of poetry. All poets, I think, recognise it, and feel that their truly immortal work is that which seems to have written itself, they cannot tell how. In Tennyson's *Life* (vol. i. p. 152) he is recorded to have said : " Keats, with his high spiritual vision, would have been, if he had lived, the greatest of us all. . . . There is something magic and of the innermost soul of poetry in almost everything which he wrote." Mr. Ruskin has given the theory his own peculiar twist, and has almost transmuted it into poetry, in these exquisite words : " Every great writer may be at once known by his guiding the mind far from himself, to the beauty which is not of his creation, and the knowledge which is past his finding out."

A paragraph in Mr. Leslie Stephen's *Studies of a Biographer* puts the same theory in a somewhat different light, and suggests a re-statement of it in somewhat less figurative terms. Mr. Stephen writes :

Arnold must, on the whole, take a lower place than Tennyson and Browning. But, though I cannot avoid falling into the method of comparison, I do not accept with satisfaction the apparently implied doctrine that poets can be satisfactorily arranged in order of merit. We cannot give so many marks for style and so many for pathos or descriptive power. It is best to look at each poet by himself. We need only distinguish between the sham and the genuine article; and my own method of distinguishing is a simple one. I believe in poetry which learns itself by heart. There are poems which dominate and haunt one ; which, once admitted, sting and cling to one ; the tune of which comes up and runs in one's head at odd moments ; and which suddenly revive, after years of forgetfulness, as vigorous and lively as ever. Such poetry, as Wordsworth told Arnold, has the characteristic of being "inevitable"—a phrase which has become something of a nuisance, but cannot always be avoided. You feel that the thing had to be said just as it was said; and that, once so said, nothing said by anybody else will ever hit just the same mark.

This is, in other words, nothing but the classical theory of "inspiration"—a true theory, no doubt, or, rather, a luminous symbol. The wise ancients recognised that a poet, at any rate in his great moments, was simply the mouthpiece of "something not himself that made for"—perfect utterance. They saw that the beauties we really value and worship in poetry are those which we feel to be unattainable by any conscious effort of will or skill, and which we therefore ascribe to the intervention of some superhuman power. To state the thing in plain prose, these beauties are the result of mental processes which transcend the experience of ordinary men and defy our gross methods of analysis. One day, perhaps, science may provide us with a formula for "inspiration," showing that it depends on some slightly abnormal volatility of the cerebral corpuscles; but in the meantime we find it shorter, more convenient, and more agreeable to use the consecrated mythological term.

One mark of inspiration, as Mr. Stephen says, is the tendency of the thing inspired to "learn itself by heart"—to sting and cling to us, to haunt and possess us. But before erecting this tendency into a law, we must reflect that some great poems are long, and that most human memories are short. Take the *Æneid*, for example. Mr. Stephen, I presume, would not restrict the term "poetry" or "inspired poetry" to those passages which every one knows by heart. Nor would he deny *The Faery Queen* to be great poetry because not one man in ten thousand can recite three whole stanzas of it. Nor would he declare *Ye Mariners of England* a greater achievement than Tennyson's *Ballad of the "Revenge,"* because fifty people, probably, could rattle it off, for one who could recite the longer and less jingling poem. I prefer, then, to modify Mr. Stephen's statement, and recognise as the mark of the true poem, not that it " learns itself by heart," but that when once we have read it and taken it in, its ghost, its disembodied spirit, released from its verbal integuments, haunts us for ever after. To think of the *Æneid*, or *The Faery Queen*, or *Paradise Lost*, is to hear, in each case, a peculiar strain of harmony, entirely divorced from words. By conscious effort, indeed, we can summon up a few fragments of the different poems, but they do not make the haunting harmonies any clearer or more unmistakable to "that inward *ear* which is the bliss of solitude." So, too, with *Ye Mariners of England* and *The "Revenge."* Campbell's song has probably run in our head from boyhood, and will remain with us, along with other "trivial fond records," to the end of our days ; but to think of Tennyson's poem is to summon up the ghost of something stately and moving and splendid, before which the actual substance of the good old ditty (of which, nevertheless, I desire to speak with respect and affection) seems to vanish into nothingness. This is simply to say, in other words, that the fundamental and imperishable quality of great poetry is style; for style is the more prosaic term for that ghostly harmony.

Let us note, too—for this must be emphasised whenever a large number of contemporary poets are to be passed in review—that style can be as clearly manifested in small as in great poetry, in the versicle as in the epic. It is unmistakable, for instance, in those three stanzas of Sir Henry Wotton's which I have quoted above. They have a physiognomy, an accent, an individuality of their own. It is not entirely unsusceptible of analysis. If it were worth while, pages might be devoted to expounding the characteristics of conception, diction, metre, and stanza which give this poem its individuality; but the ultimate secret would escape us after all. Again, if all the works of Tennyson were to vanish from earth save the nine lines of *Frater Ave atque Vale*, a critic, coming across them, would be able to say with confidence, "Here was a true poet, a man with a miraculous accent of his own." It follows, too, from the very theory of inspiration, of the miracle, that it may occur very rarely, or only once, in a whole lifetime. A man may write only one "copy of verses," and they may proclaim him incontestably a poet. Or he may doggedly turn out his tale of fifty lines a day, with never a line worth reading, until, on a particular day of days, the inspiration comes, the miracle happens, and he writes two or three stanzas which will sing in men's souls till the end of time. Such cases, of course, are very rare, perhaps purely theoretical; but they are merely over-statements of perfectly common cases. And the principle on which this book is based is that inspiration is inspiration, style is style, even if it comes to a man only half a dozen times in as many years. All poets live by their happy moments; but we are apt, in looking at the past, to lose our sense of perspective, and forget or ignore the proportion of uninspired to inspired writing in the works of all but the very greatest; thus doing injustice to the contemporaries whom we see from a different angle. The classics come to us foreshortened, like a fleet of great galleons bearing down on us from the horizon, the sunlight of renown on each high-piled tower of canvas, and the pennant of immortality floating from every main-mast-head.

Whatever the errors, oversights, or limitations of the criticism contained in the following pages, I cannot but feel that it has been my privilege to bring together, in my quotations and selections, a very remarkable body of poetry. I have already called attention to its variety, but its strength, beauty, and general originality seem to me no less striking. If the reader will bear in mind that by far the greater number of the poems here quoted have been written within the past ten years, I think he will admit that the last decade of the nineteenth century has been anything but a barren period. For my part, I do not hesitate to express my conviction that the poetry of the eighteen-nineties does no discredit whatever to a century so glorious in the annals of song that even the resplendent seventeenth century will have much ado to outshine it.

If I thought otherwise—if I believed in the decadence of which we hear so much—I should be sad indeed. It would show a strange and ominous change in the spirit of the nation if England ceased to utter her exultations and her agonies, her faith and hope and doubt and pride and love, in noble and vital verse. For three centuries and a quarter (not to go back to the very " morning star of song ") her poetry has indeed been " the breath and finer spirit of all [her] knowledge," the supreme glory of her literature.

> And were she the same England, made to feel
> A brightness gone from out those starry eyes,
> A splendour from that constellated brow?

It is a purblind practicality that thinks of poetry as one of the mere decorations of life, an idle toying with baubles of speech set in scroll-works of rhythm. Poetry is actually a great force, and potentially the greatest, in the world. It has the religion of the future in its hands. What is the vital element in the religion of the present? . Not, certainly, its dogma, not its metaphysics, not even its ethics, but simply the poetry of the life, character, and utterances of its Founder, reinforced by the more magnificent but less penetrating poetry of the lyrists and rhapsodists who preceded him, and the didactic and apocalyptic poetry of his immediate successors. In like manner must the religion of the future spring from some body of poetry potent enough to give the spirit of man a new elevation and a larger outlook upon nature and destiny.

The poet speaks to the imagination, and through the imagination to the will. Imagination is the greatest of spiritual forces. The frame of things is plastic to its touch, as clay in the hands of the potter. The world will be whatever the imagination of mankind decrees that the world shall be. It is the present impotence of man to imagine a peaceful and beautiful world that prevents or defers its realisation. If a poet mighty enough to overcome this impotence were to arise to-morrow, the world would be re-created in three generations. He need not have greater genius than the great poets of the past, but he must know more than they. Miracles do not happen, and even the poet requires knowledge as well as divination. But knowledge is being rapidly garnered; and when LAW is sufficiently ascertained, there will arise a great poet to absorb, co-ordinate, transfigure, and promulgate it, touched with magical persuasiveness, to the renovation of the spirit of man.

In the meantime, let us cherish the habit, and perfect and keep bright the mechanism, of song. One supreme world-poet—the poet of the world-pageant—has already spoken in our English tongue. The other supreme world-poet—the poet of love and law—must needs speak in the same tongue if he is to find, as it is essential to his calling that he should find, the largest possible audience. Let us, then, preserve and enrich for him, to the best of our power, the language and the rhythms of Chaucer, Shakespeare, Milton, Shelley and Tennyson.

H. C. BEECHING

THOUGH the title of Mr. H. C. Beeching's collected poems
—*In a Garden*—refers particularly to the opening sequence,
it in reality covers the whole book. An English garden is
the congenial haunt of Mr. Beeching's muse. We recognise
it at a glance as a parsonage garden. The French windows
of the drawing-room open, under a narrow verandah fes-
tooned with clematis and jasmine, upon a deep-piled lawn
of immemorial sward. A cedar in the middle of the lawn
seems, in springing from the soil, to have carried whole
swaths of turf with it into mid-air, so dense and velvety is
the verdure of its level branches. There are flower-beds on
each side, filled with old-fashioned cottage flowers :

> We turn'd our steps and loiter'd slow
> 'Twixt borders pale with later spring—
> Polyanthus crowding ring on ring,
> Love's banner, heartsease, balm for thought,
> White tulips, blue forget-me-not.
> One slim narcissus drooped his head,
> And from her closely curtain'd bed
> One lily shook out half her bells.

Below the lawn, and behind an array of rose-bushes, a
box hedge shuts off the vegetable garden, enclosed by walls
once red, long hoar with age, on which pear and peach
trees stretch their Briarean arms. The gables of modest
glass-houses peer forth in this corner and that, embowered,

28

REV. H. C. BEECHING

it may be, in raspberry and currant hedges. Through a gateway in the garden wall you reach the sloping orchard:

> Only Pomona knew no fear,
> For her white breast had brush'd the pear,
> And now her fingers 'gan to fling
> On th' apples pink enamelling.

Beyond a high laurel hedge the shingled steeple of the little church rears its rusty weather-cock—a squat old church, restored in patches, but so delicately harmonised by moss and weather stains as to seem a natural outgrowth of the soil rather than a work of human hands. Stray branches of the churchyard yews overhang the garden wall, and on winter evenings you can see through a ragged archway in the laurel hedge the glow of the old stained-glass. At the further end of the house, the bay-window of the study looks out upon a little rose-garden with a sun-dial or a trickling fountain in its centre. Over the study mantel-piece hang the arms of a college blazoned on an oaken shield, and flanked on either hand with photographs of a school eleven and a college eight. The bookshelves are well filled with general literature and eclectic theology. There is a slight haze of dust, perhaps, over the shelf of classics, but they have been well thumbed in their day, and a certain aroma exhales even from their folded leaves. But the prevalent aroma is ever that of the English garden, the English elms and limes, the English hedgerows and hayfields beyond. The influences that have produced and that tend to preserve these pastoral paradises are no doubt open to criticism; but the merely æsthetic sense cannot but rejoice in them. And if nothing more harmful than Mr. Beeching's poems ever issued from an English parsonage one could rejoice in them without afterthought or prick of conscience.

Mr. Beeching's love of nature in its homelike aspects is very genuine, his passion and his piety are alike sincere, and his lyric gift is far from insignificant. *In a Garden*—the

sequence properly so-called—consists of seventeen songs
and poems, not one of which is without merit, while several
of them show not only deep feeling but real faculty. It
must be said, too, that though Mr. Beeching's manner is not
strikingly original, it is not imitative in the bad sense. He
does not echo this poet or that, but simply works (as becomes
the editor of Milton and compiler of the charming *Paradise
of English Poetry*) on the established lines of a good poetical
tradition. The three lyrics, for example, quoted at the end
of this paper—the second, fourteenth and fifteenth of the
sequence—are no mere manufactured verse, but give spontaneous utterance to genuinely poetical moods. Of the
three I think, on the whole, that I prefer the second, but
there is at least one memorable line in the first (" And
bared the disenchanted year ") , while the third is delightfully
real and fresh in atmosphere. The sixteenth poem of the
sequence (from which I have already quoted some lines)
closes with this charming passage:

> O happy garden, two long years
> Have all thy voices charm'd our ears
> From discord, din, and rough unrest
> That drive off peace, too timorous guest.
> The ever-circling years shall bring
> Thee but more beautiful a spring ;
> (More beauteous spring, O love, to thee)
> In spite of winter's jealousy !
> Which of us twain shall sooner go
> The separate path ; ah, who can know !
> One May perhaps while thrushes call
> On Love in sweet antiphonal,
> An air shall blow, a whisper'd sigh ;
> And one the other sitting by
> Shall rise and quit this leafy place
> With backward hands, and what still face !

> Nay, tears avail not, but our love
> Avails death's terror to remove.
> Love dies not nor can lovers die ;
> And though vast worlds between them lie,

H. C. BEECHING

Th' intelligencing current thrills
From each to each the thought love wills
Remember'st not the dreary day
When I must journey, how (you say)
A nightingale, ev'n love's own bird,
In our fair garden else unheard,
Pour'd from the lilac, melting-sweet,
His throated jewels at your feet,
Till blissful night return'd me home ;
And is death more than absence ? Come,
Leave care, 'tis May, and still we are here,
And shall be, shall be, many a year,
Hearkening these swallows, and without
The struck ball, and the echoing shout
Of village children at their play,
In the quiet air at end of day.

After this, it is sad to read the concluding stanzas of the sequence, which are, however, beautiful in their simplicity :

Rose and lily, white and red
From my garden garlanded,
These I brought and thought to grace
The perfection of thy face.

Other roses, pink and pale,
Lilies of another vale,
Thou hast bound around thy head
In the garden of the dead.

There is much merit, though not without intervals of commonplace, in the *Songs and Sonnets* which form the middle section of Mr. Beeching's book. *The Night Watches* has a fine lyric movement; there is a wistful pathos in *Hope;* and this little apologue is at once pretty and significant:

ROSE-FRUIT.

They praised me when they found the new-born bud,
And all my blood
Flamed, as I burst in blossom, to requite
Their dear delight.

31

And still they praised my beauty, as I grew
    In the sun's view ;
Then what will be their joy, said I, to find
    My fruit behind !

But when the wind came, and revealed at last
    My heart set fast,
They said, " 'Twere well this cumbering thing should go ;
    New buds will blow."

Some of Mr. Beeching's best work is in his *Religious Pieces*, with which may be classed his polished and graceful " Oxford Sacred Poem," *St. Augustine at Ostia*. There is real dramatic power in *Caiaphas*, and the two sonnets entitled *Doubt* and *Creation* are admirable both in thought and movement. There is a charming artlessness about *A Song of the Three Kings*, and *The Ploughed Meadow* is an original and subtle piece of work. Why the following lines should be classed among *Religious Pieces* it is hard to say, but they are undeniably strong and beautiful :

SEPARATION.

Quis dabit mihi pennas sicut columbæ, et volabo, et requiescam.

Let us not strive, the world at least is wide ;
This way and that our different paths divide,
Perhaps to meet upon the further side.

We must not strive ; friends cannot change to foes ;
O yes, we love ; albeit winter snows
Cover the flowers, the flowers are there, God knows.

And yet I would it had been any one
Only not thou, O my companion,
My guide, mine own familiar friend, mine own !

Mr. Beeching's poetry is not of the kind that haunts the memory or imprints itself on the soul like a new experience. But even when it is least inspired it is never common or jarring. One reads it with interest and returns to it with pleasure.

H. C. BEECHING

THREE LYRICS.

I.

You came, the vernal equinox
  Brought on the solstice in a day ;
Crocuses in their beds of box
  Straight changed to tulips, striped and gay.

You went, and summer fled with you ;
  'Twas autumn, nay 'twas winter here ;
Cold winds drove snow-clouds up the blue
  And bared the disenchanted year.

Idly I mourn, or idly go
  Thro' all the wan dishevelled place,
In hope some one red rose may blow
  The harbinger of your sweet face.

II.

With dreams the sunbeams steep
  My bower that a bower will be
In a month, for March this year
  Is kind as the month of maying :
And a sound of the sea brings sleep ;
  Nay, sleep brings a sound of the sea,
For it is but the wind that I hear
  In the heavy fir-tree swaying.

What hear you as you stand,
  O love, by the shore of the sea ?
The surf, or the gull's sad cry,
  Or the shouts of children playing ?
Nay, shouts from a far-off land,
  And a plover's cry on the lea,
And the sough of the winds that sigh
  In the heavy fir-tree swaying.

III.

'Tis April, but the drought of March
  Is not yet piercèd by sweet showers;
The unsheathed sunbeams smite and parch
  The springing grass, the o'erhasting flowers.

Our lily of the valley, see,
  That hardly ripens for Mid-May,
My love's first pledge and annual fee,
  Is blown a month before the day.

The lawn grows rusty, dusty red,
  For tho' all night the gracious dew
Bathes each wan blade, that else were dead,
  It cannot their dried sap renew.

But in the orchard is a place
  Where we may lie, and feel the fall
Of apple-petals on our face,
  And drowsing hear the cuckoo's call,

The ring-dove's melancholy note,
  The blackbird's fluting, and the hum
Of bees above us, more remote,
  As slumber steals our senses. Come.

ARTHUR CHRISTOPHER BENSON

MR. A. C. BENSON'S grave and graceful talent has found expression in three substantial books of verse, *Poems* (1893), *Lyrics* (1895), and *Lord Vyet and Other Poems* (1897). He has tried, as he says in the preface to his first published book, "to present certain aspects of men and nature that have come home to him with force in an uneventful and sheltered existence." Nature he has studied to some purpose. He might be called a naturalist-poet—or perhaps a poet-naturalist—so lovingly does he describe and dwell upon the flora and fauna of an English country-side. A glance down the tables of contents of his books brings home to us the strength of this preoccupation. He has poems on

Fritillaries.	Rosemary.	The Grey Pie.
Seeds.	The Orchid.	The Yaffle.
The Thistledown.	Red Flowering Cur-	The Sparrow.
Berries of Yew.	rant.	The Ant-Heap.
The Dandelion.	The Gentian.	The Newt.
Azalea.	The Carrier Pigeon.	Live-Bait.
Knapweed.	The Mole.	The Owl.
A Lily of Annuncia-	The Toad.	The Ringdove.
tion.	The Beetle.	The Cat.
Nasturtiums.	The Dragonfly.	The Hawk.
Pines.	The Water Ouzel.	The Barbel.
	The Grasshopper.	

Had he been born a century earlier, his works might have been illustrated by Bewick. These nature-poems (and there are many others, of course, dealing with larger aspects of nature) show an observant eye and a reflective mind; for Mr. Benson seldom fails to draw a moral or to distil a sentiment from whatever subject he contemplates. If he goes to the ant, or to the newt or barbel, it is to consider his ways and be wise. I do not think, if the truth must be told, that he is equally successful in presenting those aspects of human life which his preface promises. He expresses personal moods, indeed, and sometimes moods aroused by contemplation of, or contact with, his fellow men; but he studiously avoids (or so it seems) all attempt at narrative, drama, or analysis of character, and on the whole he handles life too gingerly to take high rank as a philosophic poet.

His verse is always clear and pleasant, sometimes vivid, seldom impetuous in its movement or haunting in its cadences. His metrical skill is very considerable, and he employs some charming stanzas; but he seldom or never produces a song, a lilt, a poem that carries its own music with it and sings aloud in the reader's memory. His diction is pure, his faults of style are few. Sometimes one feels that a glaring fault would be a welcome change—only less welcome than a thrilling beauty.

Of his nature-poems this seems to me a good specimen: not quite characteristic, inasmuch as it has no particular moral; but excellently descriptive and almost dramatic in its conciseness:

THE HAWK.

The hawk slipt out of the pine, and rose in the sunlit air:
  Steady and slow he poised; his shadow slept on the grass:
And the bird's song sickened and sank; she cowered with furtive
    stare
  Dumb, till the quivering dimness should flicker and shift and
    pass.

Suddenly down he dropped: she heard the hiss of his wing,
  Fled with a scream of terror: oh, would she had dared to rest!
For the hawk at eve was full, and there was no bird to sing,
  And over the heather drifted the down from a bleeding breast.

36

· ARTHVR · C · BENSON ·

ARTHUR CHRISTOPHER BENSON

The following poem, *The Mill-Wheel*, has a certain charm, seldom lacking in Mr. Benson's verse, but illustrates at the same time the purposelessness which is its besetting weakness :

> Turn, mill-wheel, solemnly turn,
> Under the gable fringed with fern ;
> Run, swift freshet, steadily run,
> Filling the black lips one by one ;
>
> Toss and gurgle thy waters cool,
> Ere thou splash in the moss-lined pool ;
> Hark how the loud gear sullenly groans,
> Whirling, whirling the patient stones !
>
> Haste thee, rivulet, haste away,
> All that we ask thou hast done to-day ;
> Cease, O streamlet, thy chiding sound,
> Hence ! forget thou wast ever bound ;
>
> Leap and linger with fitful gleam,
> Till thou plunge in the brimming stream ;
> Thine to wander, and thine to be
> Merged at length in the monstrous sea.
>
> Only forget not, there at play,
> How in the valley, day by day,
> Under the gable fringed with ferns,
> Black and solemn the mill-wheel turns !

We read this with a general sense of pleasure, but, having read it, we feel that the mill-wheel of our intelligence has been, as Stevenson says, "grinding no grist." Its beauty of sound is not remarkable ; it is not very vividly descriptive ; and its idea is, to say the least of it, elusive. Is it quite worth while to apostrophise a mill-race and beg its waters, when they reach the sea, not to forget the mill-wheel in the valley ? They certainly will forget it, and why should they not ? Is there any esoteric and spiritual significance in the poet's appeal to the water's non-existent memory ? I think not ; I think he was, so to speak, merely " making conversation," poetic small-talk ; and too much of Mr. Benson's work partakes of this character.

Among his cradle-gifts, the instinct of experiment seems to have been omitted. He makes no effort to get out of the placidly reflective groove to which, I think, it is his lack of initiative, rather than any deeper disability, that confines him. Hence the undeniable monotony of his work. He is always brooding; sometimes half humorously, sometimes mournfully, sometimes querulously; and his broodings are almost always upon personal or purely abstract topics. The life of the nation, of the world, of the struggling and agonising individual soul, loving, hating and aspiring, find scarcely an echo in his verse. We feel that he could if he would shake off the obsession of this listless, cultured melancholy, and apply his very considerable gifts to the treatment of larger and more vital subjects. In his three books, for example, there are two poems and two only —*Lord Vyet* and *The Robin and the Credence*—which are something in the nature of ballads. Though not of striking merit, they are far from bad; if he cared to work this vein a little further, he might find it full of golden possibilities. But this is only one experiment out of a score which would be worth attempting, and from all of which he sedulously abstains. It would be something if he even achieved a fine failure; but I see no reason why he should despair of success.

Of the memorable passages scattered throughout his work, I cull a few at random. Already in the dedication of his first volume, *To my Father*, we come across a noteworthy verse of thanks for the time

> When thou, through glad laborious days,
>
> Didst nurse and kindle generous fires,
>   That, as the old earth forward runs,
> May fit the sons of hero sires,
>   To be the sires of hero sons.

There is a sense of clean, firm fingering in these lines, a

master-touch on the keyboard. Very vigorous, too, are these opening stanzas of *By the Glacier* :

> Crawl on, old ice-worm, from the solemn hills ;
>   Press deep thy burrowing snout among the stones,
> Mutter and murmur with thy turbid rills,
>   And crush the old Earth's bones.
>
> Gnaw, grind the patient cliffs with ravenous teeth,
>   The crumbling crag shall feed thy snaky spine,
> The dim unfathomed caverns gape beneath
>   Azure and crystalline.

Metrically, to my thinking, a poem entitled *My Friend* is one of Mr. Benson's happiest inspirations. I quote the last three stanzas :

> What lies here on the bed ?
> What is this pinched white thing,
> With a stony eye and a lip that's dry ?
> See I drive from the stiffened head,
> Yon fly with the buzzing wing ;
> Presently when I am fled,
> He will return and bring—
>
> Nay, but I do him wrong,
> Nothing of him I see,
> Save the shrouding dusk, the chrysalis husk,
> Oh but we loved it, we !
> He is serene and strong,
> Hath he a thought of me
> Under the angels' song ?
>
> If it be well with him,
> If it be well, I say,
> I will not try with a childish cry
> To draw him thence away :
> Only my day is dim,
> Only I long for him,
> Where is my friend to-day ?

Mr. Benson rarely essays blank verse, but he writes it well. *In the Iron Cage,* a description of an imprisoned eagle, is too long to be quoted entire. These five opening lines strike me as singularly strong and beautiful :

> The saddest sight ! oh, there are sights and sounds
> And thoughts enough in this brief world of ours
> To wet with tears the stony face of Time,
> Who has seen the suns flame out, the mountains piled,
> And guesses at the vast designs of God.

More than once Mr. Benson has described very graphically the sensation of speeding through an English landscape in a railway train. For example :

> Through this bleak hour that brings the dark
> > Ere daylight fade,
> We fly on iron wheels, and mark
> > The changing glade.
> Northward the shuddering axles reel
> > With merry din ;
> Like moving spokes on some slow wheel
> > The furrows spin.
> The copse, the farmstead shifts ; and both
> > Fly like the wind.
> Swift runs the distant spire, as loth
> > To lag behind.

This poem, entitled *Northwards*, occurs in Mr. Benson's first book ; in his last, we find a piece entitled *The Railway*, of which I quote the last four stanzas :

> But best of all, when, in the sullen night,
> > Along the dim embankment, hung in air,
> Shoots the red streamer, linked with cheerful light ;
> > The wide-flung furnace-glare
>
> Lights the dim hedges and the rolling steam :—
> > Then passes, and in narrowing distance dies,
> Tracked by the watchful lanterns' lessening gleam—
> > Two red resentful eyes.
>
> And some are borne to dim and alien shores,
> > And some return to merriment and home :—
> These, while the train through slumbering homestead roars
> > Thrill with delight :—and some

> Fly from the horror that their hands have wrought,
>   And shudder, as the shivering engine reels;
> They fly, but falter: one red-throated thought
>   Pants ever at their heels.

This final stanza is really admirable, an imaginative inspiration. Mr. Benson has done nothing finer.

A little further on in the same book there occurs a poem, remarkable in conception rather than execution, entitled *The Artist in Church*. The last three stanzas will indicate its drift:

> Lo, in our eyes the tear-drops start,
>   We swim in stormy seas:
> Hast Thou within Thine ample heart,
> No shelter for the sons of art,
>   No room for such as these?
>
> Or wert Thou silent of design,
>   Because Thy thought was cold?
> Doth love of word, of hue, of line,
> Sequester from Thy power divine,
>   Dissociate from Thy fold?
>
> O words of Power, O gracious deeds!
>   When Thou didst dwell with men,
> Thou didst divine their deepest needs:
> I marvel, and my spirit bleeds
>   That Thou wast silent then.

The reason why Jesus had nothing to say to plastic and pictorial artists is, of course, obvious enough: Judaism banned the making of images, and Jesus never came in contact with either the art or the artists of Greece and Rome. He was too intent on a moral and spiritual revolution to give any thought to æsthetics, which nowhere thrust themselves on his attention. Still, it is curious to speculate how different the gospels and the world might have been had the Jews happened to be an artistic people, or had Jesus himself gone forth into the porticos and forums of the Gentiles. Mr. Benson suggests this speculation; why should he not elaborate it?

I quote at the end of this article the two poems, *The Shepherd* and *My Poet*, which seem to me, as a whole, to show Mr. Benson at his best. There are finer lines and stanzas in other poems, but these are, to my thinking, at once his most concrete and his most sustained efforts. Both, it will be seen, are portraits; both are entirely objective. Therein, I think, lies their superiority. It is not in his favourite exercises of reflection and introspection that Mr. Benson really shines. He is not a strong thinker, and if he feels deeply, he has not sufficient self-abandonment to give passionate utterance to his emotion. But he is a real artist: he sees things clearly and can depict them vividly. It is when he gets out of himself that he is at his best. There are, as I have above suggested, many directions in which he might get out of himself. Why should he not try them all and choose that, or those, which he finds best suited to his genius?

ARTHUR CHRISTOPHER BENSON

THE SHEPHERD.

The shepherd is an ancient man,
　　His back is bent, his foot is slow;
Although the heavens he doth not scan,
　　He scents what winds shall blow.

His face is like the pippin, grown
　　Red ripe, in frosty suns that shone;
'Tis hard and wrinkled, as a stone
　　The rains have rained upon.

When tempests sweep the dripping plain,
　　He stands unmoved beneath the hedge,
And sees the columns of the rain,
　　The storm-cloud's shattered edge.

When frosts among the misty farms
　　Make crisp the surface of the loam,
He shivering claps his creaking arms,
　　But would not sit at home.

Short speech he hath for man and beast;
　　Some fifty words are all his store.
Why should his language be increased?
　　He hath no need for more.

There is no change he doth desire,
　　Of far-off lands he hath not heard;
Beside his wife, before the fire,
　　He sits, and speaks no word.

He holds no converse with his kind,
　　On birds and beasts his mind is bent;
He knows the thoughts that stir their mind,
　　Love, hunger, hate, content.

Of kings and wars he doth not hear.
　　He tells the seasons that have been
By stricken oaks and hunted deer,
　　And strange fowl he has seen.

43

In Church, some muttering he doth make,
  Well-pleased when hymns harmonious rise
He doth not strive to overtake
  The hurrying litanies.

He hears the music of the wind,
  His prayer is brief, and scant his creed ;
The shadow, and what lurks behind,
  He doth not greatly heed.

MY POET.

I.

He came ; I met him face to face,
  And shrank amazed, dismayed ; I saw
No patient depth, no tender grace,
  No prophet of the eternal law.

But weakness fretting to be great,
  Self-consciousness with side-long eye,
The impotence that dares not wait
  For honour, crying " This is I."

The tyrant of a sullen hour,
  He frowned away our mild content ;
And insight only gave him power
  To see the slights that were not meant.

II.

And was it, then, some trick of hand,
  Some deft mechanical control,
That bridged the aching gulf, and spanned
  The roaring torrent of the soul?

And when convention's trivial bond
  Was severed by the trenchant pen,
Was there no single heart beyond ?
  No hero's pulse ? And art thou then

The vision of that brutish king,
  A tortured dream at break of day,
A monstrous, misbegotten thing,
  With head of gold and heart of clay

44

LAURENCE BINYON

FROM somewhat commonplace beginnings, Mr. Laurence Binyon has ripened into a poet of great promise and no inconsiderable performance. His Newdigate Poem of 1890, *Persephone*, was a Newdigate like any other. Save for a certain dignity of movement, it had nothing to distinguish it. His *Lyric Poems* of 1894 were gracefully contemplative and pleasantly Matthew-Arnoldish. There was still a good deal of feeble and commonplace work in them. He was still capable of writing :

> So, on the mountains, hapless Niobe
>
>   *   *   *   *   *
>
> Bewailed her children, by dread deities slain ;
> Those jealous deities *whose bright shafts ne'er miss,*
> Phœbus, and his stern sister, Artemis.

He still thought it worth while not only to write—that is the common lot--but to publish such verses as these :

> Ask me not, dear, what thing it is
>   That makes me love you so ;
> What graces, what sweet qualities,
>   That from your spirit flow ;
> For I have but this old reply,
> That you are you, that I am I.
>
> My heart leaps when you look on me,
>   And thrills to hear your voice,
> Lies, then, in these the mystery
>   That makes my soul rejoice ?

> I only know, I love you true ;
> Since I am I, and you are you.

But in many individual passages and phrases he already shows imaginative vision and verbal felicity. The admiration with which one reads such lines as these :

> The gathering dusk, and one pure star
> Deep in the visionary west,

is tempered by the reflection that this solitary star has shone in many a poet's skies, if not in "the visionary west," at least in some cognate quarter of the heavens. Still, a poet can show his sense of beauty in his borrowings no less than in his inventions. Even the beautiful phrase (from an unnamed poem on London at night):

> Sleep, to how many spent-out spirits, yields
> Life's only sweetness, to forget they live,

has somehow a familiar cadence. More convincingly original is the following from a poem entitled *Tintagel* :

> See ye, knights, your ancient home
> Chafed and spoiled and fallen asunder ?
> Hear ye now, as then of old
> Waters rolled, and wrath of foam,
> Where the waves beneath your graves
> Snow themselves abroad in thunder.

Here, again, are two stanzas from an otherwise rather commonplace poem of some length, which make a charming little lyric in themselves :

> Ah, now this happy month is gone,
>   Not now, my heart, complain,
> Nor rail at Time, because so soon
>   He takes his own again.
>
> He takes his own, the weeks, the hours,
>   But leaves the best with thee :
> Seeds of imperishable flowers
>   In fields of memory,

· LAVRENCE · BINYON ·

LAURENCE BINYON

Is it quite fanciful to suspect that these verses may owe
their particular melody to an unconscious reminiscence of
Rose Aylmer :

> Ah, what avails the sceptred race !
> Ah, what the form divine !
> What every virtue, every grace !
> Rose Aylmer, all were thine.
>
> Rose Aylmer, whom these wakeful eyes
> May weep, but never see,
> A night of memories and sighs
> I consecrate to thee.

If Landor's verses have been set to music, as no doubt they
have (for nothing is sacred to your composer), Mr. Binyon's
lines could be sung to the same melody with scarcely a
change in the phrasing. The poems towards the end of the
little book are notably stronger than those at the beginning,
an excellent sign if the arrangement be chronological.

Since 1894 Mr. Binyon has published four books of
verse: *Poems*, printed at the Daniel Press, Oxford, in
1895 ; *London Visions* and *The Praise of Life*, booklets of
the " Shilling Garland," both dated 1896 ; and *Porphyrion
and other Poems*, 1898. These books, however, do not all
consist of new matter, considerable portions of the Oxford
Poems being included in the *London Visions* and in the
Porphyrion volume.

Porphyrion is, in my estimation, so much the best thing
Mr. Binyon has done that I am inclined to think his talent
essentially epic. In the pure lyric, the dramatic sketch,
the descriptive and reflective poem, his work is good and
forcible, but scarcely masterly. His reflections are estim-
able rather than luminous ; in his descriptions the effort
sometimes outweighs the result. Incomparably the best of
his *London Visions*, to my mind, is the one which I am
permitted to quote at the end of this article, entitled *The
Fire*. We have here the direct, unconventional vivacity of

47

touch required for realistic landscape, or rather townscape, if I may coin an uncouth term. In the other poems of this series there are many striking passages, but scarcely any piece that, as a whole, imprints itself on the mind. We seem to see the painter plant himself resolutely at his easel, and labour away intelligently, competently; but the sudden, vivifying flash of colour, which should put immortal light and air into the picture, somehow does not arrive. Here are two characteristic stanzas which usher in a poem of contemplation, entitled *The Threshold*. The workmanship is good, the stanzas are admirably fashioned, and the concluding lines of each are really fine; but, for all their merits, they give us a sense of effort rather than of inspiration:

I walked beside full-flooding Thames to-night
Westward, where on my face the sunset fell.
The hour, the spacious evening, pleased me well.
Buoyant the air breathed after rain, and kind
To senses flattered with soft sound and light
From merry waves that leapt against the wind,
As broadly heaving barge and boat at rest
The River came at flood, from burning skies
Issuing through arches, black upon the West,
To flame beneath the sunset's mysteries.

Far off to-night, as in a tender dream,
That different Thames, familiar as a friend,
That youthful Thames, to whom his willows bend
With secret whisper, where my boat would come
Heaped with fresh flowers, and down the noiseless stream
Follow his green banks through the twilight home.
Far from these paven shores, these haughty towers,
Where waves with beams glorying together run,
As though they would disown those cradling flowers,
And gushed immediate from the molten sun.

Touches of fine imagination are scattered every here and there; for instance:

They pause: above, the northern skies
Are pale with a furnace light.
London with upcast, sleepless eyes
Possesses the brief night.

48

For the sake of these occasional felicities, Mr. Binyon's work is always worth reading; especially as it is always distinguished, seldom jars, and never offends. Nor is Mr. Binyon's thought without its stimulating moments. A poem entitled *The Renewal*, for instance, is a really noteworthy philosophic utterance.

At one period in his development, Mr. Binyon coquetted with a strange retarded measure—exemplified in such poems as *Fog* and *In the British Museum*—suggestive of the paces of a hobbled horse, or of one tightly reined-in and chafing at the curb. As soon as the verse promises to get into swing, it is deliberately checked, to the reader's continual disappointment. But the poet seems soon to have tired of this waltzing in fetters, and as it is practically unrepresented in his latest volume, I shall not discuss it further. Of the lyrics of this period —the period of the Oxford *Poems*—the following little specimen may suffice:

FIRST DAY OF WINTER.

Like the bloom on a grape is the evening air;
  And a first faint frost the Wind has bound;
Yet the fear of his breath avails to scare
  The withered leaves on the cold ground.

For they huddle and whisper in phantom throngs,
  I hear them beneath the branches bare:
We danced with the Wind, we sang his songs;
  Now, he pursues us, we know not where!

A group of poems inspired (it would seem) by a visit to Portugal, forms a sort of half-way house between the realism of the *London Visions* and the pure romance of *Porphyrion*. They are full of light, colour, and the joy of life. One of the best in point of movement, *Granja Beach*, is, oddly enough, not reprinted in the *Porphyrion* volume. The most characteristic of all, I think, is *Carvalhos*, of which these two stanzas may serve as a specimen :

> To the sun the sun-bathed pines
> Their strength and sweetness render.
> From where the far foam shines
> Like the rim of a dazzling shield,
> All fervent things and tender
> Life, joy, and perfume yield.
>
> Me, too, with mastering charm
> From husks of dead days freeing,
> The sun draws up, to be warm
> And to bloom in this sweet hour ;
> The stem of all my being
> Waited to bear this flower.

The last two lines are a memorable inspiration.

We turn now to *Porphyrion*, a blank verse narrative poem of about 1500 lines. It is a thing of real beauty, remarkable in itself, still more remarkable if, as one cannot but hope, it should prove to be the prelude to more sustained effort in the same direction. Though nominally complete, since it ends with the death of the hero, it may best be regarded as an epic fragment ; and I do not know that anything more clearly indicative of the true epic faculty has been published of recent years. A great work it is not. It lacks vitality, because the subject is, in the literal sense of the word, insignificant. The poem, as it stands, is neither a romance, a legend, nor a parable. It is possible, no doubt, to extract an allegoric meaning from it, to make Porphyrion's quest adumbrate the pursuit of the Ideal ; but its significance on the allegoric plane is neither very clear nor very deep. Simply as a story, again, it seems totally unconditioned. We cannot even divine the nature or intent of the unseen powers that mould Porphyrion's fate. Mr. Binyon admits that he has "adapted to his own uses" the legend which suggested the poem ; but, practically, the uses to which he has put it are purely decorative. The poem is little more than a series of pictures; but many of the pictures are magnificent.

The argument is this:

A young man of Antioch, flying from the world, in that enthusiasm for the ascetic life which fascinated early Christendom, dwells some years a hermit in the Syrian desert; till, by an apparition of magical loveliness, his life is broken up, and his nature changed; returning to the world, he embraces every vicissitude, hoping to find again the lost vision of that ideal beauty.

The poem opens with a description of Porphyrion in the desert whither he has fled because

> Tumultuous life,
> Full of sweet peril, thronged with rich alarms,
> Dismayed his soul, too suddenly revealed.

After a day of toil in the plot before his cell

> He stood immersed in the sweet falling hush.
> Over him liquid gloom quivered with stars
> Appearing endlessly, as each its place
> Remembered, and in order tranquil shone.
>
>   *   *   *   *   *
>
> Then he, that with such anguish of desire
> Had supplicated peace, now peace was come,
> Of all forgetful save of his strange joy,
> That dear guest in his bosom entertained;
> From trouble and from the stealing steps of time
> Sequestered; housed within a blissful mood
> Of contemplation, like a sacred shrine;
> And poured his soul out, into gratitude
> Released: how long, there was no tongue to tell,
> Nor was himself aware; no warning voice
> Admonished, and the great stars altered heaven
> Unnoted, and the hours moved over him,
> When on his ear and slowly into his soul
> Deliciously distilling, stole a sigh.

It is the sigh of a woman faint and hungry, craving for

105182

shelter. Porphyrion admits her, and, looking on her, is troubled by an " unknown sweetness " :

> He gazed: and as wine blushes through a cup
> Of water slowly, in sure-winding coils
> Of crimson, the pale solitude of his soul
> Was filled and flushed, and he was born anew.

It would not be easy to find a more exquisite simile than this ; but it stands not alone in *Porphyrion.*

To trace the growth of his fascination would be to quote the whole canto. The visitant bids him " Defend his soul with prayers, Nor hazard for a dream his holy calm " ; but he is not to be warned. " Rain on my thirsty heart," he cries,

> Rain on my thirsty heart
> Thy charm, and by so much as was my loss
> By so much more enrich me. I have stript
> My days, imprisoned wandering desires,
> Made of my mind a jealous solitude,
> Pruned overrunning thoughts, and rooted up
> Delight, and the vain weeds of memory,
> Imagining far off to capture peace.
> Blind fool! But O no, let me rather praise
> Foreseeing Fate, that kept so fast a watch
> Over my bliss, and of my heart prepared
> A wilderness to bloom with only thee!

Then, as he seeks to embrace her, she vanishes away and he falls in a deep swoon.

When he awakes on the morrow :

> The steep noon
> Had all the cool shade into fire devoured.
> Then quailed Porphyrion. Lost was his new joy,
> An apparition frail as a bright flame
> Seen in the sun.

Here again is an admirable image, simple and unpretentious but absolutely right. Porphyrion sets out to recapture the vision, and his first day's journey is described at somewhat disproportionate length:

> Till night
> Rose in the east, and hooded the bare world.

Then Porphyrion resigned

> His senses to the huge and empty night,
> When on the infinite horizon, lo!
> Sending a herald clearness, upward stole
> Tranquil and vast, over the world, the moon.
>
> Delicately as when a sculptor charms
> The ignorant clay to liberate his dream,
> Out of the yielding dark with subtle ray
> And imperceptible touch she moulded hill
> And valley, beauteous undulation mild,
> Inlaid with silver estuary and stream,
> Until her solid world created shines
> Before her, and the hearts of men with peace,
> That is not theirs, disquiets: peopled now
> Is her dominion; she in far-off towns
> Has lighted clear a long-awaited lamp
> For many a lover, or set an end to toil,
> Or terribly invokes the brazen lip
> Of trumpets blown to Fate, where men besieged
> For desperate sally buckle their bright arms.
> All these, that the cheered wanderer on his height
> In fancy sees, the lover's secret kiss,
> The mirth-flushed faces thronging through the streets,
> And ships upon the glimmering wave, and flowers
> In sleeping gardens, and encounters fierce,
> And revellers with lifted cups, and men
> In prison bowed, that move not for their chains,
> And sacred faces of the newly dead;
> All with a mystery of gentle light
> She visits, and in her deep charm includes.

On reading such a passage as this one cannot but feel that romantic and imaginative landscape is more suited to Mr. Binyon's talent than the realistic painting he essays in his *London Visions*.

Arrived, after some days' journeying, on a height above

Antioch, Porphyrion looked out over the spacious landscape, while

> The far cloud
> Loosened her faltering tresses of dim rain,
> And broad Orontes interrupted shone.

> * * * * *

> And as a bird, alighting on a reed
> Sprung straight and slender from a lonely stream,
> Some idle morning, delicately sways
> The mirrored stem, and sings for perfect joy;
> So musical, alighted young desire
> Upon his heart, that trembled like the reed

Not in Antioch, however, does Porphyrion find the goal
of his desire. He wanders overseas into distant countries,
until at last he comes upon two armies facing each other in
battle array. A dying soldier bequeathes to him his helmet
and sword, and Porphyrion takes his place.

> In that instant the ripe war
> Broke like a tempest; the great squadrons loosed
> Shot forward glittering, like a splendid wave
> That rises out of shapeless gloom, a form
> Massy with dancing crest, threatening and huge,
> And effortlessly irresistible
> Bursts on the black rocks turbulently abroad,
> Falling, and roaring, and re-echoing far.
> So rushed that ordered fury of steeds and spears
> Under an arch of arrows hailing dark
> Against the stubborn foe: they from the slope
> Swept onward opposite with clang as fierce:
> Afar, pale women from the wall looked down.

> * * * * *

> Just on that instant when the meeting shock
> Tumultuously clashed, and cries were mixt
> With glitter of blades whirled like spirted spray,
> He came: and as the thundering ranks recoiled,
> They saw him, solitary, flushed and young,
> A radiant ghost in the dead hero's arms.

> Amazement smote them; in that pause he rode
> Forward; and shouting Orophernes' name

Jubilant the swayed host came after him.
Iron on iron gnashed: Porphyrion smote
Unwearied; the bright peril stilled his brain,
The terrible joy inspired him: by his side
Vaunting, young men over their ready graves
Were rushing glorious: many as they rushed
Drank violent draughts of darkness unawares,
And swiftly fell; but he uninjured fought.

Was I wrong in claiming for Mr. Binyon a large measure of the epic faculty ? Here, however, my citations must close, and the reader must go to the book itself to learn how Porphyrion meets his death at the hands of the soldiers he has led to victory, because he is found befriending a woman of the conquered race in whose eyes

Deep-gazing, a great anguish lay becalmed.

One word as to the versification of *Porphyrion*. Mr. Binyon is clearly a student of Milton, but he Miltonises with moderation. The trochaic second foot is the only marked abnormality in which he at all frequently indulges. For instance :

Melancholy had planned her palace here . . .
Lost the treasure of earth and all their soul . . .
All the glory of war and sounding arms . . .
Returned darkness and silence and all slept . . .
Ancient armour upon him, and unused . . .
Faint the murmur of toil ascends, and dumb.

In the first and the last of these lines there is a metrical descriptiveness in the inverted accent which is not without its value. The other lines I cannot bring myself to relish ; nor can I discover the merit in that verse of my last extract—

With glitter of blades whirled like spirted spray—

unless (and to this, as a Scotchman, I have no rooted objection) we are to pronounce the fifth word " whurruld."

Mr. Binyon cannot possibly intend the collocation " whirlëd like spirtëd," nor is it conceivable that we are to read

With glit / ter of / blades whirled / &c.

By no method of treatment, in short, can I make the line either descriptive or melodious. But it is very seldom that Mr. Binyon presents us with such a problem. He is not one of our systematic and impenitent accent-perverters. And his state is the more gracious.

If Mr. Binyon will choose a large and inspiring epic theme and put all his strength into it, I see no reason why he should not one day rank among the foremost narrative poets of his generation.

LAURENCE BINYON

THE FIRE.

With beckoning fingers bright
In heaven uplifted, from the darkness wakes,
Upon a sudden, radiant Fire,
And out of slumber shakes
Her wild hair to the night;
Bewitching all to run with hurried feet,
And stand, and gaze upon her beauty dire.

For her the shrinking gloom
Yields, and a place prepares;
An ample scene and a majestic room;
Slowly the river bares
His bank; above, in endless tier,
Glittering out of the night the windows come,
To that bright summons; and at last appear,
Hovering, enkindled, and unearthly clear,
Steeple, and tower, and the suspended dome.

But whence are these that haste
So rapt? what throngs along the street that press,
Raised by enchantment from the midnight waste,
That even now was sleeping echoless:
Men without number, lured from near and far
As by a world-portending star!
Lo, on the bright bank without interval
Faces in murmuring line,
With earnest eyes that shine,
Across the stream gaze ever; on the wall
Faces; and dense along the bridge's side
Uncounted faces; softly the wheels glide
Approaching, lest they break the burning hush
Of all that multitude aflush
With secret strange desire.

Warm in the great light, as themselves afire,
Thousands are gazing, and all silently!
How to the throbbing glare their hearts reply,
As tossing upward a dim-sparkled plume,
The beautiful swift Fury scares the sky.
The stars look changed on high,
And red the steeples waver from the gloom
Distantly clear over the water swells
The roar: the iron stanchions dribble bright,
And faltering with strong quiver to its fall,
Drops, slowly rushing, the great outer wall.
From lip to lip a wondering murmur goes,
As crouching a dark moment o'er its prey,
Swiftly again upleaps
The wild flame, and exulting madly glows;
The city burns in an enchanted day.
Still the great throng impassioned silence keeps,
Like an adoring host in ecstasy.
Did ever vision of the opened sky
Entrance more deeply, or did ever voice
Of a just wrath more terribly rejoice?

The houseless beggar gazing has forgot
His hunger: happy lovers' hands relax;
They look no more into each other's eyes.
Wrapt in its mother's shawl
The fretting child no longer cries.
And that soul-piercing flame
Melts out like wax
The prosperous schemer's busy schemes:
The reveller like a visionary gleams.
An aged wandering pair lift up their heads
Out of old memories: to each, to all,
Time and the strong world are no more the same,
But threatened, perishable, trembling, brief,
Even as themselves, an instant might destroy,
With all the builded weight of years and grief,
All that old hope and pleasant usage dear.
Glories and dooms before their eyes appear;
Upon their faces joy,
Within their bosoms fear!
Is it that even now
In all, O radiant Desolation, thou

LAURENCE BINYON

Far off prefigurest
To each obscurely wounded breast
The dream of what shall be?
And in their hearts they see
Rushing in ardent ruin out of sight
With all her splendour, with her streaming robe
Of seas, and her pale peoples, the vast globe
A sullen ember crumble into night?

MISS ALICE BROWN

So far as I am aware, Miss Alice Brown has written only one little book of poetry, *The Road to Castaly*. It runs to seventy pages, and contains about half a hundred poems. They are partly poems of nature, partly personal and dramatic lyrics; and in both classes of work there are pieces of real and striking merit. Excellent, to my thinking, is Miss Brown's strong and highly cultivated style. Her English is of the best—copious, unaffected, pure. The first poems of the collection, *Wood Longing* and *Pan*, are full of an ecstatic sense of the glory and mystery of nature. *Sunrise on Mansfield Mountain* lends itself better to quotation, and I copy the opening lines:

> O swift forerunners, rosy with the race!
> Spirits of dawn, divinely manifest
> Behind your blushing banners in the sky,
> Daring invaders of Night's tenting-ground,—
> How do ye strain on forward-bending foot,
> Each to be first in heralding of joy!
>
> With silence sandalled, so they weave their way,
> And so they stand, with silence panoplied,
> Chanting, through mystic symbollings of flame,
> Their solemn invocation to the light.
>
> O changeless guardians! O ye wizard firs!
> What strenuous philter feeds your potency,
> That thus ye rest, in sweet wood-hardiness,
> Ready to learn of all and utter naught?
> What breath may move ye, or what breeze invite

ALICE BROWN

To odorous hot lendings of the heart?
What wind—but all the winds are yet afar,
And e'en the little tricksy zephyr sprites,
That fleet before them, like their elfin locks,
Have lagged in sleep, nor stir nor waken yet
To pluck the robe of patient majesty.

This is fine verse and fine thought. How admirable are the four lines of the second paragraph! How memorable the phrase which speaks of the pine-trees' "odorous hot lendings of the heart," and the image which represents the "tricksy zephyr sprites" as the elf-locks of the great winds! The poem entitled *The Return* is a spiritual imagining of great strength and beauty. It describes the return of a soul to the room where the body lies dead, and where "one in silence sits apart" from the other mourners.

All night we watched together there;
Strange tryst we kept, my love and I!
My hurrying heart was hot with words
To teach her what it is to die.
Yet, barred within her beauty's cell,
She might not hear, she might not see;
I was alive, but not to her,
And all her soul lay dead to me.

Ah, but the end is yet to read!
When the door opens at her plaint,
When she hath set one forward step,
With bliss fordone, with languor faint,—
Closer than dreams of me have been,
More dear than her immortal breath,
My breast shall be her porch of heaven,
My face her visioning of death.

A West-Country Lover is a lyric of admirable movement, while *Lethe*, quoted at the end of this article, shows exquisite feeling and no small accomplishment. There is variety, too, in Miss Brown's inspiration. *Heimgegangen*, as its title suggests, is a simple and touching folk-song, on the German model; *In Extremis* is a passionate litany, craving deliverance, not from pain or sorrow, but from the "base empery" of fear; and in the following verses, entitled *The Slanderer*, we have a flash of no less passionate satire :

> The angels of the living God,
>   Marked, from of old, with mystic name,
> O'erveil their vision, lest they see
>   One sinner prostrate in his shame.
>
> And God Himself, the only Great,
>   Preserves in heaven one holy spot,
> Where, swept by purifying flame,
>   Transgression is remembered not.
>
> Yet thou, O banqueter on worms,
>   Who wilt not let corruption pass !—
> Dost search out mildew, mould and stain,
>   Beneath a magnifying-glass.
>
> If one lies wounded, there art thou,
>   To prick him deeper where he bleeds ;
> Thy brain, a palimpsest of crime,
>   Thy tongue, the trump of evil deeds.

Nothing that Miss Brown has written is without a certain touch of originality and distinction. But the gem of her book, beyond a doubt, is the little lyric entitled

CANDLEMAS.

> O hearken, all ye little weeds
>   That lie beneath the snow,
> (So low, dear hearts, in poverty so low !)
>   The sun hath risen for royal deeds,
>   A valiant wind the vanguard leads ;
>   Now quicken ye, lest unborn seeds
>   Before ye rise and blow.
>
> O furry living things, adream
>   On winter's drowsy breast,
> (How rest ye there, how softly, safely rest !)
>   Arise and follow where a gleam
>   Of wizard gold unbinds the stream,
>   And all the woodland windings seem
>   With sweet expectance blest.

MISS ALICE BROWN

My birds, come back ! the hollow sky
   Is weary for your note.
(Sweet throat, come back ! O liquid mellow throat !)
   Ere May's soft minions hereward fly,
Shame on ye, laggards, to deny
The brooding breast, the sun-bright eye,
   The tawny shining coat.

If the refrain (for I know not how else to describe the parenthetic third line of each stanza) is of Miss Brown's own invention, she cannot be too warmly congratulated. But be this as it may, the song is an inspiration that ought to take its place in every " Golden Treasury " of English lyrics.

LETHE.

You hope we shall remember, dear,
The happy days when we lived here?
Ah, child, what shouldst thou know of fear,
Whose soul is like a rosy leaf
Floating adown the stream of grief,
The velvet edge incurved, a boat
Unwet with woe, and made to float
Forgetful of the flood beneath,
Whose oozy waters smell of death!
Turn here thy gaze, and look on her,
Thy grandame, who wots not to stir
From her dull corner; note her face
With wrinkles lined; seek out the grace
That once adorned her heyday bloom,
Rusted and worthless in that tomb.
And think you she would greatly care,
If God should make her smooth and fair,
And round and rosy, eyes alight
With youthful pride and longing bright,
To keep that record of the years,
And trace those channels made by tears?
Saying: " In this I wept my son;
This came when old distrust begun;
That line was cut, O cruel spite!
When sweets of loving took their flight."

Nay, then, I think she'd find it good
To stand up in the lustihood
Of youthful grace and new-sprung pride,
And throw her worn-out flesh aside.
And so shall we, if in the day
When sins and ails are purged away,
The cunning record of the brain,
The hates and madness, grief and pain,

64

MISS ALICE BROWN

The murderous deed we did our friend,
The scoff for which there's no amend
May die a natural death, and we
Again like little children be ;
And caring not to understand
Our birth into that other land,
Roam through its valleys, hand in hand.

BLISS CARMAN

A FASCINATING and somewhat baffling talent is that of
Mr. Bliss Carman. His weird and fantastic imagination is
enlisted in the service of a far-reaching philosophy which
purports to gather the whole universe into its embrace; but
the precise nature of that philosophy I cannot for the life of
me discover. A half-stoical, half-rollicking Bohemianism is
one of its prevailing notes; yet every now and then it passes
over, without the slightest modulation, into a sort of grim
and cynical pessimism; while in a number of poems one is
tempted to call it sheer rigmarole, a long-drawn pageant of
symbols which symbolise nothing. I feel that here I am on
dangerous ground. It is quite possible that there may arise
—if it has not already arisen—a sect of Carmanites who, by
brooding on the enigmas of *Behind the Arras*, may hatch
out a religion from the germs of thought which are scattered
through its pages in reckless profusion. Militant sects have
been founded ere now on less cryptic, and certainly less
thoughtful, scriptures. I myself, were I casting about for a
religion, should be tempted to shut myself up for six weeks
or so in a lonely tower, with no literature in my portman-
teau but *Behind the Arras* and *Low Tide on Grand Pré*.
One might easily find much duller and less melodious
sacred books. But as I feel no pressing need for a new
revelation, I am bound to say, at the risk of figuring as an
incredible dullard in the eyes of a Carmanite posterity,

· BLISS · CARMAN ·

that I prefer the Bohemian and humorist in Mr. Carman to the metaphysician and moralist, and am more grateful to him for one whiff of downright Nova-Scotia brine, than for all his researches in the stifling caverns of symbolism.

Let me not be understood, however, to bracket together *Low Tide on Grand Pré* and *Behind the Arras*. When he wrote *Low Tide on Grand Pré* Mr. Carman was not consciously and deliberately a symbolist. This "Book of Lyrics," as he calls it, is genuinely lyrical in intention and in tone; but one respectful and indeed admiring reader must confess his inability, in most cases, to make out what the lyrics are about. Not that they are obscure; on the contrary, taken stanza by stanza, they seem as clear as daylight; but when you have read a lyric through, there is nothing for you to take hold of; nothing to bite on the mind. Even a pure lyric should tell its story, or at least suggest its situation; whereas Mr. Carman rhymes on and on, with grace, feeling and distinction, to leave us wondering at the end of a poem why it was ever begun. In saying this I probably do him injustice. I lack some key, whether of personal knowledge or local association, that should unlock for me the mystery of these Acadian lyrics. Let me quote one (chosen for its brevity, not for any exceptional vagueness in its matter), to exemplify my meaning:

A WIND-FLOWER.

Between the roadside and the wood,
  Between the dawning and the dew,
A tiny flower before the sun,
  Ephemeral in time, I grew.

And there upon the trail of spring,
  Not death nor love nor any name
Known among men in all their lands
  Could blur the wild desire with shame.

But down my dayspan of the year
  The feet of straying winds came by ;
And all my trembling soul was thrilled
  To follow one lost mountain cry.

And then my heart beat once and broke
  To hear the sweeping rain forebode
Some ruin in the April world,
  Between the woodside and the road.

To-night can bring no healing now ;
  The calm of yesternight is gone ;
Surely the wind is but the wind,
  And I a broken waif thereon.

This is chosen, let me add, not only for its brevity, but for
its beauty.   It is a delightful piece of writing ; but perspicuous I cannot think it.   That I do not know the particular flower in question is, of course, my own misfortune;
but though I have the haziest notions as to the "Small
Celandine," my lack of botanical knowledge does not hinder
my enjoyment of Wordsworth's two poems.   One is quite
willing to take the botany for granted, to rely on the poet
for information about whatever flower inspires him; but
Mr. Carman tells me nothing I can grasp or carry away
about the Wind-flower.

And there upon the trail of spring,
  Not death nor love nor any name
Known among men in all their lands
  Could blur the wild desire with shame !

What "wild desire," one asks in amaze?   One dimly con-
jectures, indeed, that this wind-flower is a feminine wind-
flower, and that the poem adumbrates a Village Tragedy.
But I submit that the situation is inadequately suggested,
that the poet expects too much of his reader.   And so it is
with almost all the poems in this book : for instance, *Pulvis
et Umbra*, *Wanderers*, and *Wayfaring*.   We begin a poem
with pleasure, and slip easily along the smooth levels of
Mr. Carman's verse; but presently we find that we have

forgotten whence we started and don't know whither we are going. Mr. Carman uses the English language with such force, freedom and distinction, that one is positively puzzled to know why so few poems in this book give permanent and substantial pleasure. Here is one of the exceptions to this general rule:

A SEA CHILD.

The lover of Child Marjory
    Had one white hour of life brim full;
Now the old nurse, the rocking sea,
    Hath him to lull.

The daughter of Child Marjory
    Hath in her veins, to beat and run,
The glad indomitable sea,
    The strong white sun.

These exquisite versicles, together with two poems at the end of the book, *Marian Drury* and *Golden Rowan*, point the way to Mr. Carman's *Ballads of Lost Haven*, an important contribution to the sea poetry of the language.

Not many poets, even in our island speech, have had a keener or more intimate feeling for the sea than breathes in this little book of Mr. Carman's. The opening poem strikes the keynote: though not necessarily to be taken as a personal utterance, it could not have been written without the liveliest personal sympathy with the habit of mind to which it gives utterance.

A SON OF THE SEA.

I was born for deep sea faring;
    I was bred to put to sea;
Stories of my father's daring
    Filled me at my mother's knee.

I was sired among the surges;
    I was cubbed beside the foam;
All my heart is in its verges,
    And the sea-wind is my home.

POETS OF THE YOUNGER GENERATION

All my boyhood, far from vernal
Bourns of being, came to me
Dream-like, plangent, and eternal
Memories of the plunging sea.

This is an admirable piece of writing, and it preludes an
impressive book.   The terror of the sea appeals even more
strongly than its other allurements to Mr. Carman's mind.
His book is full of the grim superstitions of a stormy coast,
and he dwells, almost to the point of monotony, upon the
maligner aspects of the great waters.   But some of his
poems have an eerie strength, and others a haunting charm,
peculiar to themselves.   Of the former quality, these stanzas
from the second poem in the book may serve as a specimen :

THE GRAVEDIGGER.

Oh, the shambling sea is a sexton old,
    And well his work is done.
With an equal grave for lord and knave,
    He buries them every one.

    *   *   *   *   *

Oh, the ships of Greece and the ships of Tyre
    Went out, and where are they ?
In the port they made, they are delayed
    With the ships of yesterday.

He followed the ships of England far,
    As the ships of long ago ;
And the ships of France they led him a dance,
    But he laid them all arow.

Oh, a loafing, idle lubber to him
    Is the sexton of the town ;
For sure and swift, with a guiding lift,
    He shovels the dead men down.

But though he delves so fierce and grim,
    His honest graves are wide,
As well they know who sleep below
    The dredge of the deepest tide.

The grim power of this song is not more remarkable than
the tenderness of the ballad, called *The Yule Guest*, which

follows it. The ghost of a drowned seaman stands at his sweetheart's door, and cries:

> "O Yanna, Adrianna,
> They buried me away
> In the blue fathoms of the deep,
> Beyond the outer bay.
>
> "But in the yule, O Yanna,
> Up from the round dim sea
> And reeling dungeons of the fog,
> I am come back to thee!"

What a superb phrase is this of the "reeling dungeons of the fog"! It is a thing said perfectly, said once for all. Yanna knows not at first "the change that is upon him."

> "O Garvin, I have waited,—
> Have watched the red sun sink,
> And clouds of sail come flocking in
> Over the world's gray brink.
>
> "With stories of encounter
> On plank and mast and spar;
> But never the brave barque I launched
> And waved across the bar.
>
> "How come you so unsignalled,
> When I have watched so well?
> Where rides the Adrianna
> With my name on boat and bell?"
>
> "O Yanna, golden Yanna,
> The Adrianna lies
> With the sea dredging through her ports,
> The white sand through her eyes.
>
> "And strange unearthly creatures
> Make marvel of her hull,
> Where far below the gulfs of storm
> There is eternal lull."

The ballad is perhaps a little too long, but it is beautiful throughout. A similar criticism applies to *The Marring of Malyn* and *The Kelpie Riders*. Mr. Carman lacks the gift of compression, and does not excel as a narrator. He is at his best in poems that hover on the border-line between the ballad and the mere fantasy, such as *The Nancy's Pride* and *The Master of the Isles*, and in pure lyrics like *The Ships of St. John*. But though uneven in their inspiration, these poems, one and all, bring home to us with a peculiar and searching power the mystery and terror of a stormy northern seaboard.

Perhaps I ought not to write of *Behind the Arras*, for all I can say of it is, in effect, that this sort of unconditioned symbolism has for me personally little or no message. The symbols seem, as it were, to be always shifting their plane, and my mind wearies in the effort to keep, from stanza to stanza, at the right perspective. Mr. Carman's thought is certainly "undulant and diverse" to a degree. Imagine a procession in which the figures do not move steadily past the eye at a constant distance, but are for ever making huge leaps to the right and left of their line of route, now springing forward till you see the whites of their menacing eyes, and anon whisking away till they almost vanish on the far horizon! Mr. Carman's dedication "To G. H. B." runs thus :

> I shut myself in with my soul
> And the shapes come eddying forth.

A still apter motto for the book would be this, from another poet :

> Dusk grew turbulent with fires before me,
> And, like a windy arras, waved with dreams.

"Waved," however, is too tame a term; flapped and flaunted would be nearer it. There is not a wind, but a gale "behind the arras"; it "waves" as a flag waves in a hurricane. All this only means that my personal tone of mind is antagonistic to Mr. Carman's method of visioning the mysteries of the universe ; wherefore I ought, perhaps, simply to say so, and pass on. At the same time I cannot deny myself the pleasure of expressing my sense of the extraordinary individuality and fascinating literary power which mark almost every page of the book. To read it is, to me, a sort of Tantalus agony : I feel "How I should enjoy this, if only I knew what it was about!" The meaning of many of the poems, such as *The Moondial, The Face in the Stream, The Lodger* and *Beyond the Gamut*, entirely eludes me. In others the intention is visible enough, but in a flickering, inconsequent and finally wearisome fashion. The poem which gives the book its title, *Behind the Arras*, is one of the more perspicuous, and certainly not the least powerful. Compression is what it seems chiefly to lack. The fantasy is overwrought in its sixty stanzas. If the whole were as strong as some of its parts it would be a masterpiece. The poet treats of life as a house hung with a "marvellous tapestry,"

> Where such strange things are rife,
> Fancies of beasts and flowers, and love and strife,
> Woven to the life ;
>
> Degraded shapes and splendid seraph forms,
> And teeming swarms
> Of creatures gauzy dim
> That cloud the dusk, and painted fish that swim,
> At the weaver's whim ;
>
> And wonderful birds that wheel and hang in the air ;
> And beings with hair,
> And moving eyes in the face,
> And white bone teeth and hideous grins, who race
> From place to place ;
>
> They build great temples to their John-a-nod,
> And fume and plod
> To deck themselves with gold,
> And paint themselves like chattels to be sold,
> Then turn to mould.
>
> Sometimes they seem almost as real as I ;
> I hear them sigh ;

I see them bow with grief,
Or dance for joy like [to] an aspen leaf;
But that is brief.

    *   *   *   *   *

Strangest of all, they never rest.   Day long
They shift and throng,
Moved by invisible will,
Like a great breath which puffs across my sill,
And then is still;

It shakes my lovely manikins on the wall;
Squall after squall,
Gust upon crowding gust,
It sweeps them willy nilly like blown dust
With glory or lust.

A singularly grim and powerful fantasy is *The Red Wolf*, which seems, though I risk the conjecture with diffidence, to symbolise melancholia.   It is somewhat marred, to my ear, by the atrocious rhyme of " dwarf" with " laugh" which runs through it:

With the fall of the leaf comes the wolf, wolf, wolf,
    The old red wolf at my door,
And my hateful yellow dwarf, with his hideous crooked laugh,
    Cries, " Wolf, wolf, wolf! " at my door.

A little poem called *In the Wings* is so characteristic and yet (comparatively) so perspicuous that I quote it entire:

The play is Life; and this round earth
    The narrow stage whereon
We act before an audience
    Of actors dead and gone.

There is a figure in the wings
    That never goes away,
And though I cannot see his face,
    I shudder while I play.

His shadow looms behind me here,
    Or capers at my side;
And when I mouth my lines in dread,
    Those scornful lips deride.

BLISS CARMAN

Sometimes a hooting laugh breaks out,
    And startles me alone;
While all my fellows, wondering
    At my stage-fright, play on.

I fear that when my Exit comes,
    I shall encounter there,
Stronger than fate, or time, or love,
    And sterner than despair,

The Final Critic of the craft,
    As stage tradition tells;
And yet—perhaps 't will only be
    The jester with his bells.

The finest thing in the volume, to my mind, a piece of wonderfully apt, grotesque and yet impressive symbolism, is *The Juggler*, quoted at the end of this article.

It is refreshing to turn from *Behind the Arras* to the two series of *Songs from Vagabondia*, which Mr. Carman has published in fellowship with Mr. Richard Hovey. The poems are unsigned, but I am able, from private information, to set apart the contributions of the two poets. I should have been puzzled to do so from internal evidence, so cleverly has each caught the other's strain of humour. This word I use advisedly, for the note of the booklets is a freakish, devil-may-care whimsicality. Tavern staves and jingles alternate with society verses, rollicking Irish ballads, and death's-head fantasies. But there is literary power everywhere; and here and there true poetry, in the narrower sense of the word, breaks through. Among Mr. Carman's contributions there is none more truly inspired, I think, than this perfect little ditty:

DAISIES.

Over the shoulders and slopes of the dune
    I saw the white daisies go down to the sea,
A host in the sunshine, an army in June,
    The people God sends us to set our heart free.

> The bobolinks rallied them up from the dell,
> The orioles whistled them out of the wood;
> And all of their singing was, " Earth, it is well! "
> And all of their dancing was, " Life, thou art good! "

These two quatrains proclaim their author a poet, just as
clearly as many a laboured epic proclaims—the reverse.
In *Quince to Lilac* Mr. Carman pens an epistle from a
Quince-blossom, which holds conference every morning with
a certain Man, to a Lilac-flower which, as the Man tells her,
is worshipped by a certain Lady. The odd questions which
the Man asks the Quince give her " infinite amusement."
" And yet," she continues,

> And yet who knows? He may be
>   Our equal ages hence—
> With such pathetic glimmers
>   Of weird intelligence.
>
> But this your blessed alien,
>   Why strays she roving here?
> Was Orpheus not her brother,
>   Persephone her peer?
>
> Was she not once a dryad
>   Whom Syrinx lulled to sleep
> Beside the Dorian water,
>   And still her eyelids keep
>
> The glad unperished secret
>   From centuries of joy,
> And memories of the morning
>   When Helen sailed for Troy?

Returning to the subject of human absurdity, the Quince
proceeds thus:

> They have a thing called *science*,
>   With phrases strange and pat.
> My dear, can you imagine
>   Intelligence like that?
>
> And when they first discover
>   That yellows are not greens,
> They pucker up their foreheads
>   And ponder what it means.

76

And then those cave-like places,
   Churches and Capitols,
Where they all come together
   Like troops of talking dolls,

To govern, as they term it,
   (It's really very odd!)
And have what they call worship
   Of something they call God.

But Kitty, or whatever
   May be her tender name,
Is more like us. She guesses
   What sets the year aflame.

She knows beyond her senses;
   Do tell her all you can!
The funny people need it—
   At least, so says the Man.

You may class this as society verse or what you please; but
it is true poetry none the less. *The Unsainting of Kavin*
and *In the Wayland Willows* are light and daring rhythms
of the joy of life, and *Mr. Moon: A Song of the Little
People* is a fascinating jingle from Brownie-land. Here,
finally, is a characteristic little conceit, born of a more
sombre mood :

IN A GARDEN.

Thought is a garden wild and old
   For airy creatures to explore,
Where grow the great fantastic flowers
   With truth for honey at the core.

There like a wild marauding bee
   Made desperate by hungry fears,
From gorgeous *If* to dark *Perhaps*
   I blunder down the dusk of years.

In Mr. Carman's last book, *By the Aurelian Wall, and
other Poems : A Book of Elegies*, there is still a good deal of
that insubstantiality, I had almost said inconsequence, of
thought which baffles one in *Low Tide on Grand Pré.*
The name-poem, an elegy on Keats, presents a definite,
but not, I think, a very consistent or luminous image, while

The White Gull, written for the centenary of the birth of
Shelley, seems to me to say very little in a great many
words. Its measure, however, is beautiful ; witness these
two opening stanzas :

> Up by the idling reef-set bell
> The tide comes in ;
> And to the idle heart to-day
> The wind has many things to say ;
> The sea has many a tale to tell
> His younger kin.
>
> For we are his, bone of his bone,
> Breath of his breath ;
> The doom tides sway us at their will ;
> The sky of being rounds us still ;
> And over us at last is blown
> The wind of death.

There is beautiful work in *The Country of Hur,* written
for the centenary of Blake's *Songs of Innocence ;* but the
most successful poems in the book, to my mind, are those
inspired by American subjects, the elegies on Phillips
Brooks, John Eliot Bowen, and Henry George. In *Ilicet,*
an elegy on a suicide, Mr. Carman has again invented a
beautiful measure, but has left his thought too patently
under the control of his intricate rhyme-scheme. There is
wit in the address *To Raphael,* but not enough, I think, to
atone for the rhyme in the first stanza :

> Master of adored Madonnas,
>   What is this men say of thee ?
> Thou wert something less than honor's
>   Most exact epitome ?

The verses on Verlaine are clear in idea, but not
specially inspired ; and the remainder of the book is given
up to poems commemorating friendships and comradeships
in the love of wild nature, which contain many beautiful
details, but no single number that seems to me quite
masterly and satisfying.

Of Mr. Carman's remarkable gifts there can be no doubt whatever. His fluency is sometimes a little out of proportion to the substance of his thought. He is apt, now and then, to dilute his ideas to the point of extreme tenuity, or to whip them up into a shimmering but elusive froth. Of his mysticism, as aforesaid, I desire to speak with all caution, for no doubt I lack the temperamental clue to it ; but there are a good many poems of no specially mystical cast, in which the words seem to me simply to drown and disintegrate the thought. He is always a poet, however ; his vision is intense, his imagination potent, his diction strong and free ; and when he achieves compression and clarity, the result is poetry of a very high order.

THE JUGGLER.

Look how he throws them up and up,
The beautiful golden balls !
They hang aloft in the purple air,
And there never is one that falls.

He sends them hot from his steady hand,
He teaches them all their curves :
And whether the reach be little or long,
There never is one that swerves.

Some, like the tiny red one there,
He never lets go far ;
And some he has sent to the roof of the tent
To swim without a jar.

So white and still they seem to hang,
You wonder if he forgot
To reckon the time of their return
And measure their golden lot.

Can it be that, hurried or tired out,
The hand of the juggler shook ?
O never you fear, his eye is clear,
He knows them all like a book.

And they will home to his hand at last,
For he pulls them by a cord
Finer than silk and strong as fate,
That is just the bid of his word.

Was ever there such a sight in the world
Like a wonderful winding skein,—
The way he tangles them up together
And ravels them out again !

BLISS CARMAN

He has so many moving now,
You can hardly believe your eyes;
And yet they say he can handle twice
The number when he tries.

You take your choice and give me mine,
I know the one for me,
It's that great bluish one low down
Like a ship's light out at sea.

It has not moved for a minute or more.
The marvel that it can keep
As if it had been set there to spin
For a thousand years asleep!

If I could have him at the inn
All by myself some night,—
Inquire his country, and where in the world
He came by that cunning sleight!

Where do you guess he learned the trick
To hold us gaping here,
Till our minds in the spell of his maze almost
Have forgotten the time of year?

One never could have the least idea.
Yet why be disposed to twit
A fellow who does such wonderful things
With the merest lack of wit?

Likely enough, when the show is done
And the balls all back in his hand,
He'll tell us why he is smiling so,
And we shall understand.

HEM AND HAW

Hem and Haw were the sons of sin,
Created to shally and shirk;
Hem lay 'round and Haw looked on
While God did all the work.

81

F

Hem was a fogy, and Haw was a prig,
For both had the dull dull mind ;
And whenever they found a thing to do,
They yammered and went it blind.

Hem was the father of bigots and bores ;
As the sands of the sea were they.
And Haw was the father of all the tribe
Who criticise to-day.

But God was an artist from the first,
And knew what he was about ;
While over his shoulder sneered these two,
And advised him to rub it out.

They prophesied ruin ere man was made :
" Such folly must surely fail ! "
And when he was done, " Do you think, my Lord,
He's better without a tail ? "

And still in the honest working world,
With posture and hint and smirk,
These sons of the devil are standing by
While Man does all the work.

They balk endeavour and baffle reform,
In the sacred name of law ;
And over the quavering voice of Hem
Is the droning voice of Haw.

MADISON CAWEIN

EIGHT books by Mr. Madison Cawein lie before me; yet I gather from announcements they contain that several other volumes stand to his credit—or debit. The truth is, Mr. Cawein's fluency has done grave injustice to his real talent. He has written far, far too much. Seven-eighths of his work, at a low estimate, had much better have been unpublished. There are marks of the poet in everything he writes—imagination, passion, love of nature, sense of rhythm, and an opulent, not to say extravagant, vocabulary. But in his earlier books these advantages are totally unaccompanied by distinction of style, or even by the most rudimentary sense of congruity in thought and language. He will fly anywhere for a rhyme, and let reason come limping after as best it may. It is quite possible that in the eleven hundred closely-printed pages of his *Moods and Memories, Days and Dreams, Red Leaves and Roses, Poems of Nature and Love,* and *Intimations of the Beautiful,* there may lurk poems of real accomplishment, such as occur in his later volumes. I have looked into all these books; but the mind becomes so fatigued in wading through the marish jungle of Mr. Cawein's unpruned, unchastened fancy, that it presently loses all power of discrimination and cannot tell the flower from the weed. On every possible and impossible subject the poet rhymes and rhapsodises. The bent of his imagination is romantic, and he has ransacked every storehouse of myth and legend—Oriental, Græco-Latin, Scandinavian, Arthurian, Provençal, Peninsular, Mexican, Peruvian. His personal, or seemingly personal, lyrics are numberless; he has Browningesque soul-dramas in plenty, and at least one long poem of Tennysonian self-communings in a measure developed from that of *In Memoriam*. From Keats, from Poe, even from Byron and Moore, he seems, in these earlier books, to have borrowed the obvious and vicious portions of their method. Every now and then we come across a stanza or two which promises a really fine poem ; but the promise is certain to be falsified ere long by some flaccid verse, strained image or grotesque rhyme. In a sequence called *One Day and Another* (for example) there occurs the following little song, which would be pretty enough but for its fourth and fifth stanzas :

BECOMING IMPATIENT.

The owls are quavering, two, now three,
   And all the green is graying ;
The owls our trysting dials be—
   There is no time for staying.

I wait you where this buckeye throws
   Its tumbled shadow over
Wood-violet and the bramble-rose,
   Long lady-fern and clover.

Spice-seeded sassafras weighs deep
   Rough rail and broken paling,
Where all day long the lizards sleep
   Like lichen on the railing.

Behind you you will feel the moon's
   Gold stealing like young laughter ;
And mists—gray ghosts of picaroons—
   Its phantom treasures after.

And here together, youth and youth,
   Love will be doubly able ;
Each be to each as true as truth ;
   And dear as fairy fable.

· MADISON · CAWEIN ·

MADISON CAWEIN

> The owls are calling and the maize
> With fallen dew is dripping—
> Ah, girlhood, through the dewy haze
> Come like a moonbeam slipping.

The lizard sleeping all day long "like lichen on the railing" is a charming touch; but what are we to say of the picaroon mists stealing after the moon's gold which is like young laughter? Or take, again, the following:

> We stood where the fields were tawny,
> Where the redolent woodland was warm;
> And the Maytime above us, now lawny,
> Was alive with the pulse winds of storm.

That "now lawny" conveys some meaning to Mr. Cawein's mind I have no doubt, but it is clearly a meaning invented for the sake of the rhyme. I cull another characteristic stanza from these early books:

> No sail on the ocean; no sailor
> On shore, and the winds all asleep;
> And thy face in the starlight far paler
> Than women who weep.
> A mist on the deep that was ghostly;
> A moon in the deep of the skies;
> The mist and the moon they were mostly
> In thee and thine eyes.

This is not burlesque rhyming; it is a stanza from a very serious sequence of lyrics entitled *Wreckage*. The following, I am sorry to say, occurs in a comparatively recent book; it is of course purposely light in tone, but there is a point at which playfulness passes over into puerility:

> My love went berrying
> Where brooks were merrying
> And wild wings ferrying
> Heaven's amethyst;
> The wild-flowers blessed her,
> My dearest Hester,
> The winds caressed her,
> The sunbeams kissed.

And so on for six stanzas. As a final instance of what Mr. Cawein can do in the way of tastelessness, take the following :

MOONRISE AT SEA.

With lips that were hoarse with a fury
　　Of foam and of winds that were strewn,
Of storm and of turbulent hurry,
　　The ocean roared, heralding soon
A birth of miraculous glory,
　　Of madness, affection—the moon.

And soon from her waist with a slipping
　　And shudder and clinging of light,
With a loos'ning and pushing and ripping
　　Of the sable-laced bodice of Night,
With a silence of feet and a dripping
　　The wonder came, virginal white.

Had I received my first impression of Mr. Cawein from the book in which this poem occurs, I fear my first impression would have been my last.

Fortunately Mr. Cawein has in great measure belied the threat of these early effusions. He has written two little books—*Undertones* and *Myth and Romance*—in which his talent, coming apparently to sudden maturity, puts off its worst mannerisms, and puts on, from time to time at any rate, that distinction in which it had hitherto been totally lacking. Bizarrerie becomes originality, and a conventionally romantic habit of mind develops into an almost classical sense of the divinity lurking in the aspects of nature. Mr. Cawein is an eminently, exclusively American poet. His fancy has travelled far and wide, but there is nothing in his work to show that he is personally familiar with any other country than his own. It is American nature that he observes, very closely to all appearance, and lovingly depicts. His birds, flowers, trees are all American ; his landscapes are American, his seasons American. A glossary to his writings—they almost need one for the English reader—

would be a dictionary of the flora and fauna of Kentucky and Ohio. But he brings to his study of American nature (and this is the characteristic note of his work) an imagination saturated with European myth and folk-lore. He peoples the forest primeval of the New World with the elemental spirits of the Old. "The Gods in Exile," according to Mr. Cawein, have emigrated to America, and he is their fervent worshipper. This habit of mind finds fullest and most self-conscious expression in the following poem ; but it pervades the whole body of Mr. Cawein's maturer work :

MYTH AND ROMANCE.

I.

When I go forth to greet the glad-faced Spring,
　Just at the time of opening apple-buds,
When brooks are laughing, winds are whispering,
　On babbling hillsides or in warbling woods,
　There is an unseen presence that eludes—
Perhaps a Dryad, in whose tresses cling
　The loamy odors of old solitudes,
Who, from her beechen doorway, calls ; and leads
　My soul to follow ; now with dimpling word
　Of leaves ; and now with syllables of birds ;
While here and there—is it her limbs that swing ?
Or restless sunlight on the moss and weeds ?

　　*　　　*　　　*　　　*　　　*

III.

Or now it is an Oread—whose eyes
　Are constellated dusk—who stands confessed,
As naked as a flow'r ; her heart's surprise,
　Like morning's rose, mantling her brow and breast :
　She, shrinking from my presence, all distressed
Stands for a startled moment ere she flies,
　Her deep hair blowing, up the mountain crest,
Wild as a mist that trails along the dawn.
　And is't her footfalls lure me ? or the sound
　Of airs that stir the crisp leaf on the ground ?
And is't her body glimmers on yon rise ?
Or dog-wood blossoms snowing on the lawn ?

87

IV.

Now 'tis a Satyr piping serenades
   On a slim reed. Now Pan and Faun advance
Beneath green-hollowed roofs of forest glades,
    Their feet gone mad with music : now, perchance,
    Sylvanus sleeping, on whose leafy trance
The Nymphs stand gazing in dim ambuscades
   Of sun-embodied perfume.—Myth, Romance,
Where'er I turn, reach out bewildering arms,
    Compelling me to follow. Day and night
    I hear their voices and behold the light
Of their divinity that still evades,
And still allures me in a thousand forms.

I do not know whether ultra-Americans will quite approve this intrusion of Olympus into the fastnesses of "Gitche Manito the mighty"; but surely they will at least condone it, in consideration of the deep and intimate love of American nature which inspires all Mr. Cawein's singing. How delicate, both in idea and in melody, is the following lyric:

MAY.

The golden disks of the rattlesnake-weed,
   That spangle the woods and dance—
No gleam of gold that the twilights hold
   Is strong as their necromance :
For under the oaks where the wood-paths lead,
The golden disks of the rattlesnake-weed
   Are May's own utterance.

The azure stars of the bluet-bloom,
   That sprinkle the woodland's trance—
No blink of blue that a cloud lets through
   Is sweet as their countenance :
For, over the knolls that the woods perfume,
The azure stars of the bluet-bloom
   Are the light of the May's own glance.

With her wondering words and her looks she comes,
   In a sunbeam of a gown ;
She needs but think, and the blossoms wink,
   But look, and they shower down.
By orchard ways, where the wild-bee hums,
With her wondering words and her looks she comes,
   Like a little maid to town.

Nothing could be more American than this. The rattle-snake-weed and the bluet-bloom were unknown to Herrick and to Wordsworth ; but Mr. Cawein makes them at home in English poetry.

He is at his best, I think, in the quiet pastoral mood: for instance, in such poems as *The Willow Bottom*, a picture of drowsy summer, and *A Song in Season*, a companion picture of frost-bound winter. There is considerable originality of form in some of Mr. Cawein's lyrics: for instance, in *Old Homes* quoted at the end of this article, and in the following delightful little lyric :

MEETING IN SUMMER.

A tranquil bar
Of rosy twilight under dusk's first star.

A glimmering sound
Of whispering waters over grassy ground.

A sun-sweet smell
Of fresh-reaped hay from dewy field and dell.

A lazy breeze
Jostling the ripeness from the apple-trees.

A vibrant cry,
Passing, then gone, of bullbats in the sky.

And faintly now
The katydid upon the shadowy bough.

And far-off then
The little owl within the lonely glen.

And soon, full soon,
The silvery arrival of the moon.

And, to your door,
The path of roses I have trod before.

And, sweetheart, you !
Among the roses and the moonlit dew.

Though he probably excels in what may be called still-life pictures, passion and thought are by no means absent from Mr. Cawein's equipment. The stanzas in *Monochromes* beginning "Go your own ways," are very impressive in their dignified movement—witness the last of the three:

> Though sands be black and bitter black the sea,
>   Night lie before me and behind me night,
>   And God within far heaven refuse to light
> The consolation of the dawn for me,—
>   Between the shadowy bourns of Heaven and Hell,
>   It is enough love leaves my soul to dwell
>   With memory.

There are fine things among his epigrammatic *Quatrains* —notably, as it seems to me, the second of the two here quoted:

OPPORTUNITY.

> Behold a hag whom Life denies a kiss
> As he rides questward in knighterrant-wise;
> Only when he hath passed her is it his
> To know, too late, the Fairy in disguise.

BEAUTY.

> High as a star, yet lowly as a flower,
> Unknown she takes her unassuming place
> At Earth's proud masquerade—the appointed hour
> Strikes, and, behold, the marvel of her face.

The following verses express, not, certainly, a new idea, but one which I do not remember to have seen more fitly or vitally worded:

TRANSMUTATION.

> To me all beauty that I see
>   Is melody made visible;
> An earth-translated state, maybe,
>   Of music heard in Heaven or Hell.

MADISON CAWEIN

Out of some love-impassioned strain
  Of saints, the rose evolved its bloom ;
And, dreaming of it here again,
  Perhaps re-lives it as perfume.

Out of some chant that demons sing
    Of hate and pain, the sunset grew
And, haply, still remembering,
    Re-lives it here as some wild hue

Mr. Cawein, in brief, lacks none of the poet's gifts except
—a large exception !—the sense of style. So much of his
work is fatally undistinguished, that when he attains distinction we are apt to feel that he has not sought it but
stumbled upon it. This feeling, however, is in some measure
unjust, else his finer poems would be scattered throughout
his many volumes instead of being concentrated in his two
or three latest collections. It is evident that he has acquired,
or is acquiring, a delicacy of taste of which, some years ago,
he did not dream. His self-criticism still stops short on the
hither side of fastidiousness; but there is no reason to
suppose that the process of development has ceased.
Perhaps he himself may one day subject his high-piled
granary to the winnowing process it so sadly needs, and,
scattering the chaff to the winds, give us the residual treasure-
heap of pure poetic wheat.

OLD HOMES.

Old homes among the hills ! I love their gardens,
Their old rock-fences, that our day inherits;
Their doors, 'round which the great trees stand like wardens;
Their paths, down which the shadows march like spirits;
Broad doors and paths that reach bird-haunted gardens.

I see them gray among their ancient acres,
Severe of front, their gables lichen-sprinkled,
Like gentle-hearted, solitary Quakers,
Grave and religious, with kind faces wrinkled,
Serene among their memory-hallowed acres.

Their gardens, banked with roses and with lilies—
Those sweet aristocrats of all the flowers—
Where Springtime mints her gold in daffodillies,
And Autumn coins her marigolds in showers,
And all the hours are toilless as the lilies

I love their orchards where the gay woodpecker
Flits, flashing o'er you, like a winged jewel;
Their woods, whose floors of moss the squirrels checker
With half-hulled nuts; and where, in cool renewal,
The wild brooks laugh, and raps the red woodpecker.

Old homes ! old hearts ! Upon my soul forever
Their peace and gladness lie like tears and laughter;
Like love they touch me, through the years that sever,
With simple faith ; like friendship, draw me after
The dreamy patience that is theirs forever.

MADISON CAWEIN

A SONG IN SEASON.

I.

When in the wind the vane turns round,
    And round, and round ;
And in his kennel whines the hound
When all the gable eaves are bound
With icicles of ragged gray,
    A glinting gray ;
There is little to do, and much to say,
And you hug your fire and pass the day
    With a thought of the springtime, dearie.

II.

When late at night the owlet hoots,
    And hoots, and hoots ;
And wild winds make of keyholes flutes ;
When to the door the goodman's boots
Stamp through the snow the light stains red,
    The fire-light's red ;
There is nothing to do, and all is said,
And you quaff your cider and go to bed
    With a dream of the summer, dearie.

III.

When, nearing dawn, the black cock crows,
    And crows, and crows ;
And from the barn the milch-cow lows ;
And the milkmaid's cheeks have each a rose,
And the still skies show a star or two,
    Or one or two ;
There is little to say, and much to do,
And the heartier done the happier you,
    With a song of the winter, dearie.

A. T. QUILLER COUCH

MR. QUILLER COUCH was a poet before he left Clifton College. One of his school poems, *Athens*, was privately printed at Bodmin in 1881, and is treasured in the British Museum. It is not miraculous—not a *Blessed Damozel* —but it is remarkable work for a schoolboy. At Oxford he distinguished himself by the ingenious and spirited parodies collected (with other verses) under the title of *Green Bays* (1893). Up to this point, however, his verse denoted general literary capacity rather than specially poetic endowment. It is on his single volume of *Poems and Ballads* (1896) that his position as a poet is based, and based, I think, very firmly.

The journalist in Mr. Couch has done some injustice to the poet. It is much to be regretted that a man who can write such admirable verse should write so little. But the time that he gives to prose is not all a dead loss to poetry; for several of his short stories in *Noughts and Crosses*, *The Delectable Duchy*, and *Wandering Heath*, are as true poems as any in the language. My present business, however, is not with prose poems. Whatever the compensations, one cannot but regret that Mr. Couch's verse should be so scant in quantity, for in quality it is individual and often delightful. Poetry is an art which demands more leisure and a less pre-occupied mind than Mr. Couch, I suspect, is in a position to bring to it. The poet must be able to lie in

94

· A · T · QVILLER · COVCH ·

wait for his ideas and imprison them as they arise, not in mere notebook jottings, but in poetic form. When a great poem knocks at the doors of Being, it is not to be put off till a more convenient season. "Now or never" it wails, as it is reabsorbed into the vasty deep from whence it sprang. The poet who cultivates the Muse only in his leisure moments may do good work, but scarcely great. In a word, if Mr. Couch wrote more verse he would write it still better. But for what we have received I, for my part, am truly thankful.

Along with his many qualities, Mr. Couch has two limitations. The first is a lack of metrical impulse, manifesting itself in a preference for short, staccato measures, often very cunningly woven, but lacking in swing and sonority. The second limitation is an odd one in so excellent a story-teller—several of his poems do not tell their own story, or tell it but obscurely. Here is a piece, for example, which ought to be very impressive—which *is* impressive in its very vagueness—but would certainly have been none the worse for a little definition of outline :

SHADOWS.

As I walked out on Hallows' E'en,
I saw the moon swing thin and green ;
I saw beside, in Fiddler's Wynd,
Two hands that moved upon a blind.

As I walked out on Martin's Feast,
I heard a woman say to a priest—
" His grave is digged, his shroud is sewn ;
And the child shall pass for his very own."

But whiles they stood beside his tomb,
I heard the babe laugh out in her womb—
" My hair will be black as his was red,
And I have a mole where his heart bled."

There is a touch of the Border Ballad—*Clerk Saunders* or *The Twa Corbies*—in this, as in a good many others of

Mr. Couch's pieces; and their spirit is seized with excellent skill and sympathy. But the significance of the "Two hands that moved upon the blind" somehow escapes me. If Mr. Couch had hit upon a more speaking trait for this couplet, the poem would not have been less impressive for being less enigmatic. The shadow pantomime is not enough. Tennyson objected to Wordsworth's *Thorn* that there was too much "hammering to set a scene for so small a drama." Here Mr. Couch has fallen into the opposite error. After much wrestling with *Sabina* (the second poem in the book) I think I have fathomed its mystery. It is the allegory of a mother's pain on surrendering her son to the love of another woman:

> The stair was steep; the Tower was tall;
>   Sabina's strength was gone:
> She leaned a hand against the wall
>   And let her boy run on.
>
>   *   *   *   *   *
>
> "Child! Child!" she called, and "Wait for me!"
>   But ever the boy's feet ran;
> And up through the Whisp'ring Gallery
>   Came the voice of her dead man—
>
>   *   *   *   *   *
>
> The dead man said, "He will not wait.
>   High in a naked room
> A maiden listens, strong as fate,
>   And selfish as the tomb.
>
> "Her sisters, as they cross the floor,
>   Throw glances at the clock:
> Her father fumbles with the door,
>   He knows he may not lock:
>
> "Her mother pins the bridal crown,
>   And pricks her trembling thumbs:
> But the bride has laid her mirror down,
>   Her small foot drums and drums.
>
> "A minute—hark! Ah joy, ah joy!
>   The helpless door falls wide,
> The harp of God and the laugh of a boy
>   Sing aubade to the bride.

A. T. QUILLER COUCH

" The bride she rises from her chair—
Now never stretch your hands !
The harp, the voice, the climbing stair—
Naught else she understands."

The idea comes out pretty clearly in these stanzas (how
fine the third of them is, by the way !) ; but they are only
seven out of eighteen, and the remaining verses, as it seems
to me, only obscure, or, at the very least, overburden, the
allegory. As for *Doom Ferry* and *Dolor Oogo* (a very strong
piece of work, I imagine, if only one could grasp the situation), as for *The Comrade* and *The Gentle Savage*, I have
given them up in despair. To a more strenuous spirit, no
doubt, they might yield up their secret ; but I submit that,
in the first two at any rate, there ought to be no need for
fumbling after a clue. *The Comrade* and *The Gentle Savage*
are symbolical or spiritual songs, and perhaps I lack the
spiritual instinct or experience which should enable me to
interpret them. But *Doom Ferry* and *Dolor Oogo* are
simply ballads ; and a ballad which does not tell its own
story is like a clock with no hands. Be the workmanship
never so perfect, the thing does not serve its primary
purpose.

The longest of these *Poems and Ballads* is a blank-verse
monologue entitled *Columbus at Seville*. It is a strong and
even masterly piece of work. It would not be out of place
among Browning's *Dramatis Personæ*, only that the blank
verse has not Browning's spasmodic vigour, but rather the
smooth polish of Matthew Arnold. Here is a really noble
passage :

Day by day
For two long years, seated among my books,
Maps, charts, and cross-staves, in the little shop
By Seville Bridge, incessant I had watched
The Guadalquiver through a dusty pane ;
Had watched the thin mast creep around the point ;
Had watched the slow hull warp across the tide,
And the long flank fall lazy to the quay

—Levantine traders bringing Tyrian wine,
Malmsey from Crete, fine lawn of Cyprus, silk
Of Egypt and of India. Genovese,
Whose sheer I conned and knew the shipwright's name,
—Feluccas, with a world of eastern spice
Bartered of Caspian merchants on the bar
Of Poti, or of Emosaïd clans
Down the Red Sea and south to Mozambique :
True aloes of Socotra, galbanum,
Myrrh, cassia, rhubarb, scented calamus,
Sweet storax, cinnamon, attars of the rose
And jasmine. And of some the skippers wore
Skin purses belted underneath their knives
—Spoilers of Ormuz or of Serendib,
Who sought the jeweller's offices ere they slept
Or drank ashore. These from the sunrise all :
But others from the dark and narrow seas
By England and by Flanders.

Again, what could be better, in its humour and its irony, than this passage :

At Salamanca then they tested us ;
Churchmen and schoolmen and cosmogoners
In council. " Hey ! " and " What ? " " The earth a sphere ?
And two ways to Cathaia ? " " Tut and tush ! "
" Feared the Cathaians then no blood in the head
From walking upside-down ? " " Pray did I know
Of a ship 'would sail up-hill ? " " Had I not heard
Perchance of latitudes when the wheel of the sun
Kept the sea boiling ? Of the tropic point
Where white men turned hop-skip to blackamoors ? "
" And hark ye, sir, to what Augustine says,
And here is Cosmas' map. ' God built the world
As a tabernacle : sky for roof and sides,
And earth for flooring . . . Made all men to dwell
Upon the face of it '—the face, you hear,
Not several faces—' On foundations laid
The earth abides '—foundations, if you please,
Not mid-air. Soothly, sir, at your conceits
We smile, but warn you that they lie not far
On this side heresy. ' Antipodes,' hey ?
Our Mother Church annuls the Antipodes."

The whole poem, indeed, is accomplished and beautiful, with scarcely a weak line in it. Moreover, it is well constructed, working up to a pathetic and beautiful climax:

Years afterward, when black was favour's torch
And faith took bribes; when Ferdinand betrayed,
And Bobadilla, High Commissioner,
Foamed at his lunatic height, raged like a beast,
Cast us in chains, shipped us like beeves to Spain—
Then, from the pit of that most brutal fall
A voice commanded " Break his chains! He shall
In person stand before us, plead his cause."
Carefully then I dressed me as became
The Admiral of the Ocean. Squire and page
And retinue—I did abate no jot
While the purse bled. A prince, and all a prince,
I passed between the sneering chamber crowd,
The whispering abjects of the ante-rooms,
Into the presence: stood there, cold, erect.
" I am Columbus. I have left my chains
Nailed at my bed's head by the crucifix:
And come to know what further, O my King? "
Then Ferdinand—I saw him bite his lip—
Sat with pink face averted. But the Queen
Rose from her throne, silent—I would have knelt;
Too late! She stretched her hands and, silent yet,
Gazed, and the world fell from us, and we wept—
We two, together . . .
Ah, blessed hands! Ah, blessed woman's hands—
Stretched to undo irreparable wrong!
Yea, the more blest being all impotent !
A queen's I had not touched: but hers met mine
In humbleness across man's common doom,
In sadness and in wisdom beyond pride.
They are cold beside her now, and cannot stir.
Further than I have travelled she hath fared:
But I shall follow. Soon will come the call:
And I shall grip the tiller once again.

Mr. Couch always writes well in grave and classic measures. Here, for instance, is a strong and beautiful stanza from a description of the gods of old sleeping their long sleep on a green lawn beside a stilly lake:

> There the long grasses topped a banquet spread
>   —For that the turf had been their only table—
> With cates and fruit and delicate white bread,
>   Roses afloat in craters carved with fable.
>   There droop'd a wreath from each relaxèd head,
>   And there on garland and on god were shed
>   The coverlet of years innumerable.

Keats would have loved and envied the line "Roses afloat in craters carved with fable." Mr. Couch's most characteristic note, however, is not that of culture-poetry, but of primitive Keltic imagination, expressing itself in simple ballad measure. To my thinking, the most indubitably inspired of his poems is that weird transcript of a legend with which he has also dealt in prose, *The Masquer in the Street*. It is quoted in full at the end of this article. Equally characteristic, if not equally haunting, is *The Planted Heel*, a poem instinct with a very peculiar quality of imagination. The same may be said of *The Least of These* and the Carols: they are as Cornish as saffron cakes or tamarisk hedges.

One can also trace in Mr. Couch the influence of the sixteenth- and seventeenth-century lyrists. It was a genuine affinity that made him the editor of that delightful anthology, *The Golden Pomp, a Procession of English Lyrics from Surrey to Shirley*. Take, for example, this tender and exquisite little song, a trait direct from love's psychology:

THE KERCHIEF.

> When I 'gan to know thee, dear,
>   Thy faults I did espy;
> And "Sure this is a blemish here,
>   And that's a blot," said I.

> But from that hour I did resign
>   My judgment to my fate,
> Thou art no more than only mine
>   To love and vindicate.

A. T. QUILLER COUCH

> The kerchief that thou gav'st I wear
> Upon mine eyelids bound,
> And every man I meet I dare
> To find the faults I found.

This might quite well be signed by the best of the Cavalier Poets. For the form of his poem on the loss of the *Victoria* Mr. Couch has gone still further back and has adapted the stanza of Drayton's *Agincourt*. Making all allowance for deliberate quaintness of form, one has to admit that there are one or two unfortunate prosaisms in these spirited verses; notably the conclusion of this stanza:

> But She, the stricken hull,
> The doomed, the beautiful,
> Proudly to fate abased
> Her brow Titanic.
> Praise now her multitude
> Who, nursed in fortitude,
> Fell in on deck and faced
> Death without panic.

The final verses, on the other hand, are memorably noble:

> Now for the seamen whom
> Thy not degenerate womb
> Gave thus to die for thee,
> England, be tearless:
> Rise, and with front serene
> Answer, thou Spartan queen,
> " Still God is good to me :
> My sons are fearless."

> Back to the flags that fly
> Half-mast at Tripoli,
> Back on the sullen drum
> Mourning *Victoria*,
> Loud, ay, and jubilant,
> Hurl thine imperial chant—
> *In morte talium*
> *Stat Matris gloria !*

With a few amendments of detail, this poem would be worthy a place of honour in every *Lyra Heroica* of the future.

THE MASQUER IN THE STREET.

Masquer on the rainy stones,
  Jigging, twirling 'neath the rain,
Wherefore shake thine aged bones
    To that antique strain?

Limp thy locks and lank and thinned,
  Thy grey beard it floats a yard;
And thy coat tails flap i' the wind
    Like a torn placard.

"Hush!" saith he; "there was a House—
  From its porch the cressets flared:
Lads in livery called 'Carouse!
    For thy lust's prepared!'

"Like a snake the prelude wound—
  Crash! the merry waltz began:
One unto my mind I found,
    And our feet ran.

"Rubies ripped from altar-cloths
  Leered adown her silk attire;
Her mad shoes were scarlet moths
    In a rose of fire.

"Tropic scents her tresses weaved—
  Scents to lay the soul a-swoon;
On her breast the draperies heaved
    Like clouds by the moon.

"Back she bent her throat, her wet
  Southern lips, and dared, and dared—
Over them my kisses met,
    While the saxe-horn blared.

A. T. QUILLER COUCH

" Crash ! the brassy cymbal smote—
   When I would have stayed our feet,
Laughter rippled all her throat
     Like a wind on wheat.

" Every laugh it left a crease,
   Every ripple wrote her old—
Yet her arms would not release,
     Nor her feet with-hold.

" Ah ! to watch it suck and sag—
   Rosy flesh 'had breathed so warm—
Till I twirled a loveless hag
     On a tortured arm !

" Dancers, resting for a while
   Down the wall with faces white,
Watched us waltzing, mile on mile,
     In a horror of light ! "

Masquer on the rainy stones,
   What is that thy fingers fold ?
" Dead or dying, naught atones
     But I dance and hold.

" Crash ! the maddened cymbal smote—
   Are they minutes ?   Are they years,
That I hold but dust to my coat
     And a few gold hairs ? "

Masquer in the rainy close,
   God thee pity and thy bone !
Other men have danced with those,
     And now dance alone.

PREMONITION.

She sat upon the cottage stair,—
   A tender child of three,
And washed and dressed with wisest care
     The doll upon her knee.

And we, who guessed not why there grew
   In Annie's baby eyes
That little clouding of the blue,
   That shade of awed surmise,

Remembered, in the darkened room,
   Where yesterday we took
Our Annie's new-born babe, on whom
   Her eyes might never look.

FRANCIS BURDETT MONEY-COUTTS

SOME poets are primarily thinkers of thoughts, others are primarily weavers of words. Some think before they sing, others sing before they think, and are apt, indeed, to omit the latter process altogether. Only in the greatest poets do thought and melody so absolutely coalesce that it seems impossible to imagine the one without the other, or to attribute priority to either element in the perfect whole.

Mr. Money-Coutts belongs to the clan of the thinkers. His best work is to be found in his two long philosophical poems (relatively long, that is to say, for neither exceeds one thousand lines), *An Essay in a Brief Model* and *The Revelation of St. Love the Divine.* Next in order of merit come his sonnets, for he treats the sonnet, and with reason, simply as the jewelled casket of a thought. The most successful of his lyrics are those that most nearly approach the epigram. In the pure lyric, one almost prefers to feel that the singer found his initial impulse in some predestinate congruity of words to which he adapted by afterthought, as it were, the idea or emotion which his lines express. Mr. Money-Coutts's lyrics seldom or never give us this sensation. We are apt to feel rather too clearly that their initial impulse lay in some thought, fantasy, or, it may be, conceit, which has subsequently, with more or less labour, woven for itself a more or less close-fitting vesture of words. Mr. Money-Coutts, in short, is a born discourser rather than a born melodist. Many of his lyrics are original in conception and inventive in metre; but few of them can be said to flower like the lilies of the field, without either toil or spinning.

Already in the dedication, "To my Mother," of Mr. Coutts's first book, we have a foretaste of that suave dignity of expression which is this poet's finest gift. In a passage in praise of Imagination, for example, he writes:

> For this was Spenser's magic; this the might
> That turned our Milton's darkness into light;
> This ministered to Goldsmith's loneliest hour,
> And sunned the heart of Shelley into flower:
> Sweet influences! Pilgrims, to and fro
> Ranging the world, and singing as they go;
> Till men, like cattle, captive to the grass,
> Raise their slow heads to hear them, when they pass.

An Essay in a Brief Model is a dialogue between Humanity and Religion on that inexhaustible theme, the Origin of Evil, or, to put it in more general terms, the paradox of pain. In explanation of his title, Mr. Coutts cites a passage from *The Reason of Church Government*, wherein Milton speaks of "that epic form whereof the two poems of Homer . . . are a diffuse, and the book of Job a brief, model." We are thus referred at once to Job and to Milton, who are indeed, in almost equal measures, the inspirers of the poem. Humanity plays the part of Job: Religion is a veritable Job's comforter; and both speak in cadences closely and not unsuccessfully modelled on those of Milton. To say that Mr. Coutts advances any absolutely new thought, whether in arraignment or in justification of the scheme of things, would be to claim for him a unique philosophic eminence. He re-treads the mazes of speculation in which, after the adjournment of their first great Parliament, even the fallen angels lost themselves; but he brings his own mind to bear on the eternal problems, think-

· F·B · MONEY·COVTTS ·

ing them out afresh, not merely parroting the old solutions and evasions; and he finds novel and forcible imagery for his thoughts. The poem is, take it all in all, a truly noble piece of philosophic rhetoric, tense with significance, and at many points glowing with imagination. As I turn its pages, there is not one on which some line or sequence does not stand out either as a highly-condensed epigram or a luminous figure. The wonders of modern science are the outcome of

> Fierce forces, tortured to betray
> Such secrets as a wizard hardly spies
> In crystal dream, or dreaming, when he wakes
> Derides exulting, saner than his dream.

Humanity protests against the malice that would to the record of his crimes

> Add faults
> Of ignorance, omission, and the breach
> Of laws that are themselves the breach of Law
> Divine.

One rather regrets the last epithet. The phrase "Laws that are themselves the breach of Law" is very striking in its nudity. "Ah! but let me be!" Humanity cries in exasperation at the sophistries of Religion:

> Let cerement-wreathing darkness wrap me round,
> And noiseless flake on flake of feathery night
> Compose me to oblivion absolute.
> Rest, rest I crave! From wisdom and from war,
> From vanity, endeavour, and despair,
> False riddles and false oracles. I crave
> Rest from the pauseless pulses of the world!

But it cannot be said that Mr. Coutts reserves all his good things for his protagonist. Job's comforter is no less eloquent than Job himself; witness the following passage placed in the mouth of Religion:

> Repine not that effectual Wisdom works
> In secret; with innumerable threads

Weaving an intricate pattern, as immense
As that embroidery of the lacing moons
That circle circling planets ; by their suns
Drawn around other clusters ; implicate
Themselves about some mightier universe ;
Ellipse more monstrous looping huger spheres,
More frequent swarms, to all infinitude ;
All trailed in pageant, lightly as the down,
Sown on the sowing wind by provident weeds.

Humanity in his next speech demands :

For what am *I* but Revelation ?   I,
The child of God, his scholar, and his clerk ;

*   *   *   *   *

Engrossing on my soul, with iron pen,
The comedies and tragedies of God !

Towards the close of the same speech, Humanity bursts
forth into this apostrophe :

I know Thee World-wright or I know Thee Nought !
I know Thee World-wright ; yet between that hut
Of refuge and thy jasper citadel
That overcrests the pathway of the clouds,—
Palace of promulgation of the law
And seat of government o'er all the hills,
Sinai or Calvary, or before or since,—
What void envelopment of blinding mist !
What treacheries of snow and ice and storm !
What false ascents, false guides and ominous deaths !

Reverting to a thought expressed in the previous extract.
Humanity says, a little further on :

The soul-face of the World is shattered to words
In the Mind's mirror ;—how vain, with painted shards
To tesselate God's miniature !   No Art
Holds the Arch-Artist's portrait ; save myself.
I am not undivine, nor God inhuman !

Again :

My God is Truth ;
Supreme Sincerity,—whatever else !
Who hates the homage of a menial heart ;

*   *   *   *   *

> Whom argument of souls against themselves,
> Framed for their overhearing tyrant, hurts
> More than arraignment of a scurrilous tongue.

Here is the pivot-thought of pessimism very tersely expressed :

> Canst thou record a gladness as engrained,
> As indivisibly fibred into life,
> As torture is ?

Here, again, is a very apt and beautiful image, though one finds it with some surprise in the mouth of Humanity ; it seems more characteristic of his interlocutor :

> If the Whole
> By Him was fashioned and is now maintained,—
> In just proportion, just relation, fixed,
> Must every part cohere, and all consist
> Like radiant raiment, seamless-woven throughout,—
> The Seventh Day vesture that He loves to wear,—
> Which only Mind's cross lenses rend and ravel,
> Impervious to completeness ; as the prism
> Combs into separate locks a tawny tress
> Of slender-rifted sunshine.

Pedantry might find in this passage a mixed metaphor, inquiring how a lens should rend and ravel a vesture ; but as the " radiant raiment " is conceived from the first as a vesture of light, the idea of the prism does not conflict with, but rather continues, the original metaphor.

I have made no attempt to follow the reasoning of Mr. Coutts's poem. To do so would be either to copy out the whole dialogue, or to re-write the " Argument " which Mr. Coutts himself prefixes to his work. We are not here concerned with the ingenuity or the cogency of his dialectics ; my purpose has simply been to show that he touches his Miltonic instrument with dignity and skill and finds for high thoughts appropriate harmonies.

Two of Mr. Coutts's finest sonnets will be found at the end of this article. *To the Moon* seems to me especially noteworthy as an inspiration of pure poetry. It forms an exception to the rule above stated that the sonnet is to Mr. Coutts merely the carven shrine of a definite idea. Here we have no definite idea, but an almost mythopœic fantasy; in spite of which the general rule subsists.

Of the miscellaneous poems in this first volume, *Maxima Reverentia* and *Hercules and Hylas* are perhaps the most striking. Here are three stanzas characteristic at once of the poet's somewhat sombre tone of reflection, and of the concentration of his style :

THE COMMONEST LOT.

The beam that drifts about the sea,
Nosed by the dog-fish, slimed by sea-snails, draws
Into itself through seams and flaws
    The ocean imperceptibly.

Quick currents sift it through and through ;
With jelly creatures feeding on its sides ;
The sea-flower round it glooms and slides
    With languid motion, to and fro.

The wave within weighs more and more
Down, till the burden over-balance it ;
Down, till the flat-fish o'er it flit,
    The sand-worm burrow to its core.

In his second book, *The Revelation of St. Love the Divine*, Mr. Coutts may almost be said to have invented a new instrument for contemplative, philosophic, and satirical poetry. He has taken the simplest of English stanzas, the eight-syllable quatrain with alternate rhymes, and has made a new unit by grouping these quatrains in sections of four apiece. This quatrain of quatrains becomes in his hands a highly effective literary instrument, with a character and individuality of its own. In the shaping of his single stanzas, Mr. Coutts, no doubt, owes something to *In Memoriam*, despite the different arrangement of the rhymes. The cadence of his lines is distinctly Tennysonian, and

many of his stanzas might be re-arranged according to the
rhyme-scheme of *In Memoriam* without the change of a
syllable and without the slightest detriment to the sense.
Here is one, for instance, that is positively improved by the
re-arrangement:

> Him they admit; and him who brings
> A puppet-booth, where viler verse
> Than madmen to their walls rehearse
> Is screamed by dolls to villain strings!

Mr. Coutts, in accordance with his rhyme-scheme, trans-
poses the last two lines, and thus slightly obscures his
meaning. It is in squaring the quatrain, so to speak—in
making four fours his unit—that Mr. Coutts's originality
comes in. He thus obtains a form as definite as the
sonnet, but much simpler and suppler. The epigrammatic
terseness imposed by this form would be fatal to lyric
impetus and intolerable to elegiac feeling. It is inconceivable that Tennyson's threnody, for example, could
have been fashioned into a mosaic of cubes all cut to one
size. But for Mr. Coutts's dialectical and in great measure
satiric purpose, the stricter form has a marked advantage;
and he handles it with unquestionable ability.

Mr. Coutts's poem—it is worthy of a better title, by-the-
bye—falls into two parts. In the first twenty-seven sections
he inveighs against the ascetic theories of life which have
confounded Love with Lust, and have seen in Love itself
an enemy to the higher life. In the remaining twenty-three
sections his thought takes a wider range, and he discourses
of life in general and religion in particular. It is not my
business to discuss Mr. Coutts's doctrine from the religious
or moral point of view. It is with his art that I am concerned. At the same time, I cannot help pointing out
what appears to me a logical hiatus in his argument. He
seems to assume that the thorough-going naturalism he
preaches would inevitably, and in all cases, make for

monogamy; and this cannot but strike one as a large assumption. Mr. Coutts anticipates the accusations that will be brought against him, and replies :

> " Free-thinker ?" Yes; if thought be free
> Envassalled to the laws of thought !
> " Free-lover ?" Yes ; because to me
> All other loves than one are nought !

This is all very well; and if we define "love" as the perfect relation between man and woman, that perfect relation will of course be, in virtue of its perfection, immortal and immutable. But perfect relations (even if we take the word "perfect" in a practical, sublunary sense) are the rare exception in this imperfect world, and it is dangerous to deduce general principles from exceptional cases. Enough of this, however—to argue the question out would be to construct a complete system of sexual morality. It is only fair to add that Mr. Coutts does not look for the immediate fulfilment of his apocalyptic forecast. In Love, he says,

> the worlds of soul and sense
> Are destined to be reconciled
> But æons hence, but æons hence !

Whatever the absolute value of Mr. Coutts's philosophy, there can be no doubt of its earnestness and elevation. Here again he proves himself above all things a thinker— by which I mean, not necessarily a right thinker, but a man of strenuous and eager intellectual activity. He has a somewhat intolerant contempt for

> An idle song of empty days
> Made emptier by an idle song.

His view of life is essentially optimistic. However deep his discontent with the present, he is full of faith in the larger future :

I see Humanity as one
    Scarce adolescent Soul, that grows
By seasons of no moon and sun,
    Nor destined to a senile close :

From age to age still journeying on
    To God, who evermore recedes,
He hears, before, a benison ;
    Behind, he hears the crash of creeds ;

And casting off the worthless type,
    Though never quite exempt from clay,
Becomes, with less corruption ripe,
    And grows mature, with less decay ;

Till, mergent into happier state
    And nobler place than heaven or hell,
Though never wholly consummate
    He justifies the primal Spell.

At the same time, he has moods in which this course of
evolution seems barely begun :

Ye boast of Science. . . . Has it touched
    The heart of man, or woman's mind ?
Or is the poor old World as crutched
    As ever, and as deaf and blind ?

Besotted with the frantic fear
    Of poverty and crazed with greed,
To buy men cheap and sell them dear
    Is all his Gospel, all his Creed ;

From battle-field to battle-field
    He limps along his bloody way,
In vain by all the Past appealed
    And sightless of the coming Day ;

The subtlest instruments designed
    By Science leave his spirit nude ;
He worships still, in savage kind,
    His Fetish, Family, and Feud.

These two quatrain-quatrains, though not his best, may
stand as specimens of Mr. Coutts's manner. He is not an
"impeccable" poet. He will now and then use a feeble

or an obvious epithet; he will now and then say less or more than he means, for the sake of a rhyme. In the two lines quoted above,

> Becomes, with less corruption ripe,
> And grows mature, with less decay ;

I strive in vain to discover any real difference between the first proposition and the second, and must therefore regard one or other as padding. Here are two very fine stanzas, marred by a single nerveless phrase :

> For as men deemed the shining sphere
>   Was almost in their hand's assay,
> Till drawn by lens and crystal near,
>   It proved a billion leagues away,
>
> So Revelation, once supposed
>   The earthly footsteps of a God,
> Is clearer seen, *yet less enclosed*,
>   In every place that Man has trod.

The "yet less enclosed" is a mere makeshift or stop-gap, which ought to have been removed on revision. It may fairly be said, however, that not one of these groups of quatrains is without its flash of imagination, passion, or wit, while in many the compression of thought and style, the epigrammatic force, is very remarkable. I tear the following stanza from its context for the sake of its sheer beauty ;

> O ladies—ye whom passion stirs
>   No more than thunder far away,
> That round the opal mountain-spurs
>   Beats, like a summer sea, all day.

In this one image the true poet stands unmistakably revealed.

Mr. Coutts's third book of verse, *The Alhambra and other Poems*, contains nothing so large in scale or so ambitious in design as the *Essay in a Brief Model* or the *Revelation of St. Love;* nor does it show his talent in any new light.　Of the opening sequence of lyrics *The Alhambra*, only the last seems to me quite up to the poet's best mark.　It is called

LA SILLA DEL MORO.

" Farewell, farewell !　Thy doom endears
　　Thy beauty ! . . . God is just ;
Yet must I weep with woman's tears
　　Thy glory in the dust !

" To lose thee is to die !　And yet
　　I cling to life, for fear
In death's confusion I forget
　　How fair thou art, how dear ! "

So mourned Granada's latest King,
　　Deeming that Art was dead ;
But still the flowers our footsteps ring
　　And still the stars our head !

An address *To William Watson at Windermere* is marked by real dignity, both of thought and expression. In London, says the poet, contrasting his own lot with his friend's—

No " rivulets dance," no torrents flow,
　　No " forests muse " of pine or oak ;
We marvel if a floweret blow
　　Beneath a heaven so smeared with smoke.

And here no joyous impulse moves
　　The minds of men with random waves,
But up and down these stony grooves
　　We hurry, like a gang of slaves.

*　　*　　*　　*　　*

A giant, clanking golden chains ;
　　A monster, bound in torments fierce ;
Whose strong integument of pains
　　No shaft of joy is keen to pierce ;

What more than this can poet spy
　　Beneath our brave pretence and show ?
'Tis light to lift, that bravery,
　　That broidered coverlid of woe !

And yet perchance I do thee wrong ;
  Perchance, beneath immediate ill,
Thy clearer insight, trained and strong,
  May catch a deeper vision still :

Maybe, though greeting Nature's face
  In cloud and crag, in lake and glen,
At least her footsteps thou canst trace
  Among the meaner ways of men !

*   *   *   *   *

But take thou the unfinished thought,
  To mould it, in some later lay,
By finer inspiration wrought,
  And sing me all   fail to say.

Of the half-dozen sonnets in this volume, only one, I
think, shows Mr. Coutts at his best. It is inspired by *The
Arbitration Treaty, January 1897* :

" How beautiful the feet of them that bring
    Good tidings o'er the mountains, news of peace ! "
  So cried the Hebrew prophet, long release
From long captivity previsioning.
And Cyrus came, with healing on his wing
    For Israel ; but not by Persia, Greece,
    Nor Rome, God made the world from war to cease ;
No, nor by Christ, nor any Christian King !
But England, watching by her moated main,
    Yet tasting in convergent winds the taint
      Of slaughter and the tears of those that weep
The tyranny of battle, hears again,
    With spiritual ear, the far and faint
      Footfall divine, that treads the " untrampled deep."

The expression "moated main" is something of a flaw in
this fine sonnet. There is respectable precedent for it, no
doubt ; but an ounce of logic is worth a hundredweight of
precedent. The sonnet in which Mr. Coutts expresses his
indignation at the action of the American Senate is also a
strong one ; but we had better let bygones be bygones.

Many of the lyrics in this volume are original in conception and inventive in metre. *The Riddle,* for instance,

is a delightfully fanciful and playful piece; *Children* is graceful and touching; and *Ingens Æquor* has a powerful swing in it. A new version of the ballad of *The Nut-brown Maid* is very simple and pretty, and *Queen Guene-vere's Maying* and *A Ballad of Cornwall* are rhymed with quaint ingenuity. Half lyric, half epigram, the following versicles are very charmingly turned:

PERFUME.

In love's delightful hours
    We passed the mignonette,
And plucked the blue-eyed flowers
    That bade us Not Forget;

But now the blue-eyed flowers
    We pass and we forget;
The scent of those dear hours
    Comes back with mignonette.

Since reflection, as I have said, is the chief weapon in Mr. Coutts's armoury, it is not surprising to find that the graver his theme the greater is his success. He has probably not yet given us the full measure of his power in philosophic verse. He has imagination and feeling in plenty; he has vigour and sincerity of thought; and he has often a very noteworthy felicity of phrase. In brief, he is a serious and strenuous craftsman who places a fine and individual faculty at the service of a lofty ideal.

TO THE MOON.

Θέστυλι, ταὶ κύνες ἄμμιν ἀνὰ πτόλιν ὠρύονται
ἁ θεὸς ἐν τριόδοισι·

THEOCRITUS (*Idyll II. 35, 36*).

Now maddens the slumbering shepherd in thy sheen;
    The death-foreboding watch-dog distant bays
    Thy look malign; where cross the lonely ways,
The gliding spectres pace their scant demesne !
As men emerge, this summer night serene,
    From revel, sedulous to cheat the days,
    They shudder at thy cold accusing gaze,
And wish they were not, and had never been !
Warping their faint reluctant waves, thou glarest
    On fascinated seas ; no fruitful heat,
No happier race in thy bleached bosom thou bearest;
    But rangest in sad bondage to the beat
Of Earth's sad heart, and in amazement farest,
    Treading thy weary round with frozen feet.

TO A BEAUTIFUL JEWESS.

The faithful Eliezer, at the well,
    Saluted thee ; smooth Jacob, in the field ;
    For thee unhappy Abner's fate was sealed,
And stern Ahasuerus owned thy spell ;
Before thy Child the Median sages fell,
    And shining hosts of heaven his birth revealed
    To shepherds; daily art thou now appealed
As Mother of the Lord of heaven and hell !
For thus the great traditions of thy type
    Abide.   We children of corrupted breed
Snatch short successes in a time unripe;
    And if our greedy race charge thine with greed,
Thine learnt it writhing in the Egyptian's gripe,
    Ere yet our youngling nation was in seed.

118

JOHN DAVIDSON

LONG before he had gravitated to London, long before he had made himself a name, Mr. Davidson, in his Scottish wander-years, had written, and even published, five poems in dramatic form, which he afterwards collected in one volume under the title of *Plays*. The first, *An Unhistorical Pastoral*, is dated " Glasgow 1877," the last, *Scaramouch in Naxos*, "Crieff 1888"; so that for eleven years, it would seem, Mr. Davidson gave the best part of his thoughts to dramatic composition. Yet he cannot be said, in all this time, to have invented a single plot, and scarcely to have created a character. He poured forth enough pure poetry to have made him a reputation twice over, but he showed no comprehension of the most rudimentary exigencies of the particular form he had adopted. I do not merely mean that his plays were totally unsuited to the existing stage; that might be more of a reproach to the stage than to them. What I mean is that he had as yet no inkling of the essential nature of drama, but used the form merely as a vehicle for uncontrolled fantasy, lyrism, and rhetoric.

This is not a question of pitting one convention or one technique against another, and arbitrarily declaring this one excellent, that condemnable. It is not bad technique, but no technique that we find in Mr. Davidson's early plays. Technique, in drama, means the prevision of your audience, and nice adjustment of every stroke of your work towards the compassing of the desired effect ; just as, in painting, technique means a perfect understanding of the relation between the medium and the percipient eye. The dramatist, of course, can choose his own audience, which may be an absolutely ideal one. But there is one condition from which he cannot escape, one characteristic which the ideal audience shares with the most commonplace pit and gallery : to wit, ignorance of what the dramatist has to tell them. This ignorance may be total or only partial. In the case of the Greek tragedy, founded on national legend, or the Elizabethan chronicle-play, founded on national history, the audience might be assumed to know in advance the main outline of the action to be presented. What the dramatist had in this case to impart was a superior know-ledge, a novel divination and interpretation of the characters involved. But in the best, the most artistic, examples of both Greek and English national drama, it will be found, I think, that the poet relies but little on previous knowledge of legend or history on the part of his audience, telling his story as clearly and as carefully as though it were entirely his own invention. Be this as it may, in the vast majority of modern plays the assumption is and must be that the dramatist knows everything about his characters and their fortunes, while the audience (whether real or ideal) knows nothing. The problem of the technician, then, is to find the best way, in relation to a given audience, of imparting his omniscience ; the best way being that which awakens interest earliest, sustains it most evenly, and in-volves no more than a pleasurable effort of attention and thought. It makes no essential difference whether the play be primarily one of plot or of character. In either case the business of the dramatist is, in the last analysis, the well-ordered impartment of knowledge. It is like the pouring of a liquid from a full vessel into an empty one : the method must be carefully adapted to the configuration of the vessel

· JOHN · DAVIDSON ·

to be filled, with a view to spilling as little as may be in the transference.

I do not mean, of course, that this is the whole secret of the dramatist's art; I am merely trying to define and illustrate that element in it which we call technique. A man may be an excellent technician and a very poor dramatist. The knowledge he has to impart may be worthless, though he impart it never so skilfully. But the converse holds good to a very limited degree; you shall scarcely find a man of whom it can truly be said that he is an excellent dramatist but a very poor technician. If such a case occurs to you, it will probably appear on examination either that the poet in question lives in virtue of his pure poetry, which suffers rather than gains by its dramatic form; or else that his technique is good in relation to the audience (real or ideal) for whom he wrote, and seems bad only with reference to some different convention. Technique, in short, is a fundamental necessity to the dramatist. With it he may or may not do much: that will depend on his genius; but without it, be his genius never so great, he will do nothing that he could not have done to better advantage in some other form.

In order to keep the technical problem clearly before him, the young dramatist should impress upon his consciousness the formula—which Mr. Davidson seems never to have arrived at—"I know everything (it is my business to know everything) about my characters; my audience knows nothing except what, in one way or another, I tell them." The failure to bear this in mind is the besetting error of the amateur playwright. He has thought a good deal about his characters before he sits down to write; he has lived with them, he has realised them to himself, in so far as he has the faculty of realising character; above all things, he is interested in them; and he forgets that this interest has yet to be awakened in his hearers, this realisation to be imparted. He ignores the necessity of gradually unfolding his knowledge and skilfully wooing, so to speak, the curiosity, the comprehension, the sympathy of his audience. He explains trifles twice over and leaves essential matters unexplained. He fails to grasp the great rule on which comprehension and curiosity alike depend : everything that is said must either carry its own explanation, or follow naturally from something that has gone before, or seize the attention of the audience in such a way as to make it desire and eagerly anticipate an explanation and harmonisation when the right moment shall have arrived. It is because I can discern no effort whatever on Mr. Davidson's part to place himself at the point of view of any conceivable audience outside himself, that I say he has no technique. These early plays of his—four out of the five at any rate—are such as King Louis of Bavaria might have written for those celebrated performances which he enjoyed in solitary state.

An Unhistorical Pastoral, as we have seen, dates from 1877, when Mr. Davidson must have been very young. Though the plot is partly suggested by Allan Ramsay's *Gentle Shepherd*, the piece is pure Shakespeare from beginning to end. It is the fourth act of *The Winter's Tale* expanded into five acts, eked out with snippets from *A Midsummer Night's Dream* and other plays, and written in a wonderfully spirited imitation of Shakespeare's earlier, more luxuriant, rhyme-rich and " conceited " style. There is no pretence at interest in the story. Alardo, King of Belmarie, and his counsellor Conrad, return unknown to Belmarie after a year's absence, during which they are supposed to have been drowned at sea. Alardo believes that his son, Rupert, was lost in the same storm, but learns immediately on landing that he was saved and is now ruling the country. This news is conveyed by Cinthio, a shepherd, in whom Conrad recognises his own long-lost son. Rupert is bent on marrying a humble shepherdess, Eulalie, while the (supposed) humble shepherd Cinthio is plotting to carry off Faustine, the daughter of a haughty noble. All the characters assemble in a forest on Mayday, where Oberon, Titania, Puck and their fairy company join affably in the revels. The two fathers disclose themselves to the two sons, and Alardo is about to separate Rupert from his rustic love, when Eulalie's reputed mother, Martha, explains that

> This gentle lady is no child of mine.
> Her parents both were noble : how they died,
> And she, an infant, of her heritage
> Was cozened by an uncle, I'll make plain
> By names, dates, papers, birth-marks, jewellery.

We see in this speech how Mr. Davidson himself derides his pretence at a plot, much as Mr. W. S. Gilbert puts his tongue in his cheek at the heroics of his extravaganzas. And the characters are equally hollow mockeries. There is far more flesh and blood in Allan Ramsay's Roger and Patie, Peggie and Mause, than in the puppets of Mr. Davidson's galanty-show. The whole thing is simply a pretext for a young poet's wallowing, so to speak, in limitless fantasy and whim. He turns his imagination loose in the Shakespearean fairyland and lets it ramble whither it will. Even the broader humour of Shakespeare must be mimicked (not ineffectively) in a foolish nobleman, a sharp-witted clown, and two bibulous rustics. Mark, for instance, the Shakespearean echoes in this scene between Scipio the clown and two bantering noblemen :

> FELICE.　　　　　　Come hither, Scipio.
> 　　　　Beseech your mightiness to signify
> 　　　　To us, your humble servants, what's o'clock ?
> SCIPIO. The clock's hand points now to that very hour
> 　　　　It indexed at the same time yesterday.
> FELICE. Sirrah, you lie, because the clock's gone fast.

SCIPIO. Then is it very adverse to your wit. . . .
Gentlemen, I can prove you the maddest fools out of your own
mouths.

BRUNO. Indeed we are out of our own mouths; for our mouths
are within us. . . .

FELICE. Scipio, do you know where the Prince is gone?

SCIPIO. Do I know what kind of beast a lover is? Does he not
follow his mistress like a lamb to the slaughter? If she be in the
mouth of hell, I warrant you'll find him in the jaws of death, an he
be no nearer.

Even this brief extract is sufficient to show that it is not
from the graver or maturer Shakespeare that Mr. Davidson
draws his inspiration. Nevertheless he proves himself
indubitably a poet in the very force and freedom with which
he reproduces the vices, and some of the minor virtues, of
his model. His formally lyrical efforts—the fairy interlude,
for example—are not his happiest. The passage of most
sustained merit perhaps (at any rate, that which will best
bear quotation) is this speech of Sylvia's, its movement
obviously suggested by John of Gaunt's great tirade, but
none the less spirited on that account:

SYLVIA. King Oberon, a many years ago,
Divining that this grass-green, sea-green earth,
This emerald that sets off the golden sun,
Should be by mankind sadly under-priced;
That this fair hanging garden, swung for elves
And men to revel in, this glorious stage
In heaven's theatre, so gallantly
Hung out and decked for elves and men to grace,
This temple, wherein all might minister,
Should be o'er-rioted, abused, profaned;
That this globe, frescoed round by Nature's art,
Should lose its beauty in the sight of men—
Men's eyes being jaundiced by a golden lust
To prize much more the hills' bright excrement,
Than their elate and sun-gilt brows of strength;
That men, like children wearied of a toy,
Would spoil its loveliness, in pieces rending
To put it to some use, or ravish out

JOHN DAVIDSON

The useless secret of creation : he,
The fairy king, slow-winged and sad of heart,
Searched out a new home from the host of heaven,
And chose that star for him and his to dwell in.

Mr. Davidson, we see, is not pedantic in his Shakespearising, else he would have made a whole line of "The useless
secret of cre-a-ti-on."

It is worth observing that Mr. Davidson in this first play
shows a tendency to wanton archaism, neologism, and
tampering with his parts of speech, which, in his later
work, he has kept much better in check. "Wander," for
instance, appears as a transitive verb ("where childhood oft
had wandered him"); the verbs "to coy," and "to happy"
are conveyed from Shakespeare; "to chord" (in the sense
of "accord") and "to orchard" are, I fancy, coined for the
nonce; "that trifles all" is used in the Shakespearean sense
of "that makes all the rest seem trifling," and "it aches my
eyes" in the sense of "it hurts my eyes." Mr. Davidson
is, I confidently believe, the first poet who ever talked of
"interviewing the fairies," or made a Prince of Arcady
familiar with the boomerang and its habits. Already in
this play, too, we find him treating "burn" as a dissyllable,
as he afterwards treats "world" and other similar words;
but if a Scotch poet have not licence to this extent, then
Wallace bled in vain.

That hero appears, incidentally but heroically, in the
only one of these early plays which possesses the rudiments
of what I have called technique. In the case of *Bruce; a
Chronicle Play*, two circumstances help to keep Mr. Davidson's tricksy Pegasus within the traces, and impart a certain
form to his work. In the first place, he dares not too
widely depart from the data of his historic theme; in the
second place, he borrows from Shakespeare not only the
diction, but the actual structure of his play. It would
perhaps be more accurate to say that, while history told his

story for him in advance, the Elizabethan chronicle-play provided him with a model in which the element of structure touched its irreducible minimum. It cannot be alleged that there is any particular skill in the selection or ordering of the incidents; much less is there any invention of such situations as should, without absolutely flying in the face of history, bring out the latent dramatic possibilities of the theme. The strength of the play lies not in the marshalling of events; scarcely even in characterisation, though Bruce, Isabella, and the Countess of Buchan are drawn with spirit and consistency; but rather in its copious and forceful rhetoric. It harks back to an earlier stage in the evolution of the chronicle-play than that which Shakespeare ultimately attained; but, Shakespeare apart, it is not too much to call it one of the best chronicle-plays in the language, and a substantial addition to the national literature of Scotland. It contains noble and truly dramatic passages not a few. What could be simpler and yet more thrilling than this reply of Bruce's, before Bannockburn, to Randolf's reminder that the English are five to one?

> BRUCE.   Why Randolf, shame!
> You are the last who should complain of that.
>
>   *   *   *   *   *
>
> Why man, you are my cousin, Thomas Randolf;
> And this is Douglas; this, my brother Edward;
> We are men who have done deeds, God helping us.
> God helping us, we'll do a deed to-day!

In point of dramatic concentration, however, the finest thing in the play is a retort of Wallace's to Edward I. The whole third act, I should mention, is given up to Wallace, an argument of his case, and a retrospect of his early history. Absolutely indefensible from the point of view of rational design, this scene contains some vigorous speeches; while in the following passage there is more than vigour, there is a very high quality of dramatic imagination:

JOHN DAVIDSON

WALLACE. No jurisdiction have you over me
    To pardon or to doom : prisoner of war,
    No traitor, I ; and here I make demand
    For knightly treatment at the hands of knights.
EDWARD I. You shall have justice.
WALLACE.   *In the end I shall :*
    And so shall you. Death you have often faced ;
    Justice you shall see once.

I do not hesitate to call this one of the finest, one of the most genuinely heroic sayings in all historical drama. Without an atom of pose or rodomontade, in less than a score of simple words such as a child might use, it sweeps Westminster Hall to the winds, and transfers the cause from the King's Bench to the High Court of Eternity. So absolute is its fitness that, as I write, it occurs to me to wonder whether Mr. Davidson found it ready-made in his documents. But no! if history or legend attributed it to Wallace, in anything like the perfect form it here assumes, it could not fail to be world-famous. One is tempted to supplement Touchstone's categories, and call it "the repartee sublime."

The most lifelike and certainly the most charming figure in the play is Bruce's wife, Isabella. Her part is full of genuine poetry. Here, for instance, is a speech addressed to her husband :

    You do not love me as I love you; no ;
    Else you would never leave me. Love of power
    And love of me hold tourney in your breast.
    Let Will throw down the baton, and declare
    The love of me the winner, and I'll be
    Your queen of love ; and beautiful as love
    For man can make a woman. I am proud :
    When love transfigures me I can conceive
    How beautiful I am. Stay with me, then,
    That holy, sweet, and confident desire
    May light me up a pleasant bower for you :
    I am, when you are gone, a house forlorn,
    Cold, desolate, and hasting to decay :
    Stay, tenant me, preserve me in repair ;
    Only sweet uses keep sweet beauty fair.

A little further on, she has this subtle reflection :

> I have sometimes found,
> When I have spent an hour in decking me,
> But thinking more to please you in my life
> Than in my dress, that, coming then to you,
> Brimming with tenderness, some thoughtless word,
> Or even a look from you, has changed my mood,
> And made me deem the world a wilderness ;
> While this cross glance, or inauspicious tone,
> Was but a feint of yours, whose strength of love
> Withheld itself, afraid it should undo
> Its purpose by endeavouring too much :
> And we have parted, discontented both.

When she joins her husband in the Wood of Drane, she greets him in this exquisite speech :

> My dear wayfaring hero, I have come
> To share your crust, and rags, and greenwood couch :
> I'm deep in love with skied pavilions :
> I'll be your shepherdess, Arcadian king.
> This evening's journey lay throughout a wood :
> The honeysuckle incensed all the air,
> And cushats cooed in every fragrant fir ;
> Tall foxgloves nodded round the portly trees,
> Like ruffling pages in the trains of knights ;
> Above the wood sometimes a green hill peered,
> As if dame Nature on her pillow turned
> And showed a naked shoulder ; all the way,
> Whispering along, rose-bushes blushed like girls
> That pass blood-stirring secrets fearfully,
> Attending on a princess in her walk ;
> I think with rarely scented breath they said
> A loving wife was speeding to her lord.

Take her all in all, Isabella affects us as a living woman. She is somewhat modern in her colouring perhaps ; but what seems most modern in feminine human nature will often prove, on a little examination, to be as old as "any history that is written in any book."

Bruce, too, stands out boldly as a strong and thoughtful character, not very highly individualised, but something more, certainly, than a mere mouthpiece for rhetoric. Here is the concluding passage of a scene in which he has been stimulating his soldiers' patriotism by an account of the struggle of Galgacus against Agricola:

> That battle, and the ruin of her fleet,
> Held Rome behind Grahame's dyke, and kept us Scots.
> All south of us the Romans, Saxons, Danes,
> And Normans, conquering in turn, o'erthrew
> From change to change; but we are what we were
> Before Æneas came to Italy,
> Free Scots; and though this great Plantagenet
> Seems now triumphant, we will break his power.
> Shall we not, comrades?
>   FIRST SOLDIER.   Yes, your Majesty.
>   SECOND SOLDIER. But might it not have been a benefit
> If Rome had conquered Scotland too, and made
> Between the Orkneys and the Channel Isles
> One nation?
>   BRUCE.   A subtle question, soldier;
> But profitless, requiring fate unwound.
> It might be well were all the world at peace,
> One commonwealth, or governed by one king;
> It might be paradise; but on the earth
> You will not find a race so provident
> As to be slaves to benefit their heirs.
>   FIRST SOLDIER.   At least we will not.
>   BRUCE.   By St. Andrew, no!

There is something of Miltonic concentration in the phrase:

> A subtle question, soldier;
> But profitless, requiring fate unwound.

Some of the best writing in the play occurs in the description of the Battle of Bannockburn as seen from the Gillies' Hill. For instance:

> Ah! now the daze begins! I know it well.
> The cloth-yard shafts, like magic shuttles, weave
> Athwart the warped air dazzling, dire dismay,
> And the beholder's blood slinks to his heart
> Like moles from daylight; all his sinews fade
> To unsubstantial tinder.

And again :

> Now are they hand to hand !
> How short a front !   How close !   They're sewn together
> With steel cross-stitches, halbert over sword,
> Spear across lance, and death the purfled seam !

If there should ever be founded (not that I recommend it !) a Scottish Literary Theatre, like the Irish Literary Theatre of intermittent renown, its opening play is clearly designated in advance.   But indeed, with a little trimming, *Bruce* might justly claim a place in the repertory, not of a Scottish, but of a National Theatre.

Mr. Davidson's other plays must be more briefly dealt with.   The most formless of all is *A Romantic Farce*, based, the author tells us, on a story of James Hogg's.   It was written six years before *Bruce*, and only a year after *An Unhistorical Pastoral*.   Its style is one tissue of conceits after this fashion :

> CLOWN (*to* AMAZON). I might enlarge upon the periods
> On either side your nose, that put an end
> By saucy looks to any parleying
> Save that of sharp-edged words.

The time is modern and the place Scotland.   Throughout the first two acts the characters appear in fancy costume, and we are left totally in the dark as to who or what they are and what the play is all about.   Then, in the third act, the story comes straggling in—a confused and ridiculous figment about women carried off by brigands, the exchange of a living child for a dead one, and I know not what other romantic puerilities.   Mr. Davidson, of course, takes no more interest than his readers in this nursery tale.   It is the merest pretext for poetising at large—for the outpouring of a turbulent stream of images, conceits and whimsicalities. Much of the writing is pretty ; for instance :

> In your hair
> There shines more gold than ever July spent
> In gilding leagues of wheat—

and everywhere there are traces of originality and thought Mr. Davidson's mistake lies in choosing to give the outward show of drama to what is, in effect, merely a young poet's commonplace book. The outward show of drama, I say, since it is impossible to predicate dramatic " form " of what may rather be called a poetic chaos.

A very different production is *Smith : A Tragic Farce*, written in 1886, two years later than *Bruce*. Here a clear enough story, or rather a tangible enough incident, is set forth. A person named Smith meets, in a Scottish forest, a young lady named Magdalen. Neither has seen or heard of the other before, but in a conversation of ninety lines they discover that they are predestined for each other. Magdalen being betrothed against her will to a person named Brown, she and Smith determine on instant flight. Their way to the nearest railway station lies over a rugged mountain; and being overtaken in their flight by the lady's father and Brown, they cut short recriminations by together leaping over a precipice. This is a thumbnail jotting of a theme which might, by careful elaboration, analysis and motivation, be developed into a drama ; though I fail to see how, out of the given elements, the tragic conclusion could at all plausibly be evolved. Mr. Davidson, however, cares nothing for plausibility. Once more he uses his theme simply as a pretext for stringing together more or less relevant images, descriptions, and trains of thought. In spite of his jibing title, he apparently takes some real interest in his theme ; yet he seems almost to go out of his way to make it unlifelike, nightmarish. By this time, however, his style has matured, and instead of the lush fantasy of the *Unhistorical Pastoral* and *Romantic Farce*, we find a remarkable wealth of real wit, imagination and elo-quence. How happy, for instance, is this description of the

> fell machinery of Acts and Codes
> Which now we use for nipping thought in bud,

> And turning children out like nine-pins, each
> As doleful and as wooden.

Or again, this :

> I would rather be
> A shred of glass that sparkles in the sun,
> And keeps a lowly rainbow of its own,
> Than one of those so trim and patent pearls
> With hearts of sand veneered, sewed up and down
> The stiff brocade society affects.

What a charming piece of description is this, placed in the mouth of the poet Hallowes, between whom and Smith Mr. Davidson seems to have portioned out his own personality :

> Garth's in the North, a hamlet like a cave,
> Nestling unknown in tawny Merlin's side,
> A mount, brindled with scars and waterways.
> The windows, Argus-eyed with knotted panes
> That under heavy brows of roses blink
> Blind guard, have never wept with hailstones stung ;
> No antique, gnarled, and wrinkled, roundwood porch,
> Whiskered with hollyhocks in this old thorpe
> Has ever felt the razor of the East :
> No rail, no coach, no tourist passes there :
> But in the brooding evening from her seat,
> A worn tree-trunk, the toothless beldame leaps
> As lithe as superstition, says a saw,
> And kills the toad that in the channel hops ;
> Far up the mountain children's voices ring ;
> The quoiters cry ; and past the ivied inn
> A chastened brook tells all its pebbled beads ;
> Between the bourtrie-bushes and the thorns
> The commonest bird that sings is wonderful,
> So empty are the spaces of the air
> From any breath of modern weariness.

It is Hallowes, again, to whom we owe this truly magnificent outburst :

> You misconceive : fame is the breath of power :
> What valid work was ever for itself
> Wrought solely, be it war, art, statesmanship ?

132

Nothing can be its own reward and hold
Rank above patience, or whatever game,
Angling or avarice, is selfisher.
O watering palates ! and, O skyey grapes !
O purple path above the milky way !
Give me to dream dreams all would love to dream ;
To tell the world's truth ; hear the world tramp time
With satin slippers and with hob-nailed shoes
To my true singing ; fame is worth its cost,
Blood-sweats, and tears, and haggard, homeless lives.

There is delightful irony in the phrase with which Hallowes
replies to one of the diatribes of the sententious Smith :

> You know I have not always strength of wing
> To soar like you right to God's point of view.

On the other hand, it is Smith himself who ends the first
act with this ringing stroke :

> You're right: one must become
> Fanatic—be a wedge—a thunderbolt,
> To smite a passage through the close-grained world.

The following speeches from the crucial scene between
Smith and Magdalen may convey some impression both of its
strength and its weakness. When a gentleman and lady have
only ninety lines in which to effect a mutual introduction and
decide that they are fated for each other, one can scarcely
conceive them devoting so much time to philosophy and
mythology. But it is absurd to demand conceivable details
in an inconceivable situation, and the lines in themselves are
beautiful :

MAGDALEN. What do you mean ? what spells ? what sorcery ?
SMITH. The hydra-headed creeds ; the sciences,
That deem the thing is known when it is named ;
And literature, thought's palace-prison fair ;
Philosophy, the grand inquisitor
That racks ideas and is fooled with lies ;
Society, the mud wherein we stand

133

Up to the eyes, whence if I drag you forth,
Saving your soul and mine, there shall ascend
A poisonous blast that may o'ertake our lives.
    MAGDALEN. I feel a meaning in your eloquence;
I see my poor thoughts made celestial
Like faded women Jove hung in the sky.
Obey my nature, sir? How shall I know
The voice of nature from the thousand cries
That clamour in my head like piteous birds,
Filling the air about a lonely isle
With ringing terror when the hunter comes.
    SMITH. Shut out the storm, and heed the still, small voice.

Even the brief extracts I have given must have suggested
to discerning readers of Mr. Davidson's later work a similarity of tone between *Smith* and his *Fleet Street Eclogues*.
The observation is a just one. Mr. Davidson has found in
the *Eclogues* the form towards which he was blindly groping
in his *Romantic Farce* and *Tragic Farce*. What he requires
is really a vehicle for the expression of thought, vision and
fantasy, too copious and tumultuous to be imprisoned in
strictly lyrical form. He has also the Scotchman's passion
for debate. He likes to put his thought in the shape of
argument, to let truth result from the clash of eagerly con-
flicting exaggerations, rather than to expound it with the
orderly sedateness of the poetic essayist. Therefore he
naturally rushed to dialogue; but it did not at first occur to
him that dialogue, and even, up to a certain point, the de-
lineation of character, might be divorced from story, from
action—in a word, from drama. He needlessly burdened
himself with plots; but feeling them to be quite inessential, he
had not the patience to make them interesting or plausible,
or to present them with reasonable dexterity. When at last
he hit upon the idea of the Eclogue, the brief lyrical colloquy
circling freely and fancifully round a given theme, he had
found his true instrument, and he struck a clear, individual
note at which the world at once pricked up its ears. The
fine and vital things in the so-called plays had been buried

among so much inert matter that they had attracted very little attention.

Before passing on to the *Eclogues*, however, we have still a fifth play to consider. In the Prologue to *Scaramouch in Naxos : a Pantomime*, Mr. Davidson (through the mouth of Silenus) represents himself as reflecting thus :

Which of the various dramatic forms of the time may one conceive as likeliest to shoot up in the fabulous manner of the beanstalk, bearing on its branches things of earth and heaven undreamt of in philosophy ? The sensational dramas ? Perhaps from them some new development of tragic art; but Pantomime seems to be of best hope. It contains in crude forms, humour, poetry and romance. It is the childhood of a new poetical comedy.

This opinion, in very nearly these words, I have several times expressed of late years, forgetting that Mr. Davidson had been beforehand with me. I am cordially at one with him, then, in the theory which inspired his work ; but I cannot think that he has successfully exemplified it. Pantomime, like every other form of drama, ought to have an interesting story after its own kind, and ought above all things to present it clearly. Neither condition does Mr. Davidson fulfil. Scaramouch, a showman, engages Silenus to travel with his show, passing himself off as Bacchus, while a lady named Ione is to personate Ariadne. Just as the engagement is concluded the real Bacchus and Ariadne appear on the scene, and inflict various playful penalties upon the plotters. A personage named Sarmion arrives in a mother-of-pearl boat from "a star above the moon" (but in reality from the works of Shelley), and sacrifices his immortality in order to wed Ione. And that is all ; and it is all set forth in the most haphazard, confused and arbitrary fashion, mere lawless and purposeless whim being everywhere in the ascendant. Not thus should even pantomime be written, whether for the study or the stage ; and Mr. Davidson has somewhere stated that for the stage

Scaramouch in Naxos is designed. There is plenty of pretty writing in it, however, and a good deal of Mr. Davidson's rather artificial strain of humour. Here again, as in the *Unhistorical Pastoral*, the formally lyrical passages are not the most successful. Mr. Davidson does not excel in the song pure and simple. The gems are to be found in the blank-verse dialogue; this of Ione's for instance :

> O wind, and do you wander all the night,
> Moving the broad, black clouds, heavy and high,
> And lifting, there and yonder, with a kiss,
> The wet plumes of the sea ?

Or Ariadne's lines to Bacchus :

> Each day, each hour
> I am your bride ; and as the days and years
> Gather behind us, every happiness—
> And that is every minute of my life—
> Doubles the joy of that which went before :
> And yet the past is as a galaxy
> Wherein no star excels the radiant throng.
> . . . . Come away :
> Back where the water gurgles through the fern,
> Dewing the feathery fronds, and hyacinths
> Spread like a purple smoke far up the bank.

I trust Mr. Davidson will one day vindicate his theory (and mine) of the potentialities of pantomime as an art-form. One of its merits, no doubt, is its elasticity, but elasticity is one thing, incoherence another. Not merely to logic but to æsthetics a formless art-form is abhorrent.

It is worthy of note that in his last-published work, *Godfrida*, Mr. Davidson returns to the dramatic form in the fullest sense of the word. He no longer ignores technique. This play is constructed, not unskilfully, with a conceivable audience in view, the characters definitely outlined, the action developed in purposeful and orderly fashion. It is vigorously written, too, with passages of true dramatic tension. Its theme, unfortunately, has neither the depth of tragedy nor the charm of comedy. The frenzied and incredibly maladroit efforts of the Duchess Ermengarde to win Siward from Godfrida are painful without being pathetic; and the background of political intrigue is too complicated to be quite effective. At the same time the character of Godfrida is delightfully drawn, and the play proves that if Mr. Davidson could but hit on a strong and simple theme, he does not now lack the art to use it to advantage.

Mr. Davidson's first book of non-dramatic verse, entitled *In a Music-Hall*, was published in 1891, and contains poems ranging in date from 1872 to 1889. It need not detain us long. With the exception of its title-piece, consisting of half a dozen versified character-studies of music-hall "artistes," its contents show little originality and less accomplishment. The music-hall sketches are clever: no more. The sequence might have formed a modern counterpart to Burns's *Jolly Beggars*, but is very far from rivalling the vigour and spontaneity of that masterpiece. As for the remaining poems, their chief interest lies less in their promise than in their lack of it. He would be a dull critic who should fail to discern a poet born in the writer even of the *Romantic Farce*, the poorest of the plays; whereas he would be a critic of unusual penetration who should with any confidence predict future eminence for the writer of these boyish lyrics and frigid ballads. If any considerable number of them are contemporary with, or subsequent to, *Bruce* (1884) and *Smith* (1886), I can only say that such inequality of workmanship seems to me almost without parallel.

Inequality, indeed, is one of Mr. Davidson's abiding characteristics; but when we come to the *Fleet Street Eclogues*, it is the glorious inequality of a jagged Sierra. Take the very first one, *New Year's Day*. Here the moody Brian denounces the journalist's calling, while the gentle Basil interjects antiphons of nature-worship (a frequent and charming device of Mr. Davidson's) which fall like drops of oil on the troubled waters of Brian's rhetoric. For instance :

> From the muted tread of the feet,
> And the slackening wheels, I know
> The air is hung with snow,
> And carpeted the street.

One may not at first sight recognise this as an utterance of nature-worship ; but it is not the least among Mr. Davidson's merits that Nature, for him, is not shut out by the four-mile circle. At the close of his lurid diatribe, comparing newspapers to " a covey of dragons, wide-vanned " who hide the sun and pollute the air, Brian sums up in this quatrain :

> Fed by us here and groomed
> In this pestilent reeking stye,
> These dragons I say have doomed
> Religion and poetry—

whereupon Sandy retorts with the following strophe, which I venture to call perfect in imagination and cadence :

> They may doom till the moon forsakes
> Her dark, star-daisied lawn ;
> They may doom till doomsday breaks
> With angels to trumpet the dawn ;
> While love enchants the young,
> And the old have sorrow and care,
> No song shall be unsung,
> Unprayed no prayer.

Nothing could be better than this little lyric. It has character, fervour, music and excellent form. Yet a page or two farther on we find the same poet, through the mouth of the same speaker, expressing himself thus :

> If people will go bare
> They may count on bloody backs ;
> Cold are the hearts that care
> If a girl be blue-eyed or black-eyed ;
> Only to souls of hacks
> Are phrases hackneyed.

* * * * *

JOHN DAVIDSON

Nor are we warriors giftless ;
Deep magic's in our stroke ;
Ours are the shoes of swiftness :
And ours the darkling cloak.

It would be unfair to complain of the somewhat prosaic quality of the whole speech. In discursive poetry of this order, it is inevitable that there should be level, if not actually flat, passages. It would be too much to demand an unbroken sweep of lyric exaltation. But even in a professedly humorous passage it is going a little too far in the Hudibrastic direction to make such atrocious assonances pass for rhymes. A few lines further on, however, Mr. Davidson more than recovers himself in the delightful lilt and swing of the concluding passage :

BASIL. Sing hey for the journalist !
He is your true soldado ;
Both time and chance he'll lead a dance,
And find out Eldorado.

BRIAN. Sing hey for Eldorado !
BASIL. A catch, a catch we'll trowl
BRIAN. Sing hey for Eldorado !
SANDY. And bring a mazer-bowl,
With ale a-frothing brimmed.

BRIAN. We may not rest without it.
SANDY. With dainty ribbons trimmed,
And love-birds carved about it.

BASIL. With roasted apples scented,
And spiced with cloves and mace.

BRIAN. Praise him who ale invented !
SANDY. In heaven he has a place !
BASIL. Such a camarado
Heaven's hostel never missed !

BRIAN. Sing hey for Eldorado !
SANDY. Sing ho for the journalist !
BASIL. We drink them and we sing them
In mighty, humming ale.

BRIAN. May fate together bring them !
SANDY. Amen !
BASIL.   Wass hael !
BRIAN.   Drinc hael !

To the critics, then, whose method is to prod at the weak points in a poet's armour, Mr. Davidson, in his *Eclogues* and elsewhere, offers ample opportunities for their favourite exercise. For my part, I do not envy the man who can read these *Fleet Street Eclogues* without recognising in them an originality of thought, a freshness of vision, a wealth and vivacity of imagination, and in many cases a free and buoyant lyric movement, which far outweigh their worst defects of form.

St. Valentine's Eve presents a daring paradox of Love as the thrice-sufficient counter-weight to all the agonies of a tortured universe. *Good Friday* winds up with this beautiful eulogy of the daisy. Menzies, describing the approach of spring, says :

> The vanguards of the daisies come,
>   Summer's crusaders sanguine-stained,
> The only flowers that left their home
>   When happiness in Eden reigned.
>
> They strayed abroad, old writers tell,
>   Hardy and bold, east, west, south, north :
> Our guilty parents, when they fell,
>   And flaming vengeance drove them forth,
>
> Their haggard eyes in vain to God,
>   To all the stars of heaven turned ;
> But when they saw where in the sod,
>   The golden-hearted daisies burned,
>
> Sweet thoughts that still within them dwelt
>   Awoke, and tears embalmed their smart ;
> On Eden's daisies couched they felt
>   They carried Eden in their heart.

BASIL. Oh, little flower so sweet and dear !
SANDY.   Oh, humanest of flowers that grow !
BRIAN. Oh, little brave adventurer !
        We human beings love you so !

MENZIES. We human beings love it so !
            And when a maiden's dainty shoe
        Can cover nine, the gossips know
            The fulness of the Spring is due.

BRIAN. The gallant flower!
SANDY.   Its health!   Come, drink!
MENZIES. Its health!   By heaven, in Highland style!
BASIL. The daisy's health!   And now, we'll think
            Of Eden silently a while.

St. Swithin's Day declares the glory of the summer, touching its highest point, perhaps, in this quatrain:

> I would I lay beside a brook at morn,
> And watched the shepherd's clock declare the hours;
> And heard the husky whisper of the corn,
> Legions of bees in leagues of summer flowers.

Michaelmas is mainly given up to a dream, recounted by Basil, of which he himself remarks that it was " long, too long "—and one cannot but agree with him.   Far more original is *Queen Elizabeth's Day*, with its celebration of a London fog, its vision of man's secular quest of the Hesperides, and its assertion that

> God has no machine
> For punching perfect worlds from cakes of chaos.
>
>   *   *   *   *
>
> He works but as He can;
> God is an artist, not an artisan.
> Darkly imagining,
> With ice and fire and storm,
> With floods and earthquake-shocks
> He gave our sphere its form.
> The meaning of His work
> Grew as He wrought.
> In creases of the mud, in cooling rocks
> He saw ideas lurk—
> Mountains and streams.
> Of life the passionate thought
> Haunted His dreams.

Despite some imperfections of form, this is certainly one of the most notable and characteristic of the *Eclogues*— much more so than *Christmas Eve*, a lyric of winter and a Christmas carol, which brings the first series to a close.

All Hallows' Eve, which opens the second series, has a simple and beautiful rhythmic movement, but its symbolism, I own, escapes me. It sings the doleful doom of Elfland:

> For the fate of the elves is nearly the same
>   As the terrible fate of men ;
> To love ; to rue : to be and pursue
>   A flickering wisp of the fen.
>
> We must play the game with a careless smile
>   Though there's nothing in the hand ;
> We must toil as if it were worth our while
>   Spinning our ropes of sand ;
> And laugh and cry, and live and die
>   At the waft of an unseen wand.
>
> But the elves, besides the endless woe
>   Of the unfulfilled behest,
> Have only a phantom life, and so
>   They neither can die nor rest—
> Have no real being at all, and know
>   That therefore they never can rest—
> The doleful yoke of the deathless folk
>   Since first the sun went west.

The Poe-like chiming of the last stanza is rare in Mr. Davidson's work. The reiteration of whole stanzas and passages is one of his constant mannerisms; but he does not often ring the changes on a single line.

The blank-verse eclogue entitled *Lammas* is one of the most powerful things Mr. Davidson has ever done. It is vivid in description, penetrating in psychology, superb in imagination. First we have an ingenious vindication of the modern substitute for prophecy, Debate—this " most tedious Cyclops" which

> Laborious long in darkness and distress,
> Hammered and forged the adamantine chains
> That shackle tyranny, and now begins
> To smelt the ore from which shall yet be wrought
> A kingly crown for every child of man.

Then we have pictures by the hyperæsthetic Ninian of a "chill and brindled fog" sweeping over Edinburgh, and of a Kentish land- and sea-scape; leading up to a vivid and subtle diagnosis of his own spiritual case. Having long and in vain solicited from God a revelation of the meaning of things, he ultimately gave up the enigma only to find himself "obsessed" by the pageantry of the universe:

> No well-thumbed page appeared
> In the hard book of memory when I woke:
> Amazed I trembled newly into life:
> I seemed to be created every morn.
> A golden trumpet pealed along the sky:
> The sun arose; the whole earth rushed upon me.
> Sometimes the tree that stroked my window-pane
> Was more than I could grasp; sometimes my thought
> Absorbed the universe, which fell away
> And dwindled from my ken, as if my mind
> Had been the roomy continent of space.

Then in a passionate and terrible passage he bewails the lot of his children, "defeated ere they were begot." As a remedy for his woes Sandy, in the following nervous lines, recommends the Olympian egoism of the "over-man":

> Escape! I know the manner! Live at speed;
> And call your least caprice the law of God;
> Disdain the shows of things, and every love
> Whose stamen is not hate; self-centred stand;
> Accept no second thought; in every throb
> Your heart gives, every murmur of your mind,
> Listen devoutly to the trump of doom.
> You are your birthright; let it serve you well:
> Be your own star, for strength is from within,
> And one against the world will always win!

"I am not thinking solely of myself," says Ninian in reply,

> But of the groaning cataract of life,
> The ruddy stream that leaps importunate
> Out of the night, and in a moment vaults
> The immediate treacherous precipice of time,
> Splashing the stars, downward into the night.

Then Herbert puts in a word of stoic consolation, commending first the "loyal constancy" and "noble ministry" of Nature as the "true salve" for Ninian's distempered mind, and then continuing:

> Blame not yourself too much ; admit no fear
> Of madness with the sunrise in your blood ;
> And hold your own intelligence in awe
> As the most high : there is no other God—
> No God at all ; yet God is in the womb—
> A living God, no mystic deity.
> With idols in its infancy the world
> Deceived itself as maidens do with dolls,
> And as it grew pretended and believed
> That what it should bring forth already reigned.
> Now is its hour come, but it only knows
> The sick dismay and anguish, ignorant
> Of birth-pangs and an offspring more divine
> Than man has yet imagined.   I have woes,
> As you and all men have in their degree ;
> So let us think we are the tortured nerves
> Of Being in travail with a higher type.

Finally, Ninian brings the colloquy to a close with the following vision of the beauty and majesty of the world:

> See,
> They throng the room !—no spectres, but themselves:
> Sibilant depths of darkness ; avenues
> Of latticed light ; ambrosial, pine-strewn glades ;
> Ravines and waterfalls ; the grass-green turf,
> Where primroses by secret alchemy
> Distil from buried treasure golden leaves,
> And where forget-me-nots above the tombs
> Of snow-drops hang their candelabra, trimmed
> With azure light—turquoise by magic roots
> Drawn from the bowels of the earth and changed
> To living flame ; roses, laburnum, lilac ;
> Sunrise and sunset like a glowing vice
> Bloodstained that grips the world ; the restless moon
> Swung low to light us ; clouds ; the limpid sky ;
> The bourdon of the great ground-bee, athwart
> A lonely hill-side, vibrant on the air,
> And subtler than the scent of violets ;
> Sonorous winds, storm, thunder, and the sea.

If this poem be not compact of pregnant thought and luminous imagery, I know not where to look for imagery and thought.

The eclogues of *Midsummer Day* and *Mayday* are pretty but comparatively unimportant pieces of nature-celebration; the latter embodying the pathetic story of a May-morn devotee, and Basil's spirited transcript of the nightingale's song. *St. George's Day* is, both in its strength and its occasional weakness, a typical example of Mr. Davidson's manner. But its strength far outweighs its weakness, and it is, in its general effect, a noble and spirit-stirring piece of work.

There remain to be considered Mr. Davidson's three books of miscellaneous poems: *Ballads and Songs* (1894), *New Ballads* (1897), and *The Last Ballad and other Poems* (1899). These may be treated as three volumes of one work; and I propose to survey and classify, rather than criticise, their contents, before attempting, in conclusion, to sum up the characteristics of Mr. Davidson's talent.

The ballad, or more precisely the parable in quatrains, is the poet's favourite form. But more notable to my thinking than any of the quatrain poems are three dramatic narratives in blank verse: *The Making of a Poet*, *A Woman and her Son*, and *The Ordeal*. The first of these is absolutely masterly in its sustained vitality of feeling and utterance. It sets forth the rebellion of a pagan-hearted boy against the narrow Calvinism of his parents:

> His father, woman-hearted, great of soul,
> Wilful and proud, save for one little shrine
> That held a pinchbeck cross, had closed and barred
> The many mansions of his intellect.

> *   *   *   *   *

> His father's pleading done, his mother cried,
> With twitching forehead, scalding tears that broke

The seal of wrinkled eyelids, mortised hands
Where knuckles jutted white: "Almighty God!—
Almighty God!—Oh, save my foolish boy!"

The vision of Aphrodite and Adonis that floats into the
boy's mind in the midst of his parents' entreaties is very
beautifully written; but lurid intensity rather than beauty is
the note of the poem. His mother dead, his father "dying
for his sake," the boy "yields tamely" and goes to "the
table of the Lord . . . ghastly, with haunted eyes."

The stealthy elders creaked about the floor,
Guiding the cup and platter; looking down,
The children in the gallery smirked and watched
Who took the deepest draught; and ancient dames
Crumpled their folded handkerchiefs, and pressed
With knuckly fingers sprays of southernwood.

In the reaction from his hypocritical surrender, the son
rushes to his father with a full confession of unfaith, and a
doxology, not to God, but to man; whereupon, with "gaping
horror" on his face, the old man

Rose quaking; and " The unpardonable sin!—
The unpardonable sin!" he whispered hoarse.

At first the father is fain to go with his son to hell:

Boy, help me to blaspheme. I cannot face
Without you her that nursed you at her breast.

But it is as impossible for him to disbelieve as for the son to
believe; and his wonderfully dramatic and pathetic rhapsody
ends thus:

Beside the crystal river I shall walk
For ever with the Lord. The city of gold,
The jasper walls thereof, the gates of pearl,
The bright foundation-stones of emerald,
Of sapphire, chrysoprase, of every gem,
And the high triumph of unending day
Shall be but wildfire on a summer eve

Beside the exceeding glory of delight,
That shall entrance me with the constant thought
Of how in Hell through all eternity
My son performs the perfect will of God.

The father dies; and the son, wandering by the shore of the
firth, realises the emptiness of the dogma of the godhood of
man which he would have pitted against his father's creed.
"A God? a mole, a worm!" he cries:

> . . . An enchanted God,
> Whose nostrils in a palace breathe perfume,
> Whose cracking shoulders hold the palace up,
> Whose shoeless feet are rotting in the mire!

And this is the end of his cogitations:

> Our ruthless creeds that bathe the earth in blood
> Are moods by alchemy made dogmas of—
> The petrifaction of a metaphor.
> No creed for me! I am a man apart:
> A mouthpiece for the creeds of all the world;
> A soulless life that angels may possess
> Or demons haunt, wherein the foulest things
> May loll at ease beside the loveliest;
> A martyr for all mundane moods to tear;
> The slave of every passion; and the slave
> Of heat and cold, of darkness and of light;
> A trembling lyre for every wind to sound.

*   *   *   *   *

> And lo! to give me courage comes the dawn,
> Crimsoning the smoky east; and still the sun
> With fire-shod feet shall step from hill to hill
> Downward before the night; winter shall ply
> His ancient craft, soldering the years with ice;
> And spring appear, caught in a leafless brake,
> Breathless with wonder and the tears half-dried
> Upon her rosy cheek; summer shall come
> And waste his passion like a prodigal
> Right royally; and autumn spend her gold
> Free-handed as a harlot; men to know,
> Women to love are waiting everywhere.

An outwardly similar, yet essentially different, situation is that treated in *A Woman and her Son*.   Here, in a graphically indicated environment of city squalor, we find an atheist-pessimist son beside the deathbed of his mother, who has unflinchingly borne a life of drudgery, privation and sorrow, in radiant and immovable faith that the life beyond would make all good to her.   " Hard as the nether millstone " himself, her son would see her

> Harden with a hiss
> As life goes out in the cold bath of death.

She dies in the full confidence that she is going to heaven, where her husband and the seven children who have preceded her will welcome her with rapture.   But after three days, her soul returns to her body, beside which her son is still watching ; and she has nothing to report of the undiscovered country except a feeble dream which must have flickered through her mind in the moment of dissolution. Then she, in her turn, grows hard as the nether millstone, and, cursing the illusions of " love the cheat, And hope, the radiant devil pointing up," dies a second time in her son's arms :

> He, holding her,
> With sobs and laughter spoke : his mind had snapped
> Like a frayed string o'erstretched : " Mother, rejoice ;
> For I shall make you glad.   There is no heaven ;
> Your children are resolved to dust and dew :
> But, mother, I am God.   I shall create
> The heaven of your desires.   There must be heaven
> For mothers and their babes.   Let heaven be now ! "
>
> They found him conjuring chaos with mad words
> And brandished hands across his mother's corpse.
>
> Thus did he see her harden with a hiss
> As life went out in the cold bath of death ;
> Thus did she soften him before she died :
> For both were bigots—fateful souls that plague
> The gentle world.

148

The Ordeal, with its romantic setting, may stand as a sort of half-way house between these dramatic narratives and the ballads. It is longer than the other blank-verse poems, and somewhat laxer in style, but it belongs essentially to the same class inasmuch as it is an ironic indictment at once of the ordering of human life, and of the attitude of mankind towards the powers that so order it. Sir Hilary, in a fit of malignant jealousy, hales his wife, Bertha, and Sir Godfrey, knight-errant of the Phœnix, before the judgment-seat of Emanuel, King of the Golden City. He has seen Bertha give Godfrey a ring, a valueless old "hoop of pale alloy," and accept from him a kiss upon her forehead. The King sends Bertha and her children apart, and bids Godfrey give his account of the matter. The knight relates how, thirty years before, when he set out on the quest of the Phœnix, Bertha and he, boy-and-girl sweethearts, exchanged tokens; how, meeting her again on the eve of a final sally in search of the glorious bird, he begged her to restore his token, his mother's ring; and how this is all that has ever passed between them. His tale is transparently true, but Hilary in his jealous frenzy scoffs at it, and Godfrey demands trial by battle. The lists are set, and though Godfrey has both right and strength on his side, Hilary, by a sheer brute chance, pierces him through the vizor to the brain, and he falls dead. Then the King calls upon Bertha for her story. She, ignorant of what Godfrey has said, yet confirms it in every point; but, tearing the veil from her heart, she proclaims that what to Godfrey was a boyish fancy was to her the one love of her life; that she never loved or pretended to love her husband, but merely chose him, when all hope of Godfrey's return was past, to be the father of her children; that she has been faithful to him in thought and deed, but has known no passion save the passion of maternity. The King has never a doubt of her truth; but Hilary still cries that the trial by battle has declared her an adulteress.

Confident in the justice of heaven, despite its evident failure
in the overthrow of Godfrey, she demands the Ordeal by
Fire to clear her name.

> " I grant it," said the King, feeling himself
> Heroic : " I believe in God and you.
> Choose, then : the bar ; the ring ? " But Hilary said,
> " The way of ploughshares heated hot remains
> The ordeal provided by the law."
> " The ploughshares ! " said the King, held in the trap
> Of code that men will set to catch themselves.
> " None ever traverse them uncharred, and few
> Escape with life." " But I uncharred shall pass,"
> The victim said. " Sir, I appeal to God
> Within me and about me and above
> To bear me scathless through the fiercest test.
> Heat hot your ploughshares—now ! " Her children quailed :
> " No, mother—no ! " they whispered. " What ! " she cried,
> " You also doubt your mother's chastity
> And God's omnipotence and rectitude ! "
> Abashed they fell behind her.

The ordeal is prepared, and the nine ploughshares' " Deep
notes of carmine pulsed in unison Upon the hissing turf."

> " In God's great heart the issue lies. Proceed."
> This said, the King bent down his twitching face
> In prayer ; for even men of parts will pray
> Against the wrong instead of smiting it,
> Besotted with a creed. . . . She placed her foot,
> Her naked buoyant foot, dew-drenched and white,
> She placed it firmly on the first red edge,
> Leapt half her height, and with a hideous cry
> Fell down face-foremost brained upon the next.

These passages are chosen rather because they carry the
story forward than on account of any exceptional merit.
The terrible "men of parts," indeed, in the last extract, is
one of Mr. Davidson's too frequent lapses into the commonplace. But it would be easy to set against it a score of
truly noble passages in which imagination and utterance are
alike admirable ; for instance, this of Godfrey's :

JOHN DAVIDSON

I must begone—again
To feel my heart leap at the sudden foe,
The lonely battle in the wilderness ;
To come at night under the desert moon
On pillars, ghostly porches, temples, towers
Silent for centuries ; to see at dawn
The shadow of the Arab on the sand.

These three poems seem to me to rank with the *Lammas*
Eclogue among the very strongest things Mr. Davidson has
done.

His ballads run to a round dozen : all but one—the comparatively ineffective *Vengeance of the Duchess*—composed
in rhymed quatrains. The measure sometimes becomes a
little monotonous in Mr. Davidson's hands, mainly, I think,
because of his fondness for what the Shakespearometrists
call "end-stopped lines"; but he handles it with great
force, if not with absolute freedom. They are all apologues,
more or less distinctly water-marked with a moral; but
they all embody a story, or at least a situation, and generally a very finely conceived one. *A Ballad of the Exodus
from Houndsditch* is a fervid fantasy, suggested by Carlyle's
often-quoted phrase. In *A Ballad of a Nun* and *A New
Ballad of Tannhäuser* Mr. Davidson makes use of mediæval
legends to help in "laying the ghost," as he puts it, "of an
unwholesome idea that still haunts the world—the idea of the
impurity of nature." The *Ballad of a Nun* is probably the
most popular of all Mr. Davidson's writings, and has even
become somewhat hackneyed; but it merits its popularity
if only by reason of its magnificent opening :

High on a hill the convent hung,
  Across a duchy looking down,
Where everlasting mountains flung
  Their shadows over tower and town.

The jewels of their lofty snows
  In constellations flashed at night ;
Above their crests the moon arose ;
  The deep earth shuddered with delight.

Long ere she left her cloudy bed,
  Still dreaming in the orient land,
On many a mountain's happy head
  Dawn lightly laid her rosy hand.

The adventurous sun took Heaven by storm ;
  Clouds scattered largesses of rain ;
The sounding cities, rich and warm,
  Smouldered and glittered in the plain.

The third stanza is slightly marred, to my thinking, by the recurrence of the dissyllabic epithets in " y "—" cloudy bed," " happy head," " rosy hand "; but the last stanza is magnificently pictorial, a Turner in four lines. *The Last Ballad* is a parable of the soul's decline into inert, Swiftian pessimism, and its recovery from that abyss. *A Ballad of the Poet Born* and *A Ballad of Euthanasia* celebrate the sweet compensations of life. *A Ballad of a Workman* seems, as I understand it, to commend a quietism, a lowly and reverent acceptance of that state of life to which it has pleased fate to call us, which can be regarded only as a transient eddy in the stream of Mr. Davidson's philosophy. The grandiose *Ballad of Heaven* and *Ballad of an Artist's Wife* sing the praises of strenuous idealism and humble duty respectively ; while *A Ballad of a Coward* is a study of the soul-state its title suggests, and *A Ballad of Hell* sets forth the ultimate beatitude of " a soul that knew not fear." These ballads, certainly, are not all of equal merit. Two of them, the *Ballad of Heaven* and of *Euthanasia*, seem to me to fall notably below the level of the rest, while several of them contain inert and prosaic stanzas. But, taken as a whole, they show a wealth and variety of imagination, and a vivid energy of phrase, which would abundantly compensate for greater faults than can reasonably be laid to their charge.

Mr. Davidson's shorter poems may be roughly classified under five heads : poems of the Country, poems of the Town, Romantic, Political and Spiritual poems.

JOHN DAVIDSON

The Country poems and Town poems are essentially of the same stuff of which the *Fleet Street Eclogues* are composed. They are lyrics which have not happened to fit into the quasi-dramatic eclogue setting. The most noteworthy of the Country poems are *In Romney Marsh*, *A Cinque Port*, the sequence on the four seasons, *Spring Song*, *Sunset*, *A Highway Pimpernel*, *Winter Rain*, *Summer Rain*, *Afternoon*, and *The Last Rose*. Specialists have, I am told, thrown doubts on the correctness of Mr. Davidson's observation of birds, flowers, and trees. This is a matter on which I cannot pretend to arbitrate. All I can say is that Mr. Davidson, at his best, or even at his second best, brings home to me the sound and colour, the atmosphere and aroma, the homeliness and the spaciousness, of English and Scottish scenery with a peculiar poignancy. His nature-painting is all open-air work; it never smells of the lamp; it is clear-toned, racy, or, as we should say in Scotland, "caller." Note, for instance, the compulsive sense of moisture and movement conveyed in the stanzas entitled *Winter Rain*, quoted in full on p. 160.

The admirable *Song of a Train* may stand as a sort of connecting link between the Country and the Town poems. In these Mr. Davidson's originality makes itself unmistakably felt. He tries to describe things, both animate and inanimate, not hitherto attempted, at any rate in classic verse; and, like all pioneers, he meets with an occasional misadventure. But the measure of success he achieves is, on the whole, remarkable; for instance, in *A Northern Suburb*, *A Frosty Morning*, *In the Isle of Dogs*, and that tragical lyric of labour, *Piper, Play!* quoted at the end of this article.

Of purely Romantic poems there are but two or three, for Mr. Davidson very seldom sings for the mere sake of singing. The most notable, I think, is *The Prince of the Fairies*, a set of "Stanzas for Music," as the poets of the early nineteenth century were wont to say. The mood in which they were composed—an idle mood of decorative fantasy—is not at all characteristic of Mr. Davidson. We owe to it, however, the poem entitled *Serenade*; and that spirited piece of "gallows humour," *The Stoop of Rhenish*, may perhaps come under the same heading.

Among the group which I have designated Political poems, the *War Song* stands easily first, and next to it, perhaps, *The Hymn of Abdul Hamid*, powerful in conception, grimly prosaic in style. Other notable numbers in this group are *Coming*, *Waiting*, and *The Aristocrat*.

Finally, we come to the Spiritual lyrics, among which, as is only natural, we find some of Mr. Davidson's best work. There are fine ideas in the verses *To the New Women* and *To the New Men ;* but they seem, on the whole, to have missed their perfect expression. Here is the close of the address to the New Women :

> Be bold and yet be bold,
> But be not overbold,
> Although the knell be toll'd
> Of the tyranny of old.
>
> And meet your splendid doom
> On heaven-scaling wings,
> Women, from whose bright womb
> The radiant future springs !

The epithet "heaven-scaling" seems to halt both in metre and in thought; for "scaling" is essentially a pedestrian process, incompatible with the very idea of wings. Otherwise, the quatrain is fine and original; and not less so is the last line of this verse addressed to the New Men :

> Love, and hope, and know :
> Man—you must adore him :
> Let the whole past go :
> *Think God's thought before Him.*

154

JOHN DAVIDSON

I intend both compliment and criticism when I say that these two poems remind me of Emerson's excursions into metre. Less erratic in form, and certainly not less weighty in thought, are *The Badge of Men*, the impressive *Earth to Earth*, and that lyrical allegory of rare beauty and colour *The Merchantman and the Market-haunters*. But, to my thinking, no other poem of this class can rival in intense and subtle significance the two stanzas entitled

INSOMNIA.

He wakened quivering on a golden rack
    Inlaid with gems : no sign of change, no fear
    Or hope of death came near ;
Only the empty ether hovered black
    About him stretched upon his living bier,
Of old by Merlin's Master deftly wrought :
    Two Seraphim of Gabriel's helpful race
    In that far nook of space
With iron levers wrenched and held him taut.

The Seraph at his head was Agony ;
    Delight, more terrible, stood at his feet :
    Their sixfold pinions beat
The darkness, or were spread immovably,
    Poising the rack, whose jewelled fabric meet
To strain a god, did fitfully unmask
    With olive light of chrysoprases dim
    The smiling Seraphim
Implacably intent upon their task.

Where shall we look for a briefer or more luminous similitude of human destiny ?

Mr. Davidson's talent is not one that can be readily focused in a phrase or even in a paragraph. His spirit is electrically fuliginous rather than radiant and serene. There is more of Ætna than of Olympus about it. He exemplifies the perfervid, not the " canny," side of the Scottish national genius. But he is beyond all doubt a personality, a temperament, a living spirit. There is thought as well as feeling in all he does—not systematic, close-knit reasoning, but that brave, translunary intuition, that swift penetration of the husks of sublunary things, in which lies the poet's true philosophy. He is an insistent, and for the most part an indignant, critic of life. He is not content to see and set down what he sees, to feel and take his feelings on trust. His mind is for ever occupied in weighing, comparing, analysing; contrasting the actual with the ideal; turning prejudice inside out, unmasking hypocrisy, impaling falsehood. Seeing vividly and feeling intensely, he throws his perceptions and emotions into a fiery furnace of passionate idealism, and then hammers them eagerly, impatiently, sometimes rudely enough, into weapons and missiles to be used in the battle of human progress. For at heart Mr. Davidson is an ardent meliorist, though there be times when a blackness as of utter pessimism descends upon his mood. The theorists who would have art immutably serene and conciliatory must naturally regard with horror Mr. Davidson's turbulent and disquieting onslaughts upon many comfortable optimisms, euphemisms, and conspiracies of silence. Yet, though the tone of his thought is in the main gloomy, his temperamental vitality is throughout so high that the whole effect of his work is stimulant rather than depressing. He himself has given us a lightning-flash of insight into his nature in the lines prefixed to his *New Ballads*:

> Some said, "He was strong." He was weak;
> For he never could sing or speak
> Of the things beneath or the things above,
> Till his soul was touched by death or love.
>
> Some said, "He was weak." They were wrong;
> For the soul must be strong
> That can break into song
> Of the things beneath and the things above,
> At the stroke of death, at the touch of love.

This is at once authentic poetry and true psychology. It goes far to account for what may be called the main positive and negative characteristics of Mr. Davidson's work : the presence of fire and the absence of finish. Poetry is not, to him, "emotion recollected in tranquillity." It is emotion at fever-heat, a rolling, glistering lava-stream ; and when the lava has hardened it is too late to fine away the odds and ends of slag that have become embedded in the mass.

A cunning craftsman Mr. Davidson is not. It is evident that he has not given much thought to metrical technique. He does not experiment in difficult measures, weave intricate arabesques of rhyme, or build up his blank-verse periods with subtly-distributed pauses, accelerations and suspensions, overlaying the primary rhythm with numberless secondary movements, "cycle and epicycle, orb in orb." He is too much absorbed in what he has to say to consider thus curiously the manner of saying it. But his innate rhythmical faculty is very strong, and he achieves admirable effects in a large straightforward style which, with all its simplicity, is anything but artless. His diction, again, is copious, colourful, vital. He has found multitudes of superb phrases, descriptive, contemplative, emotional, which we read with a thrill of satisfaction, thinking " This thing could not be better said." He now and then declines upon a commonplace, stereotyped epithet, now and then ventures a too daring colloquialism. For instance, we are scarcely prepared to encounter the term "pal," or the expression "words they slung," in otherwise serious and dignified poems. But it must be remembered that it is part of his function as a realist, a poet of the living hour, to try to gain rights of poetic citizenship for racy-vernacular vocables and locutions ; and we ought not to complain if his experiments are not uniformly happy. His taste in imagery is not irreproachable. Even in his maturest work, he will now and then slip in a conceit which must have been left over, one would think, from his early Shakespearising days. While he is capable, for instance, of such splendid stanzas as this—

> The trumpets pealed ; *the echoes sang*
> *A tossing fugue ;* before it died,
> Again the rending trumpets rang,
> Again the phantom notes replied—

he is also capable, only a few pages further on, of such enormities as the following :

> The hostess of the sky, the moon,
> Already stoops to entertain
> The golden light of afternoon,
> And the wan earthshine of the plain.

I am far from desiring to palliate such lapses ; but I cannot but hint that, if we are going to make " impeccability " (that most peccant word) the touchstone of a poet's worth, our library of poetry will shrink into a very narrow shelf. Artistry is good ; perfection of form, delicacy of tact, imperturbable wisdom, are all desirable qualities ; but he who can enjoy no poetry in which they are not all combined and at their highest potency, is not, to my thinking, either a good critic or an enviable man.

Mr. Davidson has imagination, vision, thought, passion, eloquence and melody. He is a humanist in the best sense. Nature he loves, but it is as an accessory to, not a refuge from, human passion. One may not always agree with his thought, one cannot always admire his workmanship. But he has the root of the matter in him ; the world is alive to his eye, language is alive on his lips ; and he is withal a strong, free spirit, untrammelled by cowardice, pedantry or cant.

JOHN DAVIDSON

PIPER, PLAY!

Now the furnaces are out,
  And the aching anvils sleep;
Down the road the grimy rout
  Tramples homeward twenty deep.
    Piper, play! Piper, play!
    · Though we be o'erlaboured men,
    Ripe for rest, pipe your best!
    Let us foot it once again!

Bridled looms delay their din;
  All the humming wheels are spent;
Busy spindles cease to spin;
  Warp and woof must rest content.
    Piper, play! Piper, play!
    For a little we are free!
    Foot it girls and shake your curls,
      Haggard creatures though we be!

Racked and soiled the faded air
  Freshens in our holiday;
Clouds and tides our respite share;
  Breezes linger by the way.
    Piper, rest! Piper, rest!
    Now, a carol of the moon!
    Piper, piper, play your best!
      Melt the sun into your tune!

We are of the humblest grade;
  Yet we dare to dance our fill:
Male and female were we made—
  Fathers, mothers, lovers still!
    Piper—softly; soft and low;
      Pipe of love in mellow notes,
    Till the tears begin to flow,
      And our hearts are in our throats!

159

Nameless as the stars of night
Far in galaxies unfurled,
Yet we wield unrivalled might,
Joints and hinges of the world !
Night and day ! night and day !
Sound the song the hours rehearse !
Work and play ! work and play !
The order of the universe !

Now the furnaces are out,
And the aching anvils sleep ;
Down the road a merry rout
Dances homeward, twenty deep.
Piper, play ! Piper, play !
Wearied people though we be,
Ripe for rest, pipe your best !
For a little we are free !

WINTER RAIN.

Motionless, leaden cloud
The region roofed and walled ;
Beneath, a tempest shrieked aloud,
And the forest beckoned and called.

The blackthorn coppice was all ablaze,
And shot and garlanded,
With bronzed and wreathing bramble sprays,
And bright leaves green and red.

The dripping pollards their shock-heads hung,
And in the glistening shaws,
Lustres and glories of rubies, swung
The dark wet crimson haws.

The dead leaves pattered and stole about
Like elves in the sheltered glades,
And rushed down the broad green rides and out
O'er the fields in wintry raids.

JOHN DAVIDSON

The motionless, leaden sky
   Emptied itself amain,
And the angry east with hue and cry
   Dashed at the pouring rain.

The forest rocked and sang:
   Behind the passing blast
Far off the new blast faintly rang,
   Arrived and roared, and passed,
In the liberty of the open sea
   To find a home at last.

MRS. TYNAN HINKSON

VERY Irish, very feminine, very human, Mrs. Katharine Tynan Hinkson possesses a clear and beautiful vein of talent, which might, indeed, be too grandiloquently praised, but can scarcely be overvalued. Mrs. Hinkson is a born poetess if ever there was one. All impressions from without, whether of nature, love, patriotism, or devotion, find their spontaneous reaction in poetry, and touch her soul to song. And the note of her singing is always pure, fresh, limpid, sincere. Though not a great mistress of style, she keeps her diction untainted by commonness. Though she is anything but a purist in rhymes, her assonances are never vulgar or grotesque. Though not an ambitious metrist, she invents for herself little lilting staves that are full of lyric charm. A pedantic criticism could pick out scores of flaws and errors in her work; but her breaches of rule are never lapses of taste. However hackneyed the similitude, one can only say of her that she sings like the birds she loves.

Though unmistakable from the first, her talent has ripened gradually. Her early books contain a much smaller proportion of really vital work than those of her maturer years. We find her sometimes trying her tools on themes that bring with them only a conventional, or at best a fitful, inspiration. Yet in the first poem of her first book, *Louise de la Vallière, and other Poems* (1885), there

· KATHARINE · TYNAN · HINKSON ·

occur stanzas which clearly prophesy the nature-singer of after years. It is Louise de la Vallière who is speaking :

> And it may be my feet will go in dreams
> Down by Touraine's fair fields and pleasant streams,
> Where my white girlhood's full fleet days were spent,
> There the breeze freshens, and a great sun gleams.
>
> Sleeps the old château through the roseate hours,
> Drifts the white odorous bloom in almond bowers;
> And the long grasses, hot and indolent,
> Murmur of April and her wine-rich showers.
>
> Like little white-winged birds that fluttering fly,
> Lustrous small clouds come sailing down the sky,
> And the great cattle, breathing thymy sweet,
> Stand where gold cowslips in the grass are high.
>
> Cherries are ripe and red-lipped in the nets,
> And the old pear-tree that its youth forgets,
> Hoary with lichen, stands with aged feet
> Deep in a purple mist of violets.

This is a clearly-seen, keenly-felt picture, very noteworthy in the work of a beginner. Several other poems in the same book contain characteristic foretastes of Mrs. Hinkson's later manner; for instance, these lines from *An Answer* :

> I yearned . . .
> To hear again, 'mid leafy springtide ways,
> The sweet small footsteps of the silvern rain.

In the main, however, the individuality of the poetess is as yet but dubiously revealed. She is much taken up with romantic and devotional themes, and draws her inspiration largely from the pre-Raphaelite poets; for example, in *My Lady*, *Joan of Arc* and *King Cophetua's Queen*. She has two delightful sonnets on *Fra Angelico at Fiesole;* but to my sense, the most living things in the book are the poems of Irish patriotism, *Waiting*, which describes Fionn and his warriors biding his time, like Barbarossa, in a cavern of the Donegal hills, and *The Flight of the Wild Geese*, dealing

with the homeward yearnings of the Irish Jacobites, who, after
the Treaty of Limerick, took service in foreign lands:

> In Austria and France they roved
> Through ways as sad as death;
> In alien paths their tired feet bled,
> The laurel crowns that decked the head
> Were thorn-set underneath.

There is nothing shrill in Mrs. Hinkson's patriotism. It
is very intimate and touching.

Her second book, *Shamrocks* (1887), opens with a
longish narrative poem, *The Pursuit of Diarmuid and
Grainne*, which contains some charming details, but will
scarcely rank, as a whole, among the master-works of the
Keltic Renascence. Nor, I think, does *The Fate of King
Feargus* show the true narrative gift. On the other hand,
The Dead Mother strikes that note of intense maternal
feeling which had been anticipated, indeed, by a few of the
greatest male poets, and by certain nameless ballad-singers,
but which has naturally entered much more largely into
literature since women learned, not merely to write more
or less like men, but to make their sex articulate. *The
Sick Princess* and *After Harvest* are beautiful, each in its
kind; *Noel* is a sort of preliminary study for the much
finer *Singing Stars* of a later volume; and *The King's Cup-
bearer* is a very noble and impressive patriotic poem.

In the *Ballads and Lyrics* of 1891, Mrs. Hinkson's
individuality is much more clearly developed. Here her
main topic is what I venture to call Christian folk-lore,
treated with the utmost reverence, but, for the most part,
in a decorative Keltic key. She has several poems on the
legend of St. Francis, and others entitled *Our Lady's Exile,
The Hiding-away of Blessed Angus, All Souls' Night,
Michael the Archangel, Golden Lilies*, and *The Chapel of the
Grail*. They all contain beautiful work, but there is a
touch of artifice in their simplicity which renders them less

sympathetic to me than those pieces, such as *The Fairy Foster-Mother* and *The Witch*, in which Mrs. Hinkson treats pagan folk-lore from the point of view, not of the abstract primitive Christian, but of the concrete Irish peasant. In *The Witch*, for instance, there is a delightful touch of character. It opens with the following verse:

> Margaret Grady—I fear she will burn—
> Charmed the butter off my churn;
> 'Tis I would know it the wide world over,
> Yellow as saffron, scented as clover.

The speaker has recourse to a "fairy-man," who gives her a witch-hazel wreath, by means of which the sinister arts of Margaret Grady are brought to nothing. Then the speaker closes the episode as follows:

> I bless the fairy-man though he be evil;
> Yet fairy-spells come not from the Devil;
> And Margaret Grady—I fear she will burn—
> I do forgive her with hate and scorn.

How racy is the human nature of the last line! And this poem strikes the keynote for several other admirable sketches of peasant character and feeling in Mrs. Hinkson's later books.

In this collection, too, she has more than one of those poems of profoundly feminine emotion above alluded to. Here is the last stanza of a short piece which is simply entitled *A Woman*:

> And for that music most forlorn,
> Voices of children never born,
> And the love words that are not hers,
> Even the sweet sky-choristers
> Pleasure her not. Ah, let her be,
> She and her dreams are company.

The following poem I quote partly for its matter, partly for its measure. Mrs. Hinkson has several times used this eight-line stanza with beautiful effect. Its charm is heightened, I think, when the double rhyme occurs always in the same place—the second and sixth lines—but even in the laxer form it here assumes, it seems to me to have a very delicate accent of its own:

MARAH.

My baby was always weeping,
    From the hour it was born ;
It never leaped and crowed
    Like other babies at play ;
In waking still or in sleeping,
    It wept most dumb and forlorn.
Bearing its mother's load,
    No wonder my head is grey.

It never looked on its father;
    He is lying under the sea.
When they told me my dear was drowned,
    The midsummer was here.
I was singing in the heather,
    And the lark's song answered me ;
For his ship was homeward bound.
    We were only wed that year.

I was like a crazèd creature ;
    I wept most terribly ;
Mad laughter and mad weeping,
    Till my little one was born.
Like him in form and feature,
    With eyes like a summer sea ;
But the tears from the closed lids creeping
    Never ceased till this morn.

It would have broken my heart,
    But it was broken already ;
The Lord has taken it home ;
    There is none so tender as He.
And His mother in motherly part
    Will train the footsteps unsteady,
Nor think it too troublesome
    To rock asleep on her knee.

And teach him later to play
    And laugh and run like another;
For there are playgrounds up there,
    To please the lambs of the fold.
Nor let him forget; and some day
    He will run, beholding his mother,
And twine his hands in her hair,
    And kiss her with loving untold.

It is in *Cuckoo Songs* (1894) that Mrs. Hinkson develops her full originality. Here there is nothing in the least degree factitious or conventional, unless it be in *The Resurrection: a Miracle Play*, at the beginning, the elaborate artlessness of which, even to the almost systematic preference of false to true rhymes, somehow leaves me cold. Perhaps I am out of sympathy with the subject; but if that were so, the same idiosyncrasy ought to debar me from appreciating this carol of the Nativity, which, on the contrary, seems to me a perfectly beautiful inspiration—one of those poems whose movement, whose lilt, whose rhythmic essence, haunt the memory when the actual words are forgotten, as the perfume of a flower outlives the flower itself:

SINGING STARS.

"What sawest thou, Orion, thou hunter of the star-lands,
On that night star-sown and azure when thou cam'st in
        splendour sweeping,
And amid thy starry brethren from the near lands and the far
        lands,
All the night above a stable on the earth thy watch wert
        keeping?"

"Oh, I saw the stable surely, and the young Child and the
        Mother,
And the placid beasts still gazing with their mild eyes full of
        loving.
And I saw the trembling radiance of the Star, my lordliest
        brother,
Light the earth and all the heavens as he kept his guard
        unmoving.

" There were kings that came from Eastward with their ivory,
  spice, and sendal,
With gold fillets in their dark hair, and gold broidered robes
  and stately,
And the shepherds gazing star-ward, over yonder hill did wend
  all,
And' the silly sheep went meekly, and the wise dog marvelled
  greatly.

" Oh, we knew, we stars, the stable held our King, His glory
  shaded,
That His baby hands were poising all the spheres and constellations ;
Berenice shook her hair down, like a shower of star-dust
  braided,
And Arcturus, pale as silver, bent his brows in adorations.

" The stars sang all together, sang their love-songs with the
  angels,
With the Cherubim and Seraphim their shrilly trumpets
  blended.
They have never sung together since that night of great
  evangels,
And the young Child in the manger, and the time of bondage
  ended."

Here the quaint rhymes—"sendal, wend all," "angels,
evangels"—are absolutely appropriate. They are, so to
speak, a touch of colour, a quavering reed-note in the
orchestration. It is only fair to observe that Mrs. Hinkson
is by no means obtuse to the difference between false and
true rhyme. She feels, I imagine, that a certain conventional laxity in rhyming—coupling "summer" with
"roamer," "meadow" with "shadow," "bosom" with
"blossom," and treating "heaven," "even," "laven," and
"forgiven" as a fourfold rhyme—harmonises with the simplicity of her style. And who shall say that she is wrong ?
It is a mechanical pedantry to insist on absolute accuracy
of rhyme as essential to all poetry whatsoever. Our older
poets dreamt not of it. The ideal of accuracy has come into
vogue among the academic singers of the nineteenth century;
and though I, for my part, believe that it has come to stay,

it cannot claim a universal, and still less a retrospective, validity. The criticism, for instance, which makes Burns's laxity of rhymes a count in a belittling indictment, seems to me opposed to sound appreciation and rational enjoyment. It is impossible to set up one single and absolute standard of workmanship in poetry. Tennyson's workmanship was good for Tennyson, and no one admires it more than I ; but I hold it no reproach to Burns that his ideal of workmanship was different. If, by some miracle, the Tennysonian ideal had been implanted in Burns's mind, and he had consistently struggled up to it, he would have been by so much the less Burns and the less enjoyable. Mrs. Hinkson, I daresay, has not troubled to reason things out in this sense, or to justify herself by any individual precedent, but has simply obeyed the instinct which told her that a scrupulous accuracy of rhymes was not imperative, perhaps not even desirable, in her unassuming strains. She writes ditties rather than set and formal lyrics; and there is one law for the lyric, another for the ditty. She feels, perhaps, that her country muse ought not to be point-device in her attire, any more than a farmer ought to wear a frock-coat and a silk hat. Cockney rhymes she absolutely eschews—"caught" and "short," "saw" and "war," &c.—and she seldom or never deals in the strained Hudibrastics to which Browning gives his (I hope unavailing) sanction. Moreover, when the dignity or solemnity of the subject demands it, she is at once more careful of her rhymes. Note, for instance, the flawless workmanship of this tender little masterpiece :

THE WIDOWED HOUSE.
(*F. W.*, *obiit August 9, 1893.*)

Within your house that's widowed Love's nest is bitter cold,
Love goes with drooping pinions, his pulses slow and old ;
Your baby cries all night long for you he never knew,
The dust is over all things ; the grave dust over you.

Drear day and night go over and yet you never come,
To all that lonely weeping so obdurate and dumb.
'Twere liker you to hasten, putting the glory by,
To kiss your love's cold forehead and still your baby's cry.

'Twere liker you'd come stealing, a little ghost in white,
To rock a tiny cradle all in the hushed moonlight,
To whisper to a sleeper till he should dream and wake,
And find the strange new comfort and lose the old heart-break.

With you the years go over fleeter than words can say,
And one shall lose her lover but the half-length of a day ;
And one shall lose her baby but 'twixt a sleep and sleep.
The dead are glad in Heaven, the living 'tis that weep.

House and Home is almost equally beautiful in its frank womanliness. Of the impersonal, and specially of the Irish, ditties in this collection, *Gramachree* is, I think, the most spirited and successful; but it has several rivals.

Of Mrs. Hinkson's next book, *A Lover's Breast-Knot* (1896), I shall say little except that it gives beautiful expression to the personal side of Mrs. Hinkson's talent. These songs of a happy wife and a bereaved mother, though full of dignity and restraint, are too intimate for criticism. They are absolutely simple, spontaneous, and free from all indelicacy of self-revelation ; yet one shrinks from making a page of heart-history the subject of mere literary discussion, however sympathetic. I give merely a taste of its quality in one song, *Annus Mirabilis*, quoted at the end of this article. Not many poets who have Mrs. Hinkson's keen sense of the tears of things have also succeeded in singing the joy of life with the rapturous, and one might almost say reassuring, confidence which animates this lyric.

The Wind in the Trees (1898) is on the whole conceived in a lighter, more impersonal vein than either *A Lover's Breast-Knot* or *Cuckoo Songs*. It justifies its sub-title, "A Book of Country Verse," by being as fresh and fragrant as a May morning. I may say of it, in the conventional phrase, "I have read it from cover to cover (several times) and not found a dull page in it." This is a great deal to say of a book of verse, however small. It does not imply that there is a monotonous level of merit in Mrs. Hinkson's work. She has her happy moments, both of inspiration and execution, and she has her less happy moments. But everywhere one finds sincerity of feeling, and conventionality or commonness nowhere. In one or two places where a conventional turn of phrase occurs, it is introduced of set purpose, to recall the manner of an earlier generation of Irish lyrists, with their eighteenth-century graces and their frequent allusions to—

> Haythen goddesses most rare,
>   Homer, Plutarch, and Nebuchadnezzar,
> All standing naked in the open air.

But these deliberately rococo touches are few. As a rule Mrs. Hinkson writes with perfect straightforwardness, imitating no one and adopting no pose. Her love of the country, and of all things sweet and fresh, is heartfelt and intense, without hysterical exaggeration. It is truly interpretative; the reader who has any sense at all for such things sees and feels them with threefold intimacy in the limpid medium of Mrs. Hinkson's verse. Each poem is like a transparent little water-colour, centring our attention on some feature or aspect of the meadow, the copse, the garden, or the mountain lea. Not a page lacks its glint of colour, its wandering waft of fragrance. The human feeling is always subdued, unaffected, sometimes humorous, at other times pathetic without mawkishness; and if elaborate metrical art is lacking, a delicate and graceful metrical instinct is always present. No one who cares for the subjects suggested by the title of the book—birds and blossoms, the trees and the wind—can fail to find pleasure and refreshment in it.

There is no poem in this collection that, to my sense, clearly overtops the rest and calls aloud for quotation. Such preferences as one feels arise rather from some chance sympathy with the subject of this poem or that, than from any marked superiority of merit. Here are a few verses which may stand as a fair specimen of Mrs. Hinkson's manner:

CHANTICLEER.

Of all the birds from East to West,
    That tuneful are and dear,
I love that farmyard bird the best,
    They call him Chanticleer.

Gold plume and copper plume,
    Comb of scarlet gay;
'Tis he that scatters night and gloom
    And whistles back the day!

He is the sun's brave herald
    That, ringing his blithe horn,
Calls round a world dew-pearled
    The heavenly airs of morn.

O clear gold, shrill and bold,
    He calls through creeping mist
The mountains from the night and cold
    To rose and amethyst.

      *   *   *   *

Black fear he sends it flying,
    Black care he drives afar;
And creeping shadows sighing
    Before the morning star.

('Tis O, and woe, the lone ghost
    That glides before his call.
And huddles in its grave, so lost,
    Below the churchyard wall!)

The birds of all the forest
    Have dear and pleasant cheer,
But yet I hold the rarest
    The farmyard Chanticleer.

MRS. TYNAN HINKSON

Red cock or black cock,
  Gold cock or white,
The flower of all the feathered flock,
  He whistles back the light!

A similar touch of humour lights up Mrs. Hinkson's verses entitled *Cuckoo's Way* and *Sparrow*. I quote one or two stanzas of the latter :

When August hangs the bough with plums,
The dusty city sparrow comes
For sojourn in the country sweet,
To taste the barley and the wheat.

      *   *   *   *

His cynic wit, his mocking eye,
The innocent country ways decry ;
Though dews may wash his feathers clean
He hath the urchin's heart within.

      *   *   *   *

A little while for health he stays
Where Flora paints the country ways,
But holds that still the town is best
For men and birds of wit and taste.

Of Mrs. Hinkson's distinctively Irish poems *Modereen Rue*, to be quoted presently, is one of the most spirited. The most hardened sportsman will scarcely read it without feeling, at any rate, a momentary sympathy with the Young Lochinvar of the henroost. A deeper note is struck in *An Anthem in Heart, The Grey Mornings, The Foggy Dew, A Lost Garden, Vita Nuova, The Christmas Bird,* and several other poems ; but I have already given sufficient examples of Mrs. Hinkson's art in her more serious moods. In all moods Mrs. Hinkson is a poet, an artist, and a clear, courageous, buoyant spirit. Readers who care only for the splendours of poetry, for the banners and the big brass band, may find her unassuming strains too inartificial for their taste. Not so those simpler lovers of song who are content with the unforced notes of a fresh human voice, in whose rhythms may be felt the throbbings of a warm human heart.

173

ANNUS MIRABILIS.

(1893.)

The year that brought our hearts' desire,
  The Spring came with a sudden glow:
    No tender Spring that shyly comes
    With primroses and apple-blooms,
But garbed as with a golden fire
  Of her own daffodils a-blow.

O year beyond all years that were!
  The Summer followed fast in May;
    Scarce had the nightingales begun
    When the red rose out-burned the sun,
And scent of ripe fruit in the air
  Mixed with the honey-breath of hay.

That year the Spring came over again,
  There were two Summers in that year.
    In August there were bird-nestings
    And second broods and such sweet things,
And on the world a golden rain,
  And a new blossom on the pear.

That year the year was always May,
  Our year in whose sweet close shall come
    No winter with a waning sky,
    Nor sad leaves fall, nor roses die;
But roses, roses all the way,
  And never a nightingale be dumb.

MRS. TYNAN HINKSON

MODEREEN RUE.

(*i.e.*, THE LITTLE RED ROGUE—THE FOX.)

Och, Modereen Rue, you little red rover,
By the glint of the moon you stole out of your cover,
And now there is never an egg to be got
Nor a handsome fat chicken to put in the pot.
        Och, Modereen Rue!

With your nose to the earth and your ear on the listen,
You slunk through the stubble with frost-drops a-glisten,
With my lovely fat drake in your teeth as you went,
That your red roguish children should breakfast content.
        Och, Modereen Rue!

Och, Modereen Rue, hear the horn for a warning,
They are looking for red roguish foxes this morning;
But let them come my way, you little red rogue,
'Tis I will betray you to huntsman and dog.
        Och, Modereen Rue!

The little red rogue, he's the colour of bracken,
O'er mountains, o'er valleys, his pace will not slacken.
Tantara! tantara! he is off now, and, faith!
'Tis a race 'twixt the little red rogue and his death.
        Och, Modereen Rue!

Och, Modereen Rue, I've no cause to be grieving
For little red rogues with their tricks and their thieving.
The hounds they give tongue, and the quarry's in sight,
The hens on the roost may sleep easy to-night.
        Och, Modereen Rue!

But my blessing be on him.   He made the hounds follow
Through the woods, through the dales, over hill, over hollow,
It was Modereen Rue led them fast, led them far,
From the glint of the morning till eve's silver star.
        Och, Modereen Rue!

And he saved his red brush for his own future wearing,
He slipped into a drain, and he left the hounds swearing.
Good luck, my fine fellow, and long may you show
Such a clean pair of heels to the hounds as they go.
        Och, Modereen Rue!

175

MISS NORA HOPPER

(MRS. CHESSON)

A VERY frank, free, imaginative and melodious talent is that
of Miss Nora Hopper. She has in full measure all the
poetic qualities of her Celtic race, without the metaphysical
fanaticisms which sometimes accompany them. There is
nothing morbid, nothing overstrained about her work, unless
it be a too constant dwelling on the melancholy aspects of
Irish folk-lore. This is especially notable in her first book,
Under Quicken Boughs (1896). Here we have really
too much keening over the "dear black head," which has
become a sort of stereotype among Irish singers—a too
frequent return to such themes as *A Drowned Man's Sweet-
heart*, *A Drowned Girl to Her Lover*, and so forth. When
this vein of sentiment is overworked, it begins to seem
conventional and consequently tedious. The same remark
applies to such verses as *Roisin Dubh*, *Ma Bouchaleen
Bwee*, *The Passing of the Shee*, and the like. However
pretty they may be in themselves (and Miss Hopper never
writes otherwise than prettily), we feel, in the long run, that
there is something factitious and even fictitious about
them—that they are exercises on traditional themes rather
than genuine utterances of feeling. How often, for
instance, do we seem to have read, if not these very
lines (from *The Fairy Music*), at least equally felicitous
treatments of the same motive :

· NORA · HOPPER ·

There's many feet on the moor to-night, and they fall so light
    as they turn and pass,
So light and true that they shake no dew from the featherfew
    and the Hungry grass.
I drank no sup and I broke no crumb of their food, but dumb at
    their feast sat I,
For their dancing feet and their piping sweet, now I sit and
    greet till I'm.like to die.

Oh kind, kind folk, to the words you spoke I shut my ears and
    I would not hear,
And now all day what my own kin say falls sad and strange on
    my careless ear—
For I'm listening, listening, all day long to a fairy song that is
    blown to me,
Over the broom and the canna's bloom, and I know the doom of
    the Ceol-Sidhe.

The metrical movement of these verses (and of the two other stanzas which complete the poem) is very pretty, but their effect is discounted by our feeling that they are as conventional as a troubadour's aubade or a sixteenth-century sonnet. Even when Miss Hopper leaves Ireland behind, and betakes herself to Greece or Norway, one cannot but suspect that in her *Hymns to Pan*, and her rhapsodies on *Phæacia* and the land *East o' the Sun and West o' the Moon*, she is expressing a somewhat superficial romanticism, with no great depth of feeling behind it. Her imagination is rather too easily kindled; and though her work is not verbally imitative in any marked degree, yet it lacks spiritual individuality. She has always great fluency and sweetness of diction, and often real charm. But this first book must, on the whole, be regarded as immature—a volume of experiments. It is in *Songs of the Morning* (1900) that she gives the true measure of her talent.

Though there is much less untranslated Erse in Miss Hopper's second book than in her first, the influence of race, or rather of environment (for the odds, in any given instance, are greatly against purity of race), is none the less clearly discernible. It appears in the freshness and coolness of her diction, her sense of nature as a living thing, and her unabashed, yet never indiscreet, utterance of passion. The Keltic character, I take it, is, more clearly than any other race-character, a product of geographical conditions. The Kelt has for ages inhabited the western fringe of the world, from the mouth of the Loire to the outermost Hebrides. He has been pent between the devil and the deep sea— between hostile races to the eastward, and the haunting enigma of the trackless ocean to the west. He has dwelt in a land of mountains, of wide, windy estuaries, of clear and rushing rivers. The shifting pageantry of sky and sea has from of old encompassed him. His soul has been alternately swathed in fantastic mists and bathed in great billows of pure colour. He has for centuries seen the sun plunge, day after day, over the very edge of the world, into an abyss of waters as mysterious as the grave. And his mind has taken its imprint from this region of mountain and river and firth, of coolness and moisture and briny fragrance, bounded on the one hand by hostility, and by mystery on the other. Nature can never be the same thing to an inland as to a seaboard people. The plain-dweller, and even the mountain-dweller, knows nothing of the reduplication and etherealisation of colour that the great waters alone can give. The Kelt is the child of a volcanic coast-line and the Atlantic, as the Saxon is the child of alluvial prairies and the narrow seas. If it be objected that by this reasoning the Norseman ought to be the spiritual brother of the Kelt, I reply that he is, as a matter of fact, his spiritual cousin-german, and that such differences as exist may be clearly referred to differences in geographical and political conditions. In the first place, the Norseman has not been subjected in anything like the same degree to the pressure of hostile races from behind; in the second place, his "Ultima Thule" was not really ultimate. He had always something more than the mere dim ocean to the west and south-west of him: he had Iceland, the Faroe Isles,

Shetland, Orkney, nay, Britain and Ireland. Thus he early familiarised himself with the ocean, and made it a highway of conquest and commerce. It affected his imagination deeply, no doubt, but not with a sense of impervious mystery, finality, or (what is really the same thing) infinitude. Therefore he escaped in a great measure the wide-eyed melancholy of the Kelt, while his soul remained more earthbound and robust, less apt to soar away from the last headland of the material world and lose itself in the insubstantial colour-maze of the sunset.*

These reflections on the Keltic temperament in general may seem to have led us far away from Miss Hopper in particular. But they are really suggested by the sense of wide space, clear colour, wind, water, and the cool breath of flowers that comes to us from her poetry. May we not see in such verses as these, for instance, the quintessence of the Keltic spirit?

BEAUTY.

Beauty was born of the world's desire
For the wandering water, the wandering fire,
Under the arch of her hurrying feet
She has trodden a world full of bittersweet.

The blood of the violet is in her veins,
Her pulse has the passion of April rains.
Out of the heart of a satin flower
God made her eyelids in one sweet hour.

Out of the wind He made her feet
That they might be lovely, and luring, and fleet.
Out of a cloud He wove her hair,
Heavy and black with the rain held there.

What is her name? There's none that knows—
Mother-o'-mischief, or Mouth-o'-rose.
What is her pathway? None may tell,
But it climbs to heaven and it dips to hell.

* Would it be pressing this theory too far to suggest that the peculiar characteristics of the Welsh people, marking them off from other branches of the Keltic stock, may be traced in part to the fact that they alone did not directly confront the Atlantic, but had land, and a very solid mass of land, to the westward of them?

> The garment on her is mist and fire,
> Anger and sorrow and heart's desire,
> Her forehead-jewel's an amethyst,
> The garland to her is love-in-a-mist.
>
> Her girdle is of the beryl-stone,
> And one dark rose for her flower has grown,
> Filled to the brim with the strength o' the sun,
> A passionate rose, and only one.

I take the liberty of omitting the final stanza, which seems to me marred by a feeble last line.

There are marked inequalities in Miss Hopper's verse, flaws of technique and sometimes lapses in inspiration. Now and then she seems to force the mood instead of waiting for it to take hold of her. But in everything she writes, even in what we regard as her failures, there is a certain distinction. She is never vulgar either in matter or form—never quite commonplace. Not often does she even introduce a false or artificial note, such as we find in the following stanza :

> Her lips were red as strawberries,
> Bare feet and brown sowed jealousies
> Among the grasses that would fain
> Unto a kiss of them attain—
> And having kissed would kiss again.

She is more at home in the pure lyric, whether of nature or of passion, than in the lyrical ballad, though in this class of work *Hugh of the Hill* and *Outlaws* are poems of notable charm. Of her nature-poems the following is one of the most characteristic :

JUNE.

> Dark red roses in a honeyed wind swinging,
> Silk-soft hollyhock, coloured like the moon ;
> Larks high overhead lost in light, and singing ;
>   That's the way of June.
>
> Dark red roses in the warm wind falling,
> Velvet leaf by velvet leaf, all the breathless noon ;
> Far-off sea-waves calling, calling, calling ;
>   That's the way of June.

Sweet as scarlet strawberry under wet leaves hidden,
Honeyed as the damask rose, lavish as the moon,
Shedding lovely light on things forgotten, hope forbidden—
    That's the way of June.

There is a true and penetrating charm in almost all Miss Hopper's love-songs. Out of a whole group of almost equal merit—*A Song at Sunset, If I had been a Rose, One Way of Love, A Woman's Marriage Song, Elusion*, and *The Chrysoberyl*—I select the last two for quotation at the end of the article, as typical specimens of the poetess's suave and harmonious lyric gift.

Some of Miss Hopper's most beautiful numbers are hard to classify—such, for instance, as *The World's Desire* and the poem entitled *A Pagan*, which contains the following exquisite stanza :

Sad sobs the sea forsaken of Aphrodite ;
Hellas and Helen are not, and the slow sands fall,
Gods that were gracious and lovely, gods that were mighty,
Sky and sea and silence resume them all.

Though the allusion be to classical mythology, this yearning backward to the spirit-haunted universe of the "pagan suckled in a creed outworn" is eminently Keltic. True, it was Wordsworth who first gave imperishable utterance to the yearning ; but who shall say how much of the Kelt there was in Wordsworth ?

It is not to be denied that Miss Hopper pays the penalty of her too fertile lyric gift. One cannot hymn and re-hymn all the months of the year and all the days of the week, yet keep one's inspiration always fresh and fervid. We may apply to her that somewhat left-handed compliment of Webster to Shakespeare, and speak of her "right happy and copious industry"; but it is only just to lay the emphasis on the "happy." There is originality, sincerity, melody in all she does. She is a born singer of songs.

ELUSION.

What would you do if I should give you roses
Who gave you only lilies yesterday?
If I should leave my idle pretty play
Among my shaded sheltered lily-closes,
     And give you roses?

If in an hour I changed from girl to woman
And gave you back your kisses, each for each—
And chose, instead of music, passionate speech?
Nay, but I will not, seeing Love's but human,
     Unveil the woman.

I'll keep my mystery and keep my lover;
You who have hung with praise and dream my name,
Being mere man, would find your praise half blame,
If in my soul full measure, running over,
You saw my love for you—not flowers but flame.

THE CHRYSOBERYL.

Men say there is a stone shines green alway
Through the long hours of the indifferent day,
But blazes scarlet when the night draws on:
I and my heart are like that changing stone.

All day I hide myself in lucent green,
All the long hours of the indifferent day:
But when the moon makes beautiful and clean
The working world, I thrust my sheaths away.
I cast my veil aside and bid it be,
And let Love's scarlet flood transfigure me.

I am a chrysoberyl, and the night
Is here, and I am changed. The changeless light
Has touched me and transfigured; my own fire
Beacons me to the place of heart's desire.
I that was dark and dull am burning bright;
I am a chrysoberyl, and 'tis night.

A. E. HOUSMAN

DESPITE its association with Erasmus Darwin, Shropshire cannot be called, like Warwickshire or Devon, a county haunted by the Muses. On the spur of the moment, and without reference to books, I can think of only one great poem definitely associated with Shropshire—*Comus*, to wit, written for performance at Ludlow Castle. It is true that on Shropshire soil the doughty Sir John Falstaff slew the Hotspur of the North, after fighting a long hour by Shrewsbury clock. But this is scarcely an inherent association, native to the glebe. Falstaff could have performed the same exploit by any other clock. It was mere fortune of war that gave Shrewsbury the honour of keeping time to that immortal combat. Take it all in all, Shropshire is not one of the great literary counties of England.

But Shropshire no longer lacks its poet. Shrewsbury clock has found another place in literature, in a less delightful but still a memorable context:

> There sleeps in Shrewsbury jail to-night,
>   Or wakes, as may betide,
> A better lad, if things went right,
>   Than most that sleep outside.
>
> And naked to the hangman's noose
>   The morning clocks will ring
> A neck God made for other use
>   Than strangling in a string.

And sharp the link of life will snap,
  And dead on air will stand
Heels that held up as straight a chap
  As treads upon the land.

So here I'll watch the night and wait
  To see the morning shine,
When he will hear the stroke of eight
  And not the stroke of nine;

And wish my friend as sound a sleep
  As lads' I did not know,
That shepherded the moonlit sheep *
  A hundred years ago.

These are the concluding verses of the ninth poem in
Mr. A. E. Housman's book, *A Shropshire Lad*. They are
not his best, nor even among his best, but I place them
here because they give a sharp foretaste of his quality. His
book (his only book of verse) is a very small one. It
contains some sixty brief lyrics, occupying not quite one
hundred pages in all. You may read it in half an hour—
but there are things in it you will scarce forget in a lifetime. It tingles with an original, fascinating, melancholy
vitality.

Mr. Housman writes, for the most part, under the guise
of "A Shropshire Lad"—the rustic namefather of his book.
But this is evidently a mere mask. Mr. Housman is no
Shropshire Burns singing at his plough. He is a man of
culture. He moves in his rustic garb with no clodhopper's
gait, but with the ease of an athlete; and he has an Elzevir
classic in the pocket of his smock frock. But it is not
Theocritus, not the Georgics or the Eclogues; I rather take
it to be Lucretius. Never was there less of a "pastoral"
poet, in the artificial, Italian-Elizabethan sense of the word.
The Shropshire of Mr. Housman is no Arcadia, no Sicily,
still less a courtly pleasaunce peopled with beribboned
nymphs and swains. It is as real, as tragic, as the Wessex

* Hanging in chains was called "keeping sheep by moonlight."

· A · E · HOVSMAN ·

of Mr. Hardy. The genius, or rather the spirit, of the two writers is not dissimilar. Both have the same rapturous realisation, the same bitter resentment, of life. To both Nature is an exquisitely seductive, inexorably malign enchantress. "Life's Ironies" might be the common title of Mr. Hardy's long series of novels and Mr. Housman's little book of verse. And both have the same taste for clothing life's ironies in the bucolic attire of an English county.

Mr. Housman's strong and stern temperament finds expression in curiously simple, original, and expressive verse. In deference to his rustic mask, and probably to something fundamental in his talent as well, he attempts no metrical arabesques, no verbal enamelling. With scarcely an exception, his metres are of the homeliest; yet, in their little variations, their suspensions, their tremulous cadences, we recognise the touch of the born metrist. Mr. Housman's chief technical strength, however, lies in the directness and terseness of his style. There is nerve and fibre in every line he writes, and of superfluous tissue not a trace. He says what he wants to say, not what his measure dictates, or his rhyme; and his words seem to fall into their places with a predestinate fitness which (inconsistent as it may seem) gives us in every second stanza a little shock of pleasurable surprise. His diction and his methods are absolutely his own. He echoes no one, borrows no one's technical devices. If he reminds us of any other poet, it is (now and then) of Heine; yet he is English of the English. We divine his culture in the very simplicity of his style; but (beyond a single allusion to Milton, to be quoted presently, and a single line adapted from Shakespeare) we find no direct evidence of his ever having read another English poet. His verse might quite well be the glorified offspring of the most unsophisticated popular poetry—the chap-book ballad or the rustic stave.

Mr. Housman has three main topics: a stoical pessimism; a dogged rather than an exultant patriotism; and what I may perhaps call a wistful cynicism. His pessimism he formulates again and again.

> Therefore, since the world has still
> Much good, but much less good than ill;
> And while the sun and moon endure
> Luck's a chance, but trouble's sure,
> I'd face it as a wise man would,
> And train for ill and not for good.

This is from a poem in which he excuses himself to certain friends who have complained that he plays only "such tunes as killed the cow," and have begged him to "pipe a tune to dance to, lad." He answers:

> Why, if 'tis dancing you would be,
> There's brisker pipes than poetry.
> Say, for what were hop-yards meant,
> Or why was Burton built on Trent?
> Oh many a peer of England brews
> Livelier liquor than the Muse,
> And malt does more than Milton can
> To justify God's ways to man.
> Ale, man, ale's the stuff to drink
> For fellows whom it hurts to think:
> Look into the pewter pot
> To see the world as the world's not.

In a remarkable poem called *The Welch Marches* he seems to give an ethnological reason for this sombre strain in his temperament. At Shrewsbury, he says (in a splendid stanza):

> The flag of morn in conqueror's state
> Enters at the English gate:
> The vanquished eve, as night prevails,
> Bleeds upon the road to Wales.
>
> * * * *
>
> When Severn down to Buildwas ran
> Coloured with the death of man,
> Couched upon her brother's grave
> The Saxon got me on the slave.
>
> * * * *

A. E. HOUSMAN

In my heart it has not died,
The war that sleeps on Severn side;
They cease not fighting, east and west,
On the marches of my breast.

Whatever its origin, whether it proceed from the subjection of the Kelt to the Teuton, or from some more modern source, Mr. Housman's melancholy is inveterate and not to be shaken off. But there is nothing whining about it. Rather, it is bracing, invigorating. The poet communes with a statue in the Grecian gallery, who reminds him that—

"Years, ere you stood up from rest,
On my neck the collar prest;
Years, when you lay down your ill,
I shall stand and bear it still.
Courage, lad, 'tis not for long:
Stand, quit you like stone, be strong."
So I thought his look would say;
And light on me my trouble lay,
And I stepped out in flesh and bone
Manful like the man of stone.

Following a curious habit, of which this little book offers several examples, Mr. Housman, in another poem, presents a variation of the same thought. This poem is so noble that I must quote it entire. Metrically, it is perhaps the best thing in the book—note the masterly handling of the cæsura :

Be still, my soul, be still; the arms you bear are brittle,
    Earth and high heaven are fixt of old and founded strong.
Think rather,—call to thought, if now you grieve a little,
    The days when we had rest, O soul, for they were long.

Men loved unkindness then, but lightless in the quarry
    I slept and saw not; tears fell down, I did not mourn ;
Sweat ran and blood sprang out and I was never sorry:
    Then it was well with me, in days ere I was born.

Now, and I muse for why and never find the reason,
    I pace the earth, and drink the air, and feel the sun.
Be still, be still, my soul; it is but for a season:
    Let us endure an hour and see injustice done.

Ay, look: high heaven and earth ail from the prime foundation;
  All thoughts to rive the heart are here, and all are vain:
Horror and scorn and hate and fear and indignation—
  Oh why did I awake? when shall I sleep again?

Germane to this theme are the two poems on suicide, the one a pocket edition, so to speak, of the other. The longer is by far the finer of the two, but I quote the briefer version for the sake of its brevity:

If it chance your eye offend you,
  Pluck it out, lad, and be sound:
'Twill hurt, but here are salves to friend you,
  And many a balsam grows on ground.

If your hand or foot offend you,
  Cut it off, lad, and be whole;
But play the man, stand up and end you,
  When your sickness is your soul.

To show how Mr. Housman can touch his world-weariness to absolute beauty, I quote, before leaving this subject, a poem so delicate that even the tenderest breath of praise would only shake off some of its bloom. It has for its motto what I take to be an old local rhyme—if it be not a new one:

Clunton and Clunbury,
  Clungunford and Clun,
Are the quietest places
  Under the sun.

In valleys of springs and rivers,
  By Ony and Teme and Clun,
The country for easy livers,
  The quietest under the sun,

We still had sorrows to lighten,
  One could not be always glad,
And lads knew trouble at Knighton
  When I was a Knighton lad.

By bridges that Thames runs under,
  In London, the town built ill,
'Tis sure small matter for wonder
  If sorrow is with one still.

A. E. HOUSMAN

And if as a lad grows older
  The troubles he bears are more,
He carries his griefs on a shoulder
  That handselled them long before.

Where shall one halt to deliver
  This luggage I'd lief set down?
Not Thames, not Teme is the river,
  Nor London nor Knighton the town:

'Tis a long way further than Knighton,
  A quieter place than Clun,
Where doomsday may thunder and lighten,
  And little 'twill matter to one.

The English language is appreciably the richer for such work as this.

Mr. Housman's patriotism, as it appears in *A Shropshire Lad*, is local rather than national or imperial. His soldiers fight, not so much for the glory of England, as for the credit of Shropshire. Of the joys of battle he tells us little enough. He accepts war as the destiny of a stubborn fighting race, and as a safety-valve for energies that might find a still more noxious outlet in peace. He sings of the sacred bond of comradeship, and has a good deal to say of the price we pay for Empire in blood and tears. He tells in the opening poem of his book how—

the Nile spills his overflow
Beside the Severn's dead.

And in a spirited "Reveille," he sings:

Up, lad, up, 'tis late for lying:
  Hear the drums of morning play;
Hark, the empty highways crying
  "Who'll beyond the hills away?"

*   *   *   *

Clay lies still, but blood's a rover;
  Breath's a ware that will not keep.
Up, lad: when the journey's over
  There'll be time enough to sleep.

189

Perhaps the most characteristic, however, of all his military pieces is the following :

THE DAY OF BATTLE.

Far I hear the bugle blow
To call me where I would not go,
And the guns begin the song,
"Soldier, fly or stay for long."

Comrade, if to turn and fly
Made a soldier never die,
Fly I would, for who would not?
'Tis sure no pleasure to be shot.

But since the man that runs away
Lives to die another day,
And cowards' funerals, when they come,
Are not wept so well at home,

Therefore, though the best is bad,
Stand and do the best, my lad ;
Stand and fight and see your slain,
And take the bullet in your brain.

The third element in Mr. Housman's inspiration is what I have roughly called a wistful cynicism. He dwells, not harshly, but rather with compassion, upon the mutability of human feeling, the ease with which the dead are forgot, the anguish of love unrequited, and the danger that long life may mean slow degradation. Among the crowd at Ludlow Fair, he wishes that those who are destined to die young, "to carry back bright to the coiner the mintage of man," could bear some mark about them so that they might be honoured and envied. For :

There's chaps from the town and the field and the till and the
    cart,
  And many to count are the stalwart, and many the brave,
And many the handsome of face and the handsome of heart,
  And few that will carry their looks or their truth to the grave.

A. E. HOUSMAN

One of his most notable little groups of poems turns on the idea that

> A lad that lives and has his will
> Is worth a dozen dead.

By far the best of this group is a dialogue between a dead man and his living friend, the gist of which lies in the friend's last answer:

> Yes, lad, I lie easy,
> I lie as lads would choose;
> I cheer a dead man's sweetheart,
> Never ask me whose.

As for the pains of love misplaced, have they ever been more poignantly or more briefly expressed than in the two stanzas of this perfect song?—

> When I was one-and-twenty
> I heard a wise man say,
> " Give crowns and pounds and guineas
> But not your heart away;
> Give pearls away and rubies
> But keep your fancy free."
> But I was one-and-twenty,
> No use to talk to me.
>
> When I was one-and-twenty
> I heard him say again,
> " The heart out of the bosom
> Was never given in vain;
> 'Tis paid with sighs a plenty
> And sold for endless rue."
> And I am two-and-twenty,
> And oh, 'tis true, 'tis true.

There is a whole heart-history in this ingenious and exquisite little work of art.

In a few of Mr. Housman's poems, however, there is no touch of that bitterness of feeling which I have named, or misnamed, cynicism. *Bredon Hill*, quoted at the end of this article, seems to me almost unrivalled in its delicate, unemphatic pathos. It exemplifies one of Mr. Housman's strongest and rarest qualities—his unerring dramatic instinct. In the way of pure contemplation, apart from drama, these four stanzas are almost as good :

> When I watch the living meet,
>   And the moving pageant file
> Warm and breathing through the street
>   Where I lodge a little while,
>
> If the heats of hate and lust
>   In the house of flesh are strong,
> Let me mind the house of dust
>   Where my sojourn shall be long.
>
> In the nation that is not
>   Nothing stands that stood before ;
> There revenges are forgot,
>   And the hater hates no more ;
>
> Lovers lying two by two
>   Ask not whom they sleep beside,
> And the bridegroom all night through
>   Never turns him to the bride.

It is long since we have caught just this note in English verse—the note of intense feeling uttering itself in language of unadorned precision, uncontorted truth. Mr. Housman is a vernacular poet, if ever there was one. He employs scarcely a word that is not understanded of the people, and current on their lips. For this very reason, some readers who have come to regard decoration, and even contortion, as of the essence of poetry, may need time to acquire the taste for Mr. Housman's simplicity. But if he is vernacular, he is also classical in the best sense of the word. His simplicity is not that of weakness, but of strength and skill. He eschews extrinsic and factitious ornament because he knows how to attain beauty without it. It is good to mirror a thing in figures, but it is at least as good to express the thing itself in its essence, always provided, of course, that the method be that of poetic synthesis, not of scientific analysis. Mr. Housman has this talent in a very high degree; and cognate and complementary to it is his remarkable gift of reticence—of aposiopesis, if I may wrest the term from its rhetorical sense and apply it to poetry. He will often say more by a cunning silence than many another poet by pages of speech. That is how he has contrived to get into his tiny volume so much of the very essence and savour of life.

As I re-read Mr. Housman's poems after an interval of three years or so, I have a curious feeling of having quoted the wrong things. Not that I admire these things less, but that I admire others more. One may safely say, at any rate, that every poem here singled out could be replaced by another of equal merit without by any means exhausting the wealth even of so small a book. There is no reason why Mr. Housman should not put off his rustic mask and widen the range of his subject matter. I trust he will do so in other and larger volumes. But even should he be content to remain merely "A Shropshire Lad," his place among English poets is secure.

BREDON* HILL.

In summer time on Bredon
　The bells they sound so clear;
Round both the shires they ring them
　In steeples far and near,
　A happy noise to hear.

Here of a Sunday morning
　My love and I would lie,
And see the coloured counties,
　And hear the larks so high
　About us in the sky.

The bells would ring to call her
　In valleys miles away:
"Come all to church, good people;
　Good people, come and pray."
　But here my love would stay.

And I would turn and answer
　Among the springing thyme,
"Oh, peal upon our wedding,
　And we will hear the chime,
　And come to church in time."

But when the snows at Christmas
　On Bredon top were strown,
My love rose up so early
　And stole out unbeknown
　And went to church alone.

They tolled the one bell only,
　Groom there was none to see,
The mourners followed after,
　And so to church went she,
　And would not wait for me.

　　　* Pronounced Breedon.

194

A. E. HOUSMAN

The bells they sound on Bredon,
  And still the steeples hum:
" Come all to church, good people "—
  Oh, noisy bells, be dumb;
  I hear you, I will come.

From far, from eve and morning
  And yon twelve-winded sky,
The stuff of life to knit me
  Blew hither: here am I.

Now—for a breath I tarry
  Nor yet disperse apart—
Take my hand quick and tell me,
  What have you in your heart.

Speak now, and I will answer;
  How shall I help you, say;
Ere to the wind's twelve quarters
  I take my endless way.

LAURENCE HOUSMAN

THE distinction of Mr. Laurence Housman's workmanship, the nimbleness of his fancy, and the sombre strength of his imagination, must be patent to all readers of *Green Arras* and *Spikenard*. No one is more authentically a poet than he ; yet the forms of thought which almost exclusively preoccupy him are to me so foreign, and, to be quite frank, so uninteresting, that I must own myself incapable of doing full justice even to his purely literary merits. He envisages the world from a point of view at which I cannot place myself, even in momentary make-believe. I lack all clue, in my own experience, to the processes of his mind. Consequently, I can but apologise in advance for the inadequate and perhaps utterly mistaken appreciation of his talent which is all I can offer. In the preface to his *All Fellows*, a book of prose legends "with insets of verse," Mr. Housman says, "Unfortunately there are to be found, to sit in judgment, minds of a literal persuasion, that take from the artist his own soul, to set it in the image that he has made." In what I have to say I may fall into this error. But a single attitude of mind is so consistently maintained throughout Mr. Housman's verse, that it is impossible to conceive it a mere artistic pose.

On the contrary, it seems to me that sincerity is what distinguishes Mr. Housman from most of his school. His kinship with Rossetti, for example, is unmistakable ; but

FORTVNA

· LAVRENCE · HOVSMAN ·

what to Rossetti was mythology and decoration, is to Mr. Housman religion and tragic fact. His Catholicism is not like that of some other poets, a mere refuge from pantheism, a robe deliberately woven to clothe and confine an invisible, elusive deity. At the root of his thinking lies, I take it, a genuine Conviction of Sin. It is his instinct to prostrate and abase himself before the rulers of the universe, and to blame himself, not them, for whatever in himself he finds amiss. Not his to

> thank whatever gods there be
> For his unconquerable soul ;

not his to

> step out in flesh and bone
> Manful like the man of stone.

It is his part rather to kiss the rod, and wreathe it in garlands of flowers ; to groan in the fetters of flesh, while damascening their links. Life is to him a prison-house, and it does not occur to him to question the moral authority of the warrant that consigned him to it. The senses are tempters lurking in the darkness. He has not even the consolations of evangelical religion, the faith in another life and in personal salvation. He seems rather to conceive deity as the spirit of nothingness ; to regard existence in itself as sin, and more especially the sense of beauty in existence ; and to yearn for annihilation as the highest grace to which mankind, guilty of having been born, can possibly aspire. This spirit seems to me to inspire, not only his poems, but the designs which illustrate them : everywhere there is passionate depth of conception and great beauty of line ; but everywhere there is a sense of oppression, of contortion, of grey gloom even in the sunshine, which not seldom results in a general effect of ugliness.

Here is a characteristic utterance of Mr. Housman's, from the " Insets " in *All Fellows*. He declares this sequence to be "dramatic rather than theoretic"; but at least these verses exemplify a marked tendency in the poet's soul-dramatisation, if so we must call it :

> With me early, with me late,
>   The face of my spent youth :
> Of youth that made a friend of fate,
>   And thought the friendship truth.
>
> But now 'tis—how to bear the sun !
>   When fate demands, o'er all
> The ills I wish to do, the one
>   I struggle to let fall.
>
> With me early, with me late,
>   A bitter thing to rue :
> The wrong set down for me by fate,
>   The wrong I would not do.
>
> Send forth thy winds, O God, to blow
>   The fever from my brain ;
> Let all Thy rains and rivers flow
>   To wash away my stain !
>
> And when of all its thousand ills
>   My body is set free,
> Then in Thy mercy bid the hills
>   Bow down and cover me.
>
> And smother out this vital spark
>   That binds me in Thy sight ;
> Give darkness, that it may be dark,
>   And heal my eyes of light !

I need not dwell upon the strength, the terseness, the fine technical quality of these verses, apparent even in the irregularity of the opening line, repeated in the third stanza. From the same sequence I copy a set of four quatrains which come as near to a questioning, or even an arraignment, of the powers that be, as anything in Mr. Housman.

> Dear heart, when with a twofold mind
>   I pray for bitter grace ;
> And from my pit of torment find
>   Your breath upon my face,

And hear you without thought of fear
  Bid me to guard you well,
And guide your footsteps to win clear—
  When my feet walk in hell:

I wonder, how can God be glad
  To hear men praise Him so,
Who makes His piteous earth so sad
  A lot to undergo?

Or does He, too, dip Feet in fire,
  And share the thirster's thirst;
And listen to man's great desire
  Holding a Heart to burst?

In *Green Arras* there are touches, never of gladness, never even of stoicism, but of sheer pulsing humanity, that come upon us with a sense of refreshment in the incense-laden atmosphere of Mr. Housman's temple of art. Note, for instance, *The Keepsake*, an original and daring poem; and this haunting little stave:

STOLEN WATERS.

" But he knoweth not that the dead are there."

Up the grassed hollow, and down the deep hill,
Sweet-heart that would not, to sweet-heart that will,
Now that I draw you, enfold you, and hold you
  Warm to my heart, how the hurt heart lies still!

Tired eyes leap open, and lips bear a boon,
So loving so late that they loved me not soon,
So eager and wistful in tender surrender,
  While cresting the ricks come the rays of the moon.

Round goes the wind, and the dark branches saw;
Out on the gables the weather-vanes flaw:
Underfoot—what is it, Dearest, thou fearest?—
  Run the white rabbits like ghosts in the straw.

The weirdness, the uncanniness, of Mr. Housman's imagination is best exemplified, perhaps, in *The Corn Keeper;* but I choose rather to quote, on account of its brevity, the following:

HOLY MATRIMONY.

Within the whispering marriage-doors, which close
  To the glad bridegroom's face, they draw the bride ;
  Love's listener he stays, and hears inside
Honeyed hands part the petals of his rose.
Over the throat the unfastened hair now flows,
  And now the white reluctant garments slide :
  Then hush on hush ; and O, the door is wide,
Moon-washed, pearl-paven as the bridegroom goes !

Into what garden hath he come, what tomb ?
  There is a gazing sorrow in this place ;
  A withered fragrance breathes against his face,
    Cold dews of lost kind kisses faintly shed
Before the couch, curtained in tender gloom,
    Crowned round with roses a slain youth lies dead.

There is not a poem in the book which has not individuality and strength. Those which most appeal to me, perhaps, are *Systole-Diastole, To a Child : Michael, The Voice of the Beloved*, and *The Song of the Three Kings*, but I do not suppose that my preference is founded on any intrinsic superiority. Everywhere, as it seems to me, Mr. Housman's work is essentially poetic, but robust or exhilarating it certainly is not. " Morbid " is a word one shrinks from using, but in this context it is inevitable. One poem, *Challengers*, breathes something of energy and defiance ; but it utters an isolated mood, if it be a personal mood at all. Much more characteristic is *Failure*, quoted at the end of the article.

" A Book of Devotional Love Poems "—so Mr. Housman himself describes *Spikenard*. It is a sequence of ecstatic lyrics, each suggested by or associated with some feast of the church, and all wearing, and wearing with power and grace, a seventeenth-century form. The book leaves on my mind a sense of manufacture, of deliberate archaism in thought no less than in form, which is probably due to a lack, on my part, of imaginative sympathy. Of the merits

LAURENCE HOUSMAN

of its craftsmanship there can be no doubt. Mr. Housman always writes with distinction, sometimes with real beauty, and generally with as much perspicuity as can be demanded of a poet who dwells exclusively on matters which, by hypothesis, transcend human reason. This is how, at the end of the book, he justifies his title:

SPIKENARD.

As one who came with ointments sweet,
   Abettors to her fleshly guilt,
And brake and poured them at Thy Feet,
   And worshipped Thee with spikenard spilt:
So from a body full of blame,
And tongue too deeply versed in shame,
Do I pour speech upon Thy Name.
O Thou, if tongue may yet beseech,
Near to Thine awful Feet let reach
This broken spikenard of my speech!

One of his more elaborate devotional poems will be quoted at the end of this article. Here let me cite two shorter and simpler ones, the first perhaps more characteristic than beautiful; the second, in my judgment, a veritable gem:

THE SOUL'S OFFERINGS.
(*Holy Thursday.*)

O Christ, first let me know
   How sweet life's best can be:
Then call me to forgo
   Its sweets for Thee!

First, passion let me taste
   Which all men praise or pray:
Then bid me cast in haste
   The prize away.

From death first make me shrink
   In bodily strong dread;
Then, then the cup to drink,
   And then the bed!

THE FOUNTAIN OF LIFE.
(*Conception of the Virgin Mary.*)

Thine earth, O Lord, is full of grief:
    Thy Heaven is full of love:
Tell me what power it was in chief
    Which drew Thee from above?

Where Love stands ever, all in all,
    No entrance is for grief:
Say then how came to Thee the call
    That won the world's relief.

Since nothing mortal grief may move
    Wholly to cast out fear;
How came the marvel that pure Love
    Could ever enter here?

Thou say'st, "This Law ordains relief
    All other laws above,
That Earth cannot contain its grief,
    Nor Heaven contain its Love:

"So from the grief which has to mount,
    The Love which has to run,
There springs and spills a Living Fount,
    Till Earth and Heaven be one."

A poem which I own myself puzzled to characterise is devoted to celebrating *Christ's Letter*, *T*, and is at least a typographical curiosity. I quote eight lines of it:

This letter, Lord was shaped for Thee,
In it thine outstretched Arms I see;
Thy Life, that all things did aTone,
Made it Thy FooTsTool and Thy Throne.

    *   *   *   *   *

Therefore, dear Lord, this letter stands
A symbol of Thine ouTsTreTched Hands
To earthly joining Heavenly wiT;
Nor are they SainTs who have not it!

I fruitlessly rack my brains to discover the principle which governs the distribution of capitals in this poem—why some

Ts should be Taken while others are left. Why, for instance, do we read "outstretched" in one line, and "ouTsTreTched" in another? This also is a mystery, deeper than that of the familiar nursery enigma which the poem irresistibly suggests. On the next page we find Mr. Housman restored to typographical sanity in the following stately *Dedication*:

When I have ended, then I see
How far my words come short of Thee:
Speech heavenly cannot live on earthly lips,
Pure thoughts borne down to language bear eclipse.

Ah, Christ, what harmony will that be then,
When, in Thy likeness, all the thoughts of men
  Grow satisfied, in silence serving Thee!
  For now 'tis difference that makes us be
Each clamorous his own meaning to express:
But then all minds will wear the marriage-dress,
  Moving in meet processional degree.

Oh, Christ, come quick, and from the body loose
The long distraction of each present use!
The hands that handle, and the lips that taste
Not at Thy banquet, work but so much waste,
And at sad lingering make heedless haste!
Some day, when love of self hath lost its lust
Of living in me, Thou wilt come, I trust,
And tread my heart to Paradisal dust:
Making me glad, ere last forgetting fall,
To know myself for naught, and Christ for all in all.

The man who can write like this is certainly no mean poet. If only Mr. Housman's spirituality had less the air of an obsession!

FAILURE.

When you are dead, when all you could not do
  Leaves quiet the worn hands, the weary head,
Asking not any service more of you,
  Requiting you with peace when you are dead;

When, like a robe, you lay your body by,
  Unloosed at last,—how worn, and soiled, and frayed!—
Is it not pleasant just to let it lie
  Unused and be moth-eaten in the shade?

Folding earth's silence round you like a shroud,
  Will you just know that what you have is best:—
Thus to have slipt unfamous from the crowd;
  Thus having failed and failed, to be at rest?

O, having, not to know! Yet, O my Dear,
  Since to be quit of self is to be blest;
To cheat the world, and leave no imprint here,—
  Is this not best?

BEFORE CONFESSION.

(*Ash Wednesday.*)

As the foul flesh lays by the hindering robe,
Letting the water probe
  And purge each stain,
Till with that sweet medicinal receipt
From face to feet
  The body is made sane;
So, from my shamefaced soul, do I aside
All covering lay (who have so long denied
Thy cleansing Power), to be purified.

LAURENCE HOUSMAN

Late though I come, at last
The dress I cast
Of my deceit, which hid
  Till late
  My soiled estate:
All that I did, I did
  In secrecy.
  Lord, in my secret places cleanse Thou me!

As to the flesh laid bare, the water, led
By its own laws of life, bids cleansing spread
With subtle press and intimate caress:
And with compelling weight,
Doth gravitate
Round all which passively submits thereto,
  Leaving untouched no part;
  So to my heart,
Stripped of itself, Thine utmost healing do!
So from its falsehood wash it with Thy truth:
And from lust-loving lave it in Thy ruth:
  And with pure Waters pitiful, whose art
The virtue bears of an inborn embrace,
Wash Thou the soil of shame from off my face!

Against all outward secrecy I pray,
Let all such secrecy be put away!
Since Thou in all my secrets seest me,
Thine, not the world's, let all my secrets be!
So, in Thy secret Ear, when they are named,
I shall be naked but yet not ashamed:
And my great gain be this dear privacy—
When I shut out the world, to shut in Thee!

RICHARD HOVEY

A POET of aggressive virility, aggressive Americanism; a devotee of Nature, not in the abstract but in the concrete, keeping all his five senses in close and intimate communion with mother earth; a lover of women, but also a lover of men, to whom comradeship is more than passion, nay, *is* passion; a eulogist of vagabondage, of the roving life, of the flannel shirt and the slouch hat; a chanter of irregular rhythms and easy-going staves, inclined to rebel against the trammels of metrical no less than of social form—to whom, if not to Walt Whitman, can this description apply? It applies almost as accurately to Mr. Richard Hovey, whom I am therefore fain to regard as the wearer of Whitman's mantle, the continuer of his tradition. Mr. Hovey, for aught I know, may reject with contumely this literary affiliation. Nowhere, that I remember, does he mention Whitman, or show any consciousness of kinship with him. Nevertheless, the resemblance is unmistakable; and, in Mr. Hovey's place, I should glory in it. Whitman's poetical doctrine, or at any rate his practice, is to be followed in the spirit rather than in the letter; but it would be a misfortune and a reproach to America if his influence were to pass idly away, and leave no abiding mark upon her literature.

Let me say at once that it is the spirit rather than the letter of Whitmanism that Mr. Hovey seems to me to represent. He proves his right to throw off the bonds of strict form by the power and grace with which he comports himself under their constraint. Far from despising rhyme, he makes constant use of it, and may even be called a virtuoso in jingles, now Browningesque, now Gilbertian— for instance, the *Jongleurs* and *Barney McGee* of *More Songs from Vagabondia*. There is no lack of culture, and certainly no contempt for it, in Mr. Hovey's work. He does not, like Whitman, reject tradition, and set up to be a law unto himself; but he brings the spirit of Whitman into line with the traditions of English poetry.

First let me show what Mr. Hovey can do in ordinary stanza form. He has written two lyrics which seem to me conspicuously admirable both in spirit and in rhythm. The first is included by Mr. E. V. Lucas in his delightful anthology *The Open Road ;* but I cannot leave to Mr. Lucas the credit of having been its "discoverer" on this side of the Atlantic ; I had quoted it at least a year earlier in the *Pall Mall Magazine.* It is entitled

THE SEA GIPSY.

I am fevered with the sunset,
I am fretful with the bay,
For the wander-thirst is on me
And my soul is in Cathay.

There's a schooner in the offing,
With her topsails shot with fire,
And my heart has gone aboard her
For the Islands of Desire.

I must forth again to-morrow !
With the sunset I must be
Hull down on the trail of rapture
In the wonder of the sea.

Within its limits, this could not be bettered. It is the perfectly musical and imaginative expression of a mood. But there is a larger, deeper inspiration, and a fine individuality of form, in the following lyric from a poem entitled

Comrades, " Read at the Sixtieth Annual Convention of the Psi Upsilon Fraternity at Dartmouth College, Hanover, New Hampshire, May 18, 1893 " :

> Comrades, pour the wine to-night,
> For the parting is with dawn.
> Oh, the clink of cups together,
> With the daylight coming on !
> Greet the morn
> With a double horn,
> When strong men drink together!
>
> Comrades, gird your swords to-night,
> For the battle is with dawn.
> Oh, the clash of shields together,
> With the triumph coming on !
> Greet the foe
> And lay him low,
> When strong men fight together.
>
> Comrades, watch the tides to-night,
> For the sailing is with dawn.
> Oh, to face the spray together,
> With the tempest coming on !
> Greet the Sea
> With a shout of glee,
> When strong men roam together.
>
> Comrades, give a cheer to-night,
> For the dying is with dawn.
> Oh, to meet the stars together,
> With the silence coming on !
> Greet the end
> As a friend a friend,
> When strong men die together.

This is not only genuine poetry, but highly original in the true sense of the word. Though staves of a similar tenor have been chanted by the score, Mr. Hovey's song rings out clearly from among them with a note that is all its own. It is not an echo, but a new thing, an absolute addition to our poetical wealth. Good in its way, yet not *so* good, is the drinking-song in another Dartmouth ode :

> Give a rouse, then, in the Maytime
> For a life that knows no fear !

Other utterances of the same Viking spirit, if I may call it so, are to be found in *The Buccaneers*, in the fine lyrical ballad entitled *Discovery*, and in the song of defeat " There is no escape by the river," quoted at the end of this article.

A good deal of Mr. Hovey's best work is to be found in his college odes. The finest, perhaps, is that entitled *Spring*, written for a Convention of the Psi Upsilon Fraternity, not at Dartmouth, but at the University of Michigan, Ann Arbor. This is one of the pieces in which Mr. Hovey's kinship with Whitman comes out most unmistakably. It opens thus :

> I said in my heart, "I am sick of four walls and a ceiling.
> I have need of the sky.
> I have business with the grass.
> I will up and get me away where the hawk is wheeling,
> Lone and high,
> And the slow clouds go by.
> I will get me away to the waters that glass
> The clouds as they pass,
> To the waters that lie
> Like the heart of a maiden aware of a doom drawing nigh
> And dumb for sorcery of impending joy.
> I will get me away to the woods.
> Spring, like a huntsman's boy,
> Halloos along the hillsides and unhoods
> The falcon in my will.
> The dogwood calls me, and the sudden thrill
> That breaks in apple blooms down country roads
> Plucks me by the sleeve and nudges me away.
> The sap is in the boles to-day,
> And in my veins a pulse that yearns and goads."

In the next strophe there occurs this striking image :

> And out of the frieze
> Of the chestnut trees
> I heard
> The sky and the fields and the thicket find voice in a bird.
> The goldenwing—hark !
> How he drives his song
> Like a golden nail
> Through the hush of the air !
> I thrill to his cry in the leafage there ;
> I respond to the new life mounting under the bark.

The poet then goes on to find in the thrill of spring a type of a stirring of new life which he divines in the soul of man, with its three great attendant spirits, Science, Art, and Religion :

> For all the bonds shall be broken and rent in sunder,
> And the soul of man go free
> Forth with those three
> Into the lands of wonder ;
> Like some undaunted youth,
> Afield in quest of truth,
> Rejoicing in the road he journeys on
> As much as in the hope of journey done.
> And the road runs east, and the road runs west,
> That his vagrant feet explore ;
> And he knows no haste and he knows no rest,
> And every mile has a stranger zest
> Than the miles he trod before ;
> And his heart leaps high in the nascent year
> When he sees the purple buds appear ;
> For he knows, though the great black frost may blight
> The hope of May in a single night,
> That the spring, though it shrink back under the bark,
> But bides its time somewhere in the dark—
> Though it come not now to its blossoming,
> By the thrill in his heart he knows the spring ;
> And the promise it makes perchance too soon,
> I shall keep with its roses yet in June ;
> For the ages fret not over a day,
> And the greater to-morrow is on its way.

With all its simplicity, this last couplet gives memorable form to a truly American optimism.

It is in a Dartmouth ode—an ode to the poet's Alma Mater—that the following fine passage occurs:

> O justly proud of thy first strenuous years!
> Be not content that thou hast nurtured well
> The hardy prowess of thy pioneers.
> Among thy fellows bold, be thou the first,
> Still guarding sacredly the antique well,
> To seek new springs to quench the ages' thirst.
> Take up the axe, O woodman of the soul,
> And break new paths through tangled ignorance;
> Dare the unknown, till on thy jubilant glance
> The prairies of the spirit shall unroll.
> For thou mayest teach us all that thou hast taught,
> Nor slay the earlier instinct of the Faun,
> Whose intimacy with earth and air withdrawn,
> There rests but hearsay knowledge in our thought.
> And thou mayest make us the familiars of
> The woodlands of desire, the crags of fate,
> The lakes of worship and the dells of love,
> Even as the Faun is Nature's intimate.
> For God lacks not his seers, and Art is strong,
> And spirit unto spirit utters speech,
> Nor is there any heaven beyond the reach
> Of them that know the masteries of Song.

What can be more Whitmanesque than this rooted conviction, running through all Mr. Hovey's work, that a faun-like intimacy with nature is the beginning of all wisdom, without which "there rests but hearsay knowledge in our thought"? This feeling inspires his poem *The Faun*, from which I quote one strophe:

> Brother, lost brother!
> Thou of mine ancient kin!
> Thou of the swift will that no ponderings smother!
> The dumb life in me fumbles out to the shade
> Thou lurkest in.
> In vain—evasive ever through the glade

Departing footsteps fail;
And only where the grasses have been pressed
Or by snapt twigs I follow a fruitless trail.
So—give o'er the quest!
Sprawl on the roots and moss!
Let the lithe garter squirm across my throat!
Let the slow clouds and leaves above me float
Into mine eyeballs and across,—
Nor think them further! Lo, the marvel! now,
Thou whom my soul desireth, even thou
Sprawl'st by my side, who fled'st at my pursuit.
I hear thy fluting; at my shoulder there
I see the sharp ears through the tangled hair,
And birds and bunnies at thy music mute.

The feeling here expressed is notably different from Wordsworthian nature-moralising. It is to be traced in several
other transatlantic singers, and is inspired—if we must seek
literary inspiration for it—not only by Whitman, but also, in
some measure, by Emerson. One is tempted to call it
American neo-paganism.

There is also a strongly patriotic strain in Mr. Hovey's
work. In his poems on the Spanish-American war we find
a good deal that is ephemeral, but also a good deal of true
impetus and imagination. Here is the opening of *The Call
of the Bugles*:

Bugles!
And the Great Nation thrills and leaps to arms!
Prompt, unconstrained, immediate,
Without misgiving and without debate,
Too calm, too strong for fury or alarms,
The people blossoms armies and puts forth
The splendid summer of its noiseless might;
For the old sap of fight
Mounts up in South and North.

There is more than a touch of poetic licence in this description of America's response to the call to arms. No modern
nation, and least of all the United States, goes to war
"without debate," without "fury or alarms" and in "noise-

less might." The poet must have written in some deep
seclusion, remote from newspapers and bulletin-boards ; but
his vision, if idealistic, is undeniably impressive. Further
on in the same poem occurs this fine passage :

> I hear the tread
> Of the great armies of the Past go by ;
> I hear,
> Across the wide sea wash of years between,
> Concord and Valley Forge shout back from the unseen,
> And Vicksburg give a cheer.
>
> Our cheer goes back to them, the valiant dead !
> Laurels and roses on their graves to-day,
> Lilies and laurels over them we lay,
> And violets o'er each unforgotten head.
> Their honour still with the returning May
> Puts on its springtime in our memories,
> Nor till the last American with them lies
> Shall the young year forget to strew their bed.

Of all Mr. Hovey's patriotic utterances, *Unmanifest
Destiny*, quoted at the end of this article, seems to me the
finest : a simple yet weighty utterance, in that sternly
unadorned measure which Emerson has consecrated to the
uses of American patriotism.

Mr. Hovey's true lyrical gift is specially apparent in his
philosophico-Bohemian love-songs, such as *The Wander-
Lovers* and *Launa Dee*. The influence of Browning makes
itself felt in several of his minor pieces, such as *The Two
Lovers*, *Dead*, *Forgiven*, *Love and Change*, and even in
Shakespeare Himself. There is strength in all he writes,
even if it be sometimes a little unchastened, as, for example,
in the following quatorzain :

FAITH AND FATE.

> To horse, my dear, and out into the night !
> Stirrup and saddle and away, away !
> Into the darkness, into the affright,
> Into the unknown on our trackless way !

Past bridge and town missiled with flying feet,
Into the wilderness our riding thrills ;
The gallop echoes through the startled street,
And shrieks like laughter in the demoned hills ;
Things come to meet us with fantastic frown,
And hurry past with maniac despair ;
Death from the stars looks ominously down—
Ho, ho, the dauntless riding that we dare !
 East, to the dawn, or west or south or north !
 Loose rein upon the neck of Fate—and forth !

The last line, with that ringing phrase " Loose rein upon the neck of Fate," seems to me magnificent, and there is movement and strength in the whole poem ; but I wish Mr. Hovey could have got on without his " missiled bridge " and " demoned hills." Such audacities are seldom justified by real success. The simple rule " Let your nouns be nouns and your verbs be verbs " seems to me worthy of all acceptation, even at the hands of poets. An occasional licence in the very greatest yields no sufficient precedent for unrestricted neologism in lesser men. Mr. Hovey talks of a man being " self-elsewhered " and of a peak which " dominions " a valley ; while, conversely, a " dare " and an " urge " are among his favourite nouns. Then, again, he is apt to use words and phrases with no clear perception of their meaning. I think (though I have lost the reference) that he is guilty of that favourite Anglo-American blunder, abhorrent to a Scottish soul : using the phrase " of that ilk " * as though it meant " of that kind " or " of that kidney." One reads of " So-and-so and people of his ilk " —an absolutely meaningless expression. I may be bearing

* " Of that ilk " means " of that same," and implies that a man takes his name from his estate ; thus " Spottiswoode of that ilk " means Mr. Spottiswoode of Spottiswoode. As this idea has seldom to be expressed in English or American writings, the writer who wants to say what he means had best avoid the phrase altogether ; though, by the way, Dr. Johnson correctly described himself as " Johnson of that ilk," because he lived in Johnson's Court, Fleet Street.

false witness against Mr. Hovey in accusing him of this
blunder; but I can give chapter and verse for his use of the
expression "what ails" in a way which shows that he totally
misunderstands it; for instance:

> I command you to show
> All the veils may conceal
> That it ails me to know;

and again:

> LANCELOT. Peace, peace! What ails that I
> Should e'er be false to Arthur?

Still more unfortunate is this attempt at archaism:

> There is no one wisteth
> The way that it goeth.
> The wind bloweth
> Whither it listeth.

There can be no doubt, I take it, that " wist " is a preterite;
so that Mr. Hovey might as well write "wenteth" or
" dideth." It may be a cisatlantic illusion, but I think that
American poets are more apt than English poets of the
same standing to use words without strict inquiry into their
meaning.

The last two examples are taken from Mr. Hovey's long
"Poem in Dramas" entitled *Lancelot and Guenevere*. This
I cannot think a fortunate effort. The first of the three
volumes is entitled *The Quest of Merlin*—a mystical
Walpurgis Night, the style of which does not encourage one
to expend upon it the time and thought required for the
solution of its enigmas. It serves as a prologue to *The
Marriage of Guenevere: a Tragedy* and *The Birth of Galahad: a Romantic Drama*. In another place * I have
stated the reasons which seem to me to render the Arthurian
legend almost impossible for dramatic purposes; and
certainly Mr. Hovey's dramas leave my generalisation intact.

* See p. 284.

There are truly imaginative passages in them, as in all he does ; but the general tendency of the plays is to deprive the story of Lancelot and Guenevere of all tragic elevation and reduce it to the level of a vulgar intrigue. The third play, indeed, *The Birth of Galahad*, is a wild romance in which the Britons conquer Rome and Arthur is crowned Emperor. Guenevere having secretly given birth to Galahad, joins the army, and shares in Arthur's triumph. Just as the crown is placed on her head, a messenger arrives with letters from Merlin, who has obligingly undertaken the charge of the baby Galahad.

> [*The messenger delivers the letters, which* ARTHUR *and* GUENEVERE *severally open and scan.*]
> GUENEVERE [*apart to* LANCELOT]. All's well with him.

And the curtain falls upon this reassuring bulletin. Mr. Hovey's intention in writing this play I cannot divine. The best thing in it, to my thinking, is the character of Dagonet, who figures as a sort of Elizabethan clown, and Shakespearises with a good deal of spirit and ingenuity. I am sorry to add that Mr. Hovey's sense of style frequently deserts him at critical moments, and suffers him to introduce words which would be more in place in a parody of Whitman than in an Arthurian drama. It is a little disconcerting to find Arthur himself remarking :

> This rings the curtain down
> Upon the first act of our purposes.

When Morgause of Orkney talks of

> This upstart queen and that false-hearted prig
> Who calls himself her husband and my brother,

we feel that she might just as well have called him a snob while she was about it. Her son, Gawaine, seems to inherit his vocabulary from her, for he talks of the Roman ambassador, Publius, as " an old glub." But the most startling utterance of all is this of Guenevere's :

> Oh, why should we bring forth
> Children in weakness, not in strength? Why not
> Be free and mighty, bearing mighty men,
> Yielding our increase as the teeming earth
> That faints not—nay, rather exults and splurges
> In her fecundity?

Mr. Hovey's blank verse, too, though sometimes strong, is full of meaningless irregularities, and he is greatly addicted to that incomprehensible eccentricity, a trochee in the fifth foot; for example:

> Shall be a knight without a peer, stainless . . .
> His little arms about my neck, never . . .
> A people like an oyster, all stomach.

Let me take leave of these dramas with a brief quotation which will show Mr. Hovey's blank verse in a better light:

> GUENEVERE.   Oh, were Launcelot here,
> I could content me, wo_ 'i a hermitage,
> And think myself the mistress of the world.
> YLEN.   And I, whose lord and lover bivouacs
> By camp-fires whence no tidings ever come,
> With the unreturning armies of the dead,
> What bird of all the heavens could lend me wings
> Would serve me?

This speech of Ylen's seems to me memorably beautiful.

AT THE END OF THE DAY.

There is no escape by the river,
There is no flight left by the fen ;
We are compassed about by the shiver
Of the night of their marching men.
Give a cheer !
For our hearts shall not give way.
Here's to a dark to-morrow,
And here's to a brave to-day !

The tale of their hosts is countless,
And the tale of ours a score ;
But the palm is nought to the dauntless,
And the cause is more and more.
Give a cheer !
We may die, but not give way.
Here's to a silent to-morrow,
And here's to a stout to-day !

God has said : " Ye shall fail and perish,
But the thrill ye have felt to-night
I shall keep in my heart and cherish
When the worlds have passed in night."
Give a cheer !
For the soul shall not give way.
Here's to the greater to-morrow
That is born of a great to-day !

Now shame on the craven truckler
And the puling things that mope !
We've a rapture for our buckler
That outwears the wings of hope.
Give a cheer !
For our joy shall not give way.
Here's in the teeth of to-morrow
To the glory of to-day !

RICHARD HOVEY

UNMANIFEST DESTINY.

To what new fates, my country, far
   And unforeseen of foe or friend,
Beneath what unexpected star,
   Compelled to what unchosen end,

Across the sea that knows no beach
   The Admiral of Nations guides
Thy blind obedient keels to reach
   The harbour where thy future rides!

The guns that spoke at Lexington
   Knew not that God was planning then
The trumpet word of Jefferson
   To bugle forth the rights of men.

To them that wept and cursed Bull Run,
   What was it but despair and shame?
Who saw behind the cloud the sun?
   Who knew that God was in the flame?

Had not defeat upon defeat,
   Disaster on disaster come,
The slave's emancipated feet
   Had never marched behind the drum.

There is a Hand that bends our deeds
   To mightier issues than we planned,
Each son that triumphs, each that bleeds,
   My country, serves Its dark command.

I do not know beneath what sky
   Nor on what seas shall be thy fate;
I only know it shall be high,
   I only know it shall be great.

RUDYARD KIPLING

INASMUCH as he defies classification, Mr. Rudyard Kipling has incurred the just resentment of criticism. When we know precisely what a man is trying to do, it is comparatively easy to make up our minds as to whether he has done it or not. But when he employs methods of his own to achieve "things unattempted yet in prose or rhyme," he upsets our preconceptions and stultifies our standards. We know not whether to praise or blame; we are fascinated and irritated in about equal measures; and, human nature being what it is, the irritation is apt to get the upper hand in our utterances. In saying this, I am partly making a personal confession, but mainly interpreting certain symbolic utterances of Mr. Kipling's own, which I take to imply that critics in general have felt themselves baffled much as I myself have been. Again and again in reading Mr. Kipling's work, whether in prose or verse, I have said to myself: " This is remarkable, this is powerful, this is even beautiful—but is it literature? Is it not journalism raised to its highest potency? Does this writer own due allegiance to the great traditions of the language? Can he claim a place in the august procession of our poets? Is he of the tribe of Chaucer, Milton, and Wordsworth? What's Tennyson to him, or he to Tennyson?"

Such questionings have now and then flitted through my mind, and have apparently been uttered by other critics, for

• RVDYARD • KIPLING •

Mr. Kipling has made more than one rejoinder to them in his own allegoric fashion. Already in his *Barrack-Room Ballads* of 1892, he published this transparent apologue :

When the flush of a new-born sun fell first on Eden's green and
gold,
Our father Adam sat under the Tree and scratched with a stick in
the mould ;
And the first rude sketch that the world had seen was joy to his
mighty heart,
Till the Devil whispered behind the leaves, "It's pretty, but is it
Art?"

Wherefore he called to his wife, and fled to fashion his work anew—
The first of his race who cared a fig for the first, most dread review;
And he left his lore to the use of his sons—and that was a glorious
gain
When the Devil chuckled "Is it Art?" in the ear of the branded
Cain.

They builded a tower to shiver the sky and wrench the stars apart,
Till the Devil grunted behind the bricks : "It's striking, but is it
Art?"
The stone was dropped at the quarry-side and the idle derrick
swung,
While each man talked of the aims of Art, and each in an alien
tongue.

    *   *   *   *   *

The tale is as old as the Eden Tree—and new as the new-cut
tooth—
For each man knows ere his lip-thatch grows he is master of Art
and Truth ;
And each man hears as the twilight nears, to the beat of his dying
heart,
The Devil drum on the darkened pane : "You did it, but was it
Art?"

Yes, this is the question the fiend is for ever whispering in our ears as we read Mr. Kipling's amazingly spirited rhythms : " It's pretty—or (more often, perhaps) it's ugly—but is it Art?" Art of a sort it is, undoubtedly, and brilliant, masterly art. But is it good Art? Is it right Art? Is it Art in the noblest sense of the word? Again Mr.

Kipling takes up the parable, this time in *The Seven Seas* (1896). The poem is entitled *The Neolithic Age*. I quote (from the fourth edition) the first stanzas of it, which are complete in themselves, though Mr. Kipling rubs in the moral in five additional verses :

In the Neolithic Age savage warfare did I wage
  For food and fame and woolly horses' pelt ;
I was a singer to my clan in that dim, red Dawn of Man,
  And I sang of all we fought and feared and felt.

Yea, I sang as now I sing, when the Prehistoric spring
  Made the piled Biscayan ice-pack split and shove ;
And the troll and gnome and dwerg, and the Gods of Cliff and Berg
  Were about me and beneath me and above.

But a rival, of Solutré, told the tribe my style was *outré*—
  'Neath a tomahawk, of diorite, he fell.
And I left my views on Art, barbed and tanged, below the heart
  Of a mammothistic etcher at Grenelle.

Then I stripped them, scalp from skull, and my hunting dogs fed
    full,
  And their teeth I threaded neatly on a thong ;
And I wiped my mouth and said, " It is well that they are dead,
  For I know my work is right and theirs was wrong."

But my Totem saw the shame ; from his ridgepole shrine he came,
  And he told me in a vision of the night :—
" There are nine and sixty ways of constructing tribal lays,
  And every single one of them is right ! "

It is not quite clear how the Totem emphasised his deliverance. Is the stress on *tribal?* Is it only for " tribal " poetry that this Universalist doctrine holds good ? Or are we to understand that criticism as a whole is a survival of savagery, and that one sort of poetry is as good as another, and probably better ? To question so is to demand too great explicitness of the fabulist. Suffice it that he puts in his protest clearly against the method of criticism which would confine excellence to one groove, and massacre individuality.

Still a cultured Christian age sees us scuffle, squeak, and rage,
　　Still we pinch and slap and jabber, scratch and dirk ;
Still we let our business slide—as we dropped the half-dressed hide—
　　To show a fellow-savage how to work.

Oh yes! but Mr. Kipling should make some allowance for the point of view of the particular savage whose business is precisely the dressing of literary hides: who is not letting his business slide, but conscientiously performing it, when he shows a fellow-savage how to work—or *not* to work.

This sceptical prolusion is designed rather to let Mr. Kipling say his own say than to express any lingering doubt on my part as to his position in literature. Personally, I dismissed all such doubt on the appearance of his *Barrack-Room Ballads* nine years ago. Mr. Henley's *Song of the Sword* appearing about the same time, I reviewed the two books together in the *Pall Mall Gazette* of May, 7, 1892, under the somewhat catchpenny title of " The New Poetry." As the position I then took up with regard to Mr. Kipling still seems to me in the main a just one, I quote without alteration such portions of the review as chiefly concern him :

" As though in preparation for the new century, every branch of intellectual activity is, or purports to be, rejuvenescent. We have the New Journalism, the New Criticism, the New Humour ; we are eagerly awaiting the New Fiction and the New Drama ; and some of us are fain to scent the New Poetry in the air. The technique of English poetry has completed its evolution. After Tennyson, Arnold, Rossetti, and Swinburne, any further advance in form must be an advance *beyond* form—a disintegration of the traditional foot, line, and stanza. It is possible, then, that the New Poetry may burst the old forms—that a

Whitman of less 'barbaric yawp,' of finer culture and subtler originality, may do for poetry what Wagner has done for music. It seems more probable, however, that the coming race will seek for novelty of substance rather than of form. Into the traditional moulds—the simpler ones, perhaps, by preference—it will pour its new observations, experiences, aspirations. And in the first instance (the prediction is a tolerably safe one) it will obey the common impulse towards what, in fiction and painting, is loosely described as Realism. Take it all in all, the Old Poetry is essentially idealistic, or, if realistic, only in the pre-Raphaelite sense. It has always preferred to dwell in periods and places to which distance lends enchantment. Of contemporary life it has reproduced only the more elegant aspects; if it has touched on aught that is common or unclean, it has done so apologetically and with a direct eye to an edifying moral; and its vocabulary has been recruited from the study, not from the street. The New Poetry will probably aim at an Impressionist, not a pre-Raphaelite, realism. It will take contemporary life for its province, and will bring to bear upon it a novel directness of vision and frankness of psychology. It will look for the characteristic term—the 'mot propre'—rather than the graceful, the consecrated phrase. Science, reputed its mortal foe, it will make its ally and contributory. The beauty, the charm, which is, in the last resort, the be-all and end-all of art, it will seek, not in elegance of subject or elaborate finish, but in rightness of touch and vitality of workmanship.

"This forecast is in great measure a prophecy after the event. The realistic tendency was very marked in Mr. W. E. Henley's first book of verses, in those simple, direct, unvarnished but always masterly hospital-pictures, which were to some of us as a new experience both in life and literature. The same tendency informs his second book

The Song of the Sword and other Poems; and close upon
its heels comes Mr. Kipling's collection of *Barrack-Room
Ballads* to prove that the impulse is felt in more quarters
than one. Mr. Henley would have done well to let his book
take its title from the four *London Voluntaries* which are
indubitably its distinction and its strength. London, we
may say, is Mr. Henley's subject as Tommy Atkins is
Mr. Kipling's. Neither subject is poetic in the conventional
sense; for it is not a symbolic, personified Titan-London
that Mr. Henley gives us, but the very brick-and-plaster
wilderness of our daily omnibus-rides; and it is not the
abstract, the monumental soldier whom Mr. Kipling studies,
but the actual fighting-man of commerce, a thing of ordinary,
often of beer-soaked clay, coarse in grain, rude in utterance,
compact of childish frailties and mute, mechanical heroisms.
But though their aim is identical—to extract the latent poetry
of the very life we live—their methods are very different.
Mr. Henley is before everything a classic. He has struck
deep roots into the literature of the past. He may be said
to innovate on an academic basis. Mr. Kipling, on the other
hand, is the consummate journalist, the self-made man of
letters. His astounding vision and faculty are schooled
only in the school of life. The contrast-in-similarity between
the two writers might form the subject of an interesting
critical study.

"Some critics may wonder at our classing Mr. Kipling's
Barrack-Room Ballads as poetry, whether new or old.
'Clever rhymes,' they may say, 'for the most part comic,'
often grotesque, sometimes terrible; but, poetry!—pooh!'
This criticism is not unjust as applied to the 'Other Verses'
in this volume. Mr. Kipling's ballads, *East and West, The
Last Suttee*, &c., are full of vigorous writing. At their best
they are as good as Macaulay, at their worst they are much
better than Mr. George R. Sims. His political, philosophic,
and, we must add, his patriotic effusions are excellent

journalism—no more. But it is precisely in his *Barrack-Room Ballads*, coarse, grotesque, and comic though they be, that Mr. Kipling, to our thinking, proves himself no mere metrical rhetorician, but a true poet. They interpret for us, in terse, tense, literary form, the thoughts and feelings, pleasures and pains, of a class of men who have hitherto, in spite of all that has been written about war and its instruments, 'lacked their sacred poet.' The ballads teem with imagination, they palpitate with emotion. We read them with laughter and tears; the metres throb in our pulses, the cunningly-ordered words tingle with life; and if this be not poetry, what is?"

The only thing that now seems to me essentially unjust in this passage is the remark about Mr. Kipling's "patriotic effusions." Indeed, it is worse than unjust—it is meaningless. It implies a quite untenable distinction between his "patriotic effusions" and his *Barrack-Room Ballads*. I can only suppose that I had specially in mind the verses entitled *The English Flag*, which, fine as they are, and containing as they do the memorable line

What should they know of England who only England know?

must yet be admitted to smack of journalism, partly on account of the controversial aggressiveness of their tone, and especially by reason of the party politics which find somewhat bitter expression in the second verse. Whatever may have been in my mind, I expressed it imperfectly; for it would be the very paradox of pedantry to attempt to exclude the *Barrack-Room Ballads* from the sphere of patriotic poetry. They are more than that, but they are that or nothing. They present a new aspect of patriotism, and they are studies in military psychology to boot; but first and last they are "tribal lays," and it is scarcely too much to say that, from that point of view, "every single one of them is right." Their main disadvantage as "tribal lays" is that they are too long for any one of them to fix itself, as a whole, in any ordinary memory. Mr. Kipling, in his verse, errs on the side of copiousness. He has written odes and ballads and psalms and chanteys ; he has invented numberless refrains ; but he can scarcely be said to have added a song to the language. He is more a rhapsodist than a pure lyrist.

If ever man arrived in the nick of time and on the crest of the wave it was Mr. Kipling. He is the poet of the Expansion of England, of the Imperial Idea. Born thirty years earlier he would have been born before his time ; for the fact of empire preceded the idea (as, given the English character, it naturally would), and Mr. Kipling's advent was nicely timed to coincide with the awakening of imperial self-consciousness. I am not here discussing whether that awakening was to be rejoiced in or deplored. I do not inquire whether the Little Englanders or the Great Englanders are the wise politicians and the true patriots. Putting politics aside, I simply note the historic fact of an extraordinary quickening of the national imagination some fifteen years ago—a novel realisation, whether exultant or the reverse, of the vastness of the British Empire and of the responsibilities it involves. Formerly Great Britain had been the unit in the popular conception, and "possessions and dependencies" only the odd fractions. Great Britain was the £., the Colonies and India the s. d. ; and many people, without being theoretically Little Englanders, were inclined to say with Mr. Mantilini, "The halfpennies be demd." The great poets of the last generation, though they each and all were patriots in their way, wrote of England down to 1885 very much as they might have written of her in 1815. She was still the England of Nelson and Welling-ton, the free England of a steady-going Whig ideal, mistress of the sea, meddling and making a good deal, no doubt, in other parts of the world, but essentially a single island with such and such items of property that happened to be situated abroad. To Tennyson " it was the land that free-men till, that sober-suited Freedom chose," and he was a good deal troubled from time to time by a conjectured degeneracy of the race of freemen. Browning, passing Cape St. Vincent and Trafalgar Bay, reflected that " Here and here had England helped him," but would probably have been a good deal astonished at the conception that what she had mainly done there and elsewhere was to help herself to a colonial dominion. Mr. Swinburne has cele-brated England's maritime supremacy in many billowy strophes, but it sometimes seems as though he thought of the sea rather as an expansive swimming-bath than as the highway of empire. Matthew Arnold, in his famous " weary Titan " passage, perhaps comes nearer than any other poet of his generation to expressing a sense of the immensity of the issues connoted in the word England ; but even that noble image presents "the too vast orb of her fate " as something external to herself. It misrepresents (or so an Imperialist would say) the solidarity of the empire. That idea—the idea of Greater Britain as no mere mechanical appendage to our island, but flesh of her flesh and blood of her blood—did not clearly emerge in the national consciousness until about the time I have indicated. When it did emerge and become a living force, Mr. Kipling emerged with it. Those who believe in it may well say " Si Kipling n'existait pas, il faudrait l'inventer."

Mr. Kipling was born (as appears from the Dedication of *The Seven Seas*) in Bombay :

> Surely in toil or fray
> Under an alien sky
> Comfort it is to say
> " Of no mean city am I ! "

Bombay, in truth, is at the very centre of the empire. Per-haps—who can tell?—she may one day play Constantinople to London's Rome. At any rate, the poet of Tommy Atkins and of the Seven Seas could have had no more fitting birthplace. Fate had fixed his horoscope, and he was born an empire-trotter. He had the rarest opportunities for seeing both the romance and the reality of the British Raj ; and he had the rarest eyes to see with. His ears, too, were no less remarkable organs than his eyes, and at least as indispensable. If I read Mr. Kipling's mental history aright, he is simply the greatest Interviewer that ever trod the earth or sailed the seas. He is the Shakespeare of Special Correspondents. One whole lobe of his brain is a myriad-leaved note-book, where is indelibly recorded every self-revealing or self-concealing syllable he ever heard uttered in all his peregrinations—

> For to admire an' for to see,
> For to be'old this world so wide.

In the other lobe is located an always nimble, always vivid, sometimes grandiose, violent, and spectacular imagination, incessantly drawing upon and recombining and duplicating and expanding the records of the indelible pages. Thus equipped from the outset, he has opened his eyes, pricked up his ears, and set his imagination to work in depicting the doings and sufferings of his "tribe" throughout the world, with a breadth of vision and intensity of realisation hitherto unapproached. His work is in the main pictorial rather than (as patriotic poetry is apt to be) fulminant and dithyrambic. Here and there we find a touch of undisguised swagger, or a page of bluster about "The Blood." But as a rule Mr. Kipling does his swaggering by delicate implication. He is a master of the brag inferential, as Bob Acres might say. The picture he draws is far more sombre than exultant. His soldiers are no rollicking, daredevil "death-or-glory boys," his sailors have to face far grimmer alternatives than victory or Westminster Abbey. A foreigner reading Mr. Kipling (but can any foreigner read him?) might say, "If the English take their pleasures sadly, they take their pride more sadly still." We of "The Blood," Mr. Kipling seems to say, have a very hard row to hoe; but our fathers set us to it, and they toiled at it in their day with might and main; let us, too, clench our teeth and put our backs into it, each remembering that though his own little patch may be stony and squalid enough, the light of the greatest romance in the world's history is over us and our work.

It is this vision of the eternally romantic in the unflinchingly real that is the mark of Mr. Kipling's genius. Look at his most popular piece, for instance, which sets out to be a comic remonstrance addressed by Tommy Atkins to his inappreciative countrymen : who can fail to see that what has imprinted it on every one's memory is the note of romance so skilfully inwoven in the refrain? Take a single stanza, and observe how the grimy commonplace of the first four lines is lifted into a new significance by contrast with the vision of the sea and the great troopships :

I went into a theatre as sober as could be,
They gave a drunk civilian room, but 'adn't none for me;
They sent me to the gallery or round the music-'alls,
But when it comes to fightin', Lord! they'll shove me in the stalls !
    For it's Tommy this, an' Tommy that, an' " Tommy, wait
        outside ";
    But it's " Special train for Atkins " when the trooper's on
        the tide,
    When the troopship's on the tide, my boys, the troopship's
        on the tide,
    O its " Special train for Atkins " when the trooper's on the
        tide.

Each of these different refrains is an inspiration :

O, it's Tommy this, an' Tommy that, an' " Tommy, go away ";
But it's " Thank you, Mister Atkins " when the band begins to
   play . . . .

Then it's Tommy this, an' Tommy that, an' "Tommy, 'ow's yer
    soul ? "
But it's "Thin red line of 'eroes" when the drums begin to
    roll . . . .

For it's Tommy this, an' Tommy that, an' "Chuck him out, the
    brute! "
But it's "Saviour of 'is country" when the guns begin to
    shoot . . . .

Even in the less good—the more commonplace—of the
Barrack-Room Ballads, we find a sense of vastness and a
sense of sadness underlying the grotesque exterior, that are
new to patriotic verse.   For instance—

Walk wide o' the Widow at Windsor,
    For 'alf o' Creation she owns:
We 'ave bought 'er the same with the sword an' the flame,
    An' we've salted it down with our bones.
        (Poor beggars !—it's blue with our bones !)
Hands off o' the sons o' the Widow,
    Hands off o' the goods in 'er shop,
For the Kings must come down an' the Emperors frown
    When the Widow at Windsor says " Stop ! "
        (Poor beggars !—we're sent to say " Stop !")
     *   *   *   *   *
There's 'er nick on the cavalry 'orses,
    There's 'er mark on the medical stores—
An' 'er troopers you'll find with a fair wind be'ind
    That takes us to various wars.
        (Poor beggars !—barbarious wars !)

Or take, again, the last three stanzas of *The Widow's Party*,
an account of a " picnic lay "

To Gawd knows where from Gosport Hard,
And you can't refuse when you git the card
      And the Widow gives the party.

" What ha' you done with half your mess,
      Johnnie, Johnnie ? "
They couldn't do more and they wouldn't do less,
      Johnnie, my Johnnie, aha !

They ate their whack and they drank their fill,
And I think the rations has made them ill,
For half my comp'ny's lying still
   Where the Widow give the party.

" How did you get away—away,
   Johnnie, Johnnie ? "
On the broad o' my back at the end o' the day,
   Johnnie, my Johnnie, aha !
I comed away like a bleedin' toff,
For I got four niggers to carry me off,
As I lay in the bight of a canvas trough,
   When the Widow give the party.

" What was the end of all the show,
   Johnnie, Johnnie ? "
Ask my Colonel, for I don't know,
   Johnnie, my Johnnie, aha !
We broke a King and we built a road—
A court-house stands where the reg'ment goed,
And the river's clean where the raw blood flowed
   When the Widow give the party.

The last line is a good example of Mr. Kipling's peculiar power of grimly realistic pathos. His eyes see not the conventional "red" blood, but the still trickling "raw" blood ; and the epithet, in its masterful crudity, is symbolic of his talent. There is a certain rawness over all his work. I am not going to say "It's gory—but is it Art?"—on that point I have already committed myself. But there are passages where one doubts whether a still greater artist might not have produced an equal effect without laying on his colours quite so raw. For instance, there is a use of the word "juicy," in that powerful and terrible ballad *Snarleyow*, which may be a stroke of genius, but goes far to console one for not possessing the genius that imposes it.

Romance is the prevailing note in the justly famous *Mandalay* and in *Ford o' Kabul River ;* a terrible and almost morbid pathos in *Birds of Prey March* in *Soldier, soldier, come from the wars* (a masterly adaptation of an old

folk-song motive), and in several others. Many of the
ballads are simply pictures (enormously spirited but scarcely
exhilarating) of military life in India—such as *Screw-Guns*,
Cells, *Oonts*, *Loot*, *Gunga Din*, *Troopin'*, *Route Marchin'*,
and *Cholera Camp*. It is to be remarked that in all Mr.
Kipling's lyrics there is never a word of contempt for the
enemy, or even of hatred, unless we reckon as hatred (which
would be false psychology) the sheer Berserk rage of hand-
to-hand fighting. The " one jolly Englishman could lick
them all three" spirit is quite absent from his writings. In
Fuzzy-Wuzzy (an admirable piece) he makes Tommy Atkins
pay chivalrous tribute to that " pore benighted 'eathen but
first-class fightin' man "—a sublimated form of bragging, no
doubt, but greatly preferable to the crude article. In
That Day he gives a very frank picture of a disgraceful
panic :

> I 'eard the knives be'ind me, but I durstn't face my man,
> Nor I don't know where I went to, 'cause I didn't 'alt to see,
> Till I 'eard a beggar squealin' out for quarter as 'e ran,
> An' I thought I knew the voice—an' it was me !

In this and a host of other traits we see a spirit of stern
veracity that must certainly be accounted unto Mr. Kipling
for righteousness. I mean moral rather than artistic
veracity. He will not, of his own consent, be a windbag or
a dealer in shoddy. Artistic veracity is not always (not
ever, one might say) to be compassed by an effort of will.
It is quite an open question—it is *the* open question of
æsthetics—whether "raw" realism such as Mr. Kipling's is
the truest veracity ; but there cannot be the least doubt of
the artist's unswerving will

> To draw the Thing as he sees It for the God of Things as They
> Are.

It is this will to see the fact and to speak the truth that
redeems Mr. Kipling's patriotism from the charge of being

mere cheap rodomontade, to which so much patriotic verse is fatally exposed. Far be it from me to disparage *Scots wha hae*, but I am not sure that it possesses the tonic quality of the refrain of Mr. Kipling's song of defeat:

> *An' there ain't no chorus 'ere to give,*
> *Nor there ain't no band to play;*
> *But I wish I was dead 'fore I done what I did,*
> *Or seen what I seed that day!*

Not his showiest, but to my mind perhaps his ablest and most pointed numbers, are what may be called his Songs of Discipline, especially *The Young British Soldier* in the first series of ballads, and *The 'Eathen* in the second. The former tells how—

> When the 'arf-made recruity goes out to the East
> 'E acts like a babe an' 'e drinks like a beast,
> An' 'e wonders because 'e is frequent deceased
>   Ere 'e's fit for to serve as a soldier.

> Now all you recruities what's drafted to-day,
> You shut up your rag-box an' 'ark to my lay,
> An' I'll sing you a soldier as far as I may :
>   A soldier what's fit for a soldier.

There follow a number of sagacious recommendations as to the personal conduct and morals of the Young British Soldier in cantonment : and then the Mentor proceeds :

> When first under fire an' you're wishful to duck,
> Don't look nor take 'eed at the man that is struck,
> Be thankful you're livin', and trust to your luck
>   And march to your front like a soldier.

> When 'arf of your bullets fly wide in the ditch,
> Don't call your Martini a crossed-eyed old bitch ;
> She's human as you are—you treat her as sich,
>   An' she'll fight for the young British soldier.

When shakin' their bustles like ladies so fine,
The guns o' the enemy wheel into line,
Shoot low at the limbers an' don't mind the shine,
 For noise never startles the soldier.

If your officer's dead and the sergeants look white,
Remember it's ruin to run from a fight :
So take open order, lie down, and sit tight,
 And wait for supports like a soldier.

When you're wounded and left on Afghanistan's plains,
And the women come out to cut up what remains,
Jest roll to your rifle and blow out your brains,
 An' go to your Gawd like a soldier.

In all the poetry of warfare, was there ever a more exactly observed and yet imaginative touch than that which describes the guns of the enemy "shaking their bustles like ladies so fine"? It is grotesque, and it is magnificent.

The 'Eathen begins by setting forth how—

The 'eathen in 'is blindness bows down to wood an' stone;
'E don't obey no orders unless they is 'is own ;
'E keeps 'is side-arms awful : 'e leaves 'em all about,
An' then comes up the regiment an' pokes the 'eathen out.
 All along o' dirtiness, all along o' mess,
 All along o' doin' things rather-more-or-less,
 All along of abby-nay,* kul,† an' hazar-ho,‡
 Mind you keep your rifle an' yourself jus' so !

With these bad habits of the 'eathen the poet then contrasts the progress in smartness, sense of duty, regimental spirit, and skill of a good non-commissioned officer who rises to be colour-sergeant. He thus depicts this worthy's part in a battle:

'E knows each talkin' corpril that leads a squad astray ;
'E feels 'is innards 'eavin', 'is bowels givin' way ;
'E sees the blue-white faces all tryin' 'ard to grin,
An' 'e stands an' waits an' suffers till it's time to cap 'em in.

---

* Not now. † To-morrow. ‡ Wait a bit.

An' now the hugly bullets come peckin' through the dust,
An' no one wants to face 'em, but every beggar must ;
So, like a man in irons which isn't glad to go,
They moves 'em off by companies uncommon stiff an' slow.

Of all 'is five years' schoolin' they don't remember much
Excep' the not retreatin', the step an' keepin' touch.
It looks like teachin' wasted when they duck an' spread an' 'op,
But if 'e 'adn't learned 'em they'd be all about the shop !

An' now it's " 'Oo goes backward ? " an' now it's " 'Oo comes on ? "
And now it's " Get the doolies," an' now the captain's gone ;
An' now it's bloody murder, but all the while they 'ear
'Is voice, the same as barrick drill, a shepherdin' the rear.

'E's just as sick as they are, 'is 'eart is like to split,
But 'e works 'em, works 'em, works 'em till he feels 'em take the
      bit ;
The rest is 'oldin' steady till the watchful bugles play,
An' 'e lifts 'em, lifts 'em, lifts 'em through the charge that wins the
      day !

In the last stanza we have again an instance of Mr. Kipling's
fine art of climax; but the whole picture is surely admirable
in its stern sobriety.

It is natural to inquire whether the armies of other
nations have their Kiplings, and, if so, what manner of men
they be. A German Kipling I have not discovered, but in
France M. Paul Déroulède seems to be accepted as the
laureate of the army. He is a spirited writer, no doubt,
full of an effervescent enthusiasm beside which Mr. Kipling's cynical stoicism is as bitter beer unto champagne.
But his talent seems to me infinitely more commonplace,
more rhetorical, less biting and stimulant than Mr. Kipling's. M. Déroulède, it is true, fought with distinction in
the war of 1870–71, whereas I have not heard that Mr.
Kipling has personally figured in the stricken field ; yet the
younger man and the civilian strikes me as much the older
soldier of the two. M. Déroulède is like the Sergius
Saranoff, and Mr. Kipling the Bluntschli, of Mr. Bernard

Shaw's farce ; only that Mr. Kipling knows a thousand times more of the realities of warfare than ever Bluntschli did. It is perhaps a mere national prejudice, but it seems to me that where the Frenchman is hysterical the Englishman is resolute ; while the Frenchman's watchword is " Gloire," the Englishman's is " Grit." Here, for example, is one of M. Déroulède's lyrics :

EN AVANT

Le tambour bat, le clairon sonne ;
Qui reste en arrière ?—Personne !
C'est un peuple qui se défend.
    En avant !

Gronde canon, crache mitraille !
Fiers bûcherons de la bataille,
Ouvrez nous un chemin sanglant !
    En avant !

Le chemin est fait : qu'on y passe !
Qu'on les écrase, qu'on les chasse !
Qu'on soit libre au soleil levant !
    En avant !

*   *   *   *   *

Leur nombre est grand dans cette plaine :
Est-il plus grand que notre haine ?
Nous le saurons en arrivant !
    En avant !

*   *   *   *   *

En avant ! tant pis pour qui tombe,
La mort n'est rien, vive la tombe !
Quand le pays en soit vivant.
    En avant !

Mr. Kipling, I have said, is not quite guiltless of bombast, but you shall search his poems in vain for a piece of such empty rhetoric as :

Leur nombre est grand dans cette plaine :
Est-il plus grand que notre haine ?

And as for stimulating and bracing effect (which, after all, must be reckoned among the essential qualities of the " tribal lay "), I should be sorry to exchange two verses such as these, from *Soldier an' Sailor too*, for a whole regiment of songs to the tune of *En Avant*:

To take your chance in the thick of a rush, with firing all about,
Is nothing so bad when you've cover to 'and, an' leave an' likin' to shout;
But to stand an' be still to the *Birken'ead* drill is a damn tough bullet to chew,
An' they done it, the Jollies—'Er Majesty's Jollies—soldier an' sailor too!
Their work was done when it 'adn't begun; they was younger nor me an' you;
Their choice it was plain between drownin' in 'eaps an' bein' mopped by the screw,
So they stood an' was still to the *Birken'ead* drill, soldier an' sailor too!

We're most of us liars, we're 'arf of us thieves, an' the rest are as rank as can be,
But once in a while we can finish in style (which I 'ope it won't 'appen to me).
But it makes you think better o' you an' your friends, an' the work you may 'ave to do,
When you think o' the sinkin' *Victorier's* Jollies—soldier an' sailor too!
Now there isn't no room for to say ye don't know—they 'ave proved it plain and true—
That whether it's Widow, or whether it's ship, Victorier's work is to do,
An' they done it, the Jollies—'Er Majesty's Jollies—soldier an' sailor too!

Mr. Kipling's songs of the sea, though still full of a vivid realism, are naturally more grandiose and rhetorical than his barrack-room ballads. Here he wears no dramatic mask, but speaks either in his own person, or in that of the abstract, conventional sailor, or through the mouth of personifications such as " The Coastwise Lights," "The Deep

Sea Cables," the Cities of the Empire. Here, too, he is apt to get into his apocalyptic mood, in which I own (though this is a mere personal idiosyncrasy) that he seldom appeals to me. We owe to it one of his very finest poems, it is true, *The Last Chantey*, but also his very worst—the fearful and wonderful dedication *To Wolcott Balestier*. We have it on the authority of Mr. Atkins that east of Suez " there aren't no Ten Commandments," which perhaps accounts for the fact that Mr. Kipling does not seem to have learnt the third decree of the Decalogue. Whatever the ethical basis of that decree, it certainly holds good in literature, for the name of God loses its force and significance when it is handled too freely. It should be as a rare medal reverently shown, not as a coin to be worn and defaced in the every-day traffic even of poetry.* Yet, with all reservations, it must be admitted that Mr. Kipling has nobly celebrated the part played by the sea in our history, or rather the part in its history which England has played, and plays, and must play so long as she is England. This, I think, is the finest, as it is certainly the simplest, verse of all his sea lyrics and odes:

> We have fed our sea for a thousand years
> And she calls us, still unfed,
> Though there's never a wave of all her waves
> But marks our English dead:
> We have strawed our best to the weed's unrest
> To the shark and the sheering gull.
> If blood be the price of Admiralty,
> Lord God, we ha' paid in full!

The spirit of the roving Englishman, too, finds admirable expression (admirable especially from the metrical point of

* I am not here speaking of the word as it occurs dramatically in the vernacular of Mr. Atkins, but (for instance) of
> our wise Lord God, master of every trade,
> Who tells them tales of His daily toil, of Edens newly made;
> And they rise to their feet as He passes by, gentlemen unafraid!

view) in *L'Envoi* to the *Barrack-Room Ballads* volume, of which I quote the last three verses :

O the blazing tropic night, when the wake's a welt of light
    That holds the hot sky tame,
And the steady fore-foot snores through the planet-powdered floors
    Where the scared whale flukes in flame!
        Her plates are scarred by the sun, dear lass,
        And her ropes are taunt with the dew,
        For we're booming down on the old trail, our own
          trail, the out trail,
        We're sagging south on the Long Trail—the trail that
          is always new.

Then home, get her home, where the drunken rollers comb,
    And the shouting seas drive by,
And the engines stamp and ring, and the wet bows reel and swing,
    And the Southern Cross rides high!
        Yes, the old lost stars wheel back, dear lass,
        That blaze in the velvet blue.
        They're all old friends on the old trail, our own trail,
          the out trail,
        They're God's own guides on the Long Trail—the trail
          that is always new.

Fly forward, O my heart, from the Foreland to the Start—
    We're steaming all-too slow,
And it's twenty thousand mile to our little lazy isle
    Where the trumpet-orchids blow!
        You have heard the call of the off-shore wind
        And the voice of the deep-sea rain ;
        You have heard the song—how long, how long ?
        Pull out on the trail again!

        The Lord knows what we may find, dear lass,
        And The Deuce knows what we may do—
        But we're back once more on the old trail, our own
          trail, the out trail,
        We're down, hull down on the Long Trail—the trail
          that is always new.

These verses scarcely exemplify one of Mr. Kipling's most marked characteristics—fault or merit, who can tell ?—

his overpowering fondness for technical terms. Take this
verse, for example, from his *Anchor Song* :

Heh! Tally on. Aft and walk away with her!
  Handsome to the cathead, now; O tally on the fall!
Stop, seize and fish, and easy on the davit-guy.
  Up, well up the fluke of her, and inboard haul!
Well, ah! fare you well, for the Channel wind's took hold of us,
  Choking down our voices as we snatch the gaskets free.
        And it's blowing up for night,
        And she's dropping light on light,
And she's snorting under bonnets for a breath of open sea.

One could imagine this stanza "set" in a second mate's
examination for comment and (if necessary) correction; to
the landsman it irresistibly suggests a parody, or rather
seems to have been parodied in advance—in *The Hunting
of the Snark*. At the same time, I am far from hastily
writing down Mr. Kipling's technicalism as a plain error in
art. The jargon of to-day may be the language of to-
morrow; and one sometimes wonders whether Mr. Kipling
be not a mighty master of the English of the Future. Who
was it that said, " I should be a great poet if only I knew
the names of things"? Whoever he may have been, he
was probably in the right. It is half the art of literature—
nay, of life itself—to know the names of things. Which of
us, if he wants a carpenter to make him a bookcase, or a
builder to throw out a bow-window to his study, can
describe in English words just the thing he wants? We
have to fumble around with pencils and rude diagrams,
expressing ourselves in a sort of hieroglyphic language
which must often afford no small entertainment to the
artificers we employ. The rudiments of technical termin-
ology—mechanical, scientific, maritime, military, legal, com-
mercial, artistic—ought to form a regular branch of education; and when it does, Mr. Kipling will come into his
kingdom. If poetry is to describe the heaving of an
anchor—and surely there are few events that appeal more

to the imagination—there can be no reason in the nature of things why the objects and actions involved should not be called by their names. If the poet happens to know these names, the question he has to consider is simply one of expediency : how far he ought to compromise with the presumable ignorance of the majority of his readers.* Mr, Kipling is a man of no compromise ; and, in this class of poetry at any rate, which purports simply to versify the thoughts of men to whom the technical terms are professionally familiar, who shall say that he is wrong? It must be remembered that the most ignorant reader will often receive an impression, and even a certain pictorial effect, from terms of which he has but the haziest comprehension. In *McAndrews' Hymn* there is a really superb passage in which the old Scotch engineer expresses his feelings towards the great engines under his charge. For my own part, I have not the least idea what the "crank-throws" or the "main eccentrics" are, or what part is played in the economy of the engine-room by the "thrust-block" and the "guides"; but the poetry impresses me none the less on that account :

Romance! Those first-class passengers they like it very well
Printed and bound in little books; but why don't poets tell?
I'm sick of all their quirks an' turns—the loves and doves they
     dream—
Lord, send a man like Bobby Burns to sing the Song o' Steam!
To match wi' Scotia's noblest speech yon orchestra sublime
Whaurto—uplifted like the Just—the tail-rods mark the time.
The crank-throws give the double-bass, the feed-pump sobs an'
     heaves,
An' now the main eccentrics start their quarrel on the sheaves:
Her time, her own appointed time, the rocking link-head bides,
Till—hear that note?—the rod's return whings glimmering through
     the guides.

---

* Falconer's *Shipwreck* is full of nautical technicalities, and his use of them is praised by Byron. But they are explained in elaborate foot-notes.

They're all awa! True beat, full power, the clangin' chorus goes
Clear to the tunnel where they sit, my purrin' dynamoes.
Interdependence absolute, foreseen, ordained, decreed,
To work, ye'll note, at any tilt an' every rate o' speed.
Fra skylight-lift to furnace-bars, backed, bolted, braced, an' stayed,
An' singin' like the Mornin' Stars for joy that they are made;
While, out o' touch o' vanity, the sweatin' thrust-block says:
"Not unto us the praise, or man—not unto us the praise!"
Now, a' together, hear them lift their lesson—theirs an' mine:
"Law, Order, Duty an' Restraint, Obedience, Discipline!"
Mill, forge, an' try-pit taught them that when roarin' they arose,
An' whiles I wonder if a soul was gied them wi' the blows.
Oh for a man to weld it, then, in one trip-hammer strain,
Till even first-class passengers could tell the meanin' plain!
But no one cares except mysel' that serve an' understand
My seven thousand horse-power here. Eh, Lord! They're grand
   —they're grand!

Only by some narrow trick of definition can such work as this be excluded from the sphere of poetry; and, poetry or no poetry, it is certainly very strong and vital literature.*

This predilection for technical terms is only a phase of a larger characteristic—that omniscience which astounds all Mr. Kipling's readers and annoys many. In his younger days, and especially with reference to his *Departmental Ditties* and *Plain Tales*, people called it "knowingness"; now it merits a term at once larger and less disparaging. Just as Shakespearolaters have averred that Shakespeare was an adept in all the learning and all the arts and crafts of his time, until at last they have gone to the opposite extreme, and made up their minds that Shakespeare was an

* Mr. Kipling's rhymes, by the way (and not merely when he is writing in the person of Mr. Atkins) are apt to be of the cockney order. He makes "brought" rhyme with "pianoforte," "Sahib" with "garb," "quarters" with "daughters," "sword" with "abroad," "court" with "wrought," "mashers" with "sashes," "pork" with "walk." Even if English usage be held to sanction these rhymes, it is a gross error in dialect to make "port" rhyme with "thought" in the mouth of a Glasgow engineer. Mr. McAndrews undoubtedly said "porrrt" and "thawt" if not "thocht."

ignoramus who lent his name to Francis Bacon; so Kip-lingolaters three centuries hence may very likely discover that Rudyard Kipling had no real existence, and was merely a pseudonym of Mr. Herbert Spencer's. The drawbacks of this omniscience are two: in the first place, it abashes and humiliates us; in the second place, it canno but arouse suspicions of superficiality. We feel as if Mr. Kipling must have "crammed" all his multiplicity of accomplishments with an eye to "copy"; and if his technical knowledge is crammed, why not his psychology as well? This criticism, too, Mr. Kipling has allegorically rebutted in *The Story of Ung*. Ung was an artist of the Ice Age who fashioned an image of snow. His tribe, seeing it, cried:

> Verily this is a man!
> Thus do we carry our lances—thus is a war-belt slung.
> Lo! it is even as we are. Glory and honour to Ung!

But then Ung, proceeding further afield in his studies, depicted an aurochs, a bear, a mammoth, and a sabre-toothed tiger dragging a man to his lair. His tribe, gathering to his exhibition, "presently whispered low, 'Yes, they are like—and it may be—— But how does the Picture-man know?'"

> "Ung—hath he slept with the Aurochs — watched where the Mastodon roam?
> Spoke on the ice with the Bow-head—followed the Sabre-tooth home?
> Nay! These are toys of his fancy! If he have cheated us so,
> How is there truth in his image—the man that he fashioned of snow?"

> Wroth was that maker of pictures—hotly he answered the call:
> "Hunters and fishers and trappers, children and fools are ye all:
> Look at the beasts when ye hunt them!" Swift from the tumult he broke,
> Ran to the cave of his father and told him the shame that they spoke

And the father of Ung gave answer, that was old and wise in the
craft,
Maker of pictures aforetime, he leaned on his lance and laughed ;
" If they could see as thou seest they would do what thou hast
done,
And each man would make him a picture, and—what would become
of my son ?

" There would be no pelts of the reindeer flung down at thy cave
for a gift,
Nor dole of the oily timber that comes on the Baltic drift ;
No store of well-drilled needles, nor ouches of amber pale ;
No new-cut tongues of the bison, nor meat of the stranded whale.

" *Thou* hast not toiled at the fishing when the sodden trammels
freeze,
Nor worked the war-boats outward through the rush of the rock-
staked seas,
Yet they bring thee fish and plunder—full meal and an easy bed—
And all for the sake of thy pictures." And Ung held down his
head.

And Ung looked down at his deerskins—their broad shell-tasselled
bands—
And Ung drew downward his mitten and looked at his naked hands ;
And he gloved himself and departed, and he heard his father,
behind :
" Son that can see so clearly, rejoice that thy tribe is blind ! "

The retort is apt and witty, but it does not quite cover the
ground. If Ung's aurochs and mastodon obtruded their
rightness of detail, impressing upon the observer, not so
much the animal in its quiddity as the marvellous observation and memory of the Picture-man, then his tribe might
say, not without reason, "It's knowing—but is it Art?"
It is only modern Shakespearolatry that, by aid of microscopic scrutiny helped out by imagination, has discovered
Shakespeare's omniscience. He dissembled it so well,
harmonised it so thoroughly, that the plain man of his
own age never dreamed of regarding him as a prodigy of
knowledge. He was praised in his lifetime for his " right

happy and copious industry," and shortly afterwards for his
" native wood-notes wild." On the other hand, there is no
mistaking when " Jonson's learned sock was on." He was
always bidding you observe how accurate were the curls of
his aurochs, how closely observed the heart of his mastodon ;
and an ungrateful posterity says " It's learned—but is it
Art ? " Would I had the skill to versify this fable, as a
pendant to *The Story of Ung !*

Mr. Kipling is still young; he has time before him to
falsify rash generalisations, and I hope he may put this one
to shame. But I cannot help thinking that he is, and
that it is in his character to be, the inspired Journalist, the
mighty Interviewer before the Lord, rather than the seer
and creator of pure beauty. His art is Art, and he has
very notably enriched our literature ; but his work does not,
on the whole, stand on the level it might quite well have
reached had he been content to know a little less and
harmonise a little more. His intelligence is appalling, his
insight and his power of divination are very remarkable.
Sometimes we say to ourselves, as we come across some
new instance of his marvellous memory and imagination :
" This man ought to be another Shakespeare and something
over"; yet he remains only the Shakespeare of special
correspondents. In one of his sketches, called *The Finest
Story in the World*, he gives us a curious little glimpse into
his workshop. The writer falls in with a city clerk who, in
a previous state of existence, has been a slave on board a
Greek galley, and who relates his recollections, taking them
for a dream. He is describing a battle in which his galley
is rammed by another :

"The moving galley's bow was plumping the oars back through
their own oar-holes, and I could hear no end of a shindy in the
decks below. Then her nose caught us nearly in the middle and we
tilted sideways . . . . and the right side dipped, and I twisted my
head round and saw the water stand still as it topped the right

bulwarks, and then it curled over and crashed down on the whole lot of us on the right side, and I felt it hit my back, and I woke."

"One minute, Charlie. When the sea topped the bulwarks, what did it look like?" I had my reasons for asking. A man of my acquaintance had once gone down with a leaking ship in a still sea, and had seen the water-level pause for an instant ere it fell on the deck.

"It looked just like a banjo string drawn tight, and it seemed to stay there for years," said Charlie.

Exactly! The other man had said: "It looked like a silver wire laid down along the bulwarks, and I thought it was never going to break." He had paid everything except the bare life for this little valueless piece of knowledge, and I had travelled ten thousand weary miles to meet him, and take his knowledge at second-hand.

Here we have the secret of Mr. Kipling's inspiration. He has the art of extracting from the " men of his acquaintance " the vividest and most intimate details of their experience ; and he has the still greater art of remembering and recombining them. It needed no wizard to divine the fact, even without the aid of this chance confession. We seem to see the " men of his acquaintance " flocking around him from every quarter of the habitable and uninhabitable globe, each bringing his (often unconscious) tribute of anecdote, observation, or experience. We seem to see this, I say ; and it is just what we ought not to see. Wonder at an artist's knowledge should always come to us as an after-thought ; in Mr. Kipling's case it is apt to get between us and the illusion of reality.

It is because he approaches literature from the journalistic side that Mr. Kipling seems, in his collected poems, to lack self-criticism. He includes even in his latest volume of poems a good deal of work that was excellent journalism in its day, but scarcely deserves to take rank as literature. For instance, *The Three-Decker*, a set of comic rhymes on the extinction of the three-volume novel, certainly ought not to sail in *The Seven Seas*. Such verse as this is not

for all time, nor even for an age, but rather for a week
or a day :

> By ways no gaze could follow, a course unspoiled of cook,
> Per Fancy, fleetest in man, our titled berths we took
> With maids of matchless beauty and parentage unguessed,
> And a Church of England parson, for the Islands of the Blest.

Mr. Kipling does himself some injustice in lowering the
average merit of his collections by the inclusion of such
journey-work as this. It is reassuring, however, to note
that the average rises with each volume. *Departmental
Ditties* consisted for the most part of mere smart society
verses, very rarely aspiring to the level of poetry. In
Barrack-Room Ballads the proportions were reversed, the
element of literature largely preponderating over that of
mere journalism ; while in *The Seven Seas* journalism pure
and simple is reduced to a minimum.

Of Mr. Kipling's technique the main thing to be noted is
that he excels in rhythm rather than in sonority. The
"love of lovely words," which infallibly marks the poet
born, is not very strong in him. He will always choose
the racy and precise rather than the nobly harmonious
vocable. Where his verse attains real grandeur it comes
mainly from his study of the Bible; and even then he
seems to give us Isaiah to a banjo accompaniment. Not
without a peculiar fitness has he sung *The Song of the
Banjo,* that " war-drum of the White Man round the world ":

> With my " *Billy-willy-winky-winky-pop !* "
> (Oh, it's any tune that comes into my head !)
> So I keep 'em moving forward till they drop ;
> So I play 'em up to water and to bed.
>
>   * * * * *
>
> With my " *Tinka-tinka-tinka-tinka-tink !* "
> (What d'ye lack, my noble masters ? What d'ye lack ?)
> So I draw the world together link by link :
> Yea, from Delos up to Limerick and back

There is a good deal of the "Tinka-tinka-tinka-tinka-tink" in Mr. Kipling's metrical art. He is always playing pizzicato; we miss what another poet has finely called

> The continuity, the long slow slope
> And vast curves of the gradual violin—

and still more the shuddering swell of the great organ.

But on his own instrument he is a consummate master, inventive, various, delightful. There are no greater triumphs of vernacular rhythm (if I may call it so) in the English language than *The Last Chantey* and *Mandalay*. Even in the early *Departmental Ditties* there are fine and memorable things, such as *Arithmetic on the Frontier*, and especially *The Galley-Slaves*; while in each of his later volumes he seems to take a larger and sincerer view of life, and to rise ever nearer at certain points to what, rather snobbishly perhaps, we are apt to call the grand manner—in other words, to real dignity and simplicity. And whatever may be his ultimate place in literature, there can be no doubt that his poems have won for him what perhaps he values more—a place in the history of his country.

RECESSIONAL.

God of our fathers, known of old—
   Lord of our far-flung battle-line—
Beneath whose awful Hand we hold
   Dominion over palm and pine—
Lord God of Hosts, be with us yet,
Lest we forget, lest we forget!

The tumult and the shouting dies—
   The captains and the kings depart—
Still stands Thine ancient sacrifice,
   An humble and a contrite heart.
Lord God of Hosts, be with us yet,
Lest we forget, lest we forget!

Far-call'd our navies melt away—
   On dune and headland sinks the fire—
Lo, all our pomp of yesterday
   Is one with Nineveh and Tyre!
Judge of the Nations, spare us yet,
Lest we forget, lest we forget!

If, drunk with sight of power, we loose
   Wild tongues that have not Thee in awe—
Such boasting as the Gentiles use,
   Or lesser breeds without the Law—
Lord God of Hosts, be with us yet,
Lest we forget, lest we forget!

For heathen heart that puts her trust
   In reeking tube and iron shard—
All valiant dust that builds on dust,
   And guarding calls not Thee to guard—
For frantic boast and foolish word,
Thy Mercy on Thy People, Lord!

RICHARD LE GALLIENNE

THERE is such a thing as looking a part too well; and Mr. Le Gallienne's eminently poetical exterior, taken along with his liquid and exotic name, have done some injustice to his real talent. Such a name and such a physiognomy are hard to live up to. People instinctively, though quite unjustly, look for pose and affectation in their possessor, and decline to take his work simply on its merits. If Mr. Henry Arthur Jones, for example, wanted to introduce a poet into one of his comedies, he would choose just such a name and suggest to the actor just such a make-up; and he would take care to give the poet a ridiculous part to play. Much better be called John Keats, and make the name (in spite of *Blackwood's* ridicule) a synonym for all that is divinest in song, than come before the world with a ready-made velveteen name, so to speak, which at once proclaims the poet, and sets a malicious world agog to find it a misfit.

Moreover, Mr. Le Gallienne himself, in the course of an industrious and voluble career, has been at no pains to live down prejudice or conciliate fastidiousness. His very considerable gift of utterance has often run ahead of reflection and of tact. He has not been guiltless of crudities both of judgment and of invention. He has given free expression to an occasionally rampant individuality, without justifying it by any convincing proof of underlying strength. His note, in the orchestra of literary journalism, has been a shrill rather than a deep one. It has attracted perhaps disproportionate attention, and has had the effect of setting a good many worthy people's teeth on edge.

But Mr. Le Gallienne is not a man to be dismissed with a grimace. His talent, his faculty, are real and rare. He has an instinctive perception of the beautiful in life, nature and art, and no common power of giving beautiful form to the thoughts and feelings engendered by this perception. His criticism, at its best, is itself a form of poetry. It is the spontaneous utterance of an inborn, unforced joy in art. Mr. Le Gallienne feels with his own nerves, thinks with his own brain. He writes about literature because he was born to love it, not because he happened to drift into an æsthetic set at college, and found editors who would send him books ere yet solicitors would send him briefs. Individual impulse, not corporate tradition, is the mainspring of his work. I am far from contesting the advantages of academic training. Many men it makes, no doubt; but some it mars in the making. It takes a very strong individuality to emerge unscathed both from the schools and from the cliques. The self-made man of letters, on the other hand, shows Nature's guarantee for the authenticity of his calling, so far as it goes. He may lack surface polish, but at least we know that his culture is not a glossy veneer. Mr. Le Gallienne, I take it, is a self-made man of letters. In his criticism, we feel that we are listening to eager and loving human talk about literature, which may not be "the better opinion," correct, judicial, certificated, but has at least the merit of being sensitive and sincere. So, too, in his *Prose Fancies*: they are perhaps a rather "rank, unweeded garden," but they have an irrepressible vitality far beyond that of many a trim parterre. There are pages of the truest poetry in these *Prose Fancies*. They are always best, indeed, when most fanciful, most poetical. But as prose

· RICHARD · LE · GALLIENNE ·

poetry does not come within the scope of the present work, I pass on without further preface to consider Mr. Le Gallienne's three books of verse.

Published in 1892, *English Poems* must be read and criticised as the work of a very young man. The book contains a good deal that Mr. Le Gallienne's maturer judgment would, I am sure, either throw into the fire or lock away in some private pigeon-hole. Its faults of style are many, its faults of taste are more. "Taste" is a word which, in this sense, I am very chary of using. It is apt to imply the mere dogmatic assertion of an unreasoned personal prejudice or system of prejudices. "Vulgarity," says the sage, "is the behaviour of other people." But I conceive it to be more than a personal prejudice which sickens at some of Mr. Le Gallienne's amatory effusions. It is one of the penalties of the poet's calling to have to make trade-capital of his heart-beats, and shout his raptures and his agonies into a megaphone for all the world to hear. But there is a limit to the duty of indiscretion, a point at which reticence may, nay must, assert its rights. Mr. Le Gallienne, in this first book, shows no consciousness of any such limit. Indiscretion is no penalty to him, but rather, it would seem, an instinctive need. "Whatever may be whispered," he seems to say, "ought to be shouted. What is fit for one ear, in one mood, must be equally fit for a million ears in any mood." Let me not be misunderstood—I am not urging a Puritan objection to the poetry of passion. A great spirit can say all things greatly. Mere tact and faculty will contrive to say much without that obtrusion of the personal element in which lies the essence of indecorum. But in such a piece as Mr. Le Gallienne's *Hesperides*, to name one typical instance, there is no tact and only the most ordinary faculty. It is the very babble of juvenile eroticism. To draw lines and lay down rules is always a dangerous business; but the study of Mr. Le Gallienne's

English Poems makes one feel that love poetry ought, so far as possible, to be dramatic, like the great lyrics in *Maud*, or at least to wear a dramatic mask and be translated "from the Portuguese." This, to be sure, is a hard saying, which, had it been acted upon, would have deprived the world of much great poetry. Non-dramatic love-poetry, I take it, may be divided into three classes: first, the ideal-passionate, as of the seventeenth-century lyrists and the pre-Raphaelites; second, the polygamous-sentimental, as of Burns and Heine; third, the domestic-sensual; and the domestic-sensual, I suggest, ought to remain in the domestic archives until, in the process of the seasons, it be found apt and proper to light the domestic fire.

Faults of style, too, and even of grammar, abound in *English Poems*. Mr. Le Gallienne speaks of Mr. Swinburne as

> That wild poet *who* so many a time
> Our hungering lips have blessed.

Asking that question which a man so often asks with regard to another man's wife, "Why did she marry him?" he writes:

> Gave she her gold for a girlish whim,
>   A freak of a foolish mood?
> Or was it some will like a snake in him,
>   *Lay* a charm upon her blood?

Such slips, and corresponding slips of metre, are not infrequent. Far more serious is an occasional tendency to write nonsense at the mere dictation of the rhyme; for instance:

> For all the silver morning is a-glimmer
>   With gleaming spears of great Apollo's host,
> *And the night fadeth like a spent out swimmer*
> *Hurled from the headlands of some shining coast.*

This is as good an instance as one could desire of an unillustrative simile. There is not the remotest resemblance between fading night and a "spent out swimmer"; and Mr. Le Gallienne would never have fancied there was, had it not happened that morning was "a-glimmer" in the first line of the quatrain. Such faults, however, are excusable enough in a young writer. Unfortunately there are greater poets than Mr. Le Gallienne who, in their maturest work, allow their imagery to be similarly conditioned by their rhyme.

But amid all Mr. Le Gallienne's youthful lapses and indiscretions, we feel every here and there the touch of the true poet. The first poem in the book is a very saccharine version in Spenserian stanzas of the story of Paolo and Francesca— merely the young poet's obligatory imitation of Keats. Still, there are several lines and passages that augur better things ; for instance this, of the husband's home-coming:

> "Fool! Fool!" he cried, "O dotard fool, indeed,
> So ho ! they wanton while the old man rides,"
> And on the night flashed pictures of the deed.
> "Come!"—and he dug his charger's panting sides,
> And all the homeward dark tore by in roaring tides.

This is dramatic, nervous writing, far above the reach of the mechanical rhymester. In *Love Platonic*, again, a sequence of amatory verses, there are some truly memorable passages. Here, for example, are two fine images from two consecutive pages :

> But we have starry business, such a grief
> As Autumn's, dead by some forgotten sheaf,
> While all the distance echoes of the wain.

This is a personification not unworthy of the poet of Autumn himself. Note especially how the last line gives spaciousness to the picture. And this, in a more fanciful way, is almost equally good :

> We sat at talk, and all the afternoon
> Whispered about in changing silences
> Of flush and sudden light and gathering shade,
> As though some Maestro drew out organ stops
> Somewhere in heaven.

A little further on in the same sequence there occurs a genuinely-felt and prettily-turned lyric, *A Lost Hour;* but on the whole, if we want to find Mr. Le Gallienne at his best, we must turn away from the personal poems, whether they be grouped as "Love Platonic" or as "Cor Cordium," to the more reflective and dramatic pieces towards the end of the book. This seems to me a thing finely conceived and executed (it may not be amiss to explain, by the way, that the "darkness" the poet has in view is that of the blind):

WHAT OF THE DARKNESS?

What of the Darkness? Is it very fair?
Are there great calms and find ye silence there?
Like soft-shut lilies all your faces glow
With some strange peace our faces never know,
With some great faith our faces never dare.
Dwells it in Darkness? Do ye find it there?

Is it a Bosom where tired heads may lie?
Is it a Mouth to kiss our weeping dry?
Is it a Hand to steal the pulse's leap?
Is it a Voice that holds the runes of sleep?
Day shows us not such comfort anywhere.
Dwells it in Darkness? Do ye find it there?

Out of the Day's deceiving light we call,
Day that shows man so great and God so small,
That hides the stars and magnifies the grass;
O is the darkness too a lying glass,
Or, undistracted, do ye find truth there?
What of the Darkness? Is it very fair?

The man who can write such a line as "Is it a Voice that holds the runes of sleep?" is not to be denied a place among the poets. Here, again, is a cool, fresh lyric, a deftly worded record of a mood:

ALL SUNG.

What shall I sing when all is sung,
And every tale is told,
And in the world is nothing young
That was not long since old?

256

RICHARD LE GALLIENNE

Why should I fret unwilling ears
　　With old things sung anew,
While voices from the old dead years
　　Still go on singing too?

A dead man singing of his maid
　　Makes all my rhymes in vain,
Yet his poor lips must fade and fade,
　　And mine shall kiss again.

Why should I strive through weary moons
　　To make my music true?
Only the dead men knew the tunes
　　The live world dances to.

There are many delicate fancies and strong phrases in the later pages of the book; for instance:

Glad as yon lark there splashing in the light;

or:

To stretch the octave 'twixt the dream and deed,
Ah, that's the thrill!

There is poetic temperament—perhaps ultra-poetic—even in the less fortunately inspired of these poems. The book, as a whole, is an unripe fruit, but at least there is a heart of promise in it.

The promise is well fulfilled in Mr. Le Gallienne's second book, dating from 1895. Still there is a certain looseness of texture in the style; still there is an occasional image of doubtful taste. But in dignity, in discretion, in concentrated force of utterance, the book marks what may even be called an astonishing advance. The opening poem, *Robert Louis Stevenson: an Elegy*, if not quite successfully sustained, contains some admirable passages. For instance:

Above his grave
Strange leaves and wings their tropic splendours wave,
While far beneath, mile after shimmering mile,
The great Pacific, with its faery deeps,
Smiles all day long its silken secret smile.

Or this:

> Death! why at last he finds his treasure isle,
> And he the pirate of its hidden hoard;
> Life! 'twas the ship he sailed to seek it in,
> And Death is but the pilot come aboard.
> Methinks I see him smile a boy's glad smile
> On maddened winds and waters, reefs unknown,
> As thunders in the sail the dread typhoon,
> And in the surf the shuddering timbers groan;
> Horror ahead, and Death beside the wheel:
> Then—spreading stillness of the broad lagoon,
> And lap of waters round the resting keel.

An Ode to Spring and *Tree-Worship* give utterance to the poet's very deep and sincere love of Nature. In each there are flaws of workmanship and even of feeling—for example:

> O winds that blow from out the fruitful mouth of God,
> O rains that softly fall from His all-loving eyes!

But in both poems there is the breath of life; whatever their faults, they are not dead exercises in versification. *A Ballad of London* is a piece of genuine imagination, and there is here a charming *Hesperides*, very differently inspired from the poem of the same name in the earlier volume. The verses on the death of Tennyson, if they contain touches of the commonplace, are at least not wholly inadequate to the occasion. I quote two stanzas for the sake of their truly noble close:

> Great wife of his great heart—'tis yours to mourn,
>   Son well-beloved, 'tis yours, who loved him so:
> But we!—hath death one perfect page out-torn
>   From that great song whereby alone we know
>
> The splendid spirit imperiously shy,—
>   Husband to you and father—we afar
> Hail poet of God, and name as one should cry:
>   "Yonder a king, and yonder, lo! a star!"

The finest thing in the book, to my thinking, is a poem entitled *If, after all.* . . . *!* a grave and passionate utterance of one of the agonised questionings which follow in the wake of a great bereavement. It speaks so directly from the soul that I somehow feel as though, if I quoted it, I should be betraying a sacred confidence; yet in this case one has none of the feeling above alluded to, that the poet himself, in publishing it, is unwarrantably blabbing the secrets of his soul. The emotion is tragic, the expression entirely dignified.

Mr. Le Gallienne's third book of verse is entitled *Rubáiyát of Omar Khayyam.* It was a foolhardy enterprise to follow in the footsteps of FitzGerald and add an apocrypha to his canon. Mr. Le Gallienne, I understand, has been severely taken to task for his impiety; whether he is properly penitent I know not. For my part, I am a lukewarm Omarian. I admire FitzGerald's work on this side idolatry, and see no reason in the world why it should not be supplemented. The Omarian spirit, in its more obvious aspect at any rate, is congenial—perhaps too congenial—to Mr. Le Gallienne, and he turns his quatrains with a very pretty grace. He does not write so well as FitzGerald at his best, but I do not find the gap between them so enormous as to make his enterprise an absurdity or a profanation. This may simply mean that I am not worthy to appreciate FitzGerald—that I have not "learned his great language, caught his clear accents, lived in his mild and magnificent eye." I speak, in short, as one of the profane; but I am not sure that I should care to be within the pale if I were thereby debarred from taking any pleasure in such verses as these:

LXI.

Of all my seeking this is all my gain:
No agony of any mortal brain
   Shall wrest the secret of the life of man;
The search has taught me that the search is vain.

LXII.

Yet sometimes on a sudden all seems clear—
Hush ! hush ! my soul, the secret draweth near ;
   Make silence ready for the speech divine—
If Heaven should speak, and there be none to hear !

LXIII.

Yea ! sometimes on the instant all seems plain,
The simple sun could tell us, or the rain ;
   The world, caught dreaming with a look of heaven,
Seems on a sudden tip-toe to explain.

It is rather hard to believe that the last two quatrains, at any rate, have any warrant in the Persian. They suggest an English landscape, they express a post-Wordsworthian mood. Omar was modern, no doubt, but was he quite so modern as all that? It boots not to inquire: Mr. Le Gallienne confesses to having embroidered pretty freely on the original fabric; and if he does so as prettily as this, I think the dust of Omar may rest undisturbed beneath its rose-bush. Here are a few more quatrains, culled almost at random :

CX.

A beauty sleeps beneath yon quiet grass
Who dreamed her face the world might not surpass ;
   Strength is her neighbour, but he boasts no more,—
And over them the wind cries out " Alas ! "

CXVI.

O weary man upon a weary earth,
What is this toil that we call living worth ?
   This dreary agitation of the dust,
And all this strange mistake of mortal birth ?

CXLV.

Nor are those sightless stars a whit more wise,
Impotent silver dots upon the dice
   The lords of heaven each night and morning throw,
In some tremendous hazard of the skies.

RICHARD LE GALLIENNE

CXLVI.

Nay ! think no more, but grip the slender waist
Of her whose kisses leave no bitter taste,
    Reason's a hag, and love a painted jade,—
Come daughter of the vine, dear and disgraced.

CLXXV.

Of all the wise wisest is he who knows
What saith the wine as in the cup it flows,
    And he alone is learnèd who can read
The little scented pages of the rose.

Like most of Mr. Le Gallienne's work, these *Rubáiyát*
would be the better for weeding; but why should the
weeds blind us to the beauty of the flowers, which shoot
up far above them?

A quick and graceful fancy, a passion for beauty in all its
manifestations, a straightforward outlook upon life, and a
gift of inventing picturesque and melodious phrases—all
these qualities Mr. Le Gallienne possesses, and they are
undeniably the qualities of a poet. He is not a great
stylist, he is not a great metrist. His faculty, indeed, is not
one which imperiously calls for verse as its only adequate
medium of expression. Neither his culture nor (perhaps)
his character fits him for the very highest flights. But he
has said some things finely, and many things beautifully;
and the power to do this, and do it in verse, seems to me the
one true criterion of the poet's calling.

TIME'S MONOTONE.

Autumn and Winter,
Summer and Spring—
Hath Time no other song to sing ?
Weary we grow of the changeless tune—
June—December,
December—June !

Time, like a bird, hath but one song,
One way to build, like a bird hath he ;
Thus hath he built so long, so long,
Thus hath he sung—Ah me !

Time, like a spider, knows, be sure,
One only wile, though he seems so wise :
Death is his web, and Love his lure,
And you and I his flies.

"Love !" he sings
In the morning clear,
"Love ! Love ! Love !"—
And you never hear
How, under his breath,
He whispers, "Death !
Death ! Death !"

Yet Time—'tis the strangest thing of all—
Knoweth not the sense of the words he saith ;
Eternity taught him his parrot-call
Of "Love and Death."

Year after year doth the old man climb
The mountainous knees of Eternity,
But Eternity telleth nothing to Time—
It may not be.

RICHARD LE GALLIENNE

ON MR. GLADSTONE'S RETIREMENT.

The world grows Lilliput, the great men go;
  If greatness be, it wears no outer sign;
  No more the signet of the mighty line
Stamps the great brow for all the world to know.
Shrunken the mould of manhood is, and lo!
  Fragments and fractions of the old divine,
  Men pert of brain, planned on a mean design,
Dapper and undistinguished—such we grow.

No more the leonine heroic head,
  The ruling arm, great heart, and kingly eye;
    No more th' alchemic tongue that turned poor themes
    Of statecraft into golden-glowing dreams;
  No more a man for man to deify:
Laurel no more—the heroic age is dead.

MRS. MEYNELL

STERN veracity, I fear, enforces the admission that few poetesses of the past have shown a very highly developed faculty for strict poetical form. I am not aware that the works of any woman in any modern language are reckoned among the consummate models of metrical style. In England, at any rate, we have had no female Milton, Coleridge, or Swinburne. Great poetesses though they were, beyond a doubt, Mrs. Browning and Miss Rossetti were incurious of formal perfection, especially in rhyme; and ladies as a rule seem to have aimed at a certain careless grace rather than a strenuous complexity or accuracy of metrical structure.

In respect of accuracy, though not of complexity, Mrs. Meynell is one of the rare exceptions to this rule. Within a carefully limited range, her form is unimpeachable. Her grace is often exquisite, but never careless. She never strays beyond two or three simple iambic or trochaic measures, and her most elaborate stanza (the sonnet excepted) is one of five lines, with rhyme-scheme either *a a b b a* or *a b a b a*. Dactylic and anapæstic rhythms and intricate rhyme-patterns she altogether eschews. The sonnet in its strictest form she writes with real accomplishment; but the sonnet is really a very easy mould to fill. This, I think, is rather a commonplace than a paradox. Who is there, in

ALICE MEYNELL

these days, that has not written one or two passable sonnets? Who is there that, if called upon to produce a copy of verses which should have a certain specious air of poetical merit, would not instantly select his double set of four rhymes and begin to weave his octave? The strict form is far more of a support than a burden. It serves as stays to a flaccid thought. It provides, so to speak, a ready-made effect of climax and antithesis, while a very little care in ordering the rhymes and distributing the pauses of the sestett will give it a highly creditable air of technical mastery. It is this amiable duplicity, if one may call it so, on the part of the sonnet—this apparent difficulty and real ease of manipulation—that has secured its vogue. I do not mean that it is easy to write sonnets as good as some of Mrs. Meynell's, but merely that her success in the sonnet form does not invalidate the remark that her metrical ambitions are carefully and judiciously limited.

Within the limits she has assigned herself, her accomplishment is real and delightful. There is scarcely a jarring note in all her measures; her rhymes, without purism, are true rhymes to the cultivated ear; and she habitually attains distinction-in-simplicity of phrase. Her diction is absolutely unaffected. There is not, in her little book of *Poems*, a single word dragged in for its own sake. Far be it from me to sneer at the poets who ransack the treasure-house of the language for jewels wherewith to encrust the hieratic vesture of their thought; but an exquisite simplicity is, in its way, at least as beautiful, and (to use the word without the slightest shade of disparagement) far more characteristically feminine. Take, for instance, these four verses—how utterly their human and intimate charm would be destroyed by a single archaic or obtrusively literary word, however beautiful in itself:

SONG.

As the inhastening tide doth roll,
Dear and desired, along the whole
  Wide shining strand, and floods the caves,
  Your love comes filling with happy waves
The open sea-shore of my soul.

But inland from the seaward spaces,
None knows, not even you, the places
  Brimmed, at your coming, out of sight,
  —The little solitudes of delight
This tide constrains in dim embraces.

You see the happy shore, wave-rimmed,
But know not of the quiet dimmed
  Rivers your coming floods and fills,
  The little pools 'mid happier hills,
My silent rivulets, over-brimmed.

What, I have secrets from you? Yes.
But, visiting sea, your love doth press
  And reach in further than you know,
  And fills all these; and when you go,
There's loneliness in loneliness.

Here the third stanza is, I think, less happy than the rest.
The three rhymes in " immed " have proved a little difficult
of manipulation, and the second of the three is a mere
makeshift, hindering the movement, without helping the
meaning, of the stanza. Otherwise the little poem seems to
me perfect—subtle and true in idea, delicate in cadence,
and full of a tender wistfulness which, in the last line, rises
to the pitch of discreet and unemphatic pathos.

This subdued distinction of tone runs through all Mrs.
Meynell's poetry and lends it a peculiar charm. What
could be more delicate than the stanzas quoted at the
end of the article, in which an image not unlike that
of the foregoing *Song* is touched to a somewhat different
issue ?

Of Mrs. Meynell's sonnets the following is, not perhaps

the most beautiful in point of form, but to my thinking the most vivid and memorable:

RENOUNCEMENT.

I must not think of thee; and, tired yet strong,
  I shun the thought that lurks in all delight—
  The thought of thee—and in the blue Heaven's height,
And in the sweetest passage of a song.

Oh, just beyond the fairest thoughts that throng
  This breast, the thought of thee waits, hidden yet bright;
  But it must never, never come in sight;
I must stop short of thee the whole day long.

But when sleep comes to close each difficult day,
  When night gives pause to the long watch I keep,
  And all my bonds I needs must loose apart,

Must doff my will as raiment laid away,—
  With the first dream that comes with the first sleep
  I run, I run, I am gathered to thy heart.

One may prefer a sonnet in which the thought is less clearly conditioned by the metrical anatomy; but this line-by-line structure is the only serious fault of an otherwise delightful piece of work.

There is not a poem of Mrs. Meynell's that is not marked by this unobtrusive grace—a quality which, if the word could be divested of its unfortunate eighteenth-century associations, one would like to call elegance. At the same time, one cannot but feel that Mrs. Meynell's verse does but scant justice to her intellectual gifts. It is deficient, not only in dramatic, but in pictorial quality; it interprets a very narrow range of experience; and the thoughts it expresses are pretty rather than luminous or searching, ingenious rather than relevant or real. The charm of the poems I have quoted lies in the discreetly sincere expression of personal feeling; but the very discretion of these utterances condemns them to a certain monotony; and beyond personal feeling, into the regions of observation and speculation, the poetess seldom strays.

But her essays have proved her capable of very keen observation and of real substantive thought, as opposed to mere air-drawn fantasy. One finds in her prose a far wider range of vision and faculty, a larger and deeper knowledge both of nature and of life, than is anywhere evidenced in her verse. Turn, for instance, to *A Letter from a Girl to her own Old Age*, one of her longest poems. The idea is ingenious, but the verses say little or nothing. There is charming sentiment, but practically no thought in them. One feels that the authoress of *The Rhythm of Life* would find something far more interesting to say were she now to approach the theme afresh. Or take again the following:

IN EARLY SPRING.

O Spring, I know thee! Seek for sweet surprise
    In the young children's eyes.
But I have learnt the years, and know the yet
    Leaf-folded violet.
Mine ear, awake to silence, can foretell
    The cuckoo's fitful bell.
I wander in a grey time that encloses
    June and the wild hedge-roses.
A year's procession of the flowers doth pass
    My feet, along the grass.
And all you sweet birds silent yet, I know
    The notes that stir you so,
Your songs yet half devised in the dim dear
    Beginnings of the year.
In these young days you meditate your part;
    I have it all by heart.

I know the secrets of the seeds of flowers
    Hidden and warm with showers,
And how, in kindling Spring, the cuckoo shall
    Alter his interval.
But not a flower or song I ponder is
    My own, but memory's.
I shall be silent in those days desired
    Before a world inspired.
O dear brown birds, compose your old song-phrases,
    Earth, thy familiar daisies.

The poet mused upon the dusky height,
        Between two stars towards night,
His purpose in his heart. I watched, a space,
        The meaning of his face:
There was a secret, fled from earth and skies,
        Hid in his grey young eyes.
My heart and all the Summer wait his choice,
        And wonder for his voice.
Who shall foretell his songs, and who aspire
        But to divine his lyre?
Sweet earth, we know thy dimmest mysteries,
        But he is lord of his.

This is, in itself, a beautiful thing, and we are duly grateful for it; but it exemplifies the insubstantiality, or, as I have called it, the unreality, of Mrs. Meynell's thought when she is no longer " A poet of one mood. . . . Ranging all life to sing one only love." It is quite true that we can foresee the whole development of the drama of spring, whereas we cannot (always) foretell a poet's songs. It is true—but does it matter? Where is the importance or significance of the thought? The poem may be delightful —is delightful, I gladly admit—though the thought is insignificant. In so far it justifies itself; but its delightfulness would be in no way impaired if it embodied an idea which took some hold upon the mind. Mrs. Meynell is capable of such ideas; she is even fertile in them; but we must seek for them elsewhere than in her poetry.

The truth is, of course, that her prose represents Mrs. Meynell's maturer experience and thought, her verse the emotion and sentiment of her girlhood. "Most of these verses," says a note appended to her *Poems*, "were written in the author's early youth, and were published in a volume called *Preludes*, now out of print. Other poems, representing the same transitory and early thoughts, which appeared in that volume, are now omitted as cruder than the rest; and their place is taken by the few verses written in maturer years." It is not at all wonderful that a girl should write like a girl; the wonder is that a very young woman should possess the technical skill which is apparent throughout these poems. My regret, then, is not that the verses of "early youth" should express "transitory and early thoughts," but that the "verses written in maturer years" should be so few. It almost seems as though Mrs. Meynell had purposely deserted verse for prose. If so, one can only hope that, without detriment to "the other harmony," her poetic impulse may override a needlessly exclusive resolution.

MRS. MEYNELL

REGRETS.

As, when the seaward ebbing tide doth pour
    Out by the low sand spaces,
The parting waves slip back to clasp the shore
    With lingering embraces,—

So in the tide of life that carries me
    From where thy true heart dwells,
Waves of my thoughts and memories turn to thee
    With lessening farewells;

Waving of hands; dreams, when the day forgets;
    A care half lost in cares;
The saddest of my verses; dim regrets;
    Thy name among my prayers.

I would the day might come, so waited for,
    So patiently besought,
When I, returning, should fill up once more
    Thy desolated thought;

And fill thy loneliness that lies apart
    In still, persistent pain.
Shall I content thee, O thou broken heart,
    As the tide comes again,

And brims the little sea-shore lakes, and sets
    Seaweeds afloat, and fills
The silent pools, rivers and rivulets
    Among the inland hills?

MISS E. NESBIT

(MRS. BLAND)

THERE is more feeling than art in the poetry of Miss E. Nesbit; but the feeling is often very genuine, and of the art one may at least say that it has ripened with every book the poetess has put forth. Miss Nesbit had from the first a remarkable fluency and a correct ear for metres. Unfortunately, her fluency was altogether too strong for her sense of style, which was originally very imperfect, and to this day leaves something to be desired. Her first collections of verse—*Lays and Legends* 1886 and 1892, and *Leaves of Life* 1888—are chiefly notable for the vigorous rhetoric of some of her revolutionary chants. She was caught on the wave, it would seem, of the Socialist movement of the 'eighties, and many of her poems breathe a deeply-felt sympathy with the toilers of the earth, and a burning sense of the inequality of social conditions. The following may serve as a specimen of her early work in this kind—a few quatrains from a poem entitled:

AT THE FEAST.

*　　　*　　　*　　　*　　　*

Yes, we have learned to know, and not to shrink
From knowing, to what depths our brothers sink.
　　And we have learned the lesson " not to feel,"
And we have learned the lesson " not to think."

We must have learned it; otherwise, to-night,
When, sped by wine and feasting, time takes flight,
　　When perfect music searches for our soul,
And all these flowers unfold for our delight,

272

·E · NESBIT·

We should not hear the music, but, instead
Hear that wild, bitter, heart-sick cry for bread,
   And in the lamps that light our lavish feast,
Should see but tapers burning for the dead.

We should not see the myriad blossoms waste;
The bloom of them would be thrust back, displaced
   By the white faces of the starving children—
Wasted and wan, who might have been flower-faced.

Among other powerful pieces in the same key may be
mentioned *Two Voices* and *A Spring Song.* There is,
perhaps, more of declamatory force than of lyric inspiration
in them, but their fervour and sincerity give them a value
of their own.

Much less notable are the narrative poems which form
the bulk of these volumes. Smooth and flowing they always
are, with occasional passages of a certain vigour; but they
have all a fatal bent towards prolixity and commonplace.
The best, I think, is *Absolution*, a story of real tragic strength.
Such legendary subjects as *Tekel* (a variation of the
St. Anthony theme) and *The Singing of the Magnificat*, Miss
Nesbit treats with occasional felicity, but also with occasional
lapses into bathos. Of the felicities I can give no better
specimen than this fine couplet, spoken by the mother of
St. Simeon Stylites to her son, in a poem entitled *Earth and
Heaven*:

At last God heard my cry—thee did I bear,
The inexorable answer to my prayer.

The lapses, on the other hand, are characteristically exemplified in the concluding couplet of this stanza:

The Angel spoke—his voice was low and sweet
   As the sea's murmur on low-lying shore—
Or whisper of the wind in ripened wheat:
   "Brother," he said, "the God we both adore
Has sent me down to ask, is all not right?—
Why was *Magnificat* not sung to-night?"

Miss Nesbit is least fortunate, to my thinking, in her modern, or semi-modern novelettes in verse, such as *The Moat House*, *Two Christmas Eves*, and *Treason*. Her literary power is always considerable. She seldom descends to mere solecisms like this :

> And then the clouds set fast again
> Into a leaden sky like this is,
> Lit by no lightnings of warm kisses—

or this :

> Her soul has held my soul, and taught
> The way of storming Fortune's fort.

Nor does she often write sheer jingling prose such as this from *The Moat House :*

> First he listened, vain and flattered that a girl as fair as she
> Should be so distinctly anxious for his lost humanity,
> Yet determined no attentions even from the Lady May
> Should delay his home returning one unnecessary day.

The last three quotations are not, I repeat, fair specimens of Miss Nesbit's manner. They are quite exceptionally bad. But, on the other hand, it is difficult to quote from these poems anything memorably good. All Miss Nesbit's narrative verse is of the nature of Christmas-number poetry. It is like the text to those highly-coloured works of art which adorn the December bookstalls. In a word, it is chromolithographic.

The poetess's true bent is clearly towards the pure lyric. Even at the height of her revolutionary fervour, she herself admitted this in the following stanza :

> Freedom we sing, and would not lose
> Her lightest footprint in life's dust.
> We sing of her because we choose,
> We sing of love because we must.

Her lyrics are pitched in many keys, and many of them, perhaps the majority, must be taken as dramatic rather than personal. They are not essentially the worse for that; but through some of them there runs a strain of Byronism which

is a little trying.   The following stanzas may serve as an
example, from a poem entitled *Bewitched* :

> You are Fate, you are love, you are longing,
>   You are music, and roses, and wine,
> You are devil, and man, and my lover,
>   You are hatefully mine and not mine.
> You are all that's infernal in loving,
>   And all that in hate is divine.
>
> *   *   *   *
>
> And all would be nothing to suffer,
>   If once at my feet you could lie,
> And offer your soul for my loving—
>   Could I know that your world was just I—
> And could laugh in your eyes and refuse you
>   And love you and hate you and die.

It is a matter of personal taste, no doubt, but for my part
I prefer to these lurid outpourings, the subdued eighteenth-
century grace of such stanzas as the following :

SONG.

> We loved, my love, and now it seems
>   Our love has brought to birth
> Friendship, the fairest child of dreams,
>   The rarest gift on earth.
>
> Soon die love's roses fresh and frail ;
>   And when their bloom is o'er,
> Not all our heart-wrung tears avail
>   To give them life once more.
>
> But when true love with friendship lives,
>   As now, for thee and me,
> Love brings the roses—Friendship gives
>   Them immortality.

More characteristic than either the Satanic or the idyllic
strain, is the note of nature-symbolism in the following verses :

HOPES.

> *   *   *   *   *
>
> In hollows where so late but dead leaves lay,
>   Through the dead leaves the primroses push up ;
> And wind-flowers fleck the copse, and fields are gay
>   With daisies and the budding buttercup.

> So in our hearts, though thick the dead leaves lie
>   Of grief—heaped up by winds of old despair—
> May there not be a spring-time by-and-by,
>   When flowers of joy shall blossom even there?
>
> So long has Winter held our hearts in his,
>   We dare not dream of Spring and all her flowers!
> Ah! the undreamed-of happiness it is
>   That comes—the dreamed-of joy is never ours.

Miss Nesbit has a real love of English nature and a keen eye for it. She seldom or never attempts formal landscape-painting, but her incidental and illustrative touches of description, as in the first of the above stanzas, are often very happy.

In *A Pomander of Verse* (1895), Miss Nesbit's style has sensibly ripened. This collection contains some fine romantic lyrics, such as *The Spider Queen*, *Inspiration*, and *The Golden Rose*, quoted at the end of this article. Of the nature-lyrics, the best, perhaps, is that entitled *A Kentish Garden*; but the following versicles are shorter and no less charming:

CHILD'S SONG IN SPRING.

> The silver birch is a dainty lady,
>   She wears a satin gown;
> The elm tree makes the old churchyard shady,
>   She will not live in town.
>
> The English oak is a sturdy fellow,
>   He gets his green coat late;
> The willow is smart in a suit of yellow,
>   While brown the beech-trees wait.
>
> Such a gay green gown God gives the larches—
>   As green as He is good!
> The hazels hold up their arms for arches
>   When Spring rides through the wood.
>
> The chestnut's proud, and the lilac's pretty,
>   The poplar's gentle and tall,
> But the plane tree's kind to the poor dull city—
>   I love him best of all.

Several of these lyrics have a dramatic—one might almost say a psychological—significance, which gives them a character of their own. That the poetess has at last learnt the art of compression we may see from the five stanzas of *Sanctuary*, of which this is the last:

> I could not speak. I touched your hand
>   At the green arch that ends the wood:
> " Ah—if she should not understand ! "
>   Ah—if you had not understood !

Here, again, is a lyric, not very happy in form perhaps, but containing the essence of a whole life-drama:

QUIETA NE MOVETE.

> Dear, if I told you, made your sorrow certain,
>   Showed you the ghosts that o'er my pillow lean,
> What joy were mine—to cast aside the curtain
>   And clasp you close with no base lies between !
>
> You have given all, and still would find to give me
>   More love, more tenderness than ever yet:
> You would forgive me—ah, you would forgive me,
>   But all your life you never would forget.
>
> And I, thank God, can still in your embraces
>   Forget the past, with all its strife and stain,
> —But, if you, too, beheld the evil faces,
>   I should forget them never, never again.

In *Songs of Love and Empire* (1898), a new note makes itself heard in Miss Nesbit's poetry. The internationalism, if I may call it so, of her early verse has now yielded a very pronounced nationalism. The political merits or demerits of the change do not here concern me; I have to consider only its literary results. My impression of the Songs of Empire—three long addresses to Queen Victoria, two songs of Trafalgar and one of Waterloo—may be summed up in the statement that they have sincerity and dignity, but lack distinction. This is not, as it may at first sight appear, a contradiction in terms. It is comparatively easy, now that

Spenser and Keats have shown the way, to weave a stately lyrical stanza of eight or ten iambic lines. It is comparatively easy to give the individual lines a certain impetus and sonority. The difficulty is to find new ideas and images, and clothe them in words that shall seem to fly together, as though at a wizard's spell, from the uttermost treasure-caves of language, and shall set up, in their collocation, a sort of elusive electricity, which not only welds them indissolubly together, but makes them glow and palpitate with light and colour. It is this magical quality of style which we do not find in Miss Nesbit's odes. Her vocabulary is restricted, and her ideas are not, as a rule, imaginative inspirations, but selections from the common stock of patriotic rhetoric. When her imagination leaves the beaten track, it is apt to go rather too far afield. In the following stanza, for instance, the first four lines are of the sonorous-commonplace order, while the last five belong rather to the imaginative-incongruous :

> Throned on the surety of a splendid past,
>> With present glory clothed as with the sun,
> Crowned with the future's hopes, you know at last
>> What treasure from the years your life has won ;
>>> Behold your hands hold fast
>> The moon of Empire, and its sway controls
> The tides of war and peace, while in those hands
> Lies tender homage out of all the lands
>> Against whose feet your furthest ocean rolls.

Here we have too much sun and moon and too many hands and feet. Queen Victoria is clothed "as with the sun," while she holds in her hands " the moon of Empire," which sways "the tides of war and peace." Even up to this point the image, for all its juggling with the orbs of heaven, is more violent than luminous. " The moon of Empire" is not a natural or illustrative figure ; it exists solely for the sake of swaying the tides, and is, therefore, a quirk of fancy,

a conceit, rather than a flash of imaginative vision.   But
when we find that the Queen holds in her hands, not only
the moon of Empire, but "tender homage" from the
Colonies, we cannot help feeling that she has altogether
too large a handful.   Then there is a distinct incongruity
in placing the Queen's "hands" on all-fours, so to speak,
with the "feet" of the Colonies.   The hands are real
hands, imaginatively conceived ; the feet are metaphoric feet,
belonging to a pure personification.   But "hands" and
"feet" are so closely associated in our mind that it gives us
a decided jolt to pass in a single sentence from one scale or
standard of imagination to another.   Here, again, is an
image which is neither novel nor congruous :

> Upon your river where, by day and night,
>   Your world-adventuring ships come home again,
> Glide ghostly galleons, manned by men of might,
>   Who plucked the wings and singed the beard of Spain.

Perhaps my ornithology is at fault, but it is surely a strange
fowl that has both wings to be plucked and a beard to be
singed.   There is, I repeat, a certain nobility of movement,
combined with real exaltation of feeling, in Miss Nesbit's
odes, but they will scarcely take lasting rank among the
poems of English patriotism.

In this, as in her earlier books, Miss Nesbit shows that
her real strength is centred in the pure lyric, whether
personal or semi-dramatic.   There is the germ of a psychological tragedy in the four stanzas of *The Refusal*, while
The Goose Girl and *The Pedlar* are quaint and delicate
ditties.   But it is in the simplicity of the sheer love-
song that Miss Nesbit touches her truest note, making
us forget her lack of verbal artistry in the fervour and intimacy of her emotion.   Here is a phase of feeling charmingly
rendered :

ENTREATY.

O Love, let us part now!
Ours is the tremulous, low-spoken vow,
Ours is the spell of meeting hands and eyes.
　　The first, involuntary, sacred kiss
Still on our lips in benediction lies.
O Love, be wise!
　　Love at its best is worth no more than this—
　　　　Let us part now!

O Love, let us part now!
Ere yet the roses wither on my brow,
Ere yet the lilies wither in your breast,
　　Ere the implacable hour shall flower to bear
The seeds of deathless anguish and unrest.
To part is best.
　　Between us still the drawn sword flameth fair—
　　　　Let us part now!

The stanzas entitled *By Faith with Thanksgiving* are more commonplace in idea, but have a genuine lyric glow; and the *Song of Long Ago*, and *Love well the Hour*, are delicate and charming pieces. This sonnet, the only one in the book, makes one regret that Miss Nesbit does not oftener cast her thoughts in sonnet form:

TOO LATE.

When Love, sweet Love, was tangled in my snare
　　I clipped his wings, and dressed his cage with flowers,
　　Made him my little joy for little hours,
And fed him when I had a song to spare.
And then I saw how good life's good things were,
　　The kingdoms and the glories and the powers.
　　Flowers grew in sheaves and stars were shed in showers,
And, when the great things wearied, Love was there.

But when, within his cage, one winter day
　　I found him lying still with folded wings,
　　No longer fluttering, eager to be fed—
Kingdoms and powers and glories passed away,
　　And of life's countless, precious, priceless things
　　　　Nothing was left but Love—and love was dead!

Among the nature-poems of this collection, *Ebb-Tide* and *Chains Invisible* stand out among the most successful; and *At Evening Time there shall be Light* is a vigorous piece of aerial landscape.

The first of my quotations from Miss Nesbit showed her intense sympathy with childhood, and the last shall exemplify the same all-pervading strain in her work. It is simply entitled:

DIRGE.

Let Summer go
To other gardens; here we have no need of her.
She smiles and beckons, but we take no heed of her,
   Who love not Summer, but bare boughs and snow.

Set the snow free
To choke the insolent triumph of the year,
With birds that sing as though he still were here,
   And flowers that blow as if he still could see.

Let the rose die—
What ailed the rose to blow? She is not dear to us,
Nor all the Summer pageant that draws near to us;
   Let it be over soon, let it go by!

Let Winter come,
With the wild mourning of the wind-tossed boughs
To drown the stillness of the empty house
   To which no more the little feet come home.

Such a Song of Love as this will—or I am no prophet—outlast many Songs of Empire.

THE GOLDEN ROSE.

A poor lost princess, weary and worn,
   Came over the down by the wind-washed moor,
And the king looked out on her grace forlorn,
   And he took her in at his palace door.

He made her queen, he gave her a crown,
   Bidding her rest and be glad and gay
In his golden town, with a golden gown,
   And a new gold lily every day.

But the crown is heavy, the gold gown gray,
   And the queen's pale breast is like autumn snows;
For he brings a gold lily every day,
   But no king gathers the golden rose.

One came at last to the palace keep
   By worlds of water and leagues of land,
Gray were his garments, his eyes were deep,
   And he held the golden rose in his hand.

She left gold gown, gold town, gold crown,
   And followed him straight to a world apart,
And he left her asleep on the wind-washed down,
   With the golden rose on her quiet heart.

MISS E. NESBIT

"AT EVENING TIME THERE SHALL BE LIGHT."

The day was wild with wind and rain,
   One grey wrapped sky and sea and shore,
It seemed our marsh would never again
   Wear the rich robes that once it wore.
The scattered farms looked sad and chill,
   Their sheltering trees writhed all awry,
And waves of mist broke on the hill
   Where once the great sea thundered by.

Then God remembered this His land,
   His little land that is our own,
He caught the rain up in His hand,
   He hid the winds behind His throne,
He soothed the fretful waves to rest,
   He called the clouds to come away,
And, by blue pathways, to the west
   They went, like children tired of play.

And then God bade our marsh put on
   Its holy vestment of fine gold;
From marge to marge the glory shone
   On lichened farm and fence and fold;
In the gold sky that walled the west,
   In each transfigured stone and tree,
The glory of God was manifest,
   Plain for a little child to see!

HENRY NEWBOLT

MR. NEWBOLT is known chiefly as a writer of patriotic lyrics
and ballads; but he began his literary career with a tragedy
which must not be overlooked if we would take the just
measure of his talent. *Mordred*, to my thinking, is scarcely
a success; but it is far from being, like so many modern
blank verse plays, a mere conventional futility. Its style is
nervous and clear-cut, with a good deal of really dramatic
feeling in it. Mr. Newbolt does not, like so many poets,
mistake rhetoric for drama, or imagine that intensity of
effect is to be sought in copiousness of utterance, or even
in vividness of imagery. His men and women express
themselves in credible human speech, ennobled indeed, but
not inflated and bedizened beyond recognition. Several
scenes in the play possess genuine life and movement;
and, as blank-verse dramas go, that is saying a great deal.
The tragedy falls short of complete success for two main
reasons, as it seems to me. First, Mr. Newbolt has handi-
capped himself by his choice of a theme; secondly, he has
handled his almost impossible theme in an undecided and
somewhat baffling fashion.

The poet, and especially the dramatist, who tackles the
Arthurian legend, necessarily finds himself in an awkward
dilemma. A realistic treatment (psychologically realistic I
mean) would strike us as grotesque and irreverent; while
the possibilities of romantic sentimentalism have been

· HENRY · NEWBOLT ·

exhausted by Tennyson. We may regret (though the regret is, I think, a trifle unphilosophic) that Tennyson made Arthur a Philistine paragon, and enveloped him in a golden haze of Early Victorian idealism. But the time has not yet come to rescue him (if, indeed, he be worth rescuing) from that "light that never was on sea or land." *The Idylls of the King*, whatever their dramatic or philosophic short-comings, are great in the essentials of pure poetry, and have powerfully impressed the national imagination. Therefore, while we smile at the Tennysonian "blameless king," any attempt to humanise him has inevitably the air of a parody. If we cannot take Tennyson's Arthur seriously, still less can we yield imaginative credence to a revised and corrected Arthur. The Arthurian legend, in short, has become, like the Gospel narrative, impossible for purposes of serious art. Its conventional poetry is exhausted, while whatever uncon-ventional poetry may be extracted from it is discounted in advance by the hold the conventional poetry has taken on our imagination. A realistic Arthur, whether the Arthur of Malory or another, could not but strike us as comic in his very contrast to the glorified waxwork (but how gloriously glorified!) of the Tennysonian allegory.

Mr. Newbolt has not overcome this initial difficulty. His hero seems to me to have put off the blamelessness of Tennyson's Arthur, while retaining a good deal of the priggishness. But stay! Is Arthur the hero, or Mordred? I do not know; and no more, I take it, does Mr. Newbolt. He prefaces his play with this citation from Hegel:

"In genuine tragedy, they must be powers both alike moral and justifiable, which from this side and from that come into collision. Two opposed Rights come forth: the one breaks itself to pieces against the other: in this way both alike suffer loss: while both alike are justified, the one towards the other; not as if this were right, that other wrong."

It appears then, that Mr. Newbolt seeks to exemplify this

theory of tragedy—the Kilkenny-cat theory, one is tempted to call it. We are invited to share our sympathy equally between Arthur and Mordred; but, unfortunately, the feeling they arouse in us—in me at any rate—is not sympathy at all, but its opposite. Mordred—Arthur's son by Morgance of Orkney—appears as a sort of moral anarchist, bent on upsetting the code of honour which, nominally at any rate, governs the Round Table. Holding the secret of Arthur's intrigue with Morgance as a threat over his head, he forces him to commit the most shameful and pusillanimous perversion of justice. This surrender of the king to what, in modern parlance, is known as blackmail, lowers the whole moral tone of the court. Lancelot and Guinevere, who have determined to remain blameless while Arthur sets them the example, at once feel the shackles of duty struck off, and rush to each other's arms. Tristram brings to a head his little affair with Iseult. Lamorak is killed by the brothers of a lady "whose life he had corrupted." In short, a contagion of licence spreads around, and at last Mordred, espousing the cause of Lancelot, takes up arms against his father. There is a final interview between the two, in which Mordred presents his ultimatum:

MORDRED.   He [Lancelot] hath sinned,
But say not, past forgiveness: drive him not
To justify his deed: set him again
To climb with stronger and more patient feet
The path he fell from; and to us his pardon
Shall be an earnest of the gentler rule
For which we humbly pray.

ARTHUR.   There thou'rt asking more—
Far more—than Lancelot's pardon.

MORDRED.   We do but crave
For freedom; every current of the time
Sets toward a kindly faith and tend'rer laws;
Only these vows oppress us, crying still
"Thou shalt not," in the ear of lusty youth,
To whom no voice should call but Nature's own,

> " Desire and dread not ; life is all too short,
> Too fair, too great, to mar with meaner hopes,
> This, this thou shalt, and this ! "

ARTHUR.   Ay, but those to whom
Despite of Nature these same meaner hopes
Are still the more endeared?

MORDRED.   There would be none !
Nay then if such there might be, I would cast them
Into the prison-house of loneliness,
The pit of life disfellowed : there to shiver
Till penitence should give them tears enough
To pay their ransom.

ARTHUR.   Thy trust were vain, ay ! vain
And perilous : there's evil in our blood
Twin-born with good, and claiming soon or late
His destined share of life's inheritance :
Whom tenderness but fosters.

MORDRED.   Nay, but 'tis not so
Put it to proof : the event shall bind us all.

Needless to say, the parley comes to nought; and in the battle which ensues, Arthur kills Mordred, while Mordred inflicts on his father a mortal wound, calling for the intervention of Bedivere, the barge and the Ladies of the Lake.

It seems to me, as above hinted, that in trying to write a tragedy of two heroes, Mr. Newbolt has only succeeded in writing a drama of two villains. Mordred and his half-brothers, Gawaine and Agravaine, are little better than a gang of sorry knaves. The misdeed of Gawaine, which Mordred forces Arthur to ignore, is not an ordinary breach of morals, which a humaner code would condone, but a flagrant act of treachery towards a friend ; while Arthur, in huddling the case out of sight, plays an utterly base part, and amply earns the contempt of Guinevere. I cannot think that Hegel's definition of " genuine tragedy " (very questionable at best) is in any sense exemplified by this clash of raw anarchism with conscience-stricken pusillanimity.

The verse of *Mordred* is always strong and supple. The above extract contains several examples of that practice of making the two halves of a broken line overlap, so to speak, which Shakespeare occasionally adopted, and which Mr. Newbolt, characteristically, elevates into a principle. For instance :

    For which we humbly pray
              (There) thou'rt asking more—
Far more—than Lancelot's pardon
              (We) do but crave.

One of the most genuinely dramatic scenes of the play is that in which Lancelot and Guinevere first confess their love. I extract from it the following passage :

LANCELOT.   I must part to-night
For Joyous Gard.

GUINEVERE.   Ah, 'tis trouble calls thee home,
Not the king's service ?   Then some rebel knight,
Grudging thine overlordship, thinks it easy
To brave an absent prince ; but thou'lt be gone
How long at most ?

LANCELOT.   I shall be gone the rest
Of all my life-days.

GUINEVERE.   Now may God defend thee!
But 'tis not like thy high victorious heart
To brood on danger.

LANCELOT.   Alas! you know me not!
I have brooded long, too long, and now must fly
Lest worse befall than danger.

GUINEVERE.   Thou must fly ?
When hast thou fled ?   But stay—'tis hence thou
    goest ;
The peril's here, then ?

LANCELOT.   Ay, most truly here,
Imminent—here and now !—farewell, my queen,
Farewell, I dare not linger.

GUINEVERE [*in a low voice*].   Peril here?
I know not—what—thou sayest—

LANCELOT.   You shall not know :
Only what's weakest in me could desire
That you should know : farewell !

GUINEVERE.   Stay, art thou not
Perchance too sudden, Lancelot, too resigned

To thine own weakness, when with patient craft
Or help of strong alliance, even yet
Thou might'st endure, and by enduring break
The onset of thy foes?

LANCELOT.   Oh, stay me not!
God knows I have endured! What is there left,
What patience, what alliance?

GUINEVERE.   Mine! the queen's!

LANCELOT. Oh, mockery! most unguarded stroke of all!
Thy words against their merciful intent
Drive the steel deeper.

GUINEVERE.   Nay, Lancelot, hear me yet,
What if this secret enemy of thine
Threatened me too? What if my life with thine
Lay strangling in the toils, the self-same toils,
Wild with one hope and dumb with one despair?

LANCELOT. Guinevere! Guinevere! What hast thou said?
I dare not understand thee!

GUINEVERE.   Must my tongue
Cry it more loudly than my beating heart?
Can'st thou not read a woman's eyes?

LANCELOT.   O Death!
Remember not my blind and faithless prayers,
Let not the end be yet!

Guinevere's lines ending,

> Wild with one hope and dumb with one despair,

are as beautiful as they are dramatically true and telling.
In the battle-scene at the close, we find a foretaste of
Mr. Newbolt's later achievements as a singer of "the
strength and splendour of England's war." How fine, for
instance, is this speech of Sir Bedivere's:

> I had liefer take
> As many blows unshielded, than recall
> The hundred partings that to-day hath knelled.
> Who is not fallen? Pertilope died first,
> Cut off from rescue; like a lonely rock,
> Now bare, now hidden by the swinging seas,
> We marked his crest awhile; then with a roar
> The full tide seethed above him.

289   T

The poet of *Marmion* would have applauded this passage; and I am sure Mr. Newbolt is not one of those who would undervalue his applause.

Mordred apart, Mr. Newbolt's poetical works are all comprised in one moderate-sized volume, *The Island Race*. The title of this book is one of its chief felicities, for three-fourths at least of Mr. Newbolt's pieces treat of the struggles and achievements of the Island Race, or, as he puts it in his *Hymn in Time of War and Tumults* :

> The race that strove to rule Thine earth
>   With equal laws unbought :
> Who bore for Truth the pangs of birth,
>   And brake the bonds of Thought.

Two other stanzas of this hymn I subjoin, as giving clear expression to the spirit in which Mr. Newbolt approaches his theme :

> Remember, Lord, the years of faith,
>   The spirits humbly brave,
> The strength that died defying death,
>   The love that loved the slave :
>
> *   *   *   *
>
> Remember how, since time began,
>   Thy dark eternal mind
> Through lives of men that fear not man
>   Is light for all mankind.

Mr. Newbolt, we see, is eminently a hero-worshipper, and eminently a believer in the mission of England. A dangerous faith, some may say, and one which may be easily used as a cloak for mere lust of empire. Mr. Newbolt, however, is alive to these dangers, and does not fail to give warning against them. The first poem in his book, for example, which sings of England's *Vigil* on the eve of war, drives home the thought expressed in this stanza :

> Hast thou counted up the cost,
>   What to foeman, what to friend ?
> Glory sought is Honour lost,
>   How should this be knighthood's end ?

HENRY NEWBOLT

> Know'st thou what is Hatred's meed?
> What the surest gain of Greed?
> England! wilt thou dare to-night
> Pray that God defend the Right?

The poem, as a whole, is not one of Mr. Newbolt's best.
There is more rhetoric than music in it; the sermon gets
the better of the song; but it is an excellent sermon and
evidently sincere. The same note recurs frequently in
Mr. Newbolt's verse. He is never tired of heartening the
Island Race to "Play up!" but he does not fail to add,
"And play the game!" He is a Clifton boy, as we learn
from more than one poem, and the best spirit of the English
public school breathes throughout his work. Simple as
they are, these two stanzas from *Clifton Chapel* seem to me
notably fine and touching. A father bids his son remember
his vows:

> To set the Cause above renown,
>   To love the game beyond the prize,
> To honour, while you strike him down,
>   The foe that comes with fearless eyes:
> To count the life of battle good,
>   And dear the land that gave you birth,
> And dearer yet the brotherhood,
>   That binds the brave of all the earth—

> * * * *

> God send you fortune: yet be sure,
>   Among the lights that gleam and pass,
> You'll live to follow none more pure
>   Than that which glows on yonder brass:
> "*Qui procul hinc,*" the legend's writ,—
>   The frontier-grave is far away—
> "*Qui ante diem periit:*
>   *Sed miles, sed pro patriâ.*"

The inweaving of Latin in English verse is a device to be
used sparingly; but I know of no instance in which it is
done with greater skill or happier effect than in this
stanza.

There is nothing frothy, then, nothing blusterous or
insincere, about Mr. Newbolt's patriotism. It is sad and

earnest rather than thoughtlessly exultant. In his fervent loyalty to a great tradition, Mr. Newbolt is almost morbidly mindful of the responsibilities it imposes. Courage, in his eyes, is still courage. He does not go about with a niggling analysis to prove that because bravery is not all pure virtue, it is not virtue at all. But he never forgets that courage is not an end in itself, but only a means to a higher end; or rather an indispensable constituent in that magnanimity without which, as he clearly and rightly understands, the world will never attain to a worthy and enduring peace. It is magnanimity, and no mere Chauvinism or brute daring, that he demands of the Island Race; and where he finds it in the past he celebrates it with contagious enthusiasm.

It is perhaps unfortunate that the *Vigil*, in which, as we have seen, the emphasis is somewhat rhetorical, should hold the first place in Mr. Newbolt's book. His other poems do not all attain one level of merit; some are but semi-successes; one or two (for instance, *The Gay Gordons*) I am inclined to think failures; but in all there is the true poetic impulse, with a glow of feeling and a vitality of phrase far beyond the reach of the mere rhetorician. His poems naturally group themselves in five classes—sea songs; ballads of naval history; ballads of Indian history; lyrics of patriotic sentiment; miscellaneous lyrics—and in each of these classes he has achieved more than one conspicuous success. His poetry has the peculiar advantage of growing upon the reader. You shall read a thing once and think it pretty enough but not remarkable; a second time, and note the delicate art beneath its simplicity; and, chancing upon it a third time, you shall find it quiver with feeling and fill, as it were, a predestined place in your heart.

It needs no second reading to realise the fine inspiration of *Drake's Drum*, certainly one of the best sea-songs in the language. I print it here as it first appeared in the

HENRY NEWBOLT

St. James's Gazette; Mr. Newbolt, in republishing it, placed the second stanza first. His reason is clear enough : he feels that the line, "Drake he's in his hammock an' a thousand mile away," is necessary to give meaning to the refrain, "Capten, art tha sleepin' there below?" Logically, no doubt, this is so ; but experience overrules logic, and as a matter of experience, we feel no difficulty in divining the sense of the refrain before we have reached its formal explanation. On the other hand, as I shall attempt to show presently, the order here adopted immensely heightens the general effect, and especially the sense of climax :

DRAKE'S DRUM.

Drake he was a Devon man, an' rüled the Devon seas,
  (Capten, art tha sleepin' there below ?)
Rovin' tho' his death fell, he went wi' heart at ease,
  An' dreamin' arl the time o' Plymouth Hoe.
"Take my drum to England, hang et by the shore,
  Strike et when your powder's runnin' low ;
If the Dons sight Devon, I'll quit the port o' Heaven,
  An' drum them up the Channel as we drummed them long
    ago."

Drake he's in his hammock an' a thousand mile away,
  (Capten, art tha sleepin' there below ?)
Slung atween the round shot in Nombre Dios Bay,
  An' dreamin' arl the the time o' Plymouth Hoe.
Yarnder lumes the island, yarnder lie the ships,
  Wi' sailor lads a-dancin' heel-an'-toe,
An' the shore-lights flashin', an' the night-tide dashin',
  He sees et arl so plainly as he saw et long ago.

Drake lies in his hammock till the great Armadas come.
  (Capten, art tha sleepin' there below ?)
Slung atween the round shot, listenin' for the drum,
  An' dreamin' arl the time o' Plymouth Hoe.
Call him on the deep sea, call him up the Sound,
  Call him when ye sail to meet the foe ;
Where the old trade's plyin' an' the old flag flyin',
  They shall find him ware an' wakin', as they found him long
    ago.

Nothing can possibly convince me that this is not the right, the heaven-appointed marshalling of these stanzas. In the opening line, as we read it above, the theme is quietly, simply announced : " Drake he was a Devon man, an' rüled the Devon seas " ; then the legend which inspires the singer is rapidly indicated, and the stanza reaches its racy and half-comic, yet thrilling, close :

> If the Dons sight Devon, I'll quit the port o' Heaven,
> An' drum them up the Channel as we drummed them long ago.

The second stanza heightens the emotion, and fixes the local colour. What admirable lines, both in sound and sugges-tion, are—" Slung atween the round shot, in Nombre Dios Bay," and " Wi' sailor lads a-dancin' heel-an'-toe " ! How finely the resonant Spanish words ring out in the former ! And how perfect is the effect, at once rhythmical and pictorial, of the latter ! But the chief merit of this stanza lies in its relation to the next—a relation of which the effect is entirely lost if the two stanzas are divorced from each other. With an art that partakes of inspiration, the opening lines of the one verse are half-repeated, half-transfigured in the other :

> Drake lies in his hammock—*till the great Armadas come* . . .
> Slung atween the round shot—*listenin' for the drum.*

Truly we owe a candle to Saint James of Compostella for the gift of the word " Armada," as glorious in sound as in associations ; and no poet has made finer use of it than Mr. Newbolt in this verse. If we should fall beneath our former selves " when the great Armadas come," it will not be for want of a singer to pipe us to quarters.

Scarcely inferior to *Drake's Drum* are three at least of Mr. Newbolt's other sea-songs : *The Fighting Téméraire* (which seems to me to want an additional stanza, between

its second and its third), *Admiral Death* and *Messmates*.
Here are two stanzas from *Admiral Death* :

> Boys, are ye calling a toast to-night ?
>   (Hear what the sea-wind saith)
> Fill for a bumper strong and bright,
>   And here's to Admiral Death !
> He's sailed in a hundred builds o' boat,
> He's fought in a thousand kinds o' coat,
> He's the senior flag of all that float,
>   And his name's Admiral Death.
>
> *   *   *   *
>
> How will ye know him among the rest ?
>   (Hear what the sea-wind saith)
> By the glint o' the stars that cover his breast
>   Ye may find Admiral Death.
> By the forehead grim with an ancient scar,
> By the voice that rolls like thunder far,
> By the tenderest eyes of all that are,
>   Ye may know Admiral Death.

This is fine ; but there is a subtler melody and a more
penetrating charm in *Messmates*, which I take leave to
quote entire :

> He gave us all a good-bye cheerily,
>   At the first dawn of day ;
> We dropped him down the side full drearily
>   When the light died away.
> It's a dead dark watch that he's a-keeping there,
> And a long, long night that lags a-creeping there,
> Where the Trades and the tides roll over him
>   And the great ships go by.
>
> He's there alone with green seas rocking him
>   For a thousand miles round ;
> He's there alone with dumb things mocking him,
>   And we're homeward bound.
> It's a long, lone watch that he's a-keeping there,
> And a dead cold night that lags a-creeping there,
> While the months and the years roll over him
>   And the great ships go by.

> I wonder if the tramps come near enough
> > As they thrash to and fro,
> And the battleships' bells ring clear enough
> > To be heard down below ;
> If through all the lone watch that he's a-keeping there
> And the long, cold night that lags a-creeping there
> The voices of the sailor-men shall comfort him
> > When the great ships go by.

With (or without) music worthy of it, this ought to take an enduring place among our lyrics of the sea.

Of Mr. Newbolt's naval ballads, the finest, to my thinking, is *The Death of Admiral Blake*, quoted at the end of this article. It is written in a four-line stanza, composed of alternate Archilochean verses and ordinary iambic pentameters, which is full of elegiac dignity and beauty. The first stanza may, for the moment, serve as a specimen.

> Laden with spoil of the South, fulfilled with the glory of achievement,
> > And freshly crowned with never-dying fame,
> Sweeping by shores where the names are the names of the victories of England
> > Across the bay the squadron homeward came.

To some readers this stanza may at first sight seem unpleasing, but it will not fail to grow upon them, and their ear will presently be haunted by the rush of such lines as :

> Sweeping by shores where the names are the names of the victories of England.

This magnificent hyperbole is, however, somewhat marred, to my sense, by the fact that it is dramatically an anachronism. In Blake's time the boast would not have been even hyperbolically true ; and we feel that in order to be perfectly appropriate the idea ought to be one that might conceivably have been present to the mind of Blake or of his comrades. Think how much more effective the line would be if we could substitute " were " for " are " ! As we cannot, the

idea remains a little out of the picture. Mr. Newbolt
should have reserved this line for a poem on the last home-
coming of Nelson.

More popular in its measure is *Admirals All*, which gave
its title to the first booklet (containing only twelve poems)
which brought Mr. Newbolt into notice. It is a stirring ditty,
with the refrain :

> Admirals all, for England's sake,
>   Honour be yours and fame !
> And honour, as long as waves shall break,
>   To Nelson's peerless name !

Here are three out of its half-dozen verses :

> Drake nor devil nor Spaniard feared,
>   Their cities he put to the sack ;
> He singed His Catholic Majesty's beard,
>   And harried his ships to wrack.
> He was playing at Plymouth a rubber of bowls
>   When the great Armada came ;
> But he said, " They must wait their turn, good souls,"
>   And he stooped, and finished the game.
>
> Fifteen sail were the Dutchmen bold,
>   Duncan he had but two ;
> But he anchored them fast where the Texel shoaled,
>   And his colours aloft he flew.
> " I've taken the depth to a fathom," he cried,
>   " And I'll sink with a right good will,
> For I know when we're all of us under the tide
>   My flag will be fluttering still."
>
> * * * *
>
> Admirals all, they said their say,
>   (The echoes are ringing still)
> Admirals all, they went their way
>   To the haven under the hill.
> But they left us a kingdom none can take,
>   The realm of the circling sea,
> To be ruled by the rightful sons of Blake,
>   And the Rodneys yet to be.

The Ballad of the Bold Menelaus is full of spirit and lilting melody. Excellent, too, is *Craven*, in which Mr. Newbolt is happily inspired to celebrate a heroic incident of the American Civil War. To this I shall return when I come to consider Mr. Newbolt as a metrist.

Of the poems of Indian history, the best, beyond a doubt, is the *Ballad of John Nicholson*, quoted at the end of this article. It is, to my thinking, flawless in workmanship, and a thing of the right heroic strain. *Gillespie* is inferior to *John Nicholson* only in that it does not tell its story quite so clearly. What happened when Gillespie rode up to the gate of Vellore—where the Sergeant's Guard was, and where the rebels—remains a trifle obscure to us. But of the spirit with which the ballad is written there can be no doubt. Gillespie, riding out of Arcot, "riding at dawn, riding alone," met a single horseman "staggering blind":

> " The devil's abroad in false Vellore,
>   The devil that stabs by night," he said,
> " Women and children, rank and file,
>   Dying and dead, dying and dead."

Quick as thought, Gillespie turned about, while "The blood roared in his ears like fire, Like fire the road beneath him burned." He thundered back to Arcot gate, and into the barrack yard :

> " Trumpeter. sound for the Light Dragoons,
>   Sound to saddle and spur," he said ;
> " He that is ready may ride with me,
>   And he that can may ride ahead."
>
> Fierce and fain, fierce and fain,
>   Behind him went the troopers grim,
> They rode as ride the Light Dragoons,
>   But never a man could ride with him.
>
> Their rowels ripped their horses' sides,
>   Their hearts were red with a deeper goad,
> But ever alone before them all
>   Gillespie rode, Gillespie rode.

In the simplicity of its means and the directness of its effect, this poem is a worthy pendent to the *Ballad of John Nicholson*. These two pieces should be in every school poetry-book, for, while they are stirring stories, they are also good literature. Less excellent, in spite of several strong touches, is *Seringapatam*, which requires a long note to explain it, and even then takes some thinking out. A ballad ought to be clear as daylight at the first reading. We should re-read it, not to cipher out its enigmas, but to admire the art which has made it clear, brief, and tense with significance.

Of Mr. Newbolt's poems of patriotic sentiment, I have already given some specimens above. Chief among them stand *Clifton Chapel*, *Vitaï Lampada* (with the refrain " Play up ! play up ! and play the game ! ") and *Ionicus*, a personal tribute to one whose influence has evidently held a chief place among those which have shaped Mr. Newbolt's thought :

> Beyond the book his teaching sped,
>   He left on whom he taught the trace
> Of kinship with the deathless dead,
>   And faith in all the Island Race.
> He passed : his life a tangle seemed,
>   His age from fame and power was far ;
> But his heart was high to the end, and dreamed
>   Of the sound and splendour of England's war.

One of these poems of patriotic sentiment, entitled *Minora Sidera*, brings us face to face with the question of the metrical peculiarities to which Mr. Newbolt is, in my judgment, too much addicted. It appears odd, at first sight, that a poet who, so to speak, lives by his rhythms, whose verses seem to prick their own tune as they sweep along, should be capable of such a line as the one here italicised—

> Such as were those, dogs of an elder day,
>   Who sacked the golden ports,
> *And those later who dared grapple their prey*
>   Beneath the harbour forts.

Nor does the wonder entirely vanish when we realise that Mr. Newbolt is here experimenting in classic prosody and writing asclepiads. I am too inexpert in antique measures to form any opinion as to whether his asclepiads are good or bad in themselves; but as English verse they seem to me intolerable. Such a line as

> But cared greatly to serve God and the king

may be excellent Latin; but it would certainly be much better English with the second and third words reversed ("greatly cared"). The Archilochean lines of *The Death of Admiral Blake* are very noble in their effect; but I suggest that Mr. Newbolt should classicise with caution.

I should be willing enough to suppose my dislike for his asclepiads a mere personal limitation, if I found his metrical tact in dealing with ordinary English measures entirely beyond dispute. But here again he often bewilders me. He is a student of his art, and always knows what he is about; wherefore I remonstrate with diffidence. But remonstrate I must. For instance, in the fine ballad called *Craven*, the crucial verse is to me, I own, a mere stone of stumbling and rock of offence. Let me first quote the two final stanzas, as examples of the normal measure of the piece :

> Sidney thirsting a humbler need to slake,
>   Nelson waiting his turn for the surgeon's hand,
> Lucas crushed with chains for a comrade's sake,
>   Outram coveting right before command,

> These were paladins, these were Craven's peers,
>   These with him shall be crowned in story and song,
> Crowned with the glitter of steel and the glimmer of tears,
>   Princes of courtesy, merciful, proud and strong.

In this measure eight stanzas out of nine are written, with perfect regularity. Take, now, the two in which the situation culminates—they require no explanation :

Over the manhole, up in the ironclad tower,
  Pilot and Captain met as they turned to fly:
The hundredth part of a moment seemed an hour,
  For one could pass to be saved, and one must die.

They stood like men in a dream: Craven spoke,
  Spoke as he lived and fought, with a Captain's pride,
"After you, Pilot:" the pilot woke,
  Down the ladder he went, and Craven died.

I ask myself in vain why, in this stanza, the first line should go short of a syllable (unless we make two syllables of "dre-am") and the third line follow a totally different metrical formula from the rest. Mr. Newbolt of course has his reasons. One may dimly divine that he thinks the necessary pause after "dream" equivalent to a syllable, and that somehow or other the metrical irregularity of the third line seems to him dramatic. I can only say that in neither case do I agree with him; nor do I believe, as a general principle, that dramatic effects are to be attained by baffling and disappointing the metrical sense. "When Ajax strives some rock's vast weight to throw," by all means let "the line too labour, and the words move slow"; but it is precisely the art of the accomplished metrist to achieve this effect within the limits of the metrical scheme which he has once for all imposed on himself.

Take, again, *The Guides at Cabul*, a stirring poem written in a purely English measure. Mr. Newbolt sets the normal model in the first stanza:

Sons of the Island Race, wherever ye dwell,
  Who speak of your fathers' battles with lips that burn,
The deed of an alien legion hear me tell,
  And think not shame from the hearts ye tamed to learn,
  When succour shall fail and the tide for a season turn,
To fight with a joyful courage, a passionate pride,
To die at the last as the Guides at Cabul died.

Here we have a stanza of free and varied but perfectly smooth-flowing dactylic-trochaic lines, and this model is

followed through the four following stanzas, except in one
line, " Twice toiled in vain to drag it back." But take now
the last stanza of all :

> Then the joy that spurs the warrior's heart
>   To the last thundering gallop and sheer leap
> Came on the men of the Guides ; they flung apart
>   The doors not all their valour could longer keep ;
>   They dressed their slender line ; they breathed deep,
> And with never a foot lagging or head bent,
> To the clash and clamour and dust of death they went.

Here the first, third, fourth, and seventh lines are normal,
but the second, fifth, and sixth are—I will not say, halting,
but deliberately baffling. Mr. Newbolt, of course, has his
reasons for his divergences from the norm. He probably
thinks that, by making the monosyllable " sheer" in the
second line fill the place of a trochee, he in some way
suggests or represents the leap of a horse over a precipice.
To me the suggestion is rather that of running one's head
against a stone wall. Perhaps he intends " shee-er" to be
read as a trochee, like the Elizabethan "fi-er"; but such
elongation destroys the whole force of the word. Similarly,
the fifth line can be saved from jarring only by the absurd
expedient of saying " breathèd" instead of " breath'd," while
by no expedient can the sixth line be forced into the measure
at all. One could divine (without approving) Mr. Newbolt's
motive for writing this line, if he were saying that the feet
did lag and the heads *were* bent. But why on earth should
he choose such a leaden and lagging measure for saying the
very opposite ?

One of his poems, *Væ Victis*, is written in Spenserian
stanzas, rendered almost unrecognisable by the incessant
elisions, or, as Mr. Newbolt would perhaps prefer to say,
the frequent anapæstic feet, which break up the stately
iambic movement—to my old-fashioned sense, the glory and
beauty of the stanza. Out of sixty-three lines, only twenty-

seven are regular.   Of the rest, perhaps half a dozen contain only such elisions or redundancies as Spenser or Shelley would have recognised as legitimate and beautiful.   In the remaining lines the metre loses its iambic character altogether, and becomes, in the main, anapæstic.   In the following stanza, for example, I italicise the redundant syllables—

> Beyond, where dawn was *a* glit*te*ring carpet, rolled
>   From sky to shore on lev*el* and endless seas,
> Hardly their eyes discerned *in* a daz*zle* of gold
>   That here in fifties, yon*der* in twos and threes,
>   The ships they sought, like *a* swarm of drowning bees
> By *a* wanton gust on *the* pool of *a* mill-dam hurled,
>   Floated forsak*en* of life-giv*ing* tide and breeze,
> Their oars broken, their sails for ever furled,
> For ev*er* desert*ed* the bul*warks* that guard*ed* the wealth of *the*
>   world.

Here it will be seen that only one line, the eighth, is free from redundance of some sort ; and in it we have a marked trochee in the second place, preceding, not following, a pause—the most violent of all departures from the regular iambic scheme.   It is impossible to call these innovations illegitimate, for there is no law in the matter, and scarcely any eccentricity for which some precedent may not be found, by diligent research, in the practice of some reputable poet. The question simply is : Are Mr. Newbolt's innovations, as a rule, beautiful ?   I answer unhesitatingly : To my ear, as a rule, they are not.

There is no lack of merit or charm in Mr. Newbolt's non-patriotic pieces, such as *Gavotte, Imogen, Invasion,* all of them remarkable for their metrical originality, if for nothing else.   From *The Last Word,* a noble ballad, I cull this one unforgettable verse :

> And now he saw with lifted eyes
> The East like a great chancel rise,
> And deep through all his senses drawn,
> Received the sacred wine of dawn.

What a masterly picture is this, again, from a characteristic copy of verses entitled *Moonset* :

> Soon
> We turn through a leafless wood, and there to the right,
> Like a sun bewitched in alien realms of night,
> Mellow and yellow and rounded hangs the moon.

Mr. Newbolt's lyre may not be of the widest range, but his touch on it is peculiarly his own—clean, and crisp, and ringing. I trust that, while not neglecting to strike a patriotic chord occasionally, he will in future cultivate the softer modes as well.

HENRY NEWBOLT

THE DEATH OF ADMIRAL BLAKE.

(*August 17th, 1657.*)

Laden with spoil of the South, fulfilled with the glory of achievement,
    And freshly crowned with never-dying fame,
Sweeping by shores where the names are the names of the victories
  of England,
    Across the Bay the squadron homeward came.

Proudly they came, but their pride was the pomp of a funeral at
  midnight,
    When dreader yet the lonely morrow looms ;
Few are the words that are spoken, and faces are gaunt beneath the
  torchlight
    That does but darken more the nodding plumes.

Low on the field of his fame, past hope lay the Admiral triumphant,
    And fain to rest him after all his pain ;
Yet for the love that he bore to his own land, ever unforgotten,
    He prayed to see the Western hills again.

Fainter than stars in a sky long gray with the coming of the day-
  break,
    Or sounds of night that fade when night is done,
So in the death-dawn faded the splendour and loud renown of
  warfare,
    And life of all its longings kept but one.

"Oh ! to be there for an hour when the shade draws in beside the
  hedgerows,
    And falling apples wake the drowsy noon :
Oh ! for the hour when the elms grow sombre and human in the
  twilight,
    And gardens dream beneath the rising moon.

Only to look once more on the land of the memories of childhood,
    Forgetting weary winds and barren foam :
Only to bid farewell to the combe and the orchard and the moorland,
    And sleep at last among the fields of home ! "

So he was silently praying, till now, when his strength was ebbing
    faster
    The Lizard lay before them faintly blue ;
Now on the gleaming horizon the white cliffs laughed along the
    coast-line,
    And now the forelands took the shapes they knew.

There lay the Sound and the Island with green leaves down beside
    the water,
    The town, the Hoe, the masts, with sunset fired—
Dreams ! ay, dreams of the dead ! for the great heart faltered on
    the threshold,
    And darkness took the land his soul desired.

A BALLAD OF JOHN NICHOLSON.

It fell in the year of Mutiny,
    At darkest of the night,
John Nicholson by Jalándhar came,
    On his way to Delhi fight.

And as he by Jalándhar came
    He thought what he must do,
And he sent to the Rajah fair greeting,
    To try if he were true.

" God grant your Highness length of days,
    And friends when need shall be ;
And I pray you send your Captains hither,
    That they may speak with me."

On the morrow through Jalándhar town
    The Captains rode in state ;
They came to the house of John Nicholson
    And stood before the gate.

HENRY NEWBOLT

The chief of them was Mehtab Singh,
   He was both proud and sly;
His turban gleamed with rubies red,
   He held his chin full high.

He marked his fellows how they put
   Their shoes from off their feet;
"Now wherefore make ye such ado
   These fallen lords to greet?

"They have ruled us for a hundred years,
   In truth I know not how,
But though they be fain of mastery,
   They dare not claim it now."

Right haughtily before them all
   The durbar hall he trod,
With rubies red his turban gleamed,
   His feet with pride were shod.

They had not been an hour together,
   A scanty hour or so,
When Mehtab Singh rose in his place
   And turned about to go.

Then swiftly came John Nicholson
   Between the door and him,
With anger smouldering in his eyes
   That made the rubies dim.

"You are overhasty, Mehtab Singh,"—
   Oh, but his voice was low!
He held his wrath with a curb of iron,
   That furrowed cheek and brow.

"You are overhasty, Mehtab Singh,
   When that the rest are gone,
I have a word that may not wait
   To speak with you alone."

The Captains passed in silence forth
   And stood the door behind;
To go before the game was played
   Be sure they had no mind.

But there within John Nicholson
  Turned him on Mehtab Singh,
" So long as the soul is in my body
  You shall not do this thing.

" Have ye served us for a hundred years
  And yet ye know not why?
We brook no doubt of our mastery,
  We rule until we die.

" Were I the one last Englishman
  Drawing the breath of life,
And you the master-rebel of all
  That stir this land to strife—

" Were I," he said, " but a Corporal,
  And you a Rajput King,
So long as the soul was in my body
  You should not do this thing.

" Take off, take off, those shoes of pride,
  Carry them whence they came;
Your Captains saw your insolence
  And they shall see your shame."

When Mehtab Singh came to the door
  His shoes they burned his hand,
For there in long and silent lines
  He saw the Captains stand.

When Mehtab Singh rode from the gate
  His chin was on his breast:
The Captains said, " When the strong command
  Obedience is best."

STEPHEN PHILLIPS

MR. STEPHEN PHILLIPS blazed suddenly into fame. The conductors of the *Academy*, realising that there must be contest and emulation—in other words, a sporting interest—in whatever is to fix the attention of the British public, determined to lend a sporting interest to literature by entering our living writers, willy-nilly, in a "selling race" for one hundred sovereigns. The judges to whom they appealed (I know not on what principle selected) pronounced Mr. Phillips's *Poems* the most remarkable book of the previous year, and he became, for the moment, almost as illustrious as a successful jockey or a "century-compiling" cricketer.

He was not a beginner in poetry. He had contributed two or three pieces of no particular note to a booklet entitled *Primavera*, published at Oxford in 1890; the other contributors being Mr. Laurence Binyon, Mr. Arthur S. Cripps, and Mr. Manmohan Ghose. Then, in 1894, he published what is as yet his longest poem, *Eremus*. As he has not reprinted it, and makes no allusion to it, on the title-page or elsewhere, in his *Poems* of 1898, one may almost conclude that he wishes it to be forgotten. It is worthy of a better fate; for if it shows something of the poet's weakness, it gives more than a foretaste of his finest strength. *Eremus* is a blank-verse rhapsody of some 1300 lines, expounding, in the form of a vision, a fantastically pessimistic philosophy. It is marred by the lack of constructive and dramatic instinct which we shall notice again in Mr. Phillips's later work. The machinery is tedious and absurd. Eremus, taken suddenly ill in a cathedral, begs two friars to carry him up to "yon hills of everlasting snow." They do so; and there he relates to them how the Spirit of the Wind—an angel, not "fallen" it would seem, yet inimical to God—bore him beyond the confines of the universe into the region where Chaos

> With sounding, sad waves, everlastingly
> Breaks sullen on the walls of builded light;
> And where unpardoned, hopeless, homeless things
> Wander, no limit to their wandering set.

There, first, he met the shade of a friend of his, one Julian, and held converse with him. Then, after passing through a region infested with feeble eighteenth-century personifications—Fears, Dread, Apprehensions, Impulses, Suggestions, Doubt, Despair—he arrives with his guide in the limbo of ruined stars, woefully guttering out in the inane, and realises that the Creator is, not precisely an "Aristophanes on high," but a sort of ruthless dramaturge for ever making worlds and peopling them for his own æsthetic enjoyment, and then leaving them to drift to the ignoble end of burnt-out fireworks. On his return to earth, this discovery so haunts him that he cannot live; wherefore, after due impartment of his extra-mundane experiences to the two irrelevant but patient friars, he dies among the snows, and they, like the King of France, come down the hill again. I confess I can discover no merit of invention in this fable. It would have been hard to devise a less interesting framework for the vision; and the vision itself lacks that clear significance, that provisional plausibility, so to speak, which an artist in narrative would have given it. But the writing throughout is attractive, and there are many

· STEPHEN · PHILLIPS ·

STEPHEN PHELPS

majestic and memorable passages, especially in the later
cantos. Mr. Phillips's blank verse has not yet attained its
full individuality; it is still, on the whole, unmistakably
Tennysonian, though Miltonic pauses and constructions
break through now and then; but, on the other hand, it is
comparatively free from those metrical eccentricities which
mar some of the poet's maturer work. Here is a fine
passage before the coming of the Angel:

> As one who, in the still
> And deepest noontide, hears the far-off storm
> Crawl up the heavens; then thunder, and a hush,
> And in the pause the world is filled with rain!
> Even so I felt the distant approach of doom
> Breathless.

Here, again, is a really memorable image:

> And I beheld, far off as 'twere, mankind
> Shivering about the fire of this world's star,
> While in the darkness ranged mysterious powers;
> Like those who round a blazing circle sit
> In a vast forest watched by wild beasts' eyes.

"And hast thou power," says Eremus to the Spirit of the
Night,

> to bring me face to face
> With Truth, sad spirit, older even than God?

—surely a noble line. In these verses the voyagers' first
leap into space is vividly described:

> "Come!" said the Spirit; and even at his word
> The great earth downward flashes from our feet,
> A star, fast fading 'mid a thousand stars.

Eremus's friend Julian—a Byronic personage, one cannot
but own—is characterised in the following remarkable
image:

> On thee God flung the fires of his delight,
> But gave thee no control, and let thee drive

> Like some tall ship aflame, that, throwing off
> Spar after blazing spar upon the waves,
> Down the great melancholy waters, burns.

Perhaps the strongest thing in the poem (too long to quote) is Julian's apostrophe to his love, whom he has met in the shades only to be severed from her again. It is one of the very few really dramatic passages in Mr. Phillips's work and moves with a passionate dignity. He says:

> We met, we loved,
> And nothing evermore can alter that;
> It has been, and can never not have been.

And again:

> And in thy soul are chambers sealèd up,
> Rooms passion-haunted, sacred unto me,
> Of which I keep the key for evermore!

And yet again:

> Yet even her at times I lose awhile,
> I cannot ever cling to her, for as
> The strength of some strong word upon the tongue
> Repeated oft, in repetition dies,
> So she, whom I repeat unto myself
> For evermore, to keep me from despair,
> At length becomes far-off, impossible.

The Angel, too, is very eloquent when his turn comes. I quote the following passage for the sake of two beautiful lines in the middle and an incredible line at the close:

> Hail, elements! I call to you as friends.
> Soon comes the hour, when we and ancient Night
> Rising, shall wash away this stranger God,
> Who, in a dream of beauty glowing, rose
> And fevered darkness with a thousand stars.
> . . . . From that lax hand the thunderbolt
> Drops: he hath called, but none obeys his voice;
> Night, stride upon stride, blots out his worlds!

Scan this, men and angels!   Are we to read it

> Night, stri-ed upon stride, blots out his worlds?

But I shall return presently to the question of versification.   In the meantime let me quote the striking passage from the ninth canto in which the Angel denounces the omnipotent Nero, the sceptred "artifex," ruthless in the pursuit of æsthetic sensation, whom he sees in the Creator of the universe:

> That vast cold spirit of the Beautiful
> Which men call God, in his advance and march
> Sweeps onward, flashing out more glorious stars,
> Lighting more splendid suns, crowding new spheres
> With mightier beings ; but, ever and anon,
> If, for a moment, he may rest from toil,
> There comes into his ear the far-off cry
> Of ruined worlds that he hath left behind.
> Then he arises, shaking from his ears
> That jarring sound, and spreads once more his wings,
> Conceiving, and creating, and accursed !

There are many other fine passages in *Eremus*—for instance, the concluding lines describing the descent of the two friars from the eternal snows into the valley.   If Mr. Phillips does not care to republish it as it stands, he might do well to re-write and perhaps enlarge it.   The Vision contains much that is well worth preservation.

The verse as a whole is of smooth, firm texture.   The line above quoted is the chief stumbling-block (can it be misprinted?); but there are three lines in which Mr. Phillips places a dissyllabic participle in the last foot, thus producing, to my ear, a totally inadmissible effect.

> While worlds may come and go; falling, falling. . . .
> Who, as some prisoner after long watching. . . .
> Began to fail, and in the stars fading. . . .

There are three lines, according to Mr. Robert Bridges, in which Milton seems to sanction this "inverted fifth stress," as Mr. Bridges terms it. But a choir of Miltons chanting in unison could not make such verses other than a torture to my ear; and in fact I am convinced that in no case did Milton intend the fifth foot to be read as an "inverted stress," or, to put it more briefly if less accurately, as a trochee. Milton's lines, it should be noted, end, not with a participle or any other word which absolutely excludes the accentuation of the last syllable, but with three words of Latin origin which have only to be accented in the Latin fashion to make the required iambic foot. Here are the verses in question:

> Beyond all past example and future. . . .
> Which of us who beholds the bright surface. . . .
> Of Thrones and mighty Seraphim prostrate . . . .

Mr. Bridges assures us that elsewhere Milton accents these three words as we do, on the penult; but he may quite well have thought it admissible, on occasion, to revert to the Latin accentuation:—"futùrus," "superfìcies," "prostràtus." To say "fallìng," "watchìng," "fadìng" is manifestly absurd, emphasising as it does, not the word itself, but its inflexional appendage, and thus making the tail wag the dog. Until some such unmistakable trochee can be quoted in the fifth foot of a Miltonic line, I shall still hold that Milton's ear agreed with mine and disagreed (we must assume) with Mr. Phillips's. It is to be noted that an occasional variation of accent in words in which it does not run counter to the sense is a beauty rather than a blemish. Thus one can accept without demur this line from *Eremus:*

> Suddenly felt the wild impùlse to spring,

just as one accepts not only without demur but with delight this line of Mr. Francis Thompson's:

> But shall triùmph upon my lips in heaven.

Mr. Thompson, to be sure, has precedent in Milton and elsewhere for "triùmph"; but even if he had shifted the accent on his own responsibility, I, for one, should certainly have raised no protest.

This question of accent in verse meets us again when we come to *Christ in Hades*, Mr. Phillips's second independent publication, and the one of all his poems which has attracted most attention. I read it on its appearance in 1896, and found my pleasure in it seriously marred, I own, by the frequent shocks it inflicted on my metrical sense, or, if you will, my metrical prejudices. I rebelled against the length to which Mr. Phillips carried the modern fashion of ignoring accent and bestrewing his iambic lines with trochaic pitfalls; and it was not till his *Poems* appeared (including *Christ in Hades*) that I began truly to relish his talent. The pitfalls are not removed from *Christ in Hades*, but they are much less frequent in other, and presumably later, poems; and, in any case, he had now proved his right to a few caprices by showing himself capable, when he pleased, of sustained nobility and beauty of metre. None the less must one marvel that he should also be capable of his occasional eccentricities. It is true that he is merely following a tendency of the time, and that several other poets of real ability make a practice of slighting or deliberately misplacing accent. But the justification of this tendency I am yet to seek. Is it a mere obstinacy of conservatism to protest that to my ear the syllables "O all fresh out of beautiful sunlight" do not make a blank verse line at all? The natural accent—the accent demanded by the meaning— falls on "O" and "fresh" and "sun"; the metrical accent falls on "all" and "out" and "light"; and what becomes of the iambic pentameter when, in three out of the five feet, the natural accent and the metrical accent clash?

The art of blank verse, no doubt, lies in judiciously relieving the monotony of the insistent iambic. But this clearly cannot be done by the mere haphazard introduction of foreign feet. There must be a limit to permissible departure from the normal and regular line, and in the great poets we find very little uncertainty as to where this limit falls. What little uncertainty there is arises, I think— let me take my critical life in my hands and say it right out—from over-reverence for the authority of Milton. I yield to no one in my admiration for that noblest achievement, of the metrical genius of our race, the Miltonic period; but there are lines in *Paradise Lost*—not many; perhaps, at a venture, a hundred out of ten thousand—that appear to me frankly ugly and of evil precedent. That is only my personal feeling, indeed; but several poets of repute appear to have agreed with me, for, until recent years, these lines have not been imitated. Nowadays, it seems to be thought that the best way to rival Milton is to imitate and even outdo his audacities. Milton, for example, occasionally (but very rarely) begins a line with two trochees, or, in Mr. Bridges' phrase, with an inversion of both the first and the second stress—thus:

> Univèrsal reproach, far worse to bear. . . .
> By the wàters of life, where'er they sat. . . .

For Mr. Phillips, consequently, such a line as this has no terrors:

> Agamemnon bowed over, and from his wheel.

To my ear, this is a mere cacophony; and so it would have seemed, I have little doubt, to Shakespeare.* If we turn to *Troilus and Cressida*, we find the word " Agamemnon " always so placed as to fit into, not jar with, the iambic

---

* Note Benedick's speech (*Much Ado*, V. 2): " Leander the good swimmer, Troilus the first employer of panders, and a whole book-full of these quondam carpet-mongers, *whose names yet run smoothly in the even road of blank verse*—why, they were never so truly turned over and over as my poor self in love."

scheme of the verse, and never, consequently, beginning a
line.   For instance :

> O Agamemnon! let it not be so. . . .
> It is not Agamemnon's sleeping hour. . . .
> Sir, pardon ; 'tis for Agamemnon's ears. . . .
> Which is the high and mighty Agamemnon ? . . .

There are four positions in a blank verse line in which the
word "Agamemnon" is possible, and Shakespeare places
it repeatedly in each of these positions, and in no other.
Had he thought a fifth possible, is it to be imagined that
he would have neglected it ?   I shall no doubt be told that
the ear of Mr. Phillips and some other young poets is
cultivated to a point undreamt of by Shakespeare.   Well,
mine is not ; and that is why such lines as the following set
my teeth on edge :

> Gentle and all in*jured*.   Art thou a god ? . . .
> Reali*zes* all the uncoloured dawn. . . .
> The bird sett*ling* ?   Hath no friend covered up. . . .
> The bright glo*ry* of after-battle wine. . . .
> And one year*ning* as wide as is the world. . . .

Read these lines naturally, and they are not verse at all,
but prose ; and good verse, to my thinking, is not prose
read unnaturally.

There is great need for an examination into the psychological basis of the pleasure and displeasure we receive
from variations of normal metrical form.   Mr. Bridges'
work, which I have so often quoted, on *Milton's Prosody*, is
an invaluable contribution to such an inquiry; but Mr.
Bridges confines himself to grouping facts and deducing
rules, without inquiring into reasons.   Reasons, however,
must exist, and must surely be discoverable, for a hundred
facts of common experience.   For instance, an inversion of
stress in the first foot of a blank verse line is so unquestion-

ably agreeable that we scarcely notice it, and so frequent that it may almost be regarded as normal. For instance :

> Sìng, heavenly muse, that on the secret top. . . .
> Règions of sorrow, doleful shades, where peace. . . .

Or in Shakespeare:

> Ò, what a rogue and peasant slave am I !
> Ìs it not monstrous that this player here
> Bùt in a fiction, in a dream of passion, &c.

Or in Tennyson:

> The lily maid of Astolat,
> Hìgh in her chamber up a tower to the east
> Guàrded the sacred shield of Lancelot.

Or in Mr. Phillips :

> Kèen as a blinded man, at dawn awoke,
> Smèlls in the dark the cold odour of earth,
> Sò the excluded ghosts in Hades felt.

Equally clear is it that an inversion of stress in the second foot is most unusual and, to the majority of ears, highly unpleasing; that the stress may with much more freedom be inverted in the third or fourth place ; and that in the last foot of the line the regular iambic stress is (except to Mr. Phillips, Mr. Yeats, and one or two other young poets) absolutely imperative. The above-noted cases of a trochaic fifth foot in Milton, even if they were not extremely doubtful, are too infinitesimally few to constitute a precedent. These marked "likes and dislikes" of the metrical sense cannot be mere matters of habit or of convention. There must be some psychological law behind them. Again, it is indubitable that in any place in the line an inversion of stress is much less noticeable after a marked pause.* For instance, look at these two lines of Milton:

> For one restraint, lords of the world beside. . . .
> Which, tasted, works knowledge of good and evil. . . .

In both of these lines there is an inverted stress in the third foot; but we do not notice it at all in the former line, because the trochee ("lords of") immediately follows a marked pause. Until we consciously scan it, the line strikes us as perfectly normal; while the second line, on absolutely the same model except for the pause, at once strikes us as abnormal. Or let us take an example from Mr. Phillips. I have protested against the line—

> Gentle and all injured. Art thou a god?—

where the inversion occurs in the third foot; but here is another line, with an equally marked trochee in the third place, which is not only beautiful but does not even strike one as in the least abnormal:

> He comes, he comes! Yet with how slow a step.

What, then, is the difference between the two lines? Simply that in the latter the trochee follows, while in the former it does not follow but precedes, a marked pause. It is not any difference in quantity† or sonority that makes

---

* This principle of the pause excuses, if it does not justify, the trochaic second foot in this line from *Christ in Hades*—

> Gazing; only was heard that river steal.

It does not seem to me a beautiful line, but the pause after " Gazing " renders it tolerable.

† It cannot be doubted that quantity has often to be taken into account in these questions. For instance, though a trochee in the second place almost inevitably jars, a spondee does not. I find it a little difficult to understand why the inverted stress in the second place of the line

> Of man's first disobedience and the fruit

the difference in beauty, as we can prove by putting the very word "injured" in a line made for the purpose. For instance:

> He comes, he comes! Injured but undismayed.

This is a passable line enough. At any rate, it strikes the ear as perfectly normal in contrast to:

> Gentle and all injured. Art thou a god?

These are not, I repeat, questions of rules or convention, but of instinctive sensation; yet I am not aware that any attempt has been made to explain why one inversion of stress seems beautiful, while another is hideous, and a third practically impossible. A rational theory of this very simple phenomenon would take us a long way towards the solution of other mysteries of metre.

In the absence of such a theory, one may perhaps put this point to Mr. Phillips and his fellow innovators: These metrical eccentricities are either beautiful or not beautiful; in the former case, why use them so seldom? in the latter case, why use them at all? If, for example, the line

> The bird settling? Hath no friend covered up . . . .

is beautiful, why should there be (after all) only four or five lines of this beautiful type in a poem of over three hundred

is beautiful rather than jarring, unless it be that the almost equal stress on the syllables of the second foot (" first dis ") produces something of a spondaic effect. Again, in *Christ in Hades* there occur these lines—

> Motionless in an ecstacy of rain . . . .
> Easily from immortal torment? yet . . . .

to my ear beautiful lines, because the second foot is not trochaic but consists of two equally *un*stressed syllables. The relation (or indeed the true distinction) between accent and quantity in English verse has not yet, so far as I know, been worked out with any clearness, though Mr. T. S. Omond seems to be on the track of it.

lines? If a dissyllabic participle makes a beautiful ending to a blank verse line, as in

> While worlds may come and go ; falling, falling,

why should there be only three lines on this model out of the thirteen hundred lines of *Eremus* ? The same point may be suggested to Mr. Bridges, who, reading "surface" with its ordinary trochaic accent in the line

> Which of us who beholds the bright surface,

declares it to be "a very beautiful inversion." If Milton intended the inversion and thought it "very beautiful," why did he, on Mr. Bridges' own showing, indulge us with only three such beautiful inversions in all the ten thousand and odd lines of *Paradise Lost* ? Milton, as I have urged above, probably did not intend this particular inversion at all ; and as for our living poets, I think the very infrequency of their aberrations establishes a valid presumption against their beauty ; since it surely cannot be pretended that (for example) the three participial endings in *Eremus* produce a particular descriptive effect, which is appropriate in these three places and would have been inappropriate anywhere else. If their ears are, in truth, more highly educated than ours, the innovators (or Miltonisers) ought really to make a systematic effort to spread the gospel of the trochaic second and fifth foot.

* *
*

[Soon after this paper was written, there occurred a most interesting controversy between Mr. Stephen Phillips and Mr. James Douglas (in several numbers of the *Star* between August 16 and September 3, 1898), on the question of Mr. Phillips's metrical peculiarities. It proved, what I, for one, never doubted, that Mr. Phillips is an earnest student of metre, and Miltonises with a full knowledge of what he is about. Mr. Douglas having, by implication, accepted Milton as a supreme authority, absolutely incapable of producing an unbeautiful line, Mr. Phillips held him in the hollow of his hand. If this were purely a question of authority, discussion might cease at once. But it is not a question of one man's authority, or even of that generalised authority which we call a set of rules. It is a question of sensation. When a line hurts me—yes, physically hurts me, like a fly in my eye or a nail in my shoe—I cannot help crying out, though Milton himself should rise from his grave to swear that it is beautiful. Now that is the case with (for instance)

> O all fresh out of beautiful sunlight,

which, Mr. Phillips tells us, is certified, if not by Milton himself, at least by his terrene plenipotentiary, Mr. Robert Bridges, as "the best in the poem." Well, Mr. Bridges' ear and mine are differently constituted, it would seem: at all events differently educated: and Mr. Phillips naturally prefers pleasing himself and Mr. Bridges to pleasing me. At the same time, as I see in Mr. Phillips a poet likely to have influence upon the coming generation, not to say generations, of singers, I venture to add a few words to the humble remonstrance I have already addressed to him.

Mr. Phillips will do me the justice to recognise that my sole desire in the matter is to be able to enjoy his poetry without reservation, and that the reservations I make on these points of metre do not arise from any pedantic application of mechanical and half understood rules, but are a veritable cry of the heart, or at any rate of the nerves. I claim no special consideration for my nerves. If they are singular they must e'en suffer for it. But I think Mr. Phillips would do well to consider whether it is my nerves or his that are singular, and whether, in such lines as the one I have chosen for an example, he is not, in obedience to a personal whim, inflicting needless pain on the great majority of educated and sensitive readers. Singular, in the literal sense of the word, Mr. Phillips is not, since he has Mr. Bridges with him. But I suggest that Mr. Bridges and he have steeped themselves in Milton until our torments have become their elements, and the handful of ugly lines in *Paradise Lost*, the lines in which the poet's ear showed signs of fatigue, now seem to them the lines best worth imitating and outdoing. Yes, outdoing; for I do not remember in any regular blank verse poem of Milton's, nor do I find in Mr. Bridges' *Milton's Prosody*, a line really analogous to

O all fresh out of beautiful sunlight.

Readers of poetry may, I think, be divided into three classes: those who have no metrical sense, those who have a normal metrical sense, more or less highly developed, and those who have deliberately cultivated a taste for the abnormal and eccentric. The first class must not be entirely left out of account. They often really enjoy, and to a certain extent appreciate, poetry, though of its metrical attributes they have only the vaguest consciousness. It is a matter of total indifference to them how many feet there are in a line, and how the accents fall. And their metre-deafness is strictly analogous to colour-blindness, in that they are unconscious of it. Many actors belong to this class. They will say, "The lover, the lùnatic and the poet," and think it every bit as good a line as "The lunatic, the lover, and the poet." Mr. Phillips, I presume, does not address himself, as a metrist, to readers of this class: let him ask himself whether some of the critics who yield him unqualified applause as a metrist do not perchance belong to it? He would hardly care to allege in defence of

O all fresh out of beautiful sunlight

the approval of a reader who did not perceive the metrical
difference between this line and (say):

How fast thy words incarnadine the world.

That the normal ear is offended by such a line as "O all
fresh out of beautiful sunlight" Mr. Phillips can scarcely
doubt. Mr. James Douglas and I by no means stand
alone in our objection to it. Many other critics have cried
out upon Mr. Phillips's metrical mannerisms; and that
admirable metrist, Mr. Owen Seaman, has parodied them
most tellingly. I have scarcely ever met a reader of Mr.
Phillips's verse who did not admit that these mannerisms
tended to mar his pleasure. Mr. Phillips may perhaps
relegate Mr. Douglas, myself, and the rest of the objectors,
to the class of the verse-deaf. In that case, I can only say
that he finds among the verse-deaf the overwhelming
majority of his admirers. No; the fact is that Mr. Douglas
and I represent the second of the three classes—the people
of normal and normally-cultivated metrical sense—and
Mr. Phillips must excuse us if we regard it as a somewhat
excessive asperity on his part to reject our remonstrances
with the remark that " because *we* cannot scan a line, it by
no means follows that the line is unscannable." Any line
is "scannable" if every conceivable divagation from the
normal form is to be held legitimate. But to scan a line is
not to prove it beautiful; and all we ask is that Mr. Phillips
should be content with the ideal of beauty which is good
enough for him (and for us) in, say, ninety-seven lines out
of every hundred, and should not write the remaining three
lines for the private satisfaction of himself and Mr. Bridges.
He ought, in sheer humanity, to think of the greatest good
of the greatest number. After all, the three lines would
not positively hurt Mr. Bridges' ear if they obeyed the laws
that govern the ninety-seven; whereas in not obeying them

they do positively hurt the ear of hundreds and thousands of readers.

Mr. Phillips may possibly impugn my classification and declare that there is no class of men "who have deliberately cultivated a taste for the abnormal and eccentric" in metre. I, on the other hand, not only assert that such a class exists, but believe that I can account for its existence. It has its origin in two very obvious facts: first, the proverbial truth that Homer sometimes nods, that even the greatest poet will now and then write a cacophonous, a vicious line; second, the scarcely less obvious fact that by dwelling sufficiently long on almost anything, the human mind at last comes to find some sort of beauty and fitness in it. The metrical specialists, if I may call them so, begin by ignoring the former fact and assuming the absolute infallibility of Milton; and then, by long poring over the abnormal lines in Milton (rendered conspicuous by their very abnormality) they come at last to think them the most beautiful he ever wrote. We all know how quickly a thing encysts itself in the mind, as a bullet does in the body, and comes to seem the right thing in the right place, simply because it has made a place for itself into which it fits with seemingly predestined accuracy. For example, by the mere process of dwelling upon it, I am becoming almost reconciled to the line

> Agamemnon bowed over, and from his wheel.

My metrical education is progressing, Mr. Phillips will say. But no! I cannot lay that flattering unction to my soul. The fact is simply that the two initial trochees, which formerly set all my nerves ajar, have now hammered for themselves, as it were, a little indentation or socket in my mind, into which they slip easily, and with a sort of click. It would be straining language to say that I find the line beautiful; but it now amuses instead of distressing me. On the other hand, I do not find "O all fresh out of beautiful sunlight" perceptibly encysting itself. Life is too short for the consummation of such a process.

Is it denied that great poets are capable of writing bad lines, even in mature work? What does Mr. Phillips say, for instance, to these lines from *Aylmer's Field*?

> With a weird bright eye, sweating and trembling. . . .
> Arguing boundless forbearance: after which . . . .

Perhaps he may declare the first to be a good line, as it seems to bear out one of his own heresies; but since the writer is Tennyson, not Milton, I imagine he will confess the second to be unmelodious. Such lines are exceedingly rare in Tennyson, as they are in Milton. I own it puzzles me to conceive how Tennyson could ever have written them, since there is no reason to suppose that he was deliberately Miltonising; and indeed I do not believe that any parallels to these particular lines are to be found in Milton. Still, there they are, and there is no reason to suppose them corrupt. If, then, such lines are to be found in Tennyson, in the proportion of, say, one to a thousand (a very large admission)* is that any reason why a poet of to-day should imitate them in the proportion of two or three to a hundred, and then tell us, if we protest, that we do not read our Tennyson?

But it is really in the infrequency, rather than the frequency, of his aberrations that the weakness of Mr. Phillips's

* The line in *Lucretius*:

> For look! what is it? there? yon arbutus?

merely proves, I take it, that Tennyson accented "arbutus" on the first syllable; just as this, from *The Princess*:

> And leaning there on those balusters, high,

proves that, for the nonce at any rate, he accented "balusters" on the second. [Since writing the above, I have come across proof positive that Tennyson accented the first syllable of "arbutus." See A. J. C. Hare, *Story of My Life*, October 8, 1877.]

position seems to me to lie. To this point I inevitably return : If Mr. Phillips is battling for a principle, if he has vowed to impress upon a recalcitrant generation the beauty of "O all fresh out of beautiful sunlight," and to vindicate for poets yet unborn the liberty to invert as many stresses as they please, then it is his bounden duty to write a far larger proportion of such lines, even if his reputation perish in the attempt.]

*　*
*

My unfortunate first impression of *Christ in Hades*, due mainly to these metrical irregularities, has never entirely worn off. The poem gives me less pleasure than either its predecessor, *Eremus*, or its successor, *Marpessa*. Its craftsmanship, no doubt, is more original than that of *Eremus*, and its idea is bold and striking. But the execution, or rather the elaboration, does not seem to me worthy of the subject. It is rather a study for a *Christ in Hades* than a finished treatment of the theme. Innumerable possibilities are, of course, left undeveloped, some of which ought surely to have tempted the poet; and the few which he has selected are not developed to the pitch of their possible significance. Take, for instance, the episode of Jesus' meeting with Virgil :

> But in his path a lonely spirit stood ;
> A Roman, he who from a greater Greek
> Borrowed as beautifully as the moon
> The fire of the sun: fresh come he was, and still
> Deaf with the sound of Rome : forward he came
> Softly ; a human tear had not yet dried.
> "Whither," he said, " O whither dost thou lead
> In such a calm all these embattled dead ?
> Almost I could begin to sing again,
> To see these nations burning run through Hell,
> Magnificently anguished, by the grave
> Untired ; and this last March against the Powers.
> Who would more gladly follow thee than I ?

But over me the human trouble comes.
Dear gladiator pitted against Fate,
I fear for thee: around thee is the scent
Of over-beautiful, quick-fading things,
The pang, the gap, the briefness, all the dew,
Tremble, and suddenness of earth: I must
Remember young men dead in their hot bloom,
The sweetness of the world edged like a sword,
The melancholy knocking of those waves,
The deep unhappiness of winds, the light
That comes on things we never more shall see.
Yet I am thrilled: thou seemest like the bourne
Of all our music, of the hinting night,
Of souls under the moonlight opening."

This is fine, no doubt, or at any rate there are fine phrases
in it; but is it quite adequate to the situation? Might not
the Mantuan have found deeper and lovelier things to
say to the Galilean? Much more striking is the prophecy
of Prometheus, the most dramatic passage, certainly, in
the poem:

Prepare thee for the anguish! Thou shalt know
Trouble so exquisite, that from his wheel
Happy Ixion shall spare tears for thee;
And thou shalt envy me my shadowy crag
And softly-feeding vulture. Thou shalt stand
Gazing for ever on the earth, and watch
How fast thy words incarnadine the world!
That I know all things is my torment; nothing,
That ever shall befall, to me is new:
Already I have suffered it far-off;
And on the mind the poor event appears
The pale reflexion of some ancient pang.
Yet I foresee dim comfort, and discern
A bleak magnificence of endless hope.
It seems that even thy woe shall have an end.
It comes upon thee! O prepare thee; ah,
That wailing, those young cries, this smouldering smell!
I see the dreadful look of men unborn.
What hast thou said, that all the air is blood?

If the whole were on this level, *Christ in Hades* would be a really great poem; as it is, I should rather call it a daring and remarkable sketch.

Less ambitious in subject, *Marpessa* is more evenly accomplished in workmanship. It is beautiful throughout, now exquisite and now magnificent. On the other hand, though it consists almost entirely of dialogue, it is curiously undramatic. The argument is thus concisely stated: " Marpessa, being given by Zeus her choice between the god Apollo and Idas, a mortal, chose Idas." Mr. Phillips sets the scene, so to speak, very beautifully:

> So
> When the long day that glideth without cloud,
> The summer day, was at her deep blue hour
> Of lilies musical with busy bliss,
> When very light trembled as with excess,
> And heat was frail, and every bush and flower
> Was drooping in the glory overcome;
> They three together met; on the one side,
> Fresh from diffusing light on all the world
> Apollo; on the other without sleep
> Idas, and in the midst Marpessa stood.

As Apollo is about to embrace her,

> They
> Heard thunder, and a little afterward
> The far Paternal voice, "Let her decide."

"The far Paternal voice," preluded by thunder, is a delightful touch. One involuntarily thinks of the voice of Fafnir in *Siegfried* droning, "Lass mich schlafen!" Apollo is naturally annoyed:

> And as a flame blown backward by a gust,
> Burned to and fro in fury beautiful
> The murmuring god.

He contains himself, however, in deference to the Paternal voice, and thus beautifully he speaks:

> Marpessa, though no trouble nor any pain,
> So it is willed, can touch me; but I live

329

> For ever in a deep deliberate bliss,
> A spirit sliding through tranquillity ;
> Yet when I saw thee I imagined woe,
> That thou who art so fair, shouldst ever taste
> Of the earth-sorrow.

He warns her of the doom of humankind :

> Child, wilt thou taste of grief ?   On thee the hours
> Shall feed, and bring thy soul into the dusk :
> Even now thy face is hasting to the dark !
> For slowly shalt thou cool to all things great,
> And wisely smile at love ; and thou shalt see
> Beautiful Faith surrendering to Time,
> And fierce ingratitude of children loved,
> Ah, sting of stings !

Apollo, we see (and this is quite in character), is prescient of Lear.   " Then wilt thou die ? " he proceeds :

> . . . . Part with eternal thoughts,
> Lie without any hope beneath the grass,
> All thy imaginations in the dust ?
> And all that tint and melody and breath,
> Which in their lovely unison are thou,
> To be dispersed upon the whirling sands !
> Thy soul blown seaward on nocturnal blast !
> O brief and breathing creature, wilt thou cease
> Once having been ? . . . .
> But if thou'lt live with me, then will I kiss
> Warm immortality into thy lips ;
> And I will carry thee above the world,
> To share my ecstacy of flinging beams,
> And scattering without intermission joy.
> And thou shalt know that first leap of the sea
> Toward me ; the grateful upward look of earth,
> Emerging roseate from her bath of dew,—
> We two in heaven dancing,—Babylon
> Shall flash and murmur, and cry from under us,
> And Nineveh catch fire, and at our feet
> Be hurled with her inhabitants, and all
> Adoring Asia kindle and hugely bloom ;—
> We two in heaven running,—continents
> Shall lighten, ocean unto ocean flash,
> And rapidly laugh till all this world is warm.

So far, his speech can only be called magnificent, both in idea and movement; but he mars it, to my thinking, at the close, by a sadly modern and curate-like touch:

> Or,—for I know thy heart,—a dearer toil,—
> To lure into the air a face long sick,
> To gild the brow that from its dead looks up,
> To shine on the unforgiven of this world;
> With slow sweet surgery restore the brain,
> And to dispel shadows and shadowy fear.

Idas then makes his appeal in a speech of exquisite feeling and eloquence, though certainly more romantic than classical in thought. Here is his peroration:

> Thy voice is like to music heard ere birth,
> Some spirit lute touched on a spirit sea;
> Thy face remembered is from other worlds,
> It has been died for, though I know not when,
> It has been sung for, though I know not where.
> It has the strangeness of the luring West,
> And of sad sea-horizons; beside thee
> I am aware of other times and lands,
> Of birth far-back, of lives in many stars.
> O beauty lone and like a candle clear
> In this dark country of the world! Thou art
> My woe, my early light, my music dying.

Having heard both sides with due attention, Marpessa answers in a speech of great beauty, but, in many passages, of extraordinary inappropriateness. The first line of her apostrophe to Apollo is beyond praise:

> O gradual rose of the dim universe!

But when she proceeds,

> Male of the female earth!
> O eager bridegroom springing in this world
> As in thy bed prepared!

we feel that it is the poet speaking, and not his character. The sentiment is peculiarly inapt as addressed by a maiden

to her wooer, be he god or man.   She proceeds, in a very
magnificent but surely un-Marpessa-like strain :

> . . . . Fain would I know
> Yon heavenly wafting through the heaven wide,
> And the large view of the subjected seas,
> And famous cities, and the various toil
> Of men : all Asia at my feet spread out
> In indolent magnificence of bloom !
> Africa in her matted hair obscured,
> And India in meditation plunged !

If Apollo is prescient of Shakespeare, Marpessa (which is
more surprising) seems to have been reading Matthew
Arnold, and to have remembered :

> The East bowed low before the blast
>   In patient, deep disdain ;
> She let the legions thunder past
>   And plunged in thought again.

Be this as it may, her feeling is that she is human and
would fain think nothing human alien to her—not even
sorrow and death.   This passage is no less appropriate
than beautiful, especially the description of those men and
women who, as Marpessa has heard,

> Panted toward their end, and fell on death
> Even as sobbing runners breast the rope.

But now again the poet's sense of fitness breaks down,
while his inspiration of sheer beauty rises higher, perhaps,
then ever :

> When I remember this, how shall I know
> That I myself may not, by sorrow taught,
> Accept the perfect stillness of the ground ?
> Where, though I lie still, and stir not at all,
> Yet shall I irresistibly be kind,
> Helplessly sweet, a wandering garden bliss.
> My ashes shall console and make for peace ;
> This mind that injured, be an aimless balm.
> Or if there be some other world, with no

Bloom, neither rippling sound, nor early smell,
Nor leaves, nor pleasant exchange of human speech ;
Only a dreadful pacing to and fro
Of spirits meditating on the sun ;
A land of barèd boughs and grieving wind ;
Yet would I not forgo the doom, the place,
Whither my poets and my heroes went
Before me ; warriors that with deeds forlorn
Saddened my youth, yet made it great to live ;
Lonely antagonists of Destiny,
That went down scornful before many spears,
Who soon as we are born, are straight our friends ;
And live in simple music, country songs,
And mournful ballads by the winter fire.

The thought of the body's beneficent return to its
elements is a favourite one with Mr. Phillips. He works
it out in a separate poem, *Beautiful Death*, which contains
some of his best lines. But a conception which we owe
to modern chemistry is strangely out of place in the mouth
of Marpessa ; and the whole passage—nay, the speaker's
whole attitude—suggests the perfected life-philosophy of a
Dorothea Brooke. We almost expect her to quote, "Oh
may I join the choir invisible." The end of her speech,
the portion addressed directly to Idas, is wonderfully tender
and beautiful ; but I have quoted enough to show both
the strength and the weakness of the poem. It has
every possible charm except a sense of character and of
congruity.

A word as to its prosody. I find in its three hundred
and fifty lines only one flagrant instance of a false
accent :

My bloom fa*ded*, and waning light of eyes.

In another line, the trochee in the second place becomes,
not only tolerable, but delightful, because of the pause preceding it :

And thou, beautiful god, in that far time.

The following line I read with a certain misgiving :

> And I in silence wondered at sorrow.

If we sound the "ed" of "wondered" this line is normal ; but one cannot help suspecting that Mr. Phillips intends the "e" to be elided in "wonder'd," in which case we have that unspeakable monstrosity (so I must maintain) a trochaic fifth foot.   While I am on the subject, let me note some peculiarities of metre in the above-mentioned poem, *Beautiful Death*.   It contains one of Mr. Phillips's most memorably exquisite lines,

> Causing to fall the indolent misty peach,

but also one which no perversion of accent or extravagance of elision can by any means coax or compress into a blank verse line :

> Conspiring with the summer plans of lovers, scent. . . .

One almost suspects a misprint ; and yet the meaning of the passage seems right enough.   Can Mr. Phillips purposely have interjected a somewhat cumbrous Alexandrine into the middle of a blank verse poem?   Here, by the way, we find yet another instance of a trochaic second foot redeemed by a pause before it, in the line

> Then thou, spendthrift of time, shalt busy be.

Incomparably the finest of the shorter poems, to my thinking, is *To Milton—Blind*, quoted at the end of this essay.   It is superb in conception, flawless in melody.   The only fault I can discover in it is the use in two places of that singularly weak and prosaic epithet "special," for which Mr. Phillips has a special fondness.   In another poem he actually speaks of

> the special whisper that restored
> Pale Lazarus.

It is not a sonorous or luminous word at best, and has
become hopelessly vulgarised by its association with tele-
grams, editions, constables, and coffee. *The Wound* and
By the Sea are also beautiful pieces of blank verse; and
the lines inscribed *A. S. P.*, which I am permitted to reprint
in full, are as delicate as a tenderly-touched cameo.

In rhyme Mr. Phillips is less happily inspired. There
is beauty in his little group of lyrics, and power in *The
Question* and *The New "De Profundis"*; but I can find
little to like in *The Woman with the Dead Soul*. The
psychological study, or rather suggestion, is interesting
enough; but the setting is incomprehensible and the verse
flaccid and often prosaic. So far as we can make out, the
woman is sitting sewing in the taproom of a public-house,
among

> labourers, gnarled and splashed with mire,
> The disillusioned women sipping fire.

This is an odd place for a seamstress to ply her calling;
and, on the other hand, we can discover no symbolic
aptness of the arrangement. The scene, however, is a
detail, and would trouble us little if the verse were stronger.
There are several fine lines; for instance, those telling how
the woman's soul

> started back to life
> Now at some angel evening after rain,
> Builded like early Paradise again,
> Now at some flower, or human face, or sky
> With silent tremble of infinity,
> Or at some waft of fields in midnight sweet,
> Or soul of summer dawn in the dark street.

But, on the whole, Mr. Phillips shapes his verse on the
garrulous Morrisian model, with frequent inversions and
unlimited padding—a form which, at its best, is delightful
in long narratives, but far too easy-going for short pieces

such as this. What could be more languid than this
couplet?—

> Then hungry grew her soul; she looked around,
> And nothing to allay that famine found.

Or the following lines?—

> Yet will she seem to run
> And hurry eager in the noonday sun,
> Industrious, timed, and kempt; till she at last,
> Run down, inaccurate, aside is cast.

And if *The Woman with the Dead Soul* is but a half-
success, what shall we say of *The Wife?* For my part, I
vehemently dislike and deplore it. Mr. Phillips has re-
touched and somewhat improved it in his second edition,
but the alterations are merely verbal. Would that he had
improved it out of existence! He takes "a true story," too
hideous to be tragic; he tells us nothing about it except
the bare, abominable event; and he leaves us gasping with
wonder that, since he had nothing more to say, he did not
prefer to hold his tongue about it. I do not mean that
such a subject—a woman selling her body to buy bread for
her husband, and returning to find the husband dead—is
necessarily outside the sphere of art. Mr. Phillips might
have given us the psychology of the situation, or made it
the text for an indictment (or even a vindication) of the
mundane or extra-mundane conditions that render such
things possible. But he has attempted no such enterprise.
He has simply, as he says, "done the story into verse,"
without analysis, without comment. And even the verse is
none of the best. There is a touch of imaginative wit in

> The constable with lifted hand
> Conducting the orchestral Strand;

but what can be said for such a couplet as this?—

> With her right arm the door she pushed
> As to the dead the *widow* rushed.

(The italics are Mr. Phillips's.) This is the very essence of doggerel—a line of pure padding and a grotesque rhyme. Why tell us that she "püshed" the door with her right arm? What else should she push it with? No, no; despite some strong lines, this piece is unworthy of the author of *Eremus*, *Marpessa*, and *To Milton— Blind*.

Though not strikingly original or penetrative, Mr. Phillips's thought is always alive and interesting. His main ideas belong to the spiritual currency of the day, and could be paralleled in many quarters. This I say entirely without reproach, for I cannot see that it is the business of a poet to be at the same time a pioneer in the world of speculation. Mr. Phillips thinks competently, sees clearly, feels intensely, and writes beautifully. In a word, he is a true poet. If he comes unscathed through the ordeal of sudden success, and perfects his talent instead of cultivating his mannerisms, he may one day merit a larger epithet.

In the foregoing pages I have more than once remarked upon what seemed to me the lack of dramatic instinct in Mr. Phillips's endowment. These passages remain unaltered because they convey accurately enough the impression which the poems in question left, and still leave, upon my mind. To be quite frank, I was amazed to learn that Mr. George Alexander had commissioned Mr. Phillips to write a play. It appeared to me that whatever other Muses might have been summoned to his christening, those of Drama had been rather pointedly overlooked. Well, I was manifestly wrong—Melpomene had brought him a splendid cradle-gift. But I still think that it must have lain neglected and impotent among his treasures, until Mr. Alexander's suggestion induced him to rummage it out and furbish it up.

It is very hard as yet, with the evidence of only two plays before us, to assign Mr. Phillips to any recognised class of dramatic poets. Is he a Shakespearean? His style is too deliberately ornate. Is he a Racinian? His action is too rapid and external. Is he a Hugoesque Romantic? His psychology is too delicate and searching. All one can say with absolute assurance is that his work has nothing in common with the pseudo-Elizabethanism, either of the stage or of the study, which has for two centuries passed current as poetical drama in England. The Elizabethan tradition, after trickling impotently through the eighteenth century, gathered new force early in the nineteenth, and split into two clearly-marked currents. We had on the stage the fustian of Sheil, Sheridan Knowles, and their tribe (slightly Gallicised in Bulwer Lytton); while the " literary drama " of Browning, Swinburne, and others seized upon and exaggerated the psychological subtleties of the Elizabethans—those lightning flashes of emotional revealment which Lamb's criticisms had brought into fashion. Webster's " Cover her face; mine eyes dazzle; she died young," may be said to have struck the keynote for these poets: this was the manner of effect they all strove to emulate. It might seem to the superficial observer that what Mr. Phillips had done was to reconcile stage Elizabethanism with literary Elizabethanism; but this, I am convinced, would be a misconception. That was what Tennyson did, in some measure—what he might have done with far-reaching results had he taken to the dramatic form earlier in his career. But Mr. Phillips stands as far apart from Tennyson as from either Sheridan Knowles or Browning. He is a totally new phenomenon in English drama of the past two centuries—at once an inventor of situations and a master of language. We have had many masters of language and a few inventors of situations; but we have never had them combined in the same person. Moreover,

338

STEPHEN PHILLIPS

Mr. Phillips's imagination is not only dramatic but scenic. He has the instinct of stage effect, in which our Victorian poets have been so notably deficient. He reminds one (to employ a very rough illustration) of the elder Dumas speaking with the voice of Marlowe. Yes, Marlowe rather than Milton. Mr. Phillips will sometimes deliberately Miltonise both in vocabulary and in syntax; but he knows that the complex harmonies, the elaborate involutions, of Milton are unsuited for drama, and therefore cultivates rather the " mighty line" than the gorgeous period. But all such comparisons are but distant adumbrations of the truth. Mr. Phillips's style is neither Marlowe's nor Milton's, but his own. It is essentially epic; yet it is full of lyrical modulations which (the paradox is only apparent) render it vividly dramatic. Take, for instance, that passage in the first act of *Herod* where Mariamne has lured Herod to her arms at the very moment when her brother is dying by his command. The poet's effort is to suggest a fateful pause, and to charge the sultry evening air with an ominous electricity. First we have, in the short, almost gasping, speeches of Bathsheba and the handmaidens, a lyric of oppressive, odorous heat, beginning,

> A breeze, a breeze.   Did you not feel it?
>> Yes.

Then, after a scene between Cypros and Salome, Herod and Mariamne re-enter with these words:

HEROD. That star is languorous with divine excess!
MARIAMNE. O world of wearied passion dimly bright!
HEROD. Now the armed man doth lay his armour by,
    And now the husband hasteth to the wife.
MARIAMNE. The brother to the sister maketh home.
HEROD. Now cometh the old lion from the pool.
MARIAMNE. And the young lion having drunk enough.

This is a pure lyric, a duet; yet it is instinct with drama.
339

Or take, again, Mariamne's solo as she is about to drink the poisoned cup :

> Now farewell !
> Jerusalem, city of God, farewell,
> My cradle first, my home, and now my grave,
> For I, the last of all the Maccabees,
> I, the lone daughter of that holy line,
> I perish without fear and without cry :
> For a doom is come upon us, and an ending.
> Brother, I drink and hasten down to you.

This might quite well be set to music ; but just because of its " lyric cry " it is at the same time intensely dramatic.

In *Herod*, however, there are defects and limitations of which I shall presently have something to say. Mr. Phillips's first play, *Paolo and Francesca*, is a far nobler, rarer and more rounded creation. It seemed almost impossible that any one should take Paolo and Francesca out of the

> *Bufera infernal che mai non resta,*

and bring them back to earth again, without vulgarising them and their fate. Mr. Phillips has achieved the impossible, and in so doing has produced a play that lives and breathes in every line. Sardou could not have ordered the action more skilfully, Tennyson could not have clothed the passion in words of rarer loveliness.

Having to deal with a theme of pure passion, Mr. Phillips has steeped it in an atmosphere of pure poetry. Your ordinary playwright, even your ordinary poet, had he had the audacity to approach this perilous subject, would have given it a political background, nailed it down to a date, and included (probably in a conversation between " First Gentleman " and " Second Gentleman ") a luminous survey of the state of Italy in the thirteenth century. He would have taken all possible pains to impress upon us that these things did actually happen ; thereby awakening in us the ever present consciousness that they assuredly did not happen in this way. Not so Mr. Phillips. Whether he has gone deeply into the history of his subject I cannot tell. If he has, it was only to brush the records aside, and fall back upon his Dante (with the simplest footnote) and his imagination. He speaks from the imagination to the imagination, and never allows another faculty to get a word in edgewise. He makes his swiftly-moving story intensely real, intensely credible, intensely beautiful and desirable to the imagination. He thus solves the one essential problem of dramatic poe .ry.

Mr. Phillips has justly recognised that here was no case for a tragedy of character, but simply for a tragedy of fate. There is only one character in the play—one personage endowed with other and subtler qualities than the sheer necessities of the story demand. This is a lady named Lucrezia, a widowed cousin of the Malatestas, who regards with suppressed but burning jealousy the introduction of the girl-bride into Giovanni's palace. She is skilfully employed at two points to heighten the tragic effect; but she is not of the essence of the theme. The essential personages, Giovanni, Paolo and Francesca, are creatures of elemental passion and naught besides : Giovanni terrible, Paolo and Francesca beautiful, all three infinitely pathetic in the shadow of their impending doom. The play opens with the arrival of Francesca, escorted by Paolo, at the frowning castle of the Malatestas, where the husband she has never seen awaits her. She is chilled from the first by the gloomy hall and its stern master :

PAOLO. You are not sad?
FRANCESCA.   What is it to be sad?
           Nothing hath grieved me yet but ancient woes,
           Sea-perils, or some long-ago farewell,
           Or the last sunset cry of wounded kings.

These lines are no mere purple patch of irrelevant beauty, but subtly foreshadow the part to be played by the "ancient woes" of Lancelot and Guenevere in shaping Francesca's own fate. It must be said that the Francesca of this act is far younger than she with whom Dante held converse. She is, indeed, a mere child ; but her soul grows older with every scene. Before the marriage takes place, Paolo tells Giovanni that he must leave Rimini; but Giovanni, who loves him dearly, commands him to stay. Then Giovanni's old blind nurse, Angela—the Tiresias or Cassandra of the tragedy—comes to him prophesying doom :

> GIOVANNI. Upon what scene are those blind eyes so fixed ?
> ANGELA. A place of leaves : and ah ! how still it is !
>   She sits alone amid great roses.
> GIOVANNI.   She ?
> ANGELA. Who is he that steals in upon your bride ?
> GIOVANNI. Angela !
> ANGELA.   And no sound in all the world !
>
> *   *   *   *   *
>
> GIOVANNI. His face ? That I may know him when we meet.
> ANGELA. His face was dim : a twilight struggles back.
>   I see two lying dead upon a bier—
>   Slain suddenly, and in each other's arms.
> GIOVANNI. Are they these two that in the roses kissed ?

One is inclined to think at first that Mr. Phillips suffers his Cassandra to vaticinate too much and too clearly—that only preternatural stupidity can now keep Giovanni in the dark. But Mr. Phillips understands perfectly the due proportions of his scheme, which does not involve keeping Giovanni in the dark at all. In the second act, when Paolo has taken his courage in his hands and fled from Francesca's very innocence, Giovanni tells Lucrezia of the Sybil's warning, and she, with the keen vision of jealousy, interprets it for him clearly enough. "As to a soul new-come," he cries,

> the murk of hell
> Grows more accustomed, gradually light,

So I begin to see amid this gloom.
Let me explore the place and walk in it.

*   *   *   *   *

Henceforward let no woman bear two sons.

Paolo, however, is gone; the danger seems averted; and Giovanni bethinks him that "there are drugs to charm the hearts of women."

Paolo is indeed gone; but at the first halting-place he determines that he cannot live his life, but will return and end it:

> Under some potion gently will I die
> And they that find me dead shall lay me down
> Beautiful as a sleeper at her feet.

To the shop of the drug-seller, Pulci, comes Giovanni, disguised and by night, seeking a love-philtre. While he is there Paolo also arrives, demanding some drug

> That can fetch down on us the eternal sleep
> Anticipating the slow mind of God.

Giovanni overhears him confessing, as the reason for his wish to die, his uncontrollable love for his brother's wife, and, after a struggle, determines to let him take his life

> He has gone out upon the only road.
> And this is my relief: O dread relief!
> Thus only am I pure of brother's blood.

Almost at the same moment Giovanni is urgently summoned away to put down a rebellion in Pesaro.

But Paolo does not at once drink his potion. "Much is permitted to a man condemned," he says, and strays into Francesca's garden, hoping to see her at her lattice, or to hear her make "a music upon midnight with my name." But Francesca cannot sleep in her sultry room, and comes out into the garden with a book in her hand, her maid carrying a lamp. She bids the maid set down the lamp and leave her alone in an arbour of roses; and now ensues the culminating, the classic scene—a passage which need in no wise shrink from confrontation with its great original, or with anything of its kind in literature.

I shall not attempt to follow the fine gradations of terror which, in the masterly fourth act, lead up to the catastrophe. As ingenious dramatically as it is beautifully human is Francesca's appeal to the mother-instinct in Lucrezia, who, after inciting Giovanni to their destruction, turns about and tries in vain to save them. Everything is ordered with perfect beauty, with a classical parsimony of physical sensation; yet not the most blood-boltered romanticist could attain a higher pitch of horror, a more crushing sense of relentless and inexorable doom. Even if its diction were commonplace, the mere carpentering of this act would proclaim Mr. Phillips a born dramatist. That its diction is anything but commonplace let these few lines from Paolo's last great speech suffice to prove :

> What can we fear, we two ?
> O God, Thou seest us Thy creatures bound
> Together by that law which holds the stars
> In palpitating cosmic passion bright ;
> By which the very sun enthrals the earth,
> And all the waves of the world faint to the moon.
> Even by such attraction we two rush
> Together through the everlasting years.
>
>   *   *   *   *   *
>
> Still, still together, even when faints Thy sun,
> And past our souls Thy stars like ashes fall,
> How wilt Thou punish us who cannot part ?

Were the poem bound down to time and place, Paolo's line about the sun enthralling the earth would be as dire an anachronism as Hector's quotation from Aristotle. But the truth is that *Paolo and Francesca* can no more be fettered to thirteenth-century Rimini than *Romeo and Juliet* to fourteenth-century Verona. Their scene is the eternal

Italy of passion, their time the dateless spring of young desire.

The inferiority of *Herod* proceeds almost entirely from the subject, which is much less suited than that of *Paolo and Francesca* to Mr. Phillips's methods. Here the love-story has, and must have, a political setting; and as it is impossible to treat politics lyrically, the poet handles the political groundwork of the action in such a summary fashion as to leave it distinctly unconvincing. More than one able and well-disposed critic has observed to me that the play is rather a skeleton or scenario than a finished whole. Certain it is that we have at several points a sense that the action is being perfunctorily dismissed in order that we may the sooner arrive at the great tirades, the purple patches of lyrism. I do not doubt that Mr. Phillips, on the whole, did wisely in hurrying the political mechanism. It is far better to be sketchy than to be tedious. But the fact that this alternative presented itself to him proves that the theme was not altogether adapted to his style. A more intimate theme, with no obligatory historical background, is what his genius seems to demand.

One cannot but feel, however, that without exceeding the limits of his method, Mr. Phillips might have given us a stronger and more consistently developed first act. He has, indeed, compressed into one act matter that would amply have sufficed for two; and hence a certain superficiality of treatment. The starting-point of the play— Herod's determination to murder Mariamne's brother Aristobulus—offers opportunities for soul-searching which Mr. Phillips ignores. A man does not resolve upon an act which (to say the least of it) may fatally estrange from him the woman he worships, without some balancing of motives, some forecasting of probabilities. Unless he is impelled by an access of fury (and this is not Herod's case) he must weigh love against statecraft, and determine whether he

will risk his throne or his Mariamne. No doubt this conflict takes place in Herod's soul; but we see nothing of it.
Close on the suggestion of the murder comes the opportunity;
and we are left to divine, beneath the surface of the scene
between Herod and Aristobulus, the process by which the
boy's death is determined on. When he has despatched
Sohemus on his mission of murder, Herod is overcome by
a presentiment:

> What if the powers permit
> The doing of that deed which serves us now;
> Then of that very deed do make a spur
> To drive us to some act that we abhor?
> The first step is with us; then all the road,
> The long road, is with Fate.

Thus we see that he realises the risk he is running; but
his reasons for taking the risk remain, not precisely obscure,
but unanalysed. Then comes the situation, a most original
one, in which Herod yields himself up to Mariamne's
embraces at the very moment when he knows that her
brother is dying by his command. Fine though the situation be, however, and clad in gorgeous lyric raiment, we
are left uncertain of Herod's mental state. Does he hope
that the boy's death will pass as an accident, and that
Mariamne will not suspect his hand in it? In that case
his evident perturbation, his hints at some "necessary
violence," are unworthy of one so versed in Oriental dis-
simulation and in the sanguinary statecraft of his day. If,
on the other hand, he clearly realises that all must presently
come out, he must feel that this love-scene will, in the
retrospect, merely intensify Mariamne's horror. In short,
we have a superb situation, a piece of intense dramatic
irony, resting on an inadequate, or inadequately presented,
psychological groundwork.

In the passage which follows—the bringing in of Aristobulus drowned—I cannot but think that Mr. Phillips's

instinct of effect for once plays him false. No one expresses the slightest surprise, nor does Mariamne make the smallest inquiry into the circumstances of her brother's death or of its discovery. Now this is very good and dramatic if we are to assume that Mariamne at once knows the murder to be Herod's work, and that Herod tacitly confesses it. But if that be so, what is the use of the elaborate scene in which Mariamne, after Herod's departure, wrings from Sohemus a confession of the crime? We are bound to conclude from this that Mariamne at first only vaguely suspects Herod; in which case the reception of the body, both on her part and on his, is utterly unrealised and undramatised. These concluding passages of the first act are, I think, the weakest in the play. Mr. Phillips has left the mental state of his characters, from moment to moment, quite indeterminate. He has not definitely chosen between two possible, but mutually exclusive, processes of thought and emotion.

The second act is very much better. Here there is no longer any question of analysing conflicts of emotion or leaving them unanalysed. The conflict which runs through the act is not that of a soul at war with itself, but of two souls given over to opposing passions. It is the battle of love inflamed to frenzy against love frozen into hate.

MARIAMNE.   I am come
      From young Aristobulus that was murdered.
HEROD. Murdered!
MARIAMNE.   Or taken as we take a dog
      And strangled in that pool whose reeds I hear
      Sighing within my ears until I die.
      You like a tiger purred about me: O!
      Your part it was to soothe and hush me while
      He gasped beneath their hands—your hands— O yes,
      You were not near; 'twas yours to kiss and lie—
      But none the less your hands were round his throat,
      O liar!
HEROD.   Mariamne!
MARIAMNE.   You forest beast!

HEROD. Mariamne!
MARIAMNE.   Back, and in the jungle burn
    Whence you did leap out at my brother's throat.
    Can you deny your part in this ? O subtle
    Half suitor and half strangler, with one arm
    About the sister's neck, the other hand
    About the brother's throat !

So the scene proceeds, until Mariamne tells Herod that her love for him is utterly dead, and that :

> Even the red misery of my brother's murder,
> That extreme pang, is pale beside this loss,
> This drying up within me of my soul.

Herod tries almost by violence to reawaken her passion for him, but it is dead in very truth :

HEROD. I'll break this barrier down as I have others.
MARIAMNE. Never—never !
HEROD.   When first I wooed was I
    Not blood-stained ?
MARIAMNE. Not with blood of his !
HEROD.   O, still
    You shall forget him. He is dead and I
    Live still, and glow, and sigh, and burn for you.
MARIAMNE. Almost I am moved to laughter at that passion
    Which once could sway and thrill me to the bone.
    Terrible when we laugh at what we loved !
HEROD. My brain, my brain, I shall go mad !
                          One kiss !
MARIAMNE. Never !
HEROD.   One touch !
MARIAMNE.   No more !
HEROD.   One word !
MARIAMNE.   Farewell !

This " Farewell "—a true dramatic invention if ever there was one—is the culminating point of a noble and poignant scene. It is followed by a speech of Herod's which recalls Othello's great valediction (as a word in the above extract

recalls Blake's " Tiger, tiger "), and does not suffer unduly
by the reminiscence :

> Where's now the boast, the glory, O where now ?
> What was this triumph but in the telling of it
> To you !   And what this victory but to pour it
> Into your ears !   I had imagined all
> Meetings but this—this only I foresaw not.
> Here I disband my legions ; I arise,
> And spill the wine of glory on the ground :
> I turn my face into the night.

Most cunningly devised are the outward stimuli—each
brought to bear through the medium of a picturesque
situation—whereby Herod is little by little wrought up to
delivering the death-doom, which is, in fact, little more
than an imprecation wrung from his agony, but on which
his malignant kinsfolk are only too ready to act.   Finest of
all, however, is the invention of the concluding scene.
Fresh honours are heaped upon Herod, and his first impulse is to share his exultation with Mariamne.   We see
him, as the curtain falls, rushing into the room where we
know her to be lying dead, and reciting, to her deaf ears,
the high-sounding roll of his new dominions.   Never did
poet lay before his protagonist a more tragic banquet of
Dead Sea fruit.   This is a fitting crown to the unbroken
series of nobly imaginative dramatic inventions of which
the act consists.

The third act is totally different in character, and even
more original.   It is entirely given up to the fathoming, so
to speak—or shall we say the sifting ?—of one psychological
situation.   It presents, with a singular combination of
subtlety and strength, a case of volitional insanity.   Herod
will not know that Mariamne is dead.   In the depths of
his soul he knows it very well.   Every second word he
speaks is a spasm of pain shooting upward from that
rankling knowledge.   But he is madly determined to fight

349

down the realisation and not suffer it to take hold of his surface consciousness. So far, indeed, is his brain actually unhinged that he hopes some miracle may prove the truth a lie, and coquets in a ghastly fashion with his wilful delusion. Whether this phase of mania is known to mental science I cannot tell; I only know that Mr. Phillips makes the case pathologically plausible and poetically convincing. He has lavished upon the scene an intensity of vision and a splendour of utterance for which one must go far to find a parallel. It is a pity that the final incident should be an almost exact repetition of that which brought the previous act to a close.

Mr. Phillips's dramatic works, it must be admitted, do not escape the defects of their qualities. Their most striking qualities are rapidity of action and splendour of style; their defects—the tendencies against which the poet ought to be on his guard—are summariness of psychology and an overstrained grandiloquence. Mr. Phillips is so determined to keep his action moving that he sometimes gives us a rather bare and inadequate indication of a crucial mental conflict. We have seen an instance of this in the first act of *Herod*. Similar, though less obvious, instances occur in *Paolo and Francesca*, where Giovanni determines to let Paolo go (as it seems) to his death, and again where Giovanni resolves upon the final act of vengeance. The tendency to dismiss a critical process of thought or feeling in a few phrases, however pregnant, must not be carried too far; though it is vastly preferable to the opposite tendency, universal among modern "poetic" playwrights, to make their characters unpack their hearts in furlongs of blank verse.

The second danger—that of over-inflation of style—is one which cannot be too sedulously avoided. Sometimes, though very rarely, one feels that Mr. Phillips has let a seductive sonority lure him from the strait path of dramatic

fitness. In *Herod* especially he once or twice presents an
opening to the scoffer by the mechanical reduplication of
almost synonymous phrases. The tendency appears even
in the earlier play, in such lines as these of Lucrezia's:

> I am become a danger and a menace,
> A wandering fire, a disappointed force,
> A peril.

We have here three almost identical terms, "danger,"
"menace," and "peril," piled one upon the other without
any perceptible reason, whether from the point of view of
pure style or of dramatic effect. More notable are the
much-parodied lines in *Herod:*

> And I will think in gold and dream in silver,
> Imagine in marble and in bronze conceive.

The fact that these verbs and substantives are all interchangeable—that Herod might quite as well have conceived
in gold, imagined in silver, thought in marble, and dreamt
in bronze—indicates an unmistakable weakness in the
passage, regarded merely as a piece of rhetoric. But it
may be argued with a certain plausibility that the rhetorical
fault is a dramatic beauty, and that it would be absurd, in
the given situation, to apply the touchstone of logic to
Herod's magniloquence. This defence, however, will scarcely
apply to the lines—

> A crying of dead prophets from their tombs,
> A singing of dead poets from their graves.

These lines are undeniably beautiful; but to make them
as satisfying to the mind as they are melodious to the
ear, there ought to be some special reason why "prophets"
should rest in "tombs," "poets" in "graves." Here,
again, the terms are interchangeable—a sure mark of a
lurking weakness. The suggestion of an antithesis, or at any
rate of a distinction, where none exists, is always a fault in

style. This collocation of "tomb" and "grave" is to the mind what an identical rhyme (two lines ending with the same word) is to the ear. It jarred on me even when I first heard the speech spoken from the stage, on that memorable evening of October 31, 1900, which sent a strain of living poetry vibrating through the prose-laden atmosphere of the modern English theatre.

STEPHEN PHILLIPS

TO MILTON—BLIND.

He who said suddenly, " Let there be light ! "
To thee the dark deliberately gave ;
That those full eyes might undistracted be
By this beguiling show of sky and field,
This brilliance, that so lures us from the Truth.
He gave thee back original night, His own
Tremendous canvas, large and blank and free,
Where at each thought a star flashed out and sang.
O blinded with a special lightning, thou
Hadst once again the virgin Dark ! and when
The pleasant flowery sight, which had deterred
Thine eyes from seeing, when this recent world
Was quite withdrawn ; then burst upon thy view
The elder glory ; space again in pangs,
And Eden odorous in the early mist,
That heaving watery plain that *was* the world ;
Then the burned earth, and Christ coming in clouds.
Or rather a special leave to thee was given
By the high power, and thou with bandaged eyes
Wast guided through the glimmering camp of God.
Thy hand was taken by angels who patrol
The evening, or are sentries to the dawn,
Or pace the wide air everlastingly.
Thou wast admitted to the presence, and deep
Argument heardest, and the large design
That brings this world out of the woe to bliss.

A. S. P.

Frail was she born ; petal by petal fell
Her life : till it was strown upon the herb ;
Like petals all her fancies lay about.
And the dread Powers kept her face toward grief,
Although she swerved ; and still with many a lash
Guided her to the anguish carefully.
So bare her soul that Beauty like a lance
Pierced her, and odour full of arrows was.
She drugged her brain against realities,
And lived in dreams, and was with music fed,
Imploring to be spared e'en sweetest things.
She suffered, and resorted to the ground,
Glad to be blind, and eager to be deaf ;
Soliciting eternal apathy.
And she was swift to steep her brain in moss,
And with the heart that so had loved, to blow
Merely, and to be idle in the wind.
She craved no Paradise but only peace.

MRS. RADFORD

It is difficult to strike just the right note of praise for the
poems in Mrs. Radford's two modest little volumes. To
define them by negatives is easy enough, but scarcely
satisfactory. They are not pictorial, they are not philosophical, they are not dramatic; they are not multitudinous
in measure, or opulent in rhyme, or inventive in stanza.
Never was there poetry with less of the "big bow-wow"
style about it. Yet Mrs. Radford is a poetess certainly,
and a poetess of distinct individuality. She finds touch-
ingly sweet and simple expression for some of the moods
and emotions of a finely-tempered, delicate, courageous,
and essentially feminine nature. There is a tremulous
sincerity in her accent which often goes straight to the
reader's heart; and though she has no great technical
accomplishment, the form of her utterance is always clear,
graceful, and unaffected.

The lyric quality in her best work is very genuine. Her
songs are not mere measured speech; they carry with them
each its little wistful melody. I should not be surprised if
for this very reason they were difficult to set to music; the
verses which sing themselves are not generally those best
suited to the musician's peculiar purposes. There is a
certain exaggeration and emphasis in even the simplest
musical setting which would do some injustice to the
absolute sincerity of Mrs. Radford's singing.

Any attempt at definition of its charm would merely dust the bloom off the wings of such a song as this:

> My lover's lute has golden strings,
>   Bright as the sunlight in the air,
> My lover touches them and sings
>   His happy music everywhere.
>
> My lover's eyes see very far,
>   Through the great toiling in the street,
> To where the seas and mountains are,
>   And all the land lies still and sweet.
>
> My lover's lips are very kind,
>   He smiles on all who pass him by,
> And all who pass him leave behind
>   A greeting, with a smile or sigh.
>
> My lover's heart, ah! none may say
>   How tenderly it beats for me,
> And, if I took my love away,
>   How silent all its song would be.

Is not this the perfection of tender simplicity? If Mrs. Radford had never written another line, she would have added a lyric to the language. But she has other songlets of equal charm. Take this as an example:

> The little songs which come and go,
> In tender measures, to and fro,
> Whene'er the day brings you to me,
> Keep my heart full of melody.
>
> But on my lute I strive in vain
> To play the music o'er again,
> And you, dear love, will never know
> The little songs which come and go.

Here now is a *Spring Song* which came, and fortunately did *not* go:

> Ah love, the sweet spring blossoms cling
> To many a broken wind-tossed bough,
> And young birds among branches sing,
> That mutely hung till now.

356

DOLLIE RADFORD

MRS. RADFORD

The little new-born things which lie
In dewy meadows, sleep and dream
Beside the brook that twinkles by
To some great lonely stream.

And children, now the day is told,
From many a warm and cosy nest,
Look up to see the young moon hold
The old moon to her breast.

Dear love, my pulses throb and start
To-night with longings sweet and new.
And young hopes beat within a heart
Grown old in loving you.

But exquisite as these songs are, they come from the
surface and not from the depths of Mrs. Radford's nature.
She can find equally pure and thrilling utterance for
emotions of a far sterner order. In the following poem,
for instance, she strikes a profoundly tragic note:

Ah, Love, through what unfathomed deeps
   Thy feet have sped,
Up what bare hills and barren steeps
   Thy hands have led,
What bitter nights and burning days
Have marked thy ways.

And I have followed all the while,
   So close to thee,
Hoping thou wouldest turn and smile,
   To gladden me,
To tell me we should safely come
To thy fair home.

But thou dost ever onward press,
   With hidden face,
Ah, surely none may wear thy dress,
   Nor take thy place;
Ah tell me it is thou indeed
With whom I speed.

Dear Love, dear Love, thy tightening hand
  Is stern and cold,
I see the gates of thy great land
  Grown clear and bold,
And Death, alone, comes forth in peace,
  To my release.

Even more moving, I think, is the quiet pathos, the
simple bravery and devotion, of the following verses:

Because I built my nest so high,
    Must I despair
If a fierce wind, with bitter cry,
Passes the lower branches by,
    And mine makes bare?

Because I hung it, in my pride,
    So near the skies,
Higher than other nests abide,
Must I lament, if far and wide
    It scattered lies?

I shall but build, and build my best,
    Till, safety won,
I hang aloft my new-made nest
High as of old, and see it rest
    As near the sun.

Through generations to come, perhaps, many a suffering
woman, here or there, will find in these verses the solace of
perfect utterance for the resolute religion of her heart.

Mrs. Radford does not often touch a quite impersonal
note, but when she does she can still write charmingly.
Take, for instance, the following:

TWO SONGS.

Winds blow cold in the bright March weather,
  Yet I heard her sing in the street to-day,
And the tattered garments scarce hung together
  Round her tiny form as she turned away,
She was too little to know or care
Why she and her mother were singing there.

MRS. RADFORD

Skies are fair when the buds are springing,
  When the March sun rises up fresh and strong,
And a little maid, with her mother, singing,
  Smiled in my face as she skipped along,
She was too happy to wonder why
She laughed and sang as she passed me by.

It is not easy to say whether the following poem should be classed as personal or impersonal, but there can be no doubt as to its tenderness or its beauty :

A BRIDE.

I saw your portrait yesterday,
  Set in a golden frame ,
Around it twines a blossom-spray,
  Beneath it is your name.

And tender smiles are round your mouth,
  High thoughts are on your brow,
The world is beautiful as Youth,
  You are so happy now.

The shining gates are opened wide,
  Love stretches forth his hand
And bids the bridegroom bring his bride
  Into the promised land.

And you and he dwell there alone,
  Beneath Love's radiant sky,
While all the world's great grief and moan
  As a sad dream pass by.

Yet on Love's flowers strange and rare,
  Your saddest tears may fall,
And in Love's country you may fare
  The loneliest of all.

A delicate ear, a very true voice, though of limited range, and a brave and beautiful human spirit—these are the gifts which make Mrs. Radford a poetess. Her philosophy is love, her learning is love, her gospel is love. It is evident that love has meant to her not only joy but suffering; yet her saddest songs are neither querulous nor accusing.

The pains of love have never blinded her to its divine compensations. Her singing makes, on the whole, for steadfast serenity, courage and hope. Simple as it is, artless as it is, it adds to our stock of beautiful things, and brings us close, yet never too close, to a simply, artlessly beautiful nature.

MRS. RADFORD

OCTOBER.

From falling leaf to falling leaf,
    How strange it was, through all the year,
In all its joy and all its grief,
    You did not know I loved you dear ;
Through all the winter-time and spring,
    You smiled and watched me come and go,
Through all the summer blossoming,
    How strange it was you did not know

Your face shone from my earth and sky,
    Your voice was in my heart always,
Days were as dreams when you were by,
    And nights of dreaming linked the day ;
In my great joy I craved so much,
    My life lay trembling at your hand,
I prayed you for one magic touch,
    How strange you did not understand !

From leaf to leaf, the trees are bare,
    The autumn wind is cold and stern,
And outlined in the clear sharp air,
    Lies a new world for me to learn ;
Stranger than all, dear friend, to-day,
    You take my hand and do not know
A thousand years have passed away,
    Since last year—when I loved you so.

CHARLES G. D. ROBERTS

It is not often that one can trace the gradual evolution of
a poetic individuality so clearly as in the case of Mr.
Charles G. D. Roberts. He has written five books of
verse : the first almost entirely academic and conventional;
the second still academic, but with traces of personal feeling and observation breaking through; the third mature
and, so to speak, real, but scarcely individual; the fourth
and fifth entirely disencumbered of imitation and convention, expressing in simple, straightforward personal accents
a marked intellectual individuality. Mr. Roberts's talent
has ripened slowly, bnt it has ripened to some purpose.

In *Orion, and other Poems* (1880), we read the college
exercise on every page. Several of the poems are distinctly
able. If there was a "Newdigate" at Mr. Roberts's
university, I am sure he deserved it, and trust he won it.
In *Orion, Ariadne*, and *Memnon* we have the usual
classical themes treated in the usual romantic fashion.
Lancelot and the Four Queens is a laboured and formless
ballad; the *Ode to Drowsihead* and *Ode to Night* are the
statutory imitations of Keats; and in the *Ballades and
Rondeaus* we see nothing but a young poet toying with his
tools. Everything, as he himself says rather prettily, in a
dedication to his father, has to do with

> Alien matters in distant regions
> Wrought in the youth of the centuries.

· CHARLES · G · D · ROBERTS ·

Six years later comes his second volume, *In Divers Tones*. Still he deals largely in classical themes—*Actæon*, *The Pipes of Pan*, *Off Pelorus*, &c.—but *Actæon* is written in strong and supple blank verse, and *The Pipes of Pan* in elegiacs which are not without an accent of their own. Furthermore, he has a fervid patriotic apostrophe to *Canada*, with the usual love-songs and some well-observed sonnets of country life.

These sonnets he reprints, with a number of others tuned to the same key, in his third book, *Songs of the Common Day* (1893). By this time he has learnt to draw his inspiration direct from nature, not from books. His verse begins to smack of the soil. The greater part of it is characteristically Canadian, and several pieces are notably vivid and vigorous. The most memorable, I think, are *The Silver Thaw* and two ballads of rustic life, *A Christmas-Eve Courtin'* and *The Wood Frolic*. A poem entitled *Canadian Streams* shows, when compared with the address to Canada in the earlier volume, a great advance in imaginative vision and distinction of style—in all that makes the difference between poetry and rhetoric. In several pieces, too—notably in *A Song of Growth*—we find unmistakable indications of that strong philosophical faculty which distinguishes Mr. Roberts's later work.

It is in *The Book of the Native* (1896) that his full individuality first declares itself. *New York Nocturnes* (1898) places some admirable work to his credit, but does not reveal his talent in a new light.

A deep and intimate love of nature and a vivid metaphysical imagination are, I conceive, Mr. Roberts's master qualities. He has an equally keen eye for sublunary and for translunary things: for the dewdrop and for the universe it mirrors. There is something of Thoreau in Mr. Roberts's endowment; something too, I think, of Robert Louis Stevenson; but withal his note is original. He loves nature in detail rather than in bulk. I should not call him a great landscapist, or a chronicler of aërial pageantries. His eye is concentrated on fruits, flowers, and grasses, orchards and purling brooks—on corners of landscape rather than on mountainous or oceanic expanses. These opening stanzas of a poem entitled *Afoot* are characteristic of the aspect in which Nature usually presents herself to his eyes :

> Comes the lure of green things growing,
> Comes the call of waters flowing,—
>   And the wayfarer desire
> Moves and wakes and would be going.
>
> Hark the migrant hosts of June
> Marching nearer noon by noon !
>   Hark the gossip of the grasses
> Bivouacked beneath the moon !
>
> Hark the leaves their mirth averring ;
> Hark the buds to blossom stirring ;
>   Hark the hushed, exultant haste
> Of the wind and world conferring !
>
> Hark the sharp, insistent cry
> Where the hawk patrols the sky !
>   Hark the flapping, as of banners,
> Where the heron triumphs by !
>
> Empire in the coasts of bloom
> Humming cohorts now resume,—
>   And desire is forth to follow
> Many a vagabond perfume.

Mr. Roberts is never tired of singing the "open meadows," the "uncut hayfields,"

> Where the hot scent steams and quivers,
>   Where the hot saps thrill and stir,
> Where in leaf-cells' green pavilions
>   Quaint artificers confer ;
>
> Where the bobolinks are merry,
>   Where the beetles bask and gleam,
> Where above the powdered blossoms
>   Powdered moth-wings poise and dream ;

CHARLES G. D. ROBERTS

> Where the bead-eyed mice adventure
> In the grass roots green and dun.
> Life is good and love is eager
> In the playground of the sun !

Admirable pieces in the same key are *The Trout Brook*
(which all brothers of the angle should know by heart), *An
August Wood Road*, *Apple Song*, *The Quest of the Arbutus*,
and *An Oblation*. But Mr. Roberts does not sing of spring
and summer only. Here is a winter fantasy of exquisite
grace :

THE FROSTED PANE.

> One night came Winter noiselessly, and leaned
> Against my window-pane.
> In the deep stillness of his heart convened
> The ghosts of all his slain.
>
> Leaves, and ephemera, and stars of earth,
> And fugitives of grass,—
> White spirits loosed from bonds of mortal birth,
> He drew them on the glass.

In some poems, notably in *The Heal-All*, Mr. Roberts's
note is purely Wordsworthian. In others his spirit soars
at a single bound from contemplating the smaller loveli-
nesses of nature to dizzy heights of cosmic vision. For
instance :

THE FALLING LEAVES.

> Lightly He blows, and at His breath they fall,
> The perishing kindreds of the leaves ; they drift,
> Spent flames of scarlet, gold aerial,
> Across the hollow year, noiseless and swift.
> Lightly He blows, and countless as the falling
> Of snow by night upon a solemn sea,
> The ages circle down beyond recalling,
> To strew the hollows of Eternity.
> He sees them drifting through the spaces dim,
> And leaves and ages are as one to Him.

In *Kinship* and in *Origins* we see the poet's thought in
the act of passing from the infinitely little to the infinitely

great, or rather of demonstrating their oneness. Here,
again, is a poem of purely metaphysical inspiration—perhaps Mr. Roberts's masterpiece in this key:

THE UNSLEEPING.

I soothe to unimagined sleep
The sunless bases of the deep,
And then I stir the aching tide
That gropes in its reluctant side.

I heave aloft the smoking hill:
To silent peace its throes I still.
But ever at its heart of fire
I lurk, an unassuaged desire.

I wrap me in the sightless germ
An instant or an endless term;
And still its atoms are my care,
Dispersed in ashes or in air.

I hush the comets one by one
To sleep for ages in the sun;
The sun resumes before my face
His circuit of the shores of space.

The mount, the star, the germ, the deep,
They all shall wake, they all shall sleep.
Time, like a flurry of wild rain,
Shall drift across the darkened pane.

Space, in the dim predestined hour,
Shall crumble like a ruined tower.
I only, with unfaltering eye,
Shall watch the dreams of God go by.

It must not be supposed, however, that Nature and
metaphysics are Mr. Roberts's sole inspirers. He has
written some strong and passionate love-poetry—witness
his *Nocturnes of the Honeysuckle* and *Nocturne of Consecra-
tion*—some very spirited ballads (one of which is quoted at
the end of this article), and some admirably imaginative
miscellaneous poems, such as *At Tide Water*, *The Witches'
Flight*, and this, on

CHARLES G. D. ROBERTS

THE ATLANTIC CABLE.

This giant nerve, at whose command
    The world's great pulses throb or sleep,—
It threads the undiscerned repose
    Of the dark bases of the deep.

Around it settle in the calm
    Fine tissues that a breath might mar,
Nor dream what fiery tidings pass,
    What messages of storm and war.

Far over it, where filtered gleams
    Faintly illume the mid-sea day,
Strange, pallid forms of fish or weed
    In the obscure tide softly sway.

And higher, where the vagrant waves
    Frequent the white, indifferent sun,
Where ride the smoke-blue hordes of rain
    And the long vapors lift and run,

Passes perhaps some lonely ship
    With exile hearts that homeward ache,—
While far beneath is flashed a word
    That soon shall bid them bleed or break.

Nowhere, however, does Mr. Roberts's talent appear more original and sympathetic than in his poems on, and for, children. *The Little Field of Peace* is a delicately restrained and touching elegy; but the poet's best things in this kind are his *Wake-up Song* and *Sleepy Man*, two companion pieces which I cannot but quote entire :

A WAKE-UP SONG.

Sun's up ; wind's up ! Wake up, dearies !
    Leave your coverlets white and downy,
June's come into the world this morning.
    Wake up, Golden Head ! Wake up, Brownie !

Dew on the meadow-grass, waves on the water,
    Robins in the rowan tree, wondering about you !
Don't keep the buttercups so long waiting,
    Don't keep the bobolinks singing without you.

Wake up, Golden Head ! Wake up, Brownie !
Cat-bird wants you in the garden soon.
You and I, butterflies, bobolinks and clover,
We've a lot to do on the first of June.

SLEEPY MAN.

When the Sleepy Man comes with the dust on his eyes
    (Oh, weary, my Dearie, so weary !)
He shuts up the earth, and he opens the skies.
    (So hush-a-by, weary my Dearie !)

He smiles through his fingers, and shuts up the sun ;
    (Oh, weary, my Dearie, so weary !)
The stars that he loves he lets out one by one.
    (So hush-a-by, weary my Dearie !)

He comes from the castles of Drowsy-boy Town ;
    (Oh, weary, my Dearie, so weary !)
At the touch of his hand the tired eyelids fall down.
    (So hush-a-by, weary my Dearie !)

He comes with a murmur of dream in his wings
    (Oh, weary my Dearie, so weary !)
And whispers of mermaids and wonderful things.
    (So hush-a-by, weary my Dearie !)

Then the top is a burden, the bugle a bane
    (Oh, weary my Dearie, so weary !)
When one would be faring down Dream-a-way Lane,
    (So hush-a-by, weary my Dearie !)

When one would be wending in Lullaby Wherry
    (Oh, weary, my Dearie, so weary !)
To Sleepy Man's Castle by Comforting Ferry.
    (So hush-a-by, weary my Dearie !)

I have said little of the peculiarly Canadian strain in
Mr. Roberts's verse, for I am no naturalist, and should
doubtless reveal startling depths of ignorance if I attempted
to discuss the birds and flowers of transatlantic poets.
Let me only say that in Mr. Roberts's later books, at any
rate, there are no conventional echoes from the woods and
gardens, or even from the Lakes, of England. When the
time comes (and surely it *has* come) for a study of the

contributions of Greater Britain to the flora and fauna of English poetry, Mr. Roberts's writings will be found to merit very close examination. And I have little doubt that they will stand the test of expert criticism. He always gives one the impression of writing with his eye upon the fact—nay, with all his senses alertly percipient of every "vagrant influence" of the spring morning or the summer noon. I know few poets who transfer to their pages so much of the actual colour and aroma of coppice and meadowland as does Mr. Charles Roberts.

THE "LAUGHING SALLY."

A wind blew up from Pernambuco.
(Yeo heave ho! the " Laughing Sally "!
  Hi yeo, heave away !)
A wind blew out of the east-sou'-east
  And boomed at the break of day.

The " Laughing Sally " sped for her life,
  And a speedy craft was she.
The black flag flew at her top to tell
  How she took toll of the sea.

The wind blew up from Pernambuco;
  And in the breast of the blast
Came the King's black ship, like a hound let slip
  On the trail of the " Sally " at last.

For a day and a night, a night and a day;
  Over the blue, blue round,
Went on the chase of the pirate quarry,
  The hunt of the tireless hound.

" Land on the port bow!'' came the cry;
  And the " Sally " raced for shore,
Till she reached the bar at the river-mouth
  Where the shallow breakers roar.

She passed the bar by a secret channel
  With clear tide under her keel,—
For he knew the shoals like an open book,
  The captain at the wheel.

She passed the bar, she sped like a ghost,
  Till her sails were hid from view
By the tall, liana'd, unsunned boughs
  O'erbrooding the dark bayou.

370

CHARLES D. G. ROBERTS

At moonrise up to the river-mouth
  Came the King's black ship of war.
The red cross flapped in wrath at her peak,
  But she could not cross the bar.

And while she lay in the run of the seas,
  By the grimmest whim of chance
Out of a bay to the north came forth
  Two battleships of France.

On the English ship the twain bore down
  Like wolves that range by night;
And the breaker's roar was heard no more
  In the thunder of the fight.

The crash of the broadsides rolled and stormed
  To the " Sally," hid from view
Under the tall, liana'd boughs
  Of the moonless, dark bayou.

A boat ran out for news of the fight,
  And this was the word she brought—
" The King's ship fights the ships of France
  As the King's ships all have fought ! "

Then muttered the mate, " I'm a man of Devon ! "
  And the captain thundered then—
" There's English rope that bides for our necks,
  But we all be English men ! "

The " Sally " glided out of the gloom
  And down the moon-white river.
She stole like a gray shark over the bar
  Where the long surf seethes forever.

She hove to under a high French hull,
  And the red cross rose to her peak.
The French were looking for fight that night,
  And they hadn't far to seek.

Blood and fire on the streaming decks,
  And fire and blood below;
The heat of hell, and the reek of hell,
  And the dead men laid a-row !

And when the stars paled out of heaven
  And the red dawn-rays uprushed,
The oaths of battle, the crash of timbers,
  The roar of the guns were hushed.

With one foe beaten under his bow,
  The other afar in flight,
The English captain turned to look
  For his fellow in the fight.

The English captain turned, and stared ;—
  For where the " Sally " had been
Was a single spar upthrust from the sea
  With the red-cross flag serene !

    *   *   *   *   *

A wind blew up from Pernambuco,—
  (Yeo heave ho ! the " Laughing Sally ! "
  Hi yeo, heavy away !)
And boomed for the doom of the " Laughing Sally,"
  Gone down at the break of day.

GEORGE SANTAYANA

His name, and two lines in his *Ode to the Mediterranean* :

> For I was born where first the rills of Tagus
> Turn to the westward—

lead one to conclude that Mr. George Santayana is of Spanish parentage. There is nothing in his pure, supple, sedulously refined English to suggest that he is not writing in his native tongue. Yet perhaps the fact that he is not bound by ancestral ties to the land of his sojourn—which I take to be America—may in part account for the extremely abstract quality of his verse. The world has scarcely any objective existence for him. Though in weaving his similitudes he uses the traditional apparatus of flowers and stars, mountains, rivers and the sea, these things are pure ideas to him, divested of all material attributes. There is scarcely a line of description in his work. A single piece of half a dozen stanzas, entitled *Cape Cod*, is the exception that proves the rule ; and even here the landscape does not merely mirror, but symbolises a mood. The pageantry of life means little or nothing to him. He has no vision for external nature, but only for the summaries, essences, abstracts of phenomena, recorded in the concave of his soul. He comes near to some such confession in the lines :

> There may be chaos still around the world,
> The little world that in my thinking lies ;

373

POETS OF THE YOUNGER GENERATION

*   *   *   *   *

> Within my nature's shell I slumber curled,
> Unmindful of the changing outer skies.

It is true that the "shell" he has here in mind is moral rather than intellectual; but it is none the less true that the "little world" of his thinking pursues its orbit in disdainful aloofness from the chaos of sense-impressions. One might almost conceive the poet to have been born blind, and to treat of the visible universe merely from hearsay.

Theoretically, this characteristic ought to imply a serious defect in Mr. Santayana's work; practically, I find it no defect at all, but rather a source of distinction. It is a relief, for once in a way, to escape from the importunate details of the visible world into a sphere of pure thought and pure melody. For Mr. Santayana is a very remarkable and extremely accomplished poet. The bulk of his work is so slight—it consists, so far as I know, of some sixty sonnets and fifty pages of other verse—that large epithets seem disproportionate. Yet it is difficult, without using terms of a certain emphasis, to express one's sense of the well-nourished suavity of his style, the flawless beauty of his metrical form, the aptness of his imagery, the elevation of his thought. He is a master of the sonnet, of that there can be no doubt. On an earlier page * I have spoken of the sonnet as a form in which a certain specious air of poetical merit is easily attainable; but there is nothing specious or superficial about Mr. Santayana's workmanship. Take this as an example:

ON THE DEATH OF A METAPHYSICIAN.

> Unhappy dreamer, who outwinged in flight
> The pleasant region of the things I love,
> And soared beyond the sunshine, and above

---

* Page 264.

· GEORGE · SANTAYANA ·

The golden cornfields and the dear and bright
Warmth of the hearth—blasphemer of delight,
Was your proud bosom not at peace with Jove,
That you sought, thankless for his guarded grove,
The empty horror of abysmal night?
Ah, the thin air is cold above the moon!
I stood and saw you fall, befooled in death,
As, in your numbèd spirit's fatal swoon,
You cried you were a god, or were to be;
I heard with feeble moan your boastful breath
Bubble from depths of the Icarian sea.

With what admirable skill is the metrical scheme of this sonnet employed to emphasise its dramatic phrasing! The seventh line is perhaps a little cumbrous, and "numbèd" in the eleventh line seems to me a nerveless epithet. Otherwise it is hard to find a flaw in the poem, and harder still to find adequate praise for the splendid intensity of the close.

The main body of Mr. Santayana's sonnets falls into two sections: the first purely philosophical, the second consecrated to a spiritual love. The opening sonnet of all tells how the poet worshipped in youth at

> the piteous height
> Where God vouchsafed the death of man to share,

but afterwards descended in search of

> a garden of delight,
> Or island altar to the Sea and Air,
> Where gentle music were accounted prayer,
> And reason, veiled, performed the happy rite.

Then the next poem opens thus:

> Slow and reluctant was the long descent,
> With many farewell pious looks behind,
> And dumb misgivings where the path might wind,
> And questionings of nature, as I went.

> The greener branches that above me bent,
> The broadening valleys, quieted my mind,
> To the fair reasons of the Spring inclined
> And to the Summer's tender argument.

If there be not in such writing as this a very peculiar delicacy and suavity, I am the more deceived. It would be a fascinating task to follow the process of Mr. Santayana's thought from sonnet to sonnet; but it must not be attempted here. "Process," perhaps, is scarcely the right word; I doubt whether any logical development is traceable 'in either sonnet-sequence. Rather it would seem that, singly or in groups of two or three, the sonnets express disconnected phases of thought. At all events, as I have not space to follow out a continuous thread of reasoning, I need not go about to search for it. Each poem has certainly an individual beauty and significance of its own, quite apart from its possible relation to an ordered whole.

My last quotation was the octave of the second sonnet; here now is the sestett of Sonnet VII., which begins " I would I might forget that I am I," and deals with the burden of personality :

> Happy the dumb beast, hungering for food,
> But calling not his suffering his own ;
> Blessèd the angel, gazing on all good,
> But knowing not he sits upon a throne ;
> Wretched the mortal, pondering his mood,
> And doomed to know his aching heart alone.

There is a sort of cruelty, however, in dismembering a sonnet, even when one portion of it, like these six lines, forms an independent epigram. Why present the stem without the flower or the flower without the stem ? I feel I must renounce the attempt to pick out brief passages of more than ordinary beauty, and let one complete sonnet represent the sequence. After much hesitation, I choose

the following—the ninth. It is a noble piece of work;
yet it would be unjust to Mr. Santayana to claim for it any
singular pre-eminence.

> Have patience ; it is fit that in this wise
> The spirit purge away its proper dross.
> No endless fever doth thy watches toss,
> For by excess of evil, evil dies.
> Soon shall the faint world melt before thine eyes,
> And, all life's losses cancelled by life's loss,
> Thou shalt lay down all burdens on thy cross,
> And be that day with God in Paradise.
> Have patience ; for a long eternity
> No summons woke thee from thy happy sleep ;
> For love of God one vigil thou canst keep
> And add thy drop of sorrow to the sea.
> Having known grief, all will be well with thee,
> Ay, and thy second slumber will be deep.

The first series consists of twenty sonnets, the second of
thirty ; and the second is the finer as well as the longer of
the two, in something like the same proportion. As one
reads it, one is more and more haunted by a sense of
familiarity, not in the ideas or the images, but in the mellow
music of the verse. Original, Mr. Santayana is, beyond a
doubt ; yet the smooth, firm texture of his lines is not new
to us, his honeyed cadences bring with them some far-off
association. "That strain again!" we say, "It had a
dying fall"—and the enigma is solved. Though writing
always in the strict Petrarcan form, Mr. Santayana has
evidently steeped his mind in the melody of Shakespeare's
quatorzains. So thoroughly has he done this that a
captious criticism might borrow the epithet employed by
Francis Meres and complain that Mr. Santayana's sonnets
were over "sug'red." They have not the complex, billowy
movement of Rossetti's sonnets, but aim rather (and that
consciously, one cannot but suppose) at Shakespearean
definiteness of crystallisation. The reader may not unnaturally cry out upon this comparison as extravagant, and

to prove it, not only just, but inevitable, I should have to
reprint the whole sequence. It is a cumulative effect that
I am seeking to indicate, not one that can be adequately
exemplified in a single sonnet, or in two, or three. Yet
some hint of it may surely be conveyed by such a sonnet as
this—the sequel to one in which the poet has besought a
painter to record in line and hue his lady's beauty: "the
sweet eyes tender and the broad brow cold."

> Yet why, of one who loved thee not, command
> Thy counterfeit, for other men to see,
> When God himself did on my heart for me
> Thy face, like Christ's upon the napkin, brand?
> O how much subtler than a painter's hand
> Is love to render back the truth of thee!
> My soul should be thy glass in time to be,
> And in my thought thine effigy should stand.
> Yet, lest the churlish critics of that age
> Should flout my praise, and deem a lover's rage
> Could gild a virtue and a grace exceed,
> I bid thine image here confront my page,
> That men may look upon thee as they read,
> And cry: Such eyes a better poet need.

This sonnet exemplifies the one besetting fault of form
which can be laid to Mr. Santayana's charge. The final
couplet, essential to the Shakespearean sonnet, seems to me
to detract notably from the beauty of the Petrarcan rhyme-
scheme. It is true that Mr. Santayana scarcely ever leaves
the final couplet isolated, but is careful to attach it to a
previous line, usually (as in this case) the eleventh. Nevertheless, the chiming close is always thin and wiry in its
effect, like the twang of a final chord on the banjo, contrasted
with the gradual evanishing of a cadence on the violin.

It is not for us to speculate how much of reality and how
much of fantasy there may be in the situation adumbrated
in this second sequence. The fact that several of the
sonnets seem mutually irreconcilable in their presentment

of the relation between the poet and the lady, appears to point to a large admixture, at any rate, of pure fancy. In one poem, for instance, there seems to be a perfect understanding between them:

> Be mine, be mine in God and in the grave,
> Since naught but chance and the insensate wave
> Divides us, and the wagging tongue of men.

A little farther on, again, the lady is represented as absolutely unconscious of the poet's worship:

> For, when God tells you, you will not despise
> The love I bore you. It is better so.

But why should we be concerned to analyse the soil of fact from which sprang such a flower of poetry as this:

> As when the sceptre dangles from the hand
> Of some king doting, faction runneth wild,
> Thieves shake their chains and traitors, long exiled,
> Hover about the confines of the land,
> Till the young Prince, anointed, takes command,
> Full of high purpose, simple, trustful, mild,
> And, smitten by his radiance undefiled,
> The ruffians are abashed, the cowards stand:—
> So in my kingdom riot and despair
> Lived by thy lack, and called for thy control,
> But at thy coming all the world grew fair;
> Away before thy face the villains stole,
> And panoplied I rose to do and bear,
> When love his clarion sounded in my soul.

Is not this noble? Is not this classical? Note the perfect simplicity and purity of Mr. Santayana's diction, his resolute avoidance of verbal ostentation or metrical eccentricity. Here is English undefiled indeed, unvulgarised even by obtrusive ornament, importunate, self-conscious beauty. There is as little to surprise and startle as there is to offend us in such work as this. It is only exquisite; it is only right. And if, in the foregoing sonnet, the form is ideal, in this which follows ideal form is wedded to tragic loftiness. of thought:

> We needs must be divided in the tomb,
> For I would die among the hills of Spain,
> And o'er the treeless melancholy plain
> Await the coming of the final gloom.
> But thou—O pitiful!—wilt find scant room
> Among thy kindred by the northern main,
> And fade into the drifting mist again,
> The hemlocks' shadow, or the pines' perfume.
> Let gallants lie beside their ladies' dust
> In one cold grave, with mortal love inurned;
> Let the sea part our ashes, if it must.
> The souls fled thence which love immortal burned,
> For they were wedded without bond of lust,
> And nothing of our heart to earth returned.

If there is a flaw in this sonnet it is the twelfth line, which is perhaps not absolutely clear, not perfectly luminous. But how trivial a blemish in how lovely a piece of work!

I quote at the end of this article three sonnets from the second sequence (which are, however, interludes in the amatory theme), and a memorial sonnet *To W. P.*—one of a set of four. Let me call special attention to the daring prosaism of the last words of the second of these poems. One would imagine it a sheer impossibility to introduce the phrase "There is no knowing" into a serious sonnet without producing an effect of bathos. But to Mr. Santayana's mastery nothing is impossible. He takes this common pebble of the highway and so cunningly enchases it that we would not exchange it for an orient pearl of speech.

Mr. Santayana's other verses, though full of accomplishment, are less remarkable than his sonnets. Among them are five *Odes*, written in Sapphic and Adonic stanzas, and a very striking dramatic fragment named *Lucifer*. It consists of a dialogue between Hermes and Lucifer, partly in irregular choric measures, partly in rhymed pentameters. Lucifer, according to his own story, has been banished to the desolate, inclement region where Hermes visits him, for disturbing the complacency of heaven by tactless questions, such as—

> Tell, O Lord, the cause
> Why sluggish nature doth with Thee contend
> And Thy designs, observant of the laws,
> By tortuous paths must struggle to their end.

There is something a little comic in this conception of inopportune curiosity as the sin by which the angels fell; but the dialogue is admirably written, none the less. Lucifer in the end makes ready to return the visit of Hermes, and thus addresses his henchman, Lyal:

> We must away; this night shall have its dreams.
> Thou shalt behold a green land, watered well,
> Where large white swans swim in the lucent streams;
> And bosky thickets where the harpy screams;
> And centaurs scouring fields of asphodel,
> While young fauns pluck their beards, and start away
> At great Pan's feast to pipe an interlude.
> There mermaids with the painted dolphins play,
> Splashing blue waves for rainbows in the spray;
> And friendly poets, straying through the wood,
> Lay finger to the mouth, to watch askance
> How in wild ring the nymphs and satyrs dance.

Does such a passage as this seem to contradict my opening remarks as to the lack of objectivity in Mr Santayana's work? Surely not. We have here a picture, it is true, and a beautiful one; but its elements are entirely conventional. When Mr. Santayana wants to paint a glade in Arcady, or by the Sicilian shore, he does not dream of transferring to it a single touch studied from the woods or seaboard of Massachusetts. He goes straight to literature for his material; or rather he conjures up the required picture from an imagination impregnated with the choicest literary essences.   He lives, in short, in a Palace of Art, with little or no outlook upon the material world.   But it is a palace of all that is exquisite in art, and, shut in though it be, there is nothing sickly or stifling in its atmosphere.   If there are no windows in the frescoed walls, at least there are skylights in the dome, through which the stars shine large and clear.

GEORGE SANTAYANA

I.

As in the midst of battle there is room
For thoughts of love, and in foul sin for mirth ;
As gossips whisper of a trinket's worth
Spied by the death-bed's flickering candle-gloom ;
As in the crevices of Cæsar's tomb
The sweet herbs flourish on a little earth :
So in this great disaster of our birth
We can be happy, and forget our doom.
For morning, with a ray of tenderest joy
Gilding the iron heaven, hides the truth,
And evening gently woos us to employ
Our grief in idle catches.   Such is youth ;
Till from that summer's trance we wake, to find
Despair before us, vanity behind.

II.

Sleep hath composed the anguish of my brain,
And ere the dawn I will arise and pray.
Strengthen me, Heaven, and attune my lay
Unto my better angel's clear refrain.
For I can hear him in the night again,
The breathless night, snow-smothered, happy, grey,
With premonition of the jocund day,
Singing a quiet carol to my pain.
Slowly, saith he, the April buds are growing
In the chill core of twigs all leafless now ;
Gently, beneath the weight of last night's snowing,
Patient of winter's hand, the branches bow.
Each buried seed lacks light as much as thou.
Wait for the spring, brave heart ; there is no knowing.

III.

What riches have you that you deem me poor,
Or what large comfort that you call me sad?
Tell me what makes you so exceeding glad:
Is your earth happy or your heaven sure?
I hope for heaven, since the stars endure
And bring such tidings as our fathers had.
I know no deeper doubt to make me mad,
I need no brighter love to keep me pure.
To me the faiths of old are daily bread;
I bless their hope, I bless their will to save,
And my deep heart still meaneth what they said.
It makes me happy that the soul is brave,
And, being so much kinsman to the dead,
I walk contented to the peopled grave.

IV.

In my deep heart these chimes would still have rung
To toll your passing, had you not been dead;
For time a sadder mask than death may spread
Over the face that ever should be young.
The bough that falls with all its trophies hung
Falls not too soon, but lays its flower-crowned head
Most royal in the dust, with no leaf shed
Unhallowed or unchiselled or unsung.
And though the after world will never hear
The happy name of one so gently true,
Nor chronicles write large this fatal year,
Yet we who loved you, though we be but few,
Keep you in whatsoe'er is good, and rear
In our weak virtues monuments to you.

DUNCAN CAMPBELL SCOTT

WHY has Canada contributed so much, Australia so little, to the poetry of Greater Britain ? This question is brought home to me, not for the first time, by the chance which places the poems of Mr. Duncan Campbell Scott in my hands, immediately after I have been vainly searching for even a single poet to represent Australia in these pages. Two or three clever, even brilliant, versifiers have won no small popularity among the public of the island continent. They write spirited narratives, stirring ballads, excellent "poems for recitation." Their descriptions of life and sport in the bush are often of great merit, full of Bret Harte-like pathos and human interest. They will sing you the fabulous exploits of a racehorse or of a bushranger with admirable vigour. They have a very pretty touch at a sentimental character-sketch. But the literary note, the note of style, dignity, rhythmical refine-ment and verbal beauty, is wanting in all the Australian verse that has come in my way. I ask myself in vain why this should be. I can aver of my own knowledge that Australian nature and Australian life abound in all the elements that go to the making of poetry. A man of the talent of Mr. Campbell Scott, for instance, would find under the Southern Cross ample material for his strong and delicate art. Why has Canada three or four such men, and

Australia, so far as I can discover, not one ? Perhaps when a great Australian poet shall, in the fulness of time, arise, we may be able to discern why his coming has been delayed so long.

Meanwhile, it is evident that Canada has a certain advantage, for poetical purposes, in the greater variety of her climate. She has two extremes of temperature, Australia only one. The process of the seasons is as strongly marked in Canada as in any region of the planet ; in Australia it is much less emphasised. The cyclic drama of life and death, then, comes home more vividly to the Canadian than to the Australian observer, and perhaps stimulates more powerfully both his observation and his imagination.

In Mr. Campbell Scott both qualities are present in liberal measure. He is above everything a poet of climate and atmosphere, employing with a nimble, graphic touch the clear, pure, transparent colours of a richly-furnished palette. He leaves unrecorded no single phase in the pageant of the northern year, from the odorous heat of June to the ice-bound silence of December. His work abounds in magically luminous phrases and stanzas. Here are two detached quatrains from a poem entitled *The Voice and the Dusk* :

> The slender moon and one pale star,
>   A rose-leaf and a silver bee
> From some god's garden blown afar,
>   Go down the gold deep tranquilly.

> *   *   *   *

> A thrush is hidden in a maze
>   Of cedar buds and tamarac bloom,
> He throws his rapid flexile phrase,
>   A flash of emeralds in the gloom.

There is a rare intensity of imaginative vision in these two

· DVNCAN · CAMPBELL · SCOTT ·

stanzas; yet not more, certainly, than in this first verse of
An Impromptu:

> The stars are in the ebon sky,
>   Burning, gold, alone;
> The wind roars over the rolling earth,
>   Like water over a stone.

Take, now, this admirable picture of *A Summer Storm*:

> Last night a storm fell on the world
>   From heights of drouth and heat,
> The surly clouds for weeks were furled,
>   The air could only sway and beat.
>
> The beetles clattered at the blind,
>   The hawks fell twanging from the sky,
> The west unrolled a feathery wind,
>   And the night fell sullenly.
>
> The storm leaped roaring from its lair,
>   Like the shadow of doom,
> The poignard lightning searched the air,
>   The thunder ripped the shattered gloom,
>
> The rain came down with a roar like fire,
>   Full-voiced and clamorous and deep,
> The weary world had its heart's desire,
>   And fell asleep.

You shall go far before you find a stronger or juster piece
of description than this. The most exquisite touch, perhaps, is the "feathery wind" from the west; but how fine
is the "poignard lightning"! how palpably true the rain
coming down "with a roar like fire"! Compare with this
superb spectacular effect the silvery tenderness of the
picture in the following stanzas from a poem entitled *In
May*:

> The apple orchards, banked with bloom,
> Are drenched and dripping with the wet,
> And on the breeze their deep perfume
> Grows and fades by and lingers yet.

In some green covert far remote
The oven-bird is never still,
And, golden-throat to golden-throat,
The orioles warble on the hill.

Now over all the gem-like woods
The delicate mist is blown again,
And after dripping interludes
Lets down the lulling silver rain.

Mr. Scott is particularly happy in the phrases suggested to
him by the song of birds. Note the ingenious suspension
in the cadence of the last two lines of the following
stanzas from a poem not otherwise remarkable—a song

made for my Dear One
When we are far apart;
That she may have wherever she goes
A song of mine in her heart.

     *   *   *   *

A song that will bid her remember
The north nights cool and still,
With the thrushes fluting deep, deep,
Deep on the pine-wood hill.

This is a musical inspiration of rare and haunting charm.

There is scarcely a poem of Mr. Scott's from which one
could not cull some memorable descriptive passage. By
way of exemplifying once for all the originality and power
of his nature-painting, I shall place in juxtaposition a midsummer and a late autumn picture, which seem to me almost
equally masterly :

A NIGHT IN JUNE.

The world is heated seven times,
The sky is close above the lawn,
An oven when the coals are drawn.

There is no stir of air at all,
Only at times an inward breeze
Turns back a pale leaf in the trees.

DUNCAN CAMPBELL SCOTT

Here the syringa's rich perfume
   Covers the tulip's red retreat,
   A burning pool of scent and heat.

The pallid lightning wavers dim
   Between the trees, then deep and dense
   The darkness settles more intense.

A hawk lies panting in the grass,
   Or plunges upward through the air,
   The lightning shows him whirling there.

A bird calls madly from the eaves,
   Then stops, the silence all at once
   Disturbed, falls dead again and stuns.

A redder lightning flits about,
   But in the north a storm is rolled
   That splits the gloom with vivid gold;

Dead silence, then a little sound,
   The distance chokes the thunder down,
   It shudders faintly in the town.

A fountain plashing in the dark
   Keeps up a mimic dropping strain;
   Ah! God, if it were really rain!

A SONG.

'Tis autumn and down in the fields
The buckwheat is browning still:
Gather yourself in your cloak,
The winter is over the hill.

There's a cloud of black in the north,
The aurora is smouldering behind,
There are stars in the parting clouds,
And a touch of frost in the wind.

Down in the icy dew
The crickets are cheering shrill:
" There is time for another song,
Though winter is over the hill."

> Out of the great black cloud
> The aurora leaps and flies,
> Pushing its phosphor spikes
> In the deeps of the violet skies.
>
> The moon is wrapped in a film,
> She looks wan and chill:
> Gather yourself in your cloak,
> The winter is over the hill.

Though I have dwelt primarily on Mr. Scott's Canadian nature-poems, it must not be understood that his talent is merely descriptive. There is a philosophic and also a romantic strain in it. I confess to finding a little vague the philosophy symbolically set forth in *Labor and the Angel*, which nevertheless contains many admirable lines and passages. *The Harvest* is an impressive chant of the earth-hunger of the disinherited multitudes. Even here, however, Mr. Scott's talent seems to me stronger on the pictorial than on the reflective side. How fine, for example, is this Constable-like landscape:

> Sun on the mountain,
> Shade in the valley,
> Ripple and lightness
> Leaping along the world,
> Sun, like a gold sword
> Plucked from the scabbard,
> Striking the wheat-fields,
> Splendid and lusty,
> Close-standing, full-headed,
> Toppling with plenty;
> Shade, like a buckler
> Kindly and ample,
> Sweeping the wheat-fields
> Darkening and tossing;
> There on the world-rim
> Winds break and gather
> Heaping the mist
> For the pyre of the sunset;
> And still as a shadow,

DUNCAN CAMPBELL SCOTT

> In the dim westward,
> A cloud sloop of amethyst
> Moored to the world
> With cables of rain.

In *The Cup* and *The Happy Fatalist* we have condensed and powerful expressions of a resolutely stoical philosophy of which this is the burden :

> Follow your bent,
> Cry life is joy,
> Cry life is woe,
> The god is content,
> Impartial in power,
> Tranquil—and lo !
> Like the kernels in quern,
> Each in his turn,
> Comes to his hour,
> Nor fast nor slow :
> It is well : even so.

Of all Mr. Scott's philosophic utterances, however, the finest is the poem entitled *In the Country Churchyard : To the Memory of my Father.* This is admirable in form, serene and elevated in thought. Despite its length, I have been sorely tempted to quote it in full. Having resisted the temptation, I shall not do the poem the injustice of tearing from their context any of its stately stanzas.

Mr. Scott's purely romantic poems are not numerous, but contain some delightful writing. The suave couplets of *By the Willow Spring* tell the story of a " fragile daughter of the earth " who naiad-like, haunted a pool in the woods, and was at last found dead upon its verge.

> This is her tale, her murmurous monument
> Flows softly where her fragile life was spent,
> Not grooved in brass nor trenched in pallid stone,
> But told by water to the reeds alone.

There is a haunting beauty in *The Magic House ;* but a still

391

finer, more clear-cut piece of pure imagination is *In the House of Dream*, of which I quote the first sonnet:

> The lady Lillian knelt upon the sward,
>   Between the arbour and the almond leaves;
>   Beyond, the barley gathered into sheaves;
> A blade of gladiolus, like a sword,
> Flamed fierce against the gold; and down toward
>   The limpid west, a pallid poplar wove
>   A spell of shadow; through the meadow drove
> A deep unbroken brook without a ford.
>
> A fountain flung and poised a golden ball;
>   On the soft grass a frosted serpent lay,
> With oval spots of opal over all;
>   Upon the basin's edge within the spray,
> Lulled by some craft of laughter in the fall,
>   An ancient crow dreamed hours and hours away.

The reverberation of the vowels in the line "With oval spots of opal over all" is perhaps a little tricky and Poe-like; but it is undeniably ingenious. A second sonnet completes the dream-picture most effectively. I confess that the beautiful stanza of *Avis* does not quite compensate, in my eyes, for the extreme vagueness of the picture it presents; but *The Piper of Arll*, though its symbolism, if it has any, escapes me, is a singularly beautiful fantasy, full of jewel-like colour and tenuous, unearthly melody. "There was in Arll a little cove," the poet begins, "Where the salt wind came cool and free"; and he pictures the cove for us in these two admirable stanzas:

> A brook hung sparkling on the hill,
> The hill swept far to ring the bay;
> The bay was faithful, wild or still,
> To the heart of the ocean far away.
>
> There were three pines above the comb
> That, when the sun flared and went down,
> Grew like three warriors reaving home
> The plunder of a burning town.

I scarcely know where to look for a more brilliant flash
of romantic imagination.

There is also a purely lyric vein in Mr. Scott's talent,
represented by such charming pieces as *At the Lattice,*
Youth and Time, and *A Little Song*. He is a poet of many
gifts, and of few vices—incapable of harshness, incapable of
vulgarity. He is not incapable of an occasional touch of
commonplace, nor can he be held guiltless of now and then
letting pass a piece of makeshift workmanship, a line or two of
padding, a word or phrase imposed by the rhyme rather than
by the idea. Let me give as an instance the last two lines of the
first stanza of *The Piper of Arll*—lines which I deliberately
refrained from quoting above, so manifest was their
inferiority to the rest of the picture :

> A foamy beach that one would love,
> If he were longing for the sea.

Such flaws, however, are not really characteristic. As a
rule, Mr. Scott's workmanship is careful and highly finished.
He is before everything a colourist. He paints in hues of
a peculiar and vivid translucency. But he is also a metrist
of no mean skill, and an imaginative thinker of no common
capacity.

OFF RIVIÈRE DU LOUP.

O ship incoming from the sea
  With all your cloudy tower of sail,
Dashing the water to the lee,
  And leaning grandly to the gale ;

The sunset pageant in the west
  Has filled your canvas curves with rose,
And jewelled every topling crest
  That crashes into silver snows!

You know the joy of coming home,
  After long leagues to France or Spain ;
You feel the clear Canadian foam
  And the gulf water heave again.

Between these sombre purple hills
  That cool the sunset's molten bars,
You will go on as the wind wills,
  Beneath the river's roof of stars.

You will toss onward toward the lights
  That spangle over the lonely pier,
By hamlets glimmering on the heights,
  By level islands black and clear.

You will go on beyond the tide,
  Through brimming plains of olive sedge,
Through paler shallows light and wide,
  The rapids piled along the ledge.

At evening off some reedy bay
  You will swing slowly on your chain,
And catch the scent of dewy hay,
  Soft blowing from the pleasant plain.

DUNCAN CAMPBELL SCOTT

THE REED-PLAYER.

To B. C.

By a dim shore where water darkening
  Took the last light of spring,
I went beyond the tumult, hearkening
  For some diviner thing.

Where the bats flew from the black elms like leaves,
  Over the ebon pool
Brooded the bittern's cry, as one that grieves
  Lands ancient, bountiful.

I saw the fireflies shine below the wood,
  Above the shallows dank,
As Uriel from some great altitude,
  The planets rank on rank.

And now unseen along the shrouded mead
  One went under the hill;
He blew a cadence on his mellow reed,
  That trembled and was still.

It seemed as if a line of amber fire
  Had shot the gathered dusk,
As if had blown a wind from ancient Tyre
  Laden with myrrh and musk.

He gave his luring note amid the fern ;
  Its enigmatic fall
Haunted the hollow dusk with golden turn
  And argent interval.

I could not know the message that he bore,
  The springs of life from me
Hidden ; his incommunicable lore
  As much a mystery.

And as I followed far the magic player
  He passed the maple wood,
And when I passed the stars had risen there,
  And there was solitude.

MISS DORA SIGERSON

(MRS. CLEMENT SHORTER)

MRS. CLEMENT SHORTER'S technical accomplishment, her sense of metre and of style, do not, unfortunately, equal her inborn poetic feeling; yet her singing has an individual note which goes far to redeem its manifold imperfections of form. There is race in her work; it smacks of the soil; it is no mere imitative culture-product, but an expression of innate emotion and impulse. Mrs. Shorter has all the fanciful melancholy, the ardent spirituality, and the eerie-pathetic invention of the western Kelts. The unseen world of semi-malignant elemental beings is quite as real to her as the tangible world of her five senses. Her imagination is nourished on folk-lore, and even Christian conceptions of life and death she instinctively translates into terms of that ancient and exquisite paganism which seems like a natural emanation from the green hills and rushing waters of Ireland. In another paper * I have hazarded a perhaps fanciful theory of the historical and geographical conditions which have begotten the peculiarly Keltic spirit. All the characteristics of that spirit are exemplified in Mrs. Shorter's poetry.

So great, so all-pervading, is her incuriousness of form, that, wherever we approach her work, it meets us on the threshold. Let us face it, then, and have done with it.

* See p. 178.

· DORA · SIGERSON · SHORTER ·

Alike in prosody, in style, and in grammar Mrs. Shorter is apt to take disconcerting liberties. She gives us, for instance, a poem entitled *The Lone of Soul*, consisting of eight stanzas, seven of which are written in the following measure :

> Alone among his kind he stands alone,
>> Torn by the passions of his own strange heart,
> Stoned by continual wreckage of his dreams,
>> He in the crowd for ever is apart.

This is a perfectly simple and regular stanza, which I select as a specimen for the sake of its fine third line ; and all the stanzas are equally regular, except the fourth, which runs, or rather stumbles, thus :

> The wedded body and the single soul,
>> Beside his mate he shall most mateless stand,
> *For ever to dream of that unseen face—*
>> *For ever to sigh for that enchanted land.*

Without going into technicalities, one may simply point out that the last line can with difficulty be coerced into the metrical scheme, while the third is in itself a passable enough line, but of a totally different measure from the rest of the poem. It is like a single prancing hussar placed in rank among a company of foot-soldiers. It upsets, and to no conceivable purpose, the whole order and symmetry of the poem. Take, again, the following :

> Since Naois was dead, her belovèd, the rose on her cheek paled
>> with sorrow,
> And laughter was dead on her lips, only tears were her own
>> night and morrow,
> Till the King a new vengeance had planned to wake her strange
>> listlessness to life.

The incompressible trisyllable "listlessness" is as clearly out of place in this line as a pebble in a walking-shoe ; but it seems to occasion Mrs. Shorter no uneasiness. The first

four lines of the poem, *The Me within Thee Blind*, run
thus :

> At the convent doors, full of alarm
> She stood like a young bird quitting its nest.
> Her first flight flown right into my arm,
> Her first tears wept upon my breast.

These are jolting lines at best ; but when we note that the
remainder of the poem (some sixteen hundred verses in
all) is written in fairly regular decasyllabics, we cannot but
suspect that the poetess conceived these lines also to be
cast in the same mould.   Innumerable are the cases in
which only by resolute manipulation can a line or a stanza
be coaxed into metrical form.   There are whole poems,
indeed—*Jeanne Bras: a Ballad of Sorrow* is a notable
instance—in which one cannot perceive any merit whatever
until one has somewhat painfully inured oneself to their
rub-a-dub movement.

Of the poetess's lapses in grammar and style, the latter
are by far the more important.   Grammar is in great
measure a matter of convention, on which none but a
pedant lays imperative stress.   When Mrs. Shorter says :

> He struggles with despair
> While you beside your fire doth watch him there—

the "doth" is no more, in my eyes, than a mere misprint.
The truth is that Mrs. Shorter very often writes English
like a foreigner—in such phrases, for instance, as

> I saw much tears and the less frequent smile

or

> " Wherefore," I said, " you dare
> Disturb the people, busy with their prayer ? "

This is exactly the syntax of the Frenchman who says
" How you are ? " for " How are you ? "   So, too, with some
of Mrs. Shorter's subjunctives (for instance, " I would that
she laugh with me ")—they suggest the inexpertness of a

foreigner rather than the error or pedantry of a writer
misusing her native tongue.

On the other hand, such phrases as

> And heavy sobbing like her heart would break

and

> There to weep like her tender heart should break

are only too English. Again, such an expression as

> The little body, quickly satisfied,
> Expressed no want I did not love to give

is simply indefensible. By "give" Mrs. Shorter means
"minister to"—a totally different thing. She says "give,"
because she wants a rhyme for "live." Or take this
stanza:

> Rotten with age, here a panel unseen
>   Slips 'neath my hand;
> Into the silence of love that has been
>   I shuddering stand.

What Mrs. Shorter means is "into the silence . . . I
burst," or something to that effect; but, needing a rhyme
to "hand," she says "stand," careless of the fact that it
makes nonsense. Even more regrettable are her clumsy
and helpless inversions, such as

Who has fooled so me the glowing morning through . . . .
I am your true Dearbhorgil, glad home you are thus soon. . . .
And therefore as we do believe that which we most would fain. . . .

These are contortions of language for which no excuse can
be alleged, either of idiom or of effect. They are simply
forced upon the writer by the exigences of metre.

Peculiarities of vocabulary are almost as common in Mrs.
Shorter's verse as peculiarities of syntax. Now and then

she seems to suffer from a sort of aphasia. For instance, when she talks of

> No trammels of time on the years of our face

and

> A soul's release
> From the difficult traits of the flesh,

it is hard to suppose that "trammels" and "traits" were the words she really intended. It almost seems as if they had been transposed. "Traits" would make a sort of sense in the former line, and "trammels" in the latter; but as the lines occur in two different poems, fifty pages apart, I fear this emendation cannot be maintained. In other poems she shows curious lapses of linguistic tact. For instance, she closes a long and, on the whole, a really fine, romantic ballad with the following couplet:

> And cursed be you, Dearbhorgil, who eloped into the south
> And war made loud in Erin with the smiling of your mouth.

"Elope," indeed, is a good old Teutonic word, but its modern associations surely exclude it from romantic verse. In the same way (though this may seem a paradox) I should say that the word "romantic" has no place in a Keltic ballad, and that the immortally beautiful story of Deirdre is sadly belittled and modernised by such writing as this:

> Many sweet tales told her nurse that fed her romantic young brain,
> Till sleeping were sweet for its dreams, and waking was dreaming again.

If a Saxon had spoken of Deirdre's "romantic young brain," it might justly have been set down as another wrong to Ireland.

Finally, to bring this ungrateful task of fault-finding to a close, one cannot but note that there are a good many passages in Mrs. Shorter's work in which she seems to be manufacturing verse without inspiration and without force. Such a passage is the following:

> And so you smiled, as though 'twas to your mind,
> Saying belief sat well on womankind,
> Fed their emotions, sentiments, and so
> You loved a woman to a church to go,
> But as I did not mind, you would remain
> To write your book till I came home again.

This occurs, to be sure, not in a romantic poem, but in a novelette in verse; yet even in such a production there is a limit to permissible prosaism. Here is another case in which a little poem of real merit is ruined by the hopeless and almost incredible feebleness of the last two lines:

QUESTIONS.

> What is the secret of your life, browsing ox,
> Ox the sweet grass eating?
> Who strung the mighty sinews in your flesh?
> Who set that great heart beating?
>
> What is the secret of your death, soulless ox,
> Ox so patiently waiting?
> Why hath pain wove her net for your brain's anguish
> If for you Death will gain no life's creating?

Did I exaggerate in calling these lines incredible?

It is because I think so highly of Mrs. Shorter's powers that I have spoken so frankly of her shortcomings. Criticism seems to me to betray its trust when it gives even tacit countenance to sheer smudginess of composition. Talent may compensate for a multitude of sins, but it ought not to be allowed to cover them. If Mrs. Shorter be suffered, without protest, to rhyme "ideal" with "steal," and to talk of "standing into a room" and "giving a want," other poetesses may plead the sanction of her talent for similar slovenlinesses, to the gradual blurring of the boundary-line between good and bad English.

But not even the most exacting criticism can alter the essential fact that Mrs. Shorter has written some very beautiful and memorable poetry. Her work may fairly be said to have the merits of its defects, inasmuch as it comes from the heart, not from the head. It is not the poetry of sentimental culture, but of imagination nurtured in a treasure-house of popular mythology, and therefore in touch with the imagination of a whole race. Mrs. Shorter is always at her best in the purely Irish ballad, not only because there an occasional artlessness of phrase or cadence is not felt to be out of place, but also because her inspiration is free, effortless, and sustained. She has written some eight or ten ballads of entirely admirable quality. One of the finest, *A Ballad of Marjorie*, I am permitted to quote at the end of this article. There is perhaps a touch of modern, self-conscious irony in its close, but that does not render it any the less tragic or impressive. *The Little Brother* is another piece in the same key—an admirable invention, though slightly marred, to my mind, by its rhythmical peculiarities. Less imaginative, but not less touching, is this:

THE FAIRY CHANGELING.

Dermod O'Byrne of Omah town
In his garden strode up and down;
He pulled his beard, and he beat his breast;
And this is his trouble and woe confessed:

" The good-folk came in the night, and they
Have stolen my bonny wean away;
Have put in his place a changeling,
A weashy, weakly, wizen thing!

" From the speckled hen nine eggs I stole,
And lighting a fire of a glowing coal,
I fried the shells, and I split the yolk;
But never a word the stranger spoke:

" A bar of metal I heated red
To frighten the fairy from its bed,
To put in the place of this fretting wean
My own bright, beautiful boy again.

" But my wife had hidden it in her arms,
And cried ' For shame ! ' on my fairy charms ;
She sobs, with the strange child on her breast :
' I love the weak, wee babe the best ! ' "

To Dermod O'Byrne's, the tale to hear,
The neighbours came from far and near :
Outside his gate, in the long boreen,
They crossed themselves, and said between

Their muttered prayers, " He has no luck !
For sure the woman is fairy-struck,
To leave her child a fairy guest,
And love the weak, wee wean the best ! "

A very striking ballad, more notable, perhaps, for its theme than for its execution, is *The Fetch*—as effective a ghost-story as ever was devised. *The Priest's Brother* is a fine piece of imaginative work—stronger, I think, than *The Ballad of the Little Black Hound*, which is more common-place in idea. *The Rape of the Baron's Wine* is perhaps the poorest of the Irish ballads. The subject, indeed, has scarcely the true Keltic flavour ; it might just as well be German. Against the notably incongruous touch,

> Nothing there to satisfy
> Souls for tragedy awake,

we may place in the balance this very fine phrase,

> the silence seemed to slip
> Its threatening fingers through his hair.

But, as a whole, the ballad is not one of Mrs. Shorter's successes. On the other hand, she has done nothing better—and it would be difficult, in this style of work, to do anything much better—than the following :

THE FAIR LITTLE MAIDEN.

" There is one at the door, Wolfe O'Driscoll,
    At the door, who is bidding you come ! "
" Who is he that wakes me in the darkness,
    Calling when all the world's dumb ? "

" Six horses has he to his carriage,
    Six horses blacker than the night,
And their twelve red eyes in the shadows
    Twelve lamps he carries for his light ;

" And his coach is a coffin black and mouldy,
    A huge black coffin open wide :
He asks for your soul, Wolfe O'Driscoll,
    Who is calling at the door outside."

" Who let him thro' the gates of my gardens,
    Where stronger bolts have never been ? "
" 'Twas the father of the fair little maiden
    You drove to her grave so green."

" And who let him pass through the courtyard,
    By loosening the bar and the chain ? "
" Oh, who but the brother of the maiden,
    Who lies in the cold and the rain ! "

" Then who drew the bolts at the portal,
    And into my house bade him go ? "
" She, the mother of the poor young maiden,
    Who lies in her youth so low."

" Who stands, that he dare not enter
    The door of my chamber, between ! "
" O, the ghost of the fair little maiden,
    Who lies in the churchyard green."

The closer she keeps to simple Irish folk-lore the more happily inspired is Mrs. Shorter's work. *My Lady's Slipper* belongs not to folk-lore but to family romance. The story might have attracted Browning, and is treated in a somewhat Browningesque manner; witness this stanza:

> Was it the woman who plotted and spied,
>   Using my heart
> Just for a stone there to step where the tide
>   Kept them apart.

Unfortunately it is not of Browning at his best that the poem as a whole reminds us. *The Phantom Deer* seems like a piece of task-work; neither it nor *Jeanne Bras* can compare in value with *The White Witch* or *The Woman who went to Hell*—folk-lore pieces both. *Uisneach and Deirdre* is, as I have already hinted, a singularly inadequate treatment of one of the most beautiful stories in the world. *False Dearbhorgil* is better, but by no means touches the high-water mark of Mrs. Shorter's achievement.

Her lyrics suffer more than her ballads from the imperfections of her craftsmanship; but in almost all there is genuine feeling and a true lyrical idea. The following I quote more on account of its brevity than of any exceptional beauty. It is an average specimen of Mrs. Shorter's lyric gift:

THE WRECKAGE.

> Love lit a beacon in thine eyes,
>   And I out in the storm,
> And lo! the night had taken wings;
>   I dream me safe and warm.
>
> Love lit a beacon in thine eyes,
>   A wreckers' light for me;
> My heart is broken on the rocks;
>   I perish in the sea.

The longest work Mrs. Shorter has as yet published is a sort of novelette in rhyming pentameters, fantastically entitled (in a phrase borrowed from Omar Kháyyám) *The Me within Thee Blind.* It is very unequal in workmanship, but contains one or two memorable passages. It would be hard to find a more apt or striking image than the following, placed in the mouth of a woman whose agnostic husband has held smilingly aloof from her soul-struggles, flattering himself that all was going well with her :

> You did not hear my soul beside you cry,
> " Look to me, friend ; your help, or else I die."
> Like some wayfarer on an Alpine height,
> You with your glass would bring within your sight
> And say, " How soft he goes amidst the snow ! "
> So smile upon him, for you could not know
> That every mound a mountain was, and deep
> Each velvet crevice—where the death-wolves creep
> With purple jaws—so that to fall or rest
> Were but to die. He struggles with despair,
> While you beside your fire doth watch him there,
> And say—" How soft he goes amidst the snow ! "
> Wherein he battles, shrieking to the sky,
> " O God, your pity, lest I faint and die ! "
> I was a wife you had no time to woo,
> I was a woman—and you never knew.
> A child to you, because you could not hear
> My woman's soul that called so loud and clear.

The style of these verses is open to criticism at many points, but none but a true poet could have conceived the image.

MISS DORA SIGERSON

A BALLAD OF MARJORIE.

" What ails you that you look so pale,
  O fisher of the sea ? "
" 'Tis for a mournful tale I own,
  Fair maiden Marjorie."

" What is the dreàry tale to tell,
  O toiler of the sea ? "
" I cast my net into the waves,
  Sweet maiden Marjorie.

" I cast my net into the tide,
  Before I made for home ;
Too heavy for my hands to raise,
  I drew it through the foam."

" What saw you that you look so pale,
  Sad searcher of the sea ? "
" A dead man's body from the deep
  My haul had brought to me ! "

" And was he young, and was he fair ? "
  " O, cruel to behold !
In his white face the joy of life
  Not yet was grown a-cold."

" Oh, pale you are, and full of prayer
  For one who sails the sea."
" Because the dead looked up and spoke,
  Poor maiden Marjorie."

" What said he, that you seem so sad,
  O fisher of the sea ?
(Alack ! I know it was my love,
  Who fain would speak to me !) "

" He said, ' Beware a woman's mouth—
A rose that bears a thorn.' "
" Ah, me ! these lips shall smile no more
That gave my lover scorn."

" He said, ' Beware a woman's eyes.
They pierce you with their death.' "
" Then falling tears shall make them blind
That robbed my dear of breath."

" He said, ' Beware a woman's hair—
A serpent's coil of gold.' "
" Then will I shear the cruel locks
That crushed him in their fold."

" He said, ' Beware a woman's heart
As you would shun the reef.' "
" So let it break within my breast,
And perish of my grief."

" He raised his hands ; a woman's name
Thrice bitterly he cried :
My net had parted with the strain ;
He vanished in the tide."

" A woman's name ?   What name but mine,
O fisher of the sea ? "
" A woman's name, but not your name,
Poor maiden Marjorie."

ARTHUR SYMONS

MR. ARTHUR SYMONS has ranged far and wide through many provinces of literature in search of "emotions and sensations;" but the form of his poetical utterances has been mainly shaped by two influences: the early and transitory influence of Browning, and the later and abiding influence of Verlaine. Mr. Symons himself, I imagine, must look back with wonder, and perhaps not without a smile, to the days of his *Days and Nights* (1889), when he used to Browningise at large in dramatic fragments, monologues, and character-portraits, such as *Red Bredbury's End*, *A Brother of the Battuti*, and *A Village Mariana*. A curious essay might be written on the invention and development of the dramatic monologue. This is not the place for it, nor can I now undertake the slight effort of research, the comparison of dates and so forth, which it would involve. For my present purpose it is sufficient to point out that, as an instrument for serious poetry, the form appears to be practically extinct. Both the great poets of the mid-century used it to noble ends; but it has the inherent disadvantage of lending itself with fatal facility, not only to parody (that would matter less), but to stolid vulgarisation. It has become the favourite instrument of the writers of "poems for recitation"; it brings with it associations of the penny reading and even the music-hall; "most can grow the flower now, for all have got the seed."

But ten years can do much to complete a process of vulgarisation, and it must be remembered that, when Mr. Symons cultivated it, the form, though senescent, was not yet decrepit. In order to judge his dramatic monologues fairly, we should have to strip them of luxuriant accretions of evil association, for which Mr. Symons himself is in no way responsible.

Unfortunately, this is well-nigh impossible. It is easier to go back a century in spirit than a decade. The form has become hopelessly discounted, except in the case of those masterpieces which had once for all taken hold of us before the process of degradation set in. Who can pretend to estimate fairly poems which begin like this :

" Joe," the old man maundered, as he lay his length in the bed,
" Joe, God bless you, my son, but your dad's no better than dead.
Eh, I'm a powerful sinner, and I thank the Lord for the same, . . .
But, Joe, I'm dying, I tell you! Joe, Joe, and I can't die game."

Or this (the opening of another poem; it reads like the second stanza of the same) :

Yes, I'm dying by inches; the Devil has got his way :
I fought him fourscore years, but he's gripped me hard to-day.
No, not God, not a word of God! For I let Him be.
The Devil is waiting, I tell you, but God has forgotten me.

Or this, again :

Esther, my lass, come hither; stand there; I've a thing to say.
Lord, but your cheeks are white! So be it, Esther Bray.
Stand you there in the light o' the fire. Now answer me :
When the babe that's yours is born, whose wife'll his mother be?

Or poems which end in this fashion :

I had to leave you, child. I'm come. The agony
    I had, I too !—Farewell.
Don't sob like that, mother! I . . . . Don't die yet, Marie !
    The priest . . . . God . . . . heaven and hell.

· ARTHVR · SYMONS ·

> I don't know—some folks do . . . .—The good God, He'll be kind—
> I hope so—by-and-by,
> One kiss more, mother dear. We can't pray. Never mind!
> He'll understand. Good-bye!

Even if the psychology of such poems were other than conventional, their irretrievably conventional form would obscure it. We cannot fix our attention on them, for we seem to know them all beforehand. When the poet starts off:

> Now, this is why he killed her. First, she lied.
> He said, " You love me still? " and she replied,
> " Still——"

the whole poem floats instantly into the mind, like a hackneyed tune evoked by its opening bar, and we feel that we could write it almost as easily as read it. The very titles, *An Interruption in Court*, *An Episode under the Nihilists*, *An Altar-Piece of Master Stephan*, beget in us an instant weariness of spirit. This is a style of poetry which " dates " terribly—in Mr. Symons's eyes, I am sure, no less than in his readers'.

The real interest of this first volume lies in its foreshadowing of the future. Mr. Symons is a love poet or nothing; when he sings of love he is himself—not otherwise. Therefore the fourteen Shakespearean sonnets, entitled *A Lover's Progress*, seem to me the most living things in the book. Mr. Symons has since become a far more learned amorist; but there are rudiments of imaginative insight even here. There are also premonitions of that smilelessness, that absence of restraining humour, which is a little trying in Mr. Symons's later work. And yet, who knows? Surely Mr. Symons must have been laughing in his sleeve when he wrote this quatrain:

> Who does not long to capture, long to tame,
> The beautiful sleek tiger, full of death?
> *The unctuous cat (her cousin, all the same)*
> *Exerts in vain her fond melodious breath.*

The epithet "melodious," in this context, has at least the charm of the unexpected.

To find the real Symons, we must turn to *Silhouettes* (1892), *London Nights* (1895), and *Amoris Victima* (1897). Here we encounter a distinct personality, an individual note, and a restricted, but far from insignificant, technical accomplishment. Unfortunately, the individual note is at the same time insistently monotonous. The poet, even in recording his many moods, reveals himself as a man of one mood—a sensual melancholy. His verses impress us, one and all, as the metrical diary of a sensation-hunter; and though he disclaims all concern with morality, he is a moralist in spite of himself, inasmuch as the picture he presents of a sensation-hunter's life is distinctly deterrent. I do not doubt that a good deal of Mr. Symons's work— the *Amoris Victima* sequence, for example—is dramatic. In other words, Mr. Symons does not merely record his own actual sensations and experiences, but gives them an imaginative extension; working out in detail the data they provide, the possibilities implicit in them. This, however, is not true drama. It is only self-dramatisation, Byronism. The poet never projects himself into another personality, but only enacts his own part in imaginary circumstances. Therefore the element of drama in Mr. Symons's work does not make it any the less like a diary. These three booklets might be grouped together under the title of Turgueneff's first book: *Memoirs of a Sportsman;* and one is harassed with doubts as to whether the memoirs are always quite sportsmanlike.

As documents in erotic psychology, they are undoubtedly curious and valuable; and that, to be sure, is what they set forth to be. "I do not profess," says Mr. Symons in his preface to *London Nights* (second edition), "that any poem in this book is the record of actual fact; I declare that every poem is the sincere attempt to render a particular mood which has once been mine, and to render it as if, for the moment, there were no other mood for me in the world. I have rendered, well or ill, many moods, and without disguise or preference. If it be objected to me that some of them are moods I had better never have felt, I am ready to answer, 'Possibly'; but I must add, 'What of that? They have existed; and whatever has existed has achieved the right of artistic existence.'" So be it; in so far as Mr. Symons has achieved artistic beauty and potency in the expression of his moods, I admit the validity of his argument. None the less must one be permitted to observe that as all his moods (with the exception of a few brief nature-impressions) are connected with the satisfaction or non-satisfaction of one particular appetite, or play around the means of ministering to that appetite, their record becomes, in the long run, a trifle cloying. We are apt to cry, " Comfort me with apples, for I am sick of love."

In the expression of his moods, Mr. Symons often attains real beauty, seldom a very high potency. He writes very well—fluently, gracefully, without the slightest harshness or vulgarity of form; but his poems seldom take hold of us very strongly, thrill our imagination, or imprint themselves on our memory. To be fair, I ought to drop the plural pronoun, and say that I find Mr. Symons's verse, as a rule, lacking in that barb, that sting, which is the sign of true inspiration. One reads him with pleasure, admiring the even competence of his workmanship; but the element of the miraculous, of unaccountable beauty and predestinate fitness, seldom makes itself felt. Therefore, it is very difficult to select from his poems. All are characteristic; all have a certain merit; there is none which imposes itself as an indispensable trait in the portraiture of his talent. Take first one or two of his nature-impressions :

AFTER SUNSET.

The sea lies quieted beneath
　　The after-sunset flush
That leaves upon the heaped grey clouds
　　The grape's faint purple blush.

Pale, from a little space in heaven
　　Of delicate ivory,
The sickle moon and one gold star
　　Look down upon the sea.

AUTUMN TWILIGHT.

The long September evening dies
　　In mist along the fields and lanes ;
Only a few faint stars surprise
　　The lingering twilight as it wanes.

Night creeps across the darkening vale ;
　　On the horizon tree by tree
Fades into shadowy skies as pale
　　As moonlight on a shadowy sea.

And down the mist-enfolded lanes,
　　Grown pensive now with evening,
See, lingering as the twilight wanes,
　　Lover with lover wandering.

These are but, as it were, two pebbles from a heap; I really do not know why I pick them up rather than any of the others. Here, now, are a couple of prettily-polished pebbles from another heap :

DURING MUSIC.

The music had the heat of blood,
　　A passion that no words can reach ;
We sat together, and understood
　　Our own heart's speech.

We had no need of word or sign,
　　The music spoke for us, and said
All that her eyes could read in mine
　　Or mine in hers had read.

ARTHUR SYMONS

AFTER LOVE.

O to part now, and, parting now,
    Never to meet again;
To have done for ever, I and thou,
    With joy, and so with pain.

It is too hard, too hard to meet
    As friends, and love no more;
Those other meetings were too sweet
    That went before.

And I would have, now love is over,
    An end to all, an end:
I cannot, having been your lover,
    Stoop to become your friend.

Obvious as is the sentiment of these versicles, some equally obvious felicity of words might have sent them soaring, lark-like, into the empyrean of poetry. To my ear they seem to lack that final felicity; for other ears, perhaps, they may possess it. The individuality in Mr. Symons's work is apt to proceed from his theme rather than from his diction or his melody. He seeks inspiration in subjects which other poets eschew, and if he does not always find it, he at any rate never fails to show the touch of the accomplished literary craftsman. Unfortunately, the most "individual" passages in his work are apt to be the least quotable; for instance (in *London Nights*), the sequences entitled *Leves Amores* and *To One in Alienation*. Here are two vividly-written pieces from *Silhouettes;* I am not sure that they are poetry, but certainly they are literature:

IN BOHEMIA.

Drawn blinds and flaring gas within,
    And wine, and women, and cigars;
Without, the city's heedless din;
    Above, the white unheeding stars.

415

And we, alike from each remote,
  The world that works, the heaven that waits,
Con our brief pleasures o'er by rote,
  The favourite pastime of the Fates.

We smoke, to fancy that we dream,
  And drink, a moment's joy to prove,
And fain would love, and only seem
  To love because we cannot love.

Draw back the blinds, put out the light:
  'Tis morning, let the daylight come.
God ! how the women's cheeks are white,
  And how the sunlight strikes us dumb !

IN THE HAYMARKET.

I danced at your ball a year ago,
  To-night I pay for your bread and cheese,
  " And a glass of bitters, if you please,
For you drank my best champagne, you know ! "

Madcap ever, you laugh the while
  As you drink your bitters and munch your bread,
The face is the same, and the same old smile
  Came up at a word I said.

A year ago I danced at your ball,
  I sit down by your side in the bar to-night ;
And the luck has changed, you say—that's all !
  And the luck will change, you say—all right !

For the men go by, and the rent's to pay,
And you haven't a friend in the world to-day ;
And the money comes and the money goes :
And to-night, who cares ? and to-morrow, who knows ?

The influence of Verlaine, subtly omnipresent in these later books, comes out unmistakably in such a piece as the following, in which the feeling, both for rhythm and rhyme, is French rather than English :

MORBIDEZZA.

White girl, your flesh is lilies
Grown 'neath a frozen moon,
So still is
The rapture of your swoon
Of whiteness, snow or lilies.

The virginal revealment
Your bosom's wavering slope—
Concealment,
'Neath fainting heliotrope,
Of whitest white's revealment—

Is like a bed of lilies,
A jealous-guarded row,
Whose will is
Simply chaste dreams :—but oh,
The alluring scent of lilies !

There is one poem, as it seems to me, in which Mr. Symons, without prejudice to his individuality, outsoars his limitations, and attains to really large and passionate utterance. It is the *Magnificat* in *London Nights*, quoted at the end of this article. The same quality of work, if not in such high perfection, appears in several of the poems of *Amoris Victima*, on the whole, I think, Mr. Symons's strongest and most sustained effort. From the concluding sequence, *Mundi Victima*, I would fain quote Section X., a passage of remarkable power; but its length forbids. Instead of it, I select from the opening sequence two couplet-quatorzains, which are no less intimately felt than vividly expressed.

It is possible that the psychological insight displayed in *Amoris Victima*, and indeed throughout Mr. Symons's work, has been bought at the expense of more strictly poetic qualities, and is intimately associated with the limitations of his method. He is too sedulously self-observant ever to let himself go in that fine frenzy, that paroxysm of the imagination, which is an essential condition of the creative miracle. Perhaps it is only in the very greatest spirits that keen introspection can co-exist with the highest imaginative impulse and energy. Mr. Symons is too critical of his moods, too conscious that they *are* moods, to find the most poignant expression for them. The pulse which has always a finger upon it may beat rapidly, but not strongly, contagiously. "A lyric conception," said Oliver Wendell Holmes, "hits me like a bullet in the forehead. I have often had the blood drop from my cheeks when it struck, and felt that I turned as white as death. Then comes a creeping as of centipedes running down the spine—then a gasp and a great jump of the heart—then a sudden flush and a beating in the vessels of the head—then a long sigh—and the poem is written. . . . I said written," he proceeds, "I did not say *copied*." Mr. Symons may despise this account of the genesis of a poem as an antiquated affectation, and point to the Autocrat's own performances as a sufficient comment on his theory. Well, there are doubtless other ways in which a great lyric may come into being; I quote this passage merely to point the contrast to what one cannot but conceive to be Mr. Symons's method of production. A lyric conception, I take it does not "hit him like a bullet in the forehead," but is gradually and deliberately spun out from a mass of raw material supplied by memory and observation. If it brings with it a tingling in the spine, a jump of the heart, a pulsing in the vessels of the head, it certainly does not communicate these sensations to the reader. Mr. Symons's poetry, in short, seems to me to lack magnetic temperament —I had almost said virility. It is in the main a criticism of "life," in the narrowest sense of the latter term. It has many eminent literary qualities, but seldom, I think, that inevitableness which is the final criterion of poetry.

ARTHUR SYMONS

MAGNIFICAT.

Praise God, who wrought for you and me
 Your subtle body made for love;
God, who from all eternity
 Willed our divided ways should move
Together, and our love should be.

I wandered all these years among
 A world of women, seeking you.
Ah, when our fingers met and clung,
 The pulses of our bodies knew
Each other: our hearts leapt and sung.

It was not any word of mine,
 It was not any look of yours;
Only we knew, and knew for sign
 Of Love that comes, Love that endures,
Our veins the chalice of his wine.

Because God willed for us and planned
 One perfect love, excelling speech
To tell, or thought to understand,
 He made our bodies each for each,
Then put your hand into my hand !

From "AMORIS VICTIMA."

Dare I remember, nay, can I forget,
(Would God I could forget them all, and yet
Thank God for this the most, I have not the power !)
Of all the hours of all our love one hour ?
It is my glory, as it is my curse,
(Loveliest, best loved out of the universe !)

To have loved, to have been beloved by you above
All other loving women, made for love.
No woman ever loved me as you loved,
And now that you have from my brows removed
The heavy crown of love, and cast it down,
I cannot stoop to wear a lighter crown.
Having been crowned by you, I abdicate
Kingship, and join the beggars at your gate.

I cannot work : I dare not sit alone.
There's not a corner here that has not known
Some moment of you, and your pictured eyes
Pursue me with relentless memories.
Here was the chair you sat in ; here we lay
Until your face grew fainter with the day,
And, in a veil of kisses, swooning white,
Fell back into the mystery of night.
'Twas here I kissed you first ; 'twas there you said,
" I love you," and " Would God that I were dead ! "
And now, when you are gone for evermore,
I pace between the window and the door,
And, in the feverish folly of despair,
Stand listening for your step upon the stair.

JOHN B. TABB

In Mr. John B. Tabb we come upon a clear-cut, cameo-like poetic individuality. His poetry, so far as it is known to me, is contained in two exceedingly dainty little volumes entitled *Poems* (1894) and *Lyrics* (1897). These booklets exactly typify Mr. Tabb's dainty talent. It is in no disparaging sense that I use this phrase. Smallness of scale is the deliberately-adopted characteristic of all Mr. Tabb's work. His lyrics seldom extend beyond three quatrains, and are often compressed into one. In the booklet entitled *Poems*, for instance, out of 163 numbers, only three overrun a single page, while the great majority fill less than half of one of the diminutive pages. In truth, Mr. Tabb is an epigrammatist rather than a pure lyrist. Even when he writes what is to the eye a song, it is apt to be to the ear and the mind an expanded epigram. His metres are correct and graceful, but they have no lyric impetus—they do not sing. His exquisite measured speech neither makes its own music nor asks to be upborne on the wings of melody.

The main sources of his inspiration are three: Nature (and in especial birds and flowers); Devotional sentiment, sincere though fanciful; Personal sentiment, which finds discreet, unimpassioned, one might almost say attenuated, utterance. If one were asked to illustrate the somewhat overworked distinction between fancy and imagination, one

need but open at random either of Mr. Tabb's booklets, to
find a clear, and very often a striking, example of the
former quality. He has none of the harshness, the
violences, of the spiritual singers of the seventeenth century;
in his limpidity of form, indeed, he is much more re-
miniscent of the epicurean Herrick; but in his application
of a humourless wit to spiritual subjects he denotes himself
a true descendant of Crashaw and Herbert. I do not
employ the word "humourless" in a reproachful sense, as
meaning that he says things whereof humour would have
checked the utterance. This is seldom or never the case.
My meaning is simply to release the term wit from its
conventional but inessential association with merriment,
before applying it to the master faculty of Mr. Tabb's
sedate and pensive mind. The essence of wit is a quick
perception of analogies; but all analogies are not necessarily comic. On the other hand, when we find a poem
unmistakably inspired by a purely intellectual concept, we
are apt to doubt, not the sincerity or depth, but the
immediate poignancy, of the emotion it expresses. That
is why I call Mr. Tabb's utterances of personal sentiment
attenuated. Perhaps sublimated would be a better word.

So much I say by way of delimitation—not certainly of
disparagement. Mr. Tabb is a most admirable writer: he
has said numberless beautiful things, with an accent all his
own. He does not always avoid those pitfalls of the
concettist, frigidity and triviality; but even his frigidity is
often exquisite. Here are two conceits which are wintry in
every sense; but who can deny their beauty?—

TO THE BABE NIVA.

Niva, Child of Innocence,
  Dust to dust *we* go:
Thou, when Winter wooed thee hence,
  Wentest snow to snow.

· JOHN · B · TABB ·

JOHN B. TABB

PHANTOMS.

Are ye the ghosts of fallen leaves,
    O flakes of snow,
For which, through naked trees, the winds
    A-mourning go ?

Or are ye angels, bearing home
    The host unseen
Of truant spirits, to be clad
    Again in green ?

Here, from a sequence of Christmas versicles, is a conceit
that George Herbert, surely, would not have disowned :

OUT OF BOUNDS.

A little Boy of heavenly birth,
    But far from home to-day,
Comes down to find His ball, the Earth,
    That Sin has cast away.
O comrades, let us one and all
Join in to get Him back His ball !

If this be quaint rather than beautiful, the following seems
to me exempt from that reproach :

EASTER FLOWERS.

We are His witnesses ; out of the dim,
Dank region of Death we have risen with Him.
Back from our sepulchre rolleth the stone,
And Spring, the bright Angel, sits smiling thereon.

We are His witnesses. See, where we lay
The snow that late bound us is folded away ;
And April, fair Magdalen, weeping anon,
Stands flooded with light of the new-risen Sun !

Mr. Tabb has many other devotional pieces of a like
exquisite quality ; but this is specially characteristic in that
it blends devotional feeling with that tender worship of the

minor miracles of nature to which the poet owes some of
his happiest inspirations. For instance:

MIGNONETTE.

Give me the earth, and I might heap
   A mountain from the plain ;
Give me the waters of the deep,
   I might their strength restrain ;
But here a secret of the sod
Betrays the daintier hand of God.

STAR-JESSAMINE.

Discerning Star from Sister Star,
   We give to each its name;
But ye, O countless Blossoms, are
   In fragrance and in flame
So like, that He from whom ye came
Alone discerneth each by name.

Of nature-poems, pure and simple, let me now cull a little
bouquet :

ANTICIPATION.

The master scans the woven score
Of subtle harmonies, before
   A note is stirred ;
And Nature now is pondering
The tidal symphony of Spring,
   As yet unheard.

THE MID-DAY MOON.

Behold, whatever wind prevail,
Slow westering, a phantom sail—
The lonely soul of Yesterday—
Unpiloted, pursues her way.

As I transcribe this lovely quatrain it repents me that in
emphasising Mr. Tabb's wealth of fancy I may have seemed

JOHN B. TABB

to deny him the gift of imagination.   There is imagination, too, in this:

SAP.

> Strong as the sea, and silent as the grave,
>   It ebbs and flows unseen;
> Flooding the earth—a fragrant tidal wave—
>   With mist of deepening green.

In the following quatrains, on the other hand, we return to the realm of fancy:

HEROES.

> Against the night, a champion bright,
> The glow-worm, lifts a spear of light;
> And, undismayed, the slenderest shade
> Against the noonday bares a blade.

THE POSTULANT.

> In ashes from the wasted fires of noon,
>   Aweary of the light,
> Comes Evening, a tearful novice, soon
>   To take the veil of night.

Whether it be fancy or imagination that is at work in the following versicles, it boots not to decide.   It is sufficient to feel that they proceed from a singularly delicate poetic faculty:

THE SNOW-BIRD.

> When snow, like silence visible,
>   Hath hushed the summer bird,
> Thy voice, a never-frozen rill
>   Of melody, is heard.

> But when from winter's lethargy
>   The buds begin to blow,
> Thy voice is mute, and suddenly
>   Thou vanishest like snow.

Turning now to Mr. Tabb's more personal utterances, I

find perhaps the most remarkable of them on the first page of his first book. It is this :

AVE: SIDNEY LANIER.

Ere Time's horizon-line was set,
Somewhere in space our spirits met,
Then o'er the starry parapet
    Came wandering here.
And now that thou art gone again
Beyond the verge, I haste amain
(Lost echo of a loftier strain)
    To greet thee there.

Of the poet's remarkable gift of compression, one could scarcely find a better example than this :

ADIEU.

God speed thee, setting Sun !
Thy beams for me have spun
    Of light to-day
A memory that one
Alone could bring, and none
    Can take away.

This is no mere epigram, but a true lyric—in twenty-six words ! Something to the same purpose, though not quite so stern in its condensation, is the following :

THE PEAK.

As on some solitary height
Abides, in summer's fierce despite,
Snow-blossom that no sun can blight,
    No frost can kill ;
So, in my soul,—all else below
To change succumbing,—stands aglow
One wreath of immemorial snow,
    Unscattered still.

Twelve lines is quite an unusual amplitude of space for

the poet to allow himself; but it would be difficult to turn twelve lines more daintily than this:

EXALTATION.

O leaf upon the highest bough,
The Poet of the woods art thou
    To whom alone 'tis given—
The farthest from thy place of birth—
To hold communion with the earth,
    Nor lose the light of Heaven.

O leaf upon the topmost height,
Amid thy heritage of light
    Unsheltered by a shade,
'Tis thine the loneliness to know
That leans for sympathy below,
    Nor finds what it has made.

Mr. Tabb has written a score or so of sonnets, but for some reason which I cannot quite define, none of them greatly appeals to me. Is it, perhaps, that the sonnet requires a stronger rhythmic pulse than beats in this poet's measures? But, if he is not fortunate in the quatorzain, he excels in the quatrain. I cannot refrain from supplementing the specimens I have given already with another little miscellaneous gleaning:

THE DANDELION.

With locks of gold to-day;
To-morrow silver gray;
Then blossom-bald. Behold,
O man, thy fortune told!

LOVE'S AUTOGRAPH.

Once only did he pass my way.
  " When wilt thou come again ?
Ah, leave some token of thy stay ? "
  He wrote (and vanished) " Pain."

MY SECRET.

'Tis not what I am fain to hide
   That doth in deepest darkness dwell,
But what my tongue hath often tried,
   Alas, in vain, to tell.

MILTON.

So fair thy vision that the night
Abided with thee, lest the light,
A flaming sword before thine eyes,
Had shut thee out from Paradise.

Mr. Tabb is, I understand, a priest of the Roman Catholic Church. Though there is nothing cloistral in his spirit, which has a wide enough outlook on nature and man, yet the patient minuteness of his workmanship is not without a monkish quality. But it is the gem-engraver rather than the illuminator that Mr. Tabb recalls. He works in a hard material of somewhat limited capabilities, but he often succeeds in touching it to forms of a very tender grace.

JOHN B. TABB

A SIGH OF THE SEA.

" Why is it ? " once the Ocean asked,
    As on a summer's day,
Basking beneath a cloudless sky,
    In musing rest he lay,

" Why is it, that, unruffled still,
    The welkin's brow I see,
While mine, with racking wind and tide,
    Deep-furrowed oft must be ?

" Her richest gems, by night displayed,
    Man's filching grasp defy ;
But safety for my treasures none,
    Though buried deep they lie.

" The hands that from her diadem
    In reverence recoil,
Are bold my depths to penetrate
    And of their wealth despoil.

" A thousand ships with cruel keel
    My writhing waves divide,
But mariner hath never steered
    Athwart her tranquil tide.

" Why is it thus, that rest to her
    And toil to me is given—
That she the blessing ever meets,
    And I, the curse of Heaven ? "

The Ether heard.   Through all her depths
    A deeper azure spread,
And to the murmuring Ocean thus,
    With radiant smile, she said :

" Who cleaveth to the earth, as thou,
    Ne'er knows tranquillity ;
Naught pulses in my bosom wide
    But God, whose own am I."

COMMUNION.

Once when my heart was passion-free
    To learn of things divine,
The soul of nature suddenly
    Outpoured itself in mine.

I held the secrets of the deep,
    And of the heavens above;
I knew the harmonies of sleep,
    The mysteries of love.

And for a moment's interval
    The earth, the sky, the sea—
My soul encompassed, each and all,
    As now they compass me.

To one in all, to all in one—
    Since Love the work began—
Life's ever widening circles run,
    Revealing God and man.

FRANCIS THOMPSON

Iᴛ is very easy to cavil at, and still easier to ridicule, the poems of Mr. Francis Thompson. I am well aware of all that may be said, and not unjustly, in their disfavour. I shall in due time unpack my own little budget of grievances, and reckon up some of the bad marks I have immargined (as Mr. Thompson would say) in reading and re-reading his three books of verse. But the first thing to be done, and by far the most important, is to recognise and declare that we are here face to face with a poet of the first order—a man of imagination all compact, a seer and singer of rare genius. In the sheer essentials of poetry Mr. Thompson is rich to superfluity. He appeals mainly to the reader who loves poetry for its own sake, not for its possible but inessential accompaniments of sentiment, contemplation or passion, psychology, romance or drama. Mr. Thompson, as we shall see, is something of a psychologist and a good deal of a metaphysician. There are noble passages of thought and cosmic vision in his work. But it is not primarily for thought, ethical, metaphysical, or mystical, that one turns to Mr. Thompson. It is for the inexhaustible opulence, the superb daring, of his imagery, and for the pomp and majesty (mannered though it may often be) of his diction. If ever there was a born poet, a poet in spite of himself, who lisped in metaphors for the metaphors came, this surely

431

is he. His worst faults proceed from excess, not from defect, of poetic endowment.

To many poets rhythm is a snare, to some, imagery; Mr. Thompson belongs to the latter, and to my thinking nobler, company. He pours forth image after image in riotous, bewildering profusion ; most of them beautiful, but some incongruous, contorted, and (in a literary sense) vicious. Moderation is not included among his gifts; but, for my part, I greatly prefer poems which superabound in imagery to poems which are all rhythm. A happy image is a thing of inherent beauty, even if it lack that relation to a larger whole which should be its beauty's crown of beauty. Mr. Thompson never sacrifices coherence to a mere gallop of accents, or sets a cockboat of meaning asway on a billowy ocean of words. Every period or strophe of his work is a poem in itself, an image, or a many-petalled flower of imagery.

It is not yet ten years since he published his first book, *Poems;* and the *Sister Songs*, which form the matter of his second book, were written, he tells us, before the earlier collection appeared. These two books, then, may be grouped together; as the dates of individual poems are not given, we can scarcely hope to trace any development of style. *Sister Songs*, indeed, strike me as more superbly sustained, more evenly fraught with essential poetry, than the analogous sequence in the earlier volume, entitled *Love in Dian's Lap;* but while the resemblance is unmistakable, the difference may be fanciful. On the other hand, Mr. Thompson's third book, *New Poems*, shows a marked increase of power. There is more thought in it, less rhapsody; while the pressure of imagination to the square inch is, if possible, even higher than in the earlier volumes.

It is easy to attribute some of Mr. Thompson's peculiarities of style to the influence of Donne, Herbert, Crashaw, Vaughan, and other spiritual singers of the seven-

· FRANCIS · THOMPSON ·

teenth century. Mr. Coventry Patmore, too, had indubitably some share in making him what he is. But it would be a grave critical error to dwell with any insistence on these influences. We must not mistake affinity for discipleship. Mr. Thompson is a voice, not an echo. His style was implicit in his organisation, or, in simpler terms, was born with him. It is the inevitable expression of a very individual mind—vividly perceptive, intensely sentient, and irrepressibly alert to recombine its perceptions in unexpected interplays of analogy. He may have been encouraged by seventeenth-century example to give the rein to certain tendencies, or to cultivate, instead of chastening, certain mannerisms. He may have picked up a measure here, a cadence there; but his style, in the main, is not a thing acquired from without. It is not the more or less artificial vesture, but the organic expression, of his mental processes. The undulant procession of images, of which almost all his work consists, is no mere decoration, but presents the very substance and texture of his thought. So, too, with the Latinisms of his diction. If they are a vice, they must be put down to original sin, not superinduced iniquity. The love of majestic sonorities is fundamental in the poet's idiosyncrasy, so that he tends instinctively to employ the more sonorous factor in our composite tongue. He Latinises, not because Milton Latinised, but because his mental ear is tuned to the Miltonic key. He does not follow that great precedent, but no doubt it helps to make him (as he might say) obsequious to the trend of his own impulse.

In one of Mr. Thompson's later poems, *An Anthem of Earth*, there is a passage which is probably in fact, as it certainly is in form, autobiographical. The poet is addressing Mother Earth :

> In a little joy, in a little joy,
> We wear awhile thy sore insignia,
> Nor know thy heel o' the neck. O Mother ! Mother !

Then what use knew I of thy solemn robes,
But as a child, to play with them?   I bade thee
Leave thy great husbandries, thy grave designs,
Thy tedious state which irked my ignorant years,
Thy winter-watches, suckling of the grain,
Severe premeditation taciturn
Upon the brooded Summer, thy chill cares,
And all thy ministries majestical,
To sport with me, thy darling.   Thought I not
Thou set'st thy seasons forth processional
To pamper me with pageant,—thou thyself
My fellow-gamester, appanage of mine arms?
Then what wild Dionysia I, young Bacchanal,
Danced in thy lap!   Ah, for thy gravity!
Then, O Earth, thou rang'st beneath me,
Rocked to Eastward, rocked to Westward,
Even with the shifted
Poise and footing of my thought!
I brake through thy doors of sunset,
Ran before the hooves of sunrise,
Shook thy matron tresses down in fancies
Wild and wilful
As a poet's hand could twine them;
Caught in my fantasy's crystal chalice
The Bow, as its cataract of colours
Plashed to thee downward;
Then when thy circuit swung to nightward,
Night the abhorrèd, night was a new dawning,
Celestial dawning
Over the ultimate marges of the soul;
Dusk grew turbulent with fire before me,
And like a windy arras waved with dreams.
Sleep I took not for my bedfellow,
Who could waken
To a revel, an inexhaustible
Wassail of orgiac imageries;
Then while I wore thy sore insignia
In a little joy, O Earth, in a little joy;
Loving thy beauty in all creatures born of thee,
Children, and the sweet-essenced body of woman;
Feeling not yet upon my neck thy foot,
But breathing warm of thee as infants breathe
New from their mothers' morning bosom.   So I,
Risen from thee, restless winnower of the heaven,

Most Hermes-like, did keep
My vital and resilient path, and felt
The play of wings about my fledgèd heel—
Sure on the verges of precipitous dream,
Swift in its springing
From jut to jut of inaccessible fancies,
In a little joy.

This is clearly no imaginary presentation of the poet's childhood and boyhood. Such lines as

> Dusk grew turbulent with fire before me,
> And like a windy arras waved with dreams,

speak from the very heart of experience. It is plain that Mr. Thompson was born into the sect of the Sun-Worshippers, and holds what he justly deems his Priesthood of Apollo by hereditary right. Again and again he speaks as the Sun-God's fated devotee. Already in his first book of *Poems* he called himself the "constant Magian" of the sun. In *Sister Songs* he thus wrote of himself:

> I who can scarcely speak my fellows' speech,
> Love their love, or mine own love to them teach ;
> A bastard barred from their inheritance,
>   Who seem, in this dim shape's uneasy nook,
> Some sunflower's spirit which by luckless chance
>   Has mournfully its tenement mistook ;
> When it were better in its right abode,
> Heartless and happy lackeying its god.

"Sultan Phœbus has his Janisars," he says, and he is of the company. Again, in the *Orient Ode*:

> Not unto thee, great Image, not to thee
> Did the wise heathen bend an idle knee ;
> And in an age of faith grown frore
> If I too shall adore,
> Be it accounted unto me
> A bright sciential idolatry !

God has given thee visible thunders
To utter thine apocalypse of wonders ;
And what want I of prophecy,
That at the sounding from thy station
Of thy flagrant trumpet, see
The seals that melt, the open revelation ?

* * * * *

Yea, biune in imploring dumb,
Essential Heavens and corporal Earth await,
The Spirit and the Bride say : Come !
Lo, of thy Magians I the least
Haste with my gold, my incenses and myrrhs,
To thy desired epiphany, from the spiced
Regions and odorous of Song's traded East.
Thou, for the life of all that live
The victim daily born and sacrificed;
To whom the pinion of this longing verse
Beats but with fire which first thyself did give.
To thee, O Sun—or is't perchance, to Christ ?

We shall return presently to this point of interrogation.
In the meantime let us note Mr. Thompson's marvellous
fertility of images descriptive of the Sun-God's diurnal
progress, and the whole pageantry of the heavens.   Evening,
he says,

Bursts yon globèd yellow grape
(Which is the sun to mortals' sealèd sight)
Against her stainèd mouth.

Again :

And now, thou elder nursling of the nest,
Ere all the intertangled West
Be one magnificence
Of multitudinous blossoms that o'errun
The flaming brazen bowl o' the burnished sun
Which they do flower from,
How shall I 'stablish *thy* memorial ?

Again, we read of

The earth and all its planetary kin,
Starry buds tangled in the whirling hair
That flames round the Phoebean wassailer.

FRANCIS THOMPSON

Again :

> With lucent feet imbrued,
> If young Day tread, a glorious vintager,
> The wine-press of the purple-foamèd East ;
> Or round the nodding sun, flush-faced and sunken,
> His wild bacchantes drunken
> Reel, with rent woofs aflaunt, their westering rout.

Yet again (and how beautiful this is !) :

> The day is lingered out :
> In slow wreaths folden
> Around yon censer, spherèd, golden,
> Vague Vesper's fumes aspire ;
> And glimmering to eclipse
> The long laburnum drips
> Its honey of wild flame, its jocund spilth of fire.

Here, now, is a splendid image of the dawn—I cannot find it in my heart to tear it from its immediate context :

> Yet there is more, whereat none guesseth, love !
> Upon the ending of my deadly night
> (Whereof thou hast not the surmise, and slight
> Is all that any mortal knows thereof),
> Thou wert to me that earnest of day's light,
> When, like the back of a gold-mailèd saurian
> Heaving its slow length from Nilotic slime,
> The first long gleaming fissure runs Aurorian
> Athwart the yet dun firmament of prime.

The last five extracts are all from the second poem of *Sister Songs*. In the first of the *New Poems*, Mr. Thompson, still more daringly, translates the sunrise, not into any colour-image, but into sound :

> East, ah, east of Himalay,
> Dwell the nations underground ;
> Hiding from the shock of Day,
> For the sun's uprising-sound :

> Dare not issue from the ground
> At the tumults of the Day,
> So fearfully the sun doth sound
> Clanging up beyond Cathay ;
> For the great earthquaking sunrise rolling up beyond Cathay.

There is an amusing similarity-in-diversity between this last line and Mr. Kipling's famous—

> An' the dawn comes up like thunder outer China 'crost the Bay !

One of the most majestic of Mr. Thompson's sun-images occurs in the opening strophe of his *Orient Ode* :

> Lo, in the sanctuaried East,
> Day, a dedicated priest
> In all his robes pontifical exprest,
> Lifteth slowly, lifteth sweetly,
> From out its Orient tabernacle drawn,
> Yon orbèd sacrament confest
> Which sprinkles benediction through the dawn.
> And when the grave procession's ceased,
> The earth with due illustrious rite
> Blessed—ere the frail fingers featly
> Of twilight, violet-cassocked acolyte,
> His sacerdotal stoles unvest—
> Sets, for high close of the mysterious feast,
> The sun in august exposition meetly
> Within the flaming monstrance of the West.

These passages are enough to prove Mr. Thompson's unwearying passion for what (misappropriating the term) I am tempted to call "heliography"; yet I have made no quotation from his formal *Ode to the Setting Sun.* Sometimes his absorption in this inexhaustible theme betrays him into conceits which seem unworthy of him; as, for instance, where he talks of the sun

> like a golden bee
> Stinging the West to angry red.

But far more frequent than such lapses of taste are splendid and memorable phrases such as

> The golden vortex in the West
> Over the foundered sun.

"So stirbt ein Held, anbetungsvoll," said Schiller's Karl Moor as he gazed at the sinking orb ; and no one surely has ever been more fervent in his "Anbetung" than Mr. Thompson. A sun-worshipping Council of Divines might extract a whole liturgy from his three books of verse.

Let us note, now, that Mr. Thompson regards the sun not merely from the spectacular but also from the scientific point of view. In a highly mystical poem called *New Year's Chimes* there occurs the following stanza :

> The world above in the world below
> *(And a million worlds are but as one)*
> And the One in all ; as the sun's strength so
> Strives in all strength, glows in all glow
> Of the earth that wits not, and man thereon.

We have implicit in these lines the whole theory of the conservation of energy ; and again and again the poet returns to the thought. In the *Ode to the Setting Sun* he cries :

> Who lit the furnace of the mammoth's heart ?
> Who shagged him like Pilatus' ribbèd flanks ?
>
>   *   *   *   *   *
>
> Thou rear'dst the enormous brood ;
> Who hast with life imbued
> The lion maned in tawny majesty,
>   The tiger velvet-barred,
>   The stealthy-stepping pard,
> And the lithe panther's flexuous symmetry.

Then he goes on to ask :

> How came the entombèd tree a light-bearer,
>   Though sunk in lightless lair ?
>
>   *   *   *   *   *

Thou gavest him his light,
Though sepultured in night
Beneath the dead bones of a perished world;
Over his prostrate form
Though cold, and heat, and storm,
The mountainous wrack of a creation hurled.

This train of thought runs through the whole ode, and proves that Mr. Thompson's worship is (in a narrower sense, no doubt, than he intended) truly a "bright sciential idolatry"—that his imagination has been kindled not merely through the eye, but through an intelligence capable of grasping and glorying in the most grandiose generalisations of science. There is nothing here of the wilful obscurantism of Campbell's famous quatrain:

Triumphal arch, that fill'st the sky
When storms prepare to part,
I ask not proud Philosophy
To teach me what thou art.

And Mr. Thompson's familiarity with, and employment of, "proud Philosophy" does not end here. There is a scientific conception, very perfectly and nobly transmuted into poetry, in the couplet depicting

This labouring, vast, Tellurian galleon,
Riding at anchor off the Orient sun;

and the same thought reappears under a different image, and very much elaborated, in the *Orient Ode:*

Thou as a lion roar'st, O Sun,
Upon thy satellites' vexèd heels;
Before thy terrible hunt thy planets run;
Each in his frighted orbit wheels,
Each flies through inassuageable chase,
Since the hunt o' the world begun,
The puissant approaches of thy face,
And yet thy radiant leash he feels.
Since the hunt o' the world begun,

440

Lashed with terror, leashed with longing,
The mighty course is ever run;
Pricked with terror, leashed with longing,
Thy rein they love, and thy rebuke they shun.

It is quite natural, indeed, that the Titanic processes revealed (as Tennyson phrases it) by "Astronomy and Geology, terrible Muses," should take strong hold upon a poet's imagination. But Mr. Thompson is familiar with scientific conceptions of a much less obviously impressive order. He is as much at home in the microcosm as in the macrocosm. For instance, in a poem entitled *Contemplation*, he writes:

No hill can idler be than I;
No stone its inter-particled vibration
Investeth with a stiller lie;
No heaven with a more urgent rest betrays
The eyes that on it gaze.

*　　*　　*　　*　　*

In poets floating like a water-flower
Upon the bosom of the glassy hour,
In skies that no man sees to move,
Lurk untumultuous vortices of power.

*　　*　　*　　*　　*

From stones and poets you may know,
Nothing so active is, as that which least seems so.

Again, the dissipation of energy is as clearly present to Mr. Thompson's mind as its conservation; witness the following passage from one of his finest odes, entitled *From the Night of Forebeing:*

For as the dark, profound nativity,
God saw the end should be,
When the world's infant horoscope He cast.
Unshackled from the bright Phoebean awe,
In leaf, flower, mould, and tree,
Resolved into dividual liberty,
Most strengthless, unparticipant, inane,
Or suffered the ill peace of lethargy,

Lo, the Earth eased of rule:
Unsummered, granted to her own worst smart
The dear wish of the fool—
Disintegration, merely which man's heart
For freedom understands.

The poet is treating of winter as the symbol of this ultimate
degeneration of material energy; and proceeds to find in
spring the correlative symbol of the spiritual energy which
has once made cosmos out of chaos, and is destined, he
would have us think, to do so again:

But thou, O Earth, dost much disdain
The bondage of thy waste and futile reign,
And sweetly to the great compulsion draw
Of God's alone true-manumitting law,
And Freedom, only which the wise intend,
To work thine innate end.

I wish I could quote the whole magnificent passage in
which the waking of the world is pictured; but I must
content myself with the concluding lines:

And thou up-floatest, warm, and newly-bathed,
Earth, through delicious air,
And with thine own apparent beauties swathed,
Wringing the waters from thine arborous hair;
That all men's hearts, which do behold and see,
Grow weak with their exceeding much desire,
And turn to thee on fire,
Enamoured with their utter wish of thee,
Anadyomene!
What vine-outquickening life all creatures sup,
Feel, for the air within its sapphire cup
How it does leap, and twinkle headily!
Feel, for Earth's bosom pants, and heaves her scarfing
    sea;
And round and round in bacchanal rout reel the swift
    spheres intemperably!

Earlier in the same poem Mr. Thompson has another
442

picture of the coming of spring, from a terrene, rather than
a planetary, standpoint :

> What popular breath her coming does out-tell
> The garrulous leaves among !
> What little noises stir and pass
> From blade to blade along the voluble grass !
> O Nature, never-done
> Ungaped-at Pentecostal miracle,
> We hear thee, each man in his proper tongue !
> Break, elemental children, break ye loose
> From the strict frosty rule
> Of grey-beard Winter's school.
> Vault, O young winds, vault in your tricksome courses
> Upon the snowy steeds that reinless use
> In coerule pampas of the heaven to run ;
> Foaled of the white sea-horses,
> Washed in the lambent waters of the sun.

*   *   *   *   *

> The great-vanned Angel March
> Hath trumpeted
> His clangorous " Sleep no more " to all the dead—
> Beat his strong vans o'er earth, and air, and sea.
> And they have heard ;
> Hark to the *Jubilate* of the bird
> For them that found the dying way to life !
> And they have heard,
> And quicken to the great precursive word ;
> Green spray showers lightly down the cascade of the larch ;
> The graves are riven,
> And the Sun comes with power amid the clouds of heaven !

How admirable in idea, atmosphere, and movement is
that line about the " cascade of the larch " ! The poet
then repeats, in somewhat more diffuse and less vigorous
form, the image from his own *Sister Songs :*

> And Summer moves on Winter
> With the trumpet of the March, and the pennon of the May ;

—winding up the strophe with the daring, and to my thought
greatly daring, phrase,

> From sky to sod
> The world's unfolded blossom smells of God.

443

It would be easy to multiply indefinitely these examples of Mr. Thompson's intense realisation of all the phenomena of Nature—both of her visual appearances, and of those vaster and minuter phenomena which are conceivable only to the imagination quickened by science. How comes it, then, that a poet who sees the material universe so intensely and, up to a certain point, so intrepidly, should, when that point is reached, plunge into the theological mysticism which speaks in *The Hound of Heaven* and *To the Dead Cardinal of Westminster*, in *Assumpta Maria* and *Any Saint*, and in a hundred incidental passages throughout his work? The explanation, I think, is not far to seek. Catholicism is Mr. Thompson's refuge from Pantheism, a creed, or rather a philosophy, too cold to satisfy the poet within him. Pantheism makes no more picturesque or emotional appeal than a demonstration in Euclid. It is the product of a logical process—we might almost say of a logical quibble. Granted a certain set of definitions and axioms, a certain conclusion inevitably results; but as the whole process really takes place in the region of the Unthinkable, the spiritual sustenance it affords is somewhat attenuated. Mr. Thompson, at all events, cannot stay his stomach upon it. Having realised the unity of the force underlying all phenomena, he proceeds to visualise, to dramatise it; or rather to accept the most gorgeously spectacular dramatisation of it ever evolved by the human intelligence. We have seen him, a little way back, at what we may call the jumping-off place: where, in his *Orient Ode*, he describes himself as hasting with gold, with incenses and myrrhs, to the "desired epiphany" of the sun, and adds:

> To thee, O Sun—or is't, perchance, to Christ?

In the following strophe (the last of the ode) he thus answers his own question:

> Ay, if men say that on all high heaven's face
> The saintly signs I trace

Which round my stolèd altars hold their solemn place,
Amen, amen! For oh, how could it be—
When I with wingèd feet had run
Through all the windy earth about,
Quested its secret of the sun,
And heard what things the stars together shout,—
I should not heed thereout
Consenting counsel won :—
" By this, O Singer, know we if thou see.
When men shall say to thee : Lo! Christ is here,
When men shall say to thee : Lo! Christ is there,
Believe them : yea, and this—then art thou seer,
When all thy crying clear
Is but : Lo here! lo there! ah me, lo everywhere! "

This, it is evident, is not the evangelical Christ, so to
speak, of popular orthodoxy, and still less the divine moralist
and humanitarian of popular heterodoxy. It may be doubted
whether Mr. Thompson takes much interest in the historic
Jesus of Nazareth, or has ever troubled his head about
evidence or dogma. His religion—in so far as one can read
it in his poems—is simply a function of his imagination.
He feels it an imperious necessity to visualise the immanent
Force of the universe in a picture, not in the bare diagram
of Pantheism ; and Catholicism provides him with a ready-
made mythology, beautiful to the eye, venerable to the mind.
In his religious poems (unless I misread them) there is
far more apocalyptic pageantry than theological subtlety or
spiritual unction. Mr. Thompson can think, and think
keenly, on the physical and psychological plane ; on the
plane of theology he does not attempt to think, but aban-
dons himself to beatific vision and what he himself calls a
" wassail of orgiac imageries." Whether it be just or unjust,
this remark conveys no reproach, and still less any imputa-
tion of insincerity. I am merely trying, with some diffidence,
to bridge the chasm between Mr. Thompson's vision of
phenomena and the theories of causation and destiny which
content and even enrapture him. It is possible, of course,

that the chasm is an illusion on my part, and that there is absolute consistency and continuity between Mr. Thompson's vision and his speculation. The probability is, at all events, that the word "belief" conveys totally diverse meanings to him and to me—that we have been brought up (perhaps from generations back) on very different "Grammars of Assent."

It remains to note what seems to me the striking increase in virility and strength that distinguishes Mr. Thompson's *New Poems* from his two earlier publications. Writing of *Sister Songs* at the time of their appearance (1895) I said: "His fantasies flash forth and fade away like streamers of the Aurora Borealis, with no apparent interdependence, and to no ascertainable end. Poetry more phantasmagoric does not exist in the language." This remark was perhaps too sweeping even then, but there was a considerable measure of truth in it. *Love in Dian's Lap* and *Sister Songs* are long-drawn hyperboles of homage, beautiful, but exceedingly insubstantial. We cannot see the Lady or the Children for the incense-fumes rolling up in ever-shifting arabesques from the poet-worshipper's censer. It is not intended that we should see his divinities: adoration, not portraiture or psychology, is his purpose: he achieves with mastery what he sets forth to do, but there is very little thought-substance, very little relation to life, in the long processions of imagery. What he aims at is rather the absolute beauty of music than the beauty-in-truth of the greatest poetry. He works himself up to magnificent raptures of eulogy; but we feel that they are—not insincere, certainly, not even conventional— yet more indicative of the poet's fervour of imagination than of any unique quality in the subjects of his song. The Lady—

> Whose body other ladies well might bear
> As soul—

while rejoicing to have inspired so beautiful a conceit,

would probably be the first to disclaim it as a trait of portraiture. So, too, with unnumbered other passages:

> 'Tis not for her to hold that prize a prize,
> Or praise much praise, though proudest in its wise,
> To which even hopes of merely women rise.
> Such strife would to the vanquished laurels yield,
> Against *her* suffered to have lost a field.

> *   *   *   *   *

> How shall I gauge what beauty is her dole,
> Who cannot see her countenance for her soul,
> As birds see not the casement for the sky?
> And as 'tis check they prove its presence by,
> I know not of her body till I find
> My flight debarred the heaven of her mind.

These (and especially the second) are admirable ecstasies; yet we cannot but feel that the simple, half-humorous humanity of the following couplet (almost unique in the poem) brings us more genuinely in touch with the subject:

> If of her virtues you evade the snare,
> Then for her faults you'll fall in love with her.

Again, there is an element of truth, despite its subtlety, in this little touch, which makes it stand out from its context:

> She wears that body but as one indues
> A robe, half careless, for it is the use.

Here we feel that the poet really has his eye on his subject; at other times he is possessed, inspired, inflamed by it: he does not see it.

In *Sister Songs* we have precisely the same sensation: that the poet has been, so to speak, stung or stimulated into a dithyrambic ecstasy, but that, the impetus once given, he almost forgets where it came from, and revels on at large from fantasy to fantasy, each more gorgeous than the last.

Here, for instance, is one strophe of Mr. Thompson's
" Syllabling to Sylvia " :

Next I saw, wonder-whist,
How from the atmosphere a mist,
So it seemed, slow uprist;
And, looking from those elfin swarms,
    I was 'ware
    How the air
Was all populous with forms
Of the Hours, floating down,
Like Nereids through a watery town.
Some, with languors of waved arms,
Fluctuous oared their flexile way ;
Some were borne half resupine
On the aërial hyaline,
Their fluid limbs and rare array
Flickering on the wind, as quivers
Trailing weed in running rivers ;
And others, in far prospect seen,
Newly loosed on this terrene,
Shot in piercing swiftness came,
With hair a-stream like pale and goblin flame.
As crystàlline ice in water,
Lay in air each faint daughter ;
Inseparate (or but separate dim)
Circumfused wind from wind-like vest,
Wind-like vest from wind-like limb.
But outward from each lucid breast,
When some passion left its haunt,
Radiate surge of colour came,
Diffusing blush-wise, palpitant,
Dying all the filmy frame.
With some sweet tenderness they would
Turn to an amber-clear and glossy gold ;
Or a fine sorrow, lovely to behold,
Would sweep them as the sun and wind's joined flood
    Sweeps a greening-sapphire sea ;
    Or they would glow enamouredly
Illustrious sanguine, like a grape of blood ;
    Or with mantling poetry
Curd to the tincture which the opal hath,
Like rainbows thawing in a moonbeam bath.
So paled they, flushed they, swam they, sang melodiously.

With all its mannerism, this is magnificent work. Shelley,
I venture to say, would have held out the right hand of
fellowship to the man who wrote it. But what, the reader
may well ask, has it to do with " Sylvia " or any other little
girl? Turn to the book, and you will find that it is part of
an ordered scheme; but you will also find, I think, that the
scheme bears no relation to any individual child, but is
simply a sort of masque of imagery presumed to circle
around an abstract simulacrum of childhood. It is almost
ludicrous to imagine the bewilderment of a child in the
concrete to whom, by a telepathic miracle perhaps, some
faint conception should be conveyed of the pageantry here
conjured up in her honour. Need I say that in this remark
I intend no censure, but am merely trying to substantiate
what I have said as to the phantasmagoric character of Mr.
Thompson's earlier work? It is true that some of the
other poems in the first collection are a little more concrete.
A Judgment in Heaven is a fine and pregnant parable, ending
in an epilogue from which I cannot refrain from quoting the
following profoundly significant lines :

> Virtue may unlock hell, or even
> A sin turn in the wards of heaven
> (As ethics of the text-book go),
> So little men their own deeds know,
> Or through the intricate mêlée
> Guess whitherward draws the battle sway ;
> So little, if they know the deed,
> Discern what therefrom shall succeed.
> To wisest moralists 'tis but given
> To work rough border-law to Heaven,
> Within this narrow life of ours,
> These marches 'twixt delimitless Powers
> Is it, if Heaven the future showed,
> Is it the all-severest mode
> To see ourselves with the eyes of God ?
> God rather grant, at His assize,
> He see us not with our own eyes.

Concrete and very beautiful, too, are the five *Poems on Children*—*Daisy*, *The Making of Viola*, *To My God-child*, *The Poppy*, and *To Monica thought Dying*. But, on the whole, it may be said that in his first two books Mr. Thompson took no very firm hold upon life, suggesting rather Matthew Arnold's too-famous description of Shelley as "a beautiful ineffectual angel, beating in the void his luminous wings in vain."

To the poet of *New Poems*, on the other hand, this description would be grotesquely inapplicable. Here the great mass of the work is concrete and of universal relevance ; no mere glorified coterie-speech, like *Love in Dian's Lap* and *Sister Songs*. Of the first poem—*The Mistress of Vision*—I shall say nothing. It contains impressive passages, but its purport, as a whole, entirely eludes me. Nor do I pretend that *Assumpta Maria* conveys much definite meaning to my mind : it probably is not intended to. One or two other poems, short and (I hope) unimportant, are too utterly spiritual for my grosser apprehension. But with the two exceptions above stated, all the longer poems convey definite and tangible, often profound and noble, thought, in language which, though loaded and overloaded with imagery, readily yields up its meaning to an attentive reader. *Contemplation*, *The Dread of Height*, the *Orient Ode*, *From the Night of Forebeing*, and the *Ode to the Setting Sun*, are philosophic poems of commanding power. The more one reads them, the more one is impressed by the vigour and fecundity of the mind which produced them. But the most important poem of this group is the before mentioned *Anthem of Earth*—a stately survey, in irregular, unrhymed verse, of man's destiny on earth. Here is one of its most memorable strophes :

In a little dust, in a little dust,
Earth, thou reclaim'st us, who do all our lives
Find of thee but Egyptian villeinage.

Thou dost this body, this enhavocked realm,
Subject to ancient and ancestral shadows ;
Descended passions sway it ; it is distraught
With ghostly usurpation, dinned and fretted
With the still-tyrannous dead ; a haunted tenement,
Peopled from barrows and outworn ossuaries.
Thou giv'st us life not half so willingly
As thou undost thy giving ; thou that teem'st
The stealthy terror of the sinuous pard,
The lion maned with curlèd puissance,
The serpent, and all fair strong beasts of ravin,
Thyself most fair and potent beast of ravin ;
And thy great eaters thou, the greatest, eat'st.
Thou hast devoured mammoth and mastodon,
And many a floating bank of fangs,
The scaly scourges of thy primal brine,
And the tower-crested plesiosaure.
Thou fill'st thy mouth with nations, gorgest slow
On purple æons of kings ; man's hulking towers
Are carcase for thee, and to modern sun
Disglutt'st their splintered bones.
Rabble of Pharaohs and Arsacidæ
Keep their cold house within thee ; thou has sucked down
How many Ninevehs and Hecatompyloi,
And perished cities whose great phantasmata
O'erbrow the silent citizens of Dis :—
Hast not thy fill ?
Tarry awhile, lean Earth, for thou shalt drink,
Even till thy dull throat sicken,
The draught thou grow'st most fat on ; hear'st thou not
The world's knives bickering in their sheaths ? O patience !
Much offal of a foul world comes thy way,
And man's superfluous cloud shall soon be laid
In a little blood.

Still more impressive in its stately serenity is the concluding passage of the *Anthem :*

Now, mortal-sonlike
I thou hast suckled, Mother, I at last
Shall sustenant be to thee.   Here I untrammel,
Here I pluck loose the body's cerementing,
And break the tomb of life ; here I shake off

> The bur o' the world, man's congregation shun,
> And to the antique order of the dead
> I take the tongueless vows ; my cell is set
> Here in thy bosom ; my little trouble is ended
> In a little peace.

I have spoken of Mr. Thompson's kinship with the seventeenth century. In such a strain as this it is no minor Caroline singer he recalls, but the Jacobean Shakespeare.

It must not be supposed, however, that Mr. Thompson's Pegasus is always such a very high horse. There is considerable variety both of matter and style in these *New Poems*. In *A Narrow Vessel: Being a little Dramatic Sequence on the Aspect of Primitive Girl Nature towards a Love beyond its Capacities*, we find delicate analysis, with a light and graceful metrical touch. Witness this single stanza :

> His silence on my cheek like breath
> I felt in subtle way ;
> More sweet than aught another saith
> Was what he did not say.

Witness, too, this exquisite little poem :

THE WAY OF A MAID

> The lover whose soul shaken is
> In some decuman billow of bliss,
> Who feels his gradual-wading feet
> Sink in some sudden hollow of sweet,
> And 'mid love's used converse comes
> Sharp on a mood which all joy sums—
> An instant's fine compendium of
> The liberal-leavèd writ of love ;
> His abashed pulses beating thick
> At the exigent joy and quick,
> Is dumbed, by aiming utterance great
> Up to the miracle of his fate.
> The wise girl, such Icarian fall
> Saved by her confidence that she's small,—
> As what no kindred word will fit
> Is uttered best by opposite,

FRANCIS THOMPSON

Love in the tongue of hate exprest,
And deepest anguish in a jest,—
Feeling the infinite must be
Best said by triviality,
Speaks, where expression bates its wings,
Just happy, alien, little things;
What of all words is in excess
Implies in a sweet nothingness,
With dailiest babble shows her sense
That full speech were full impotence;
And while she feels the heavens lie bare,
She only talks about her hair.

In the *Miscellaneous Poems* we discover that Mr. Thompson is no less at home in the short lyric than in the ode. *A Question*, *Field-Flower*, *Nocturn*, and *A May Burden* are exquisite little things; *Memorat Memoria* is passionate and beautiful: *My Lady the Tyranness* is superb; and this, *To a Snow-Flake*, is simply perfect:

What heart could have thought you?—
Past our devisal
(O filigree petal!)
Fashioned so purely,
Fragilely, surely,
From what Paradisal
Imagineless metal,
Too costly for cost?
Who hammered you, wrought you,
From argentine vapour?—
"God was my shaper.
Passing surmisal,
He hammered, He wrought me,
From curled silver vapour,
To lust of His mind;—
Thou could'st not have thought me!
So purely, so palely,
Tinily, surely,
Mightily, frailly,
Insculped and embossed,
With His hammer of wind,
And His graver of frost."

453

How can one harden one's heart to remonstrate with a
poet who can write like this ? One's impulse is rather to
say, " Go on and prosper—play what pranks you please with
the English language ; Latinise, neologise, solecise as you
will ; make past-participles from nouns and verbs transitive
from adjectives ; devise gins and springes for the tongue out
of cunningly-knotted sibilants and dental consonants ; pause
not to distinguish between grotesque conceits and noble
images ; only continue to write such lines as these :

> Even the kisses of the just
> Go down not unresurgent to the dust.
> Yea, not a kiss which I have given,
> But shall triumph upon my lips in heaven,
> Or cling a shameful fungus there in hell—

and everything, everything shall be forgiven you ! "

The reader must have gathered clearly enough from the
foregoing quotations that Mr. Thompson is not a writer of
pure and perfect style, of unfailing mental equipoise, self-
critical and self-controlled. His genius is turbulent and
volcanic. It is significant that he very seldom writes in
strict stanza form. A few powerful sonnets on the Shakespearean model are, I think, his most successful attempts at
casting his thought in a definite and narrow mould. In no
respect is he to be proposed as a model to the neophyte in
verse. To any young poet who admires, and is tempted to
imitate him, I would say, " Be sure you have his genius
before you adopt his licences ; and even when you *are* sure
—think better of it." Any one can write of a "lioned
leap" or say that something "dafts him with doubt." The
difficulty is not to use such phrases, but to atone for them.
Mr. Thompson's favourite audacity is the making of past-
participles from non-existent verbs. He talks of being
"heavened" and "godded"; of "lampèd clusters of
grapes"; of a "hearted casement," an "azured daïs," a
"lethèd eon," a "calyxed heart," of "fountained poesy,"

and "unprevisioned height." When he means "suns used as shields" he says "shielded suns," which, according to all established usage, means something totally different. When he wants to say "golden gates" he says "gated golds," which, according to all established usage, means—nothing at all. Again, he cares not what part of speech he presses into service as a verb; for instance, "to nigh," "to naiad," "to dirge," "to dusk," "to sultry." He revives archaic terms for the sake of their archaism, without much thought of their harmony or beauty. "The cockshut-light," though it has Shakespearean authority, is scarcely an improvement on "twilight." "Totty" (applied to the October sun) is sanctioned by Chaucer, yet has all the air of a modern vulgarism. Again, Mr. Thompson now and then exaggerates to the point of caricature the Latinism of his diction. When he writes of

> Sinking day, which, pouring its abundance,
> *Sublimed the illuminous and volute redundance*
> Of locks that, half dissolving, floated round her face,

we could almost suspect him of deliberately parodying himself. He cannot always resist an incongruous image. For instance:

> When the snake summer casts her blazoned skin,
> We find it at the turn of autumn's path,
> And think it summer that re-winded hath,
>   Joying therein.

This is rather worse than a mixed metaphor—it is a juxtaposition of disparate metaphors, of mutually exclusive figures. Two seasons, in the same sentence, ought surely to be typified by homogeneous symbols. It does not help but hinder the imagination to find summer figuring as a snake, and autumn as a path. The inherent strength of an image will sometimes blind the poet to its grotesqueness or inappropriateness to the matter in hand.

In one passage of *Sister Songs*, for example, he suffers a note of intolerable ugliness to intrude into a context where it is fatally dissonant:

> So between thy father's knees
> I saw *thee* stand,
> And through my hazes
> Of pain and fear thine eyes' young wonder shone.
> Then, *as flies scatter from a carrion*
>
> * * * * *
>
> Fled at thy countenance, all that doubting spawn.

Again, these two stanzas from *A Judgment in Heaven*, though magnificently vigorous, give the scoffer unnecessary cause to blaspheme:

As in a secret and tenebrous cloud * the watcher from the disquiet earth
At momentary intervals * beholds from it raggèd rifts break forth
The flash of a golden perturbation,* the travelling threat of a witchèd birth:

Till heavily parts a sinister chasm,* a grisly jaw, whose verges soon,
Slowly and ominously filled* by the on-coming plenilune,
Supportlessly congest with fire,* and suddenly spit forth the moon.

The masterly movement of this poem reminds me that I have said nothing of Mr. Thompson's rare gifts as a metrist, nothing of the singularly just instinct (to my thinking) with which in his rhymes he steers a middle course between pedantic accuracy and vulgar slovenliness. These aspects of Mr. Thompson's art I must leave to other critics or another time. The purpose of the present study will have been fulfilled if I have brought home to the reader some realisation (however inadequate) of the wealth of essential poetry in Mr. Thompson's work, and proved him a poet not by personal choice but by divine election.

FRANCIS THOMPSON

DAISY.

Where the thistle lifts a purple crown
  Six foot out of the turf,
And the harebell shakes on the windy hill—
  O the breath of the distant surf!—

The hills look over on the South,
  And southward dreams the sea;
And, with the sea-breeze hand in hand,
  Came innocence and she.

Where 'mid the gorse the raspberry
  Red for the gatherer springs,
Two children did we stray and talk
  Wise, idle, childish things.

She listened with big-lipped surprise,
  Breast-deep 'mid flower and spine:
Her skin was like a grape, whose veins
  Run snow instead of wine.

She knew not those sweet words she spake,
  Nor knew her own sweet way;
But there's never a bird, so sweet a song
  Thronged in whose throat that day!

Oh, there were flowers in Storrington
  On the turf and on the spray;
But the sweetest flower on the Sussex hills
  Was the Daisy-flower that day!

Her beauty smoothed earth's furrowed face!
  She gave me tokens three:—
A look, a word of her winsome mouth,
  And a wild raspberry.

A berry red, a guileless look,
  A still word,—strings of sand !
And yet they made my wild, wild heart
  Fly down to her little hand.

For standing artless as the air,
  And candid as the skies,
She took the berries with her hand,
  And the love with her sweet eyes.

The fairest things have fleetest end :
  Their scent survives their close,
But the rose's scent is bitterness
  To him that loved the rose !

She looked a little wistfully,
  Then went her sunshine way :—
The sea's eye had a mist on it,
  And the leaves fell from the day.

She went her unremembering way,
  She went and left in me
The pang of all the partings gone,
  And partings yet to be.

She left me marvelling while my soul
  Was sad that she was glad ;
At all the sadness in the sweet,
  The sweetness in the sad.

Still, still I seemed to see her, still
  Look up with soft replies,
And take the berries with her hand,
  And the love with her lovely eyes.

Nothing begins, and nothing ends,
  That is not paid with moan ;
For we are born in others' pain,
  And perish in our own.

FRANCIS THOMPSON

LOVE DECLARED.

I looked, she drooped, and neither spoke, and cold
We stood, how unlike all forecasted thought
Of that desirèd minute! Then I leaned
Doubting; whereat she lifted—oh, brave eyes
Unfrighted:—forward like a wind-blown flame
Came bosom and mouth to mine!
                    That falling kiss
Touching long-laid expectance, all went up
Suddenly into passion; yea, the night
Caught, blazed, and wrapt us round in vibrant fire.

Time's beating wing subsided, and the winds
Caught up their breathing, and the world's great pulse
Stayed in mid-throb, and the wild train of life
Reeled by, and left us stranded on a hush.
This moment is a statue unto Love
Carved from a fair white silence.
                    Lo, he stands
Within us—are we not one now, one, one roof,
His roof, and the partition of weak flesh
Gone down before him, and no more, for ever?—
Stands like a bird new-lit, and as he lit,
Poised in our quiet being; only, only
Within our shaken hearts the air of passion,
Cleft by his sudden coming, eddies still
And whirs round his enchanted movelessness.

A film of trance between two strivings! Lo,
It bursts; yet dream's snapped links cling round the limbs
Of waking: like a running evening stream
Which no man hears, or sees, or knows to run,
(Glazed with dim quiet,) save that there the moon
Is shattered to a creamy flicker of flame,
Our eyes' sweet trouble were hid, save that the love
Trembles a little on their impassioned calms.

FREDERIC HERBERT TRENCH

THE incomparable legend of Deirdre may, for aught I
know, have found its predestined poet in the Irish tongue ;
but in English it as yet awaits him. It cannot, surely, have
long to wait ; indeed, one rather wonders that there should
not be a rush for the usufruct of so glorious a theme.
Perhaps Mr. Herbert Trench may be held to have "staked
out his claim" in *Deirdre Wed.* His poem cannot be
regarded as more than a preliminary study for the epic
yet to be ; but if he himself regards it in that light—
a point on which I have no information—one must gladly
admit it to be a preliminary study of very high promise.

"This episode of thirty hours," says Mr. Trench, "does
not occur in any of the versions of the famous ' Tragical Tale
of the Sons of Usnach.' " In other words, the episode is a
thing of his own invention, outside and apart from the
actual legend. In just such a fashion would a poet, in
doubt as to the best form in which to cast an ambitious
work, make his experimental essays. He would not care to
prove his tools on any portion of his actual theme, but would
rather choose for that purpose a piece of similar material,
which would form no necessary part of the ultimate fabric.
Mr. Trench is even at some pains, as it seems to me, to
emphasise the tentative nature of his present effort. It is
difficult to account otherwise for the elaborate and quite disproportionate machinery which he applies to the narration

· HERBERT · TRENCH ·

of so very brief and fragmentary an episode. Though he
deals only with the first stage, as it were, in the flight of
Deirdre and Naois, Mr. Trench employs no fewer than
three ghostly "Chanters" to serve as his mouthpieces.
First of all we have the "Voice of Fintan, out of the First
Century," speaking in blank verse; then the "Voice of Cir,
out of a Century more remote, but unknown," speaking in a
rugged, mainly anapæstic, four-line stanza; then the "Voice
of Urmael, out of the Sixth Century," speaking in an
elaborate ten-line stanza of iambic pentameters; and, finally,
the "Voice of Fintan," still in blank verse, takes up the tale
afresh, and brings it to the point at which Mr. Trench
chooses to leave off. As enabling the poet to experiment in
different metres and styles, this machinery has clearly its
uses. Otherwise, its artistic advantages entirely escape me.
Mr. Trench may possibly conceive that each of the voices
has a peculiar fitness for that portion of the narrative which
he assigns to it. This special adaptation is not very
apparent; but supposing it to exist, it is certainly pur-
chased at too great cost. The sense of artifice becomes
overpowering when we have to summon three "Chanters"
from their graves, in widely sundered centuries, to narrate
the events of thirty hours. The oldest of the Chanters,
indeed—Cir, to wit—was dead long before the date of the
events he narrates, and saw them from his tomb. It may
be said that there is no particular reason why he should not
do so; but is there any particular reason why he should?
The burden of proof lies on the poet. He ought, one
would think, to make us sensible of some imperative reason
for such a gigantic draft on our powers of make-believe.

When he returns to the theme, as I trust he may, and
tells the actual story of Deirdre and the Sons of Usnach,
let him by all means speak with the Voice of Fintan, or
at any rate in the measure adopted by that "chanter
divine." Mr. Trench's blank verse is very strong and

resonant : a little lacking in suppleness, perhaps ; but that would come when he warmed to his theme. His description of the preparations for the wedding feast in the palace of King Connachar, of the arrival and dismissal of Naois, and of the discovery that Deirdre has fled, is exceedingly spirited and picturesque throughout. In the following passage, the painting of the sunset is not in Mr. Trench's happiest manner ; but how admirable is the fourth line, and how original and beautiful the last three :

> But while outside the black roof on the mount
> Outwafted was the gold divinity
> On swooning wings, the Lake of Pearls far down
> Curdled beneath the unseen seed of rain.
> Ramparts run there that misty prisoners
> Bore once in bags of slime up from the lake
> For barriers of the house they most abhorr'd.
> And on the hillside, where that rampart old
> Dips lowest to the lakeward, Deirdre stood,
> Hearing from distant ridges the faint bleat
> Of lambs perturb the dusk—bleats shivering out
> Like wool from thorns—there the young Deirdre stood.

While Deirdre is in the dusk by the lake, Connachar, on the hill above, is receiving Naois and his brothers " Back from a hosting and a desperate prey " :

> Hanging on the young man's lips
> The hosts sway'd round him, and above the press
> Connachar, glittering all in torques of gold
> And writhen armlets, listen'd from the mound
> Of judgment, by the doom-oak at his door.
> His beak'd helm took the sunset, but he held
> His flint-red eyes in shadow and averse.

At once pictorial and dramatic, these two concluding lines are perfect in vision, masterly in condensation. Here, again, is an admirable image describing the moment at which Connachar divines the flight of Deirdre :

> And he, consummate lord of fear,
> Our never-counsell'd lord, the Forest-odour'd,

That kept about his heart a zone of chill,
Smiled, though within the gateway of his fort
A surmise crept, as 'neath a load of rushes
Creeps in the stabber.

No less striking, and entirely in the spirit of the saga, is the speech of the old nurse when Connachar ironically asks her if her tears can bring Deirdre back.

But she looked up and said : " How shall I bring her ?
Look now outside thy door, O Connachar !
The black oak with the vision-dripping boughs
Whose foot is in thy fathers' blood of pride
Stagger'd as I came up in the night-blast.
In vain it stretches angers to the sky :
It cannot keep the white moon from escape
To sail the tempest; nor, O king, canst thou ! "

The phrase which describes the oak " stretching angers to the sky " is probably as daring a metonymy as any in literature—perhaps a little over-intrepid.

The Voices of Cir and Urmael say many fine and memorable things, but are to me, on the whole, much less pleasing than that of Fintan. The jolting measure of Cir, though its roughness is, of course, intentional, strikes me as exceedingly wearisome. One quatrain — certainly not of the roughest—may serve as a specimen. Naois, with his two brothers, is fleeing from Connachar's hall, and hears Deirdre call him from afar :

" O Aillean, O Ardan, hark ! What cry was that ? For some cry
Rang on my soul's shield ; hark ! hear ye it now ? "
But they rein'd not their weary chariots, shouting reply,
" It was fate, 'twas the curst hag that is crouch'd on a bough ! "

The stanza of Urmael is a peculiar one. It begins with six lines of alternate rhymes ; then comes a single unrhymed line ; and finally a rhyming triplet : thus—*a b a b a b x c c c*. It does not seem to me that the beauty of this stanza compensates for its difficulty ; nor is its movement very well suited to narrative purposes. In spite of many individual passages of striking merit in this section, one is glad when the Voice of Fintan again makes itself heard, in the warnings addressed by the old Druid Cathva to Naois, and in this noble retort of Deirdre's hero-lover:

> Then spoke Naois, keeping back his wrath,
> "Strange is it one so old should threat with Death!
> Are not both thou and I, are not we all,
> By Death drawn from the wickets of the womb—
> Seal'd with the thumb of Death when we are born?
> As for friends lost (though I believe thee not),
> A man is nourish'd by his enemies
> No less than by his friends. But as for her,
> Because no man shall deem me noble still,—
> Because I like a sea-gull of the isles
> May be driven forth—branded and nationless,—
> Because I shall no more, perhaps, behold
> The deep-set eaves on that all-sacred house,—
> Because the gather'd battle of the powers
> Controlling fortune, breaks upon my head,—
> Yea! for that very cause, lack'd other cause,
> In love the closer,—quenchless,—absolute,
> Would Deirdre choose to follow me. Such pains,
> Seër, the kingdoms are of souls like hers!"
> He spoke; he felt her life-blood at his side
> Sprung of the West, the last of human shores,
> Throbbing, "Look forth on everlastingness!
> Through the coil'd waters and the ebb of light
> I'll be thy sail!"

A few lines more, and the episode comes to an abrupt end.

My quotations have left the reader in no doubt, I trust, as to the essentially poetic quality of Mr. Trench's thought and style. His work abounds in images and phrases beyond the reach of any but a true poet—this line, for instance, which tells how, on the lark-haunted upland, the lovers drank in

> from the recesses of the sun
> Tremble of those wings that beat light into music.

Or this description of Deirdre :

> Tall as a rush is she,
> Sweet as the glitter of the netted lakes !

It does not seem to me that Mr. Trench's vocabulary is always very happily attuned to his theme. He Latinises, and even Hellenises, too freely. It is hard to imagine King Connachar sneering at Naois as a "paragon," or an Irish chanter of the sixth century chanting of "diaphaneity." Such words as "argentine," "imperishable," "arrogant," "attempered," and "cirque" seem to me of questionable propriety in such a poem ; nor can I imagine Deirdre asking the grey seer Cathva if he be "numbered with things terrene." Finally, I would beg Mr. Trench to be on his guard against the fashion of the day which makes for harsh, halting and anomalous metres. His verse is generally harmonious enough ; but here and there, even in the smoother utterances of Fintan and Urmael, one is pulled up by a decidedly craggy line.

The little sheaf of occasional poems at the end of Mr. Trench's book includes many delicate and original things. In the *Ode on a Silver Birch*, in *The Nutter*, and in one or two other pieces, there is a certain suggestion of Matthew Arnold ; but the resemblance arises from spiritual sympathy, not from verbal imitation. The chief technical defect in Mr. Trench's work is an occasional lack of perspicuity. His meaning is generally clear enough, but he does not always succeed in presenting it with perfect purity of outline. The following fine poem, for example, would be finer but for a certain blurring of the contours of its thought. The first stanza especially does not seem to express quite accurately what the poet means ; and the imagery of the second and third, though it cannot be called incongruous, lacks something of that perfect visual consistency which betokens perfect mastery.

SHAKESPEARE.

If many a daring spirit must discover
The chartless world, why should they glory lack?
Because athwart the skyline they sank over
Few, few, the shipmen be that have come back.

Yet one, wreck'd oft, hath by a giddy cord
The rugged head of Destiny regain'd—
One from the maelstrom's lap hath swum aboard—
One from the polar sleep himself unchain'd.

But he, acquainted well with every tone
Of madness whining in his shroudage slender,
From storm and mutiny emerged alone
Self-righted from the dreadful self-surrender:

Rich from the isles where sojourn long is death
Won back to cool Thames and Elizabeth,
Sea-weary, yes, but human still, and whole—
A circumnavigator of the soul.

From among several deeply felt and finely expressed lyrics, I select the following, not as the best, but as the briefest:

She comes not when Noon is on the roses—
    Too bright is Day.
She comes not to the Soul till it reposes
    From work and play.

But when Night is on the hills, and the great Voices
    Roll in from Sea,
By starlight and by candlelight and dreamlight
    She comes to me.

The Night and *Come, let us make Love deathless* are intenser and more elaborate than this, but not more melodious or more truly lyrical.

Mr. Trench's work as a whole, though it certainly cannot be called unripe, strikes one as lingering a little on the hither side of complete maturity. He has all the gifts of a true poet, but he does not always develop them to the best advantage. I trust we may regard this first book as only an earnest of more sustained and perhaps more thoroughly accomplished work to follow.

466

FREDERIC HERBERT TRENCH

A CHARGE.

If thou hast squander'd years to grave a gem
   Commission'd by thy absent Lord, and while
      'Tis incomplete,
Others would bribe thy needy skill to them—
      Dismiss them to the street !

Shouldst thou at last discover Beauty's grove,
   At last be panting on the fragrant verge,
      But in the track,
Drunk with divine possession, thou meet Love—
      Turn, at her bidding, back.

When round thy ship in tempest Hell appears,
   And every spectre mutters up more dire
      To snatch control
And loose to madness thy deep-kennell'd Fears—
      Then, to the helm, O Soul !

Last ; if upon the cold green-mantling sea
   Thou cling, alone with Truth, to the last spar,
      Both castaway
And one must perish—let it not be he
      Whom thou art sworn to obey !

IN THE ROMAN AMPHITHEATRE, VERONA.

Two architects of Italy—austere
Men who could fashion nothing small—refused
To die with life, and for their purpose used
This dim and topless Amphitheatre.

Some Cæsar trench'd the orb of its ellipse
And call'd on distant provinces to swell
Resonant arches whence his World could scan,
Tier above tier, the fighters and the ships.

But Dante—having raised, as dreamer can,
Higher tenfold these walls immutable—
Sole in the night arena, grew aware
He was himself the thing spectacular
Seized by the ever-thirsting gaze of Hell,—
Here, on the empty sand, a banish'd man.

MRS. MARRIOTT-WATSON

MRS. MARRIOTT-WATSON disconcerts and discourages criticism by the absolute correctness of her writing. She is the "Andrea Senz'-Errore" of latter-day verse. Limitations she has, no doubt, but positive faults—not one. Her diction is pure, her rhymes perfect; her metres, without being mechanical, are absolutely correct; her imagery is always restrained, consistent, congruous. To some people, this faultlessness no doubt seems a blemish. Their idea of poetry is thought excruciated and language bedevilled. They love either to browse on intellectual chaff, chopped as dry and sapless as possible, or else to luxuriate in an iridescent lather of verbiage. Such readers may apply to Mrs. Marriott-Watson's work the much-misapplied phrase, "faultily faultless, splendidly null." I emphatically dissent. In reading her verse, I have the exhilarating sensation of skating over perfectly smooth, strong, and yet elastic ice, where one has not the least fear of catching one's skate in a crack, or sousing into an air-hole. Not that there is anything wintry or chill about her poetry. My metaphor refers simply to its surface texture, not to its temperature.

Without metaphor or exaggeration of any sort, Mrs. Marriott-Watson has achieved an astonishing correctness of style and perfection of technique. "Achieved" is perhaps not the right word; this sense of form is a thing innate, constitutional; culture does not generate it, but merely sets it free to work its will. One feels that an imperfect rhyme, a halting verse, a violent or incongruous metaphor would be as impossible to this poetess as the shriek of a jay to a nightingale. Yet she may fairly be said to "achieve" her perfection of form at the cost of great renunciation. She attempts nothing very elaborate in metre, very ornate in imagery. She touches a little lyre, not a great organ. Its strings being few, she can all the more easily keep them in perfect tune.

Her themes, indeed, may almost be told off on the five fingers. She praises the town, and paints it (sometimes) with an impressionist prodigality of colour; she praises the country, and paints it (generally) with classical firmness of touch and coolness of tone; she sings the fulness, the intensity of life, sighs for her full share of "the heady wine of living," and sets death at defiance; she clings to youth, shrinks from age, and owns the supremacy of death; and she lets her imagination stray among the eerie, and especially the supernatural, fantasies of romanticism. It would be too much to pretend that all her poems fall unmistakably under one or other of these rubrics; but those that remain unclassed are certainly few. The personal note in her poetry is exceedingly discreet. The heart-throb is always there, but it is not obtruded upon us. She hits the happy mean between absolute impersonality and tactless self-exposure.

The even excellence of Mrs. Marriott-Watson's workmanship renders it difficult to quote from her. There is nothing that does not seem worthy of quotation, little that seems imperatively to call for it. The fragments which I shall cite to illustrate her different moods are not chosen as being specially admirable, but at most as being specially characteristic.

· ROSAMVND · MARRIOTT · WATSON ·

MRS. MARRIOTT-WATSON

Of her town poetry the opening verses of *In the Rain*
may serve as a specimen :

Rain in the glimmering street—
Murmurous, rhythmical beat;
Shadows that flicker and fly ;
Blue of wet road, of wet sky,
(Grey in the depths and the heights) ;
Orange of numberless lights,
Shapes fleeting on, going by.

Figures, fantastical, grim—
Figures, prosaical, tame,
Each with chameleon-stain,
Dun in the crepuscle dim,
Red in the nimbus of flame—
Glance through the veil of the rain.

Rain in the measureless street—
Vistas of orange and blue ;
Music of echoing feet,
Pausing, and pacing anew.

Rain, and the clamour of wheels,
Splendour, and shadow, and sound ;
Coloured confusion that reels
Lost in the twilight around.

At this point the poem ceases to be pictorial, and becomes
an example of that dwelling on the idea of death which runs
like an almost monotonous burden through the poetess's
work.   The best-known of Mrs. Marriott-Watson's London
poems is that which begins :

The sun's on the pavement
  The current comes and goes,
And the grey streets of London
  They blossom like the rose.

Crowned with the spring sun,
  Vistas fair and free ;
What joy that waits not ?
  What that may not be ?

This is a fresh and tripping lyric ; but of a far more serious

beauty are *Aubade* and *London in October*.   Of the latter I
quote the final strophe :

> Thine are our hearts, beloved City of Mist
> Wrapped in thy veils of opal and amethyst,
> Set in thy shrine of lapis-lazuli,
> Dowered with the very language of the sea,
> Lit with a million gems of living fire—
> London, the goal of many a soul's desire.
> Goddess and sphinx, thou hold'st us safe in thrall
> Here while the dead leaves fall.

Mrs. Marriott-Watson's country poetry is very rich and
varied, ranging from the mere vignette of bird or flower to
the large ideal landscape, as in that noble poem, *On Lethe
Wharf*.   Contrast with the grey gloom of this fantasy, the
dancing fragrant sunshine of *A South Coast Idyl*, and you
will realise the wealth of colour on this painter's palette.
To my thinking, she has done nothing finer than the
following poem, entitled *On the Downs*.   It is a sort of
preliminary study for *Vespertilia*—the landscape before the
individual figures are painted in :

> Broad and bare to the skies
> The great Down-country lies,
> Green in the glance of the sun,
> Fresh with the clean salt air ;
> Screaming the gulls rise from the fresh-turned mould,
> Where the round bosom of the wind-swept wold
> Slopes to the valley fair.
>
> Where the pale stubble shines with golden gleam
> The silver ploughshare cleaves its hard-won way
> Behind the patient team,
> The slow black oxen toiling through the day
> Tireless, impassive still,
> From dawning dust and chill
> To twilight grey.
>
> Far off, the pearly sheep
> Along the upland steep

MRS. MARRIOTT-WATSON

Follow their shepherd from the wattled fold,
With tinkling bell-notes falling sweet and cold
As a stream's cadence, while a skylark sings
High in the blue, with eager, outstretched wings,
Till the strong passion of his joy be told.

But when the day grows old,
And night cometh fold on fold,
Dulling the western gold,
Blackening bush and tree,
Veiling the ranks of cloud,
In their pallid pomp and proud,
That hasten home from the sea,
Listen—now and again, if the night be still enow,
You may hear the distant sea range to and fro
Tearing the shingly bourne of his bounden track,
Moaning with hate as he fails and falleth back;
The Downs are peopled then;
Fugitive, low-browed men
Start from the slopes around;
Over the murky ground
Crouching they run with rough-wrought bow and spear,
Now seen, now hid, they rise and disappear,
Lost in the gloom again.

Soft on the dew-fall damp
Scarce sounds the measured tramp
Of bronze-mailed sentinels,
Dark on the darkened fells
Guarding the camp.

The Roman watch-fires glow
Red on the dusk; and harsh
Cries a heron flitting slow
Over the valley marsh
Where the sea-mist gathers low

Closer, and closer yet
Draweth the night's dim net
Hiding the troubled dead:
No more to see or know
But a black waste lying below,
And a glimmering blank o'erhead.

473

In a very different key, *A Midnight Harvest* is equally imaginative and impressive.

Mrs. Marriott-Watson's somewhat stoical joy of life may seem to some readers not clearly distinguishable from melancholy. It is resolute rather than instinctive, sudden and fierce rather than habitual and serene. *Open Sesame* expresses

> Joy in our part in all—in life's possession
> Joy in the Joy of Life beyond expression.
> Joy in the task beloved tho' unavailing,
> Joy in the splendid steeps too high for scaling,
> Joy in the fleeting glimpse, the vain endeavour,
> Tho' Almost meadows flower at the gates of Never.

Of the Earth, Earthy, leads up to this moral :

> Life and Life's worst and best be ours to share,
> Charm of the motley ! undefined and rare ;
> Melodious discord in the heart o' the tune,
> Sweet with the hoarse note jarring everywhere !
> Let us but live, and every field shall bear
> Fruit for our joy ; for Life is Life's best boon,

This mood finds its strongest expression in *Resurgam*, a lyric of remarkable individuality and power.

Much more frequent, as already hinted, are the poems which express, not so much the fear of death, as wonder and a touch of resentment at the thought of it. In this simple quatrain the poetess strikes the keynote of many of her moods :

> O sad, O strange in the sunshine,
> To think that the day must be !
> To think of the fragrant autumns
> I shall not feel nor see.

The thought of death is the motive of those fine poems, *Hic Jacet*, *Armistice*, *The Wind's Summons*, and many others. It is on account of its brevity that I choose the following, which, though almost hackneyed in idea, is charming in expression:

REQUIESCAT.

Bury me deep when I am dead,
Far from the woods where sweet birds sing;
Lay me in sullen stone and lead,
Lest my poor dust should feel the Spring.

Never a flower be near me set,
Nor starry cup nor slender stem,
Anemone nor violet,
Lest my poor dust remember them.

And you—wherever you may fare—
Dearer than birds, or flowers, or dew—
Never, ah me, pass never there,
Lest my poor dust should dream of you.

Correlative to this preoccupation with the thought of death is the shrinking from "grey Eld," the yearning towards Youth, that find touching expression in such poems as *Ave atque Vale* and *The Isle of Voices*.

Several of Mrs. Marriott-Watson's ballads and shorter poems on romantic themes show a depth and sincerity of feeling not often attained in a form so purely imitative, so anachronistic as this. Not that all ballads are necessarily anachronisms. It is quite possible to treat modern themes in ballad form, or to put modern thought and feeling into ballads of the conventional "past which never was present." But this is not what Mrs. Marriott-Watson essays to do. Her effort, in such pieces as *Borderland* and *A Ballad of the Were-Wolf*, is to place herself absolutely at the point of view, and in the frame of mind, of the old ballad-makers, to produce work on which the intervening centuries shall have left no mark. Not so strictly imitative, and therefore, perhaps, more vital and genuinely tragic, are *The Moor Girl's Well* and the *Ballad of the Willow Pool*, two admirable poems. The following exquisite little lyric, though scarcely to be called a ballad, will suffice to show the poetess in her purely romantic mood:

AN ENCHANTED PRINCESS.

I found her deep in the forest,
  The beeches and elms between,
A delicate amber-plane tree
  'Mid masses of bronze and green;

A sorrowful, spell-bound princess
  Awaiting her lover there.
She said: "He will know me, surely,
  By the veil of my yellow hair.

"He seeks me the wide world over,
  He seeks me the whole year through,
To loosen the charm that binds me—
  My prince, and my lover true!"

She shivered beneath her foliage
  And sighed in the twilight chill:
"Ay me! wilt thou find me never,
  Thy love that thou seekest still?"

"I saw him," chirruped a blackbird,
  "He passed by this very spot;
He is come and gone, O princess!
  He passed—and he knew you not."

The cold wind rustled her branches
  Till the yellow leaves fell slow—
"He is dead and gone, O princess
  Many a year ago."

Vespertilia—perhaps on the whole the strongest thing Mrs. Marriott-Watson has done—is not in form a ballad, though it makes a ballad-like appeal to our sense of the eerie and the mysterious. Perhaps the poetess felt, and with justice, that where there was a question of evoking, however vaguely, the phantom of old Rome, it was best to avoid a form so definitely mediæval or post-mediæval as that of the ballad. Be this as it may, she chose that

Protean measure, the iambic pentameter, which takes on with equal ease whatever attribute the poet has the genius to impress upon it, from foppish elegance to Olympian majesty. For her present purpose, Mrs. Marriott-Watson imbued it with a wistful elegiac tenderness, cunningly accentuated by the occasional six-syllable lines, like sighs set to music, which break without marring the stately flow of the decasyllables. Alike in conception and in workmanship, the poem is masterly. It ranks among those which, once read, will haunt the memory for ever.

When the foregoing lines were written, I was unacquainted with Mrs. Marriott-Watson's first book of verses, *The Bird Bride: a Volume of Ballads and Sonnets*, published in 1889. It does not require me to modify my estimate of the poetess's talent. Distinctly less mature than her later volumes, it contains nothing, except perhaps a few sonnets, that would claim a place in a representative selection of her best work. But it already shows that scrupulous refinement and accuracy of form which is so striking in the later books. Although she does a good deal of work in complex rhyme-schemes (ballades, villanelles, &c.) she scarcely ever allows herself the licence of an imperfect rhyme. "Poor" rhyming to "shore" and "more," and "come" to "home," are the only flaws I have noted, and they are microscopic. As for a halting line, or even a line which requires to be unnaturally accented in order to fit into the metrical scheme, I have discovered not one in all three books. One feels that the white kid gloves presented to a judge at a "maiden assize" ought to be worn by the critic who handles Mrs. Marriott-Watson's poetry.

VESPERTILIA.

In the late autumn's dusky-golden prime,
When sickles gleam and rusts the idle plough,
The time of apples dropping from the bough,
And yellow leaves on sycamore and lime ;
O'er grassy uplands far above the sea
Often at twilight would my footsteps fare,
And oft I met a stranger-woman there
    Who stayed and spake with me :
Hard by the ancient barrow smooth and green,
Whose rounded burg swells dark upon the sky
Lording it high o'er dusky dell and dene,
    We wandered—she and I.

Ay, many a time as came the evening hour
And the red moon rose up behind the sheaves,
I found her straying by that barren bower,
Her fair face glimmering like a white wood-flower
That gleams through withered leaves,
Her mouth was redder than the pimpernel,
Her eyes seemed darker than the purple air
'Neath brows half hidden—I remember well—
'Mid mists of cloudy hair.

And all about her breast, around her head,
Was wound a wide veil shadowing cheek and chin,
Woven like the ancient grave-gear of the dead :
    A twisted clasp and pin
Confined her long blue mantle's heavy fold
Of splendid tissue dropping to decay,
    Faded like some rich raiment worn of old,
With rents and tatters gaping to the day.
Her sandals wrought about with threads of gold,
Scarce held together still, so worn were they,
Yet sewn with winking gems of green and blue,
And pale as pearls her naked feet shone through.

And all her talk was of some outland rare,
Where myrtles blossom by the blue sea's rim,
And life is ever good and sunny and fair ;
" Long since," she sighed, " I sought this island grey—
Here, where the winds moan and the sun is dim,
When his beaked galleys cleft the ocean spray,
For love I followed him."

Once, as we stood, we heard the nightingale
Pipe from a thicket on the sheer hillside,
Breathless she hearkened, still and marble-pale,
Then turned to me with strange eyes open wide—
" Now I remember ! . . . Now I know !" said she,
" Love will be life . . . ah, Love *is* Life !" she cried,
" And thou—thou lovest me ? "

I took her chill hands gently in mine own,
" Dear, but no love is mine to give," I said,
" My heart is colder than the granite stone
That guards my true-love in her grassy bed ;
My faith and troth are hers, and hers alone,
Are hers . . . and she is dead."

Weeping, she drew her veil about her face,
And faint her accents were and dull with pain ;
" Poor Vespertilia ! gone her days of grace,
Now doth she plead for love—and plead in vain :
None praise her beauty now, or woo her smile !

          .   .   .   .   .

Ah, hadst thou loved me but a little while,
    I might have lived again."

Then slowly as a wave along the shore
She glided from me to yon sullen mound ;
My frozen heart, relenting, smote me sore—
Too late—I searched the hollow slopes around
Swiftly I followed her, but nothing found
    Nor saw nor heard her more.

And now, alas, my true love's memory
Even as a dream of night-time half-forgot,
    Fades faint and far from me,
And all my thoughts are of the stranger still,
    Yea, though I loved her not :
I loved her not—and yet—I fain would see,
Upon the wind-swept hill,

Her dark veil fluttering in the autumn breeze ;
Fain would I hear her changeful voice awhile,
Soft as the wind of spring-tide in the trees,
And watch her slow, sweet smile.

Ever the thought of her abides with me
Unceasing as the murmur of the sea ;
When the round moon is low and night-birds flit,
When sink the stubble-fires with smouldering flame,
Over and o'er the sea-wind sighs her name,
    And the leaves whisper it.

" *Poor Vespertilia,*" sing the grasses sere,
" *Poor Vespertilia,*" moans the surf-beat shore ;
Almost I feel her very presence near—
    Yet she comes nevermore.

WILLIAM WATSON

In attempting an estimate of Mr. William Watson's talent, one is somewhat embarrassed by the fact that he has already formed the subject of a masterly and conclusive critical study. It is entitled *Apologia;* it appears in a book called *The Father of the Forest;* and it is written by Mr. William Watson. Apart from a phrase or two of obligatory self-depreciation, there is nothing in this poem that is not just, that is not right. I do not mean that the modesty with which it is written is conventional or insincere. It is not so much modesty, indeed, as modest pride: a totally different thing from "the pride that apes humility." At the same time, the mere exigences of rhetoric compel a little over-emphasis here and there, for which the candid reader will make allowance. This done, he will find the poem an admirably accurate piece of self-criticism. It may be amplified, indeed; it can scarcely be amended.

The very fact that Mr. Watson should criticise himself, and in doing so produce a really fine poem, abounding in memorable lines and passages, is in itself characteristic. The differentia of his talent is the intimate blending of logic with imagination. He would possibly have been a greater (certainly a more productive) poet, had the imaginative element in his composition been less exactly balanced by the logical element. But the imaginative element is in

itself very strong; and there is one of his poems, not
sufficiently appreciated, I think, even by his admirers, in
which we find it without any admixture of the logical
element, and can study it by itself.

Need I add that it is his first poem?—"written in great
part during his teens," says the Publishers' Note to the
second edition. On its appearance in 1880, the Note
proceeds, *The Prince's Quest* "attracted the attention of a
few excellent judges," chief among whom was Dante
Gabriel Rossetti. He must have been the reverse of an
"excellent judge" who could read ten pages of this poem
without feeling himself in the presence of a true poet.
Rossetti's own *Blessed Damozel* gave no clearer prognostic
of genius. *The Prince's Quest* is a romantic narrative, a
fairy-tale, of something like two thousand lines. It is very
immature, very wordy, very saccharine. There are passages
which flow idly on and on, like a thread of syrup dribbling
from a spoon—nor is the syrup always "tinct with cinnamon." I cannot even agree with Rossetti that Mr. Watson
"goes right back to Keats." The intermediary influence of
William Morris seems to me unmistakable.

None the less does one feel assured that this writer is
an original poet in the truest sense of the word. There
is scarcely a page in which individual inspiration does
not break through the borrowed mannerism. Take, for
instance, this picture:

> So hour by hour (thus ran the Prince's dream)
> Glided the boat along the broadening stream.
>
>   *   *   *   *   *
>
> Over the errant water wandering free,
> As some lone sea-bird over a lone sea.
>
> And Morn pale-haired with watery wide eyes
> Look'd up. And starting with a swift surprise,
> Sprang to his feet the Prince, and forward leant,
> His gaze on something right before him bent

· WILLIAM · WATSON ·

> That like a towered and templed city showed,
> Afar off, dim with very light, and glowed
> As burnished seas at sundawn when the waves
> Make amber lightnings all in dim-roof'd caves
> That fling mock-thunder back. Long leagues away,
> Down by the river's green right bank it lay,
> Set like a jewel in the golden morn:
> But ever as the Prince was onward borne,
> Nearer and nearer danced the dizzy fires
> Of domes innumerable and sun-tipped spires
> And many a sky-acquainted pinnacle,
> Splendid beyond what mortal tongue may tell.

All Paris went into ecstasies the other day over Jean Richepin's line,

> Et tous les forêts avec tous leurs oiseaux

In England we take no notice of such trifles, and the north-country lad who wrote

> As some lone sea-bird over a lone sea

had to wait many a year before he met with any real encouragement. But besides the exquisite gift of verbal melody displayed in this passage, we cannot but recognise that vitality of vision which more than anything else denotes the poet. It is evident that the writer has a luminous and vivid picture in his mind's eye when he writes of the city

> Set like a jewel in the golden morn:

and describes how,

> Nearer and nearer danced the dizzy fires
> Of domes innumerable and sun-tipped spires.

This is a "chose vue" beyond a doubt. I do not mean that Mr. Watson's physical eye had scanned a faery city, or even, perhaps, a seaboard city of the Orient. But he had noted the effect of a blaze of morning light on the towers and spires of some, perhaps quite commonplace, town, and had stored in his memory the picture which, when the time came, he amplified and idealised. Such are the true uses of imagination.

Vitality of all the senses, indeed, is the pervading charm of this poem. Except in a few mechanical passages, Mr. Watson not only sees but feels all that he is describing. For instance:

> And all about their feet were woods bespread,
> Hoarding the cool and leafy silentness
> In many an unsunned hollow and hid recess.

> The sea-line grew
> O'erhazed with visible heat, and no wind blew,
> And the half-stifled morning dropped aswoon
> Into the panting bosom of the noon.

> There wilding orchards faced the beach, and bare
> All manner of delicious fruits and rare,
> Such as in gardens of kings' palaces
> Trembles upon the sultry-scented trees,
> The soul of many sunbeams at its core.

> And so the days, the sultry summer days,
> Went by, and wimpled over with fine haze
> The noiseless nights stole after them.

> And 'fore his eyes the world began to swim
> All vague, and doubtful as a dream that lies
> Folded with another, petal-wise.
> And therewithal himself but half believed
> His own eyes' testimony, and perceived
> The things that were about him as who hears
> A distant music throbbing towards his ears
> At noontide, in a flowery hollow of June,
> And listens till he knows not if the tune
> And he be one or twain, or near or far,
> But only feels that sound and perfume are,
> And tremulous light and leafy umbrage : so
> The Prince beheld unknowing, nor fain to know.

Not less remarkable than the sensuous colour and aroma of *The Prince's Quest* are its frequent passages of imaginative intensity. Note, for example, the whole description of the Demon Bird whose "false sweet song"

> dropped
> As honey changed to music;

but when he revealed himself in all his balefulness

> his eyes
> Were wandering wells of lightning to the skies.

How admirable, again, is the last couplet of the passage describing the speed of the magic pinnace:

> A moment was a league in that wild flight
> From vast to vast of ocean and the night.

The poem includes two very beautiful lyrics: the song of "the crystal-hearted cool sweet sea," and the final chant of the

> Sooth-tongued singers, throated like the bird
> All darkness holds its breath to hear.

Neither of these songs, however, is quite suited for quotation, for part of their charm lies in their perfect harmony with their context.

Youthful as it is in every respect, *The Prince's Quest* is no mere boyish experiment, without any interest save such as is reflected from the writer's maturer performance. It has a substantive and inherent value, and would deserve honourable mention among the poems of the period, if Mr. Watson had never written another line. It is full of light and heat, colour and melody. I should not be surprised if a sect or coterie should one day arise which should declare it the finest thing Mr. Watson ever wrote, and make admiration for it their shibboleth.

The remaining poems in this first volume are of inferior value. *Angelo*, a short narrative in blank verse, is youthful to the point of crudity; and the lyrics and sonnets are chiefly remarkable for their metrical finish, not without a touch of inventiveness. In the *Song of Three Singers*, an empty enough jingle in itself, the little unexpected sob of rhyme in the fourth line strikes me as an inspiration:

> Wave and wind and willow-tree
> Speak a speech that no man knoweth,
> Tree that sigheth, wind that bloweth,
> Wave that floweth to the sea :
> Wave and wind and willow-tree.
>
> Peerless perfect poets ye,
> Singing songs all songs excelling,
> Fine as crystal music dwelling
> In a welling fountain free :
> Peerless perfect poets three !

Everywhere, even in his crudest passages, Mr. Watson's workmanship, at this early stage of his career, is already distinguished. Flaccid his style may be, but never unrefined. There is not a vulgar rhyme in the whole book. In the following sonnet, the fourth and fifth lines are surely remarkable as the work of a mere youth, while the poise and impetus of the whole foretell the singer of the *Year of Shame* :—

SKYFARING.

> Drifting through vacant spaces vast of sleep,
> One overtook me like a flying star
> And whirled me onward in his glistering car.
> From shade to shade the wingèd steeds did leap,
> And clomb the midnight like a mountain-steep ;
> Till that vague world where men and women are,
> Ev'n as a rushlight down the gulfs afar,
> Paled and went out, upswallowed of the deep.
>
> Then I to that ethereal charioteer :
> " O whither through the vastness are we bound ?
> O bear me back to yonder blinded sphere ! "
> Therewith I heard the ends of night resound ;
> And, wakened by ten thousand echoes, found
> That far-off planet lying all too near.

The odd thing is, however, that, in the main, Mr. Watson has falsified the prediction of this first volume.

The poet it foretells is curiously different from the poet we
know. It foretells a garrulous, sensuous, flamboyant romanticist; and behold! we have to deal with an austere,
concise, fastidious classicist. And, strangest of all, the
metamorphosis was not gradual, but sudden and complete.
Mr. Watson's biographer may one day be able to throw
some light on the temperamental change which seems to
have taken place in him during his first years of manhood.
In the meantime, we can but divine it from its results.
We part from the facile honey-tongued rhapsodist of *The
Prince's Quest*, to meet him again, with astonishment, as
the chastened critical elegist of *Wordsworth's Grave*, the
laconic philosopher of the *Epigrams*. It is true that, on
looking back in the light of this reincarnation, we find a
certain vague foreshadowing of it in *The Prince's Quest*.
Comparing it either with *Endymion* or with one of William
Morris's romances, we note in it a decided bent towards
epigrammatic neatness of diction, antithesis, and verbal
equipoise. Diffuse though the whole poem undoubtedly is,
there are notably terse couplets in it. Already we can
trace a proclivity towards the cult of the jewelled line;
and in the vicious and strained conceits which now and
then crop up, we recognise in germ that imaginative wit
which is among the most characteristic of Mr. Watson's
gifts. At the very beginning of the poem we come across
this couplet :

> Till, being widowed of the sun, her lord,
> The purblind day went groping evenward.

Mr. Watson's maturer taste would doubtless have rejected
this conceit; yet it is, as he would say, a "fore-whispering"
of his poetic destiny. So are many couplets in the passages
quoted above; so, too, are such lines as these :

> What then were left for him to do? . . . .
> Wander unresting, reft of hope and bliss,

A mariner on a sea that hath no coast,
Seeking a shade, himself a shade, and lost
In shadows, as a wave is lost i' the sea?

A strange mute sea, where never wave hath stirred,
Nor sound of any wandering wind is heard,
Nor voice of sailors sailing merrily :
A sea untraversed, an enchanted sea
From all the world fate-folden ; hemmed about
Of linkèd Dreams ; encompassed with a Doubt.

The tendency towards what may be called a high surface polish is here unmistakable ; and this surface polish is the omnipresent quality of Mr. Watson's later work.

Nevertheless, the transition from *The Prince's Quest* of 1880 to the *Epigrams* of 1884 is startling in its abruptness. Of the hundred quatrains published in that year, Mr. Watson has included just half in his *Poems* of 1892 ; and in the main, I think, he has selected and rejected rightly. It is a little surprising, certainly, that he should include a trivially facetious quatrain on *The Metropolitan Underground Railway*, and should omit these lines :

WRITTEN IN A VOLUME OF CHRISTINA G. ROSSETTI'S POEMS.

Songstress, in all times ended and begun,
  Thy billowy-bosomed fellows are not three.
Of those sweet peers, the grass grows green o'er one,
  And blue above the other is the sea.

Here one epithet would bear amendment ; but, even as they stand, there is a haunting quality in the lines which would redeem a greater defect. There are perhaps half a dozen of the rejected epigrams that, without being heart-broken at their loss, one would like to see recovered. None of them, however, can for a moment compare with these :

In mid whirl of the dance of Time ye start,
  Start at the cold touch of Eternity,
And cast your cloaks about you, and depart.—
  The minstrels pause not in their minstrelsy.

The beasts in field are glad, and have not wit
  To know why leapt their hearts when springtime shone.
Man looks at his own bliss, considers it,
  Weighs it with curious fingers; and 'tis gone.

Momentous to himself as I to me
  Hath each man been that ever woman bore;
Once, in a lightning-flash of sympathy,
  I *felt* this truth, an instant, and no more.

Toiling and yearning, 'tis man's doom to see
  No perfect creature fashion'd of his hands.
Insulted by a flower's immaculacy,
  And mock'd at by the flawless stars he stands.

Onward the chariot of the Untarrying moves;
  Nor day divulges him nor night conceals;
Thou hear'st the echo of unreturning hooves
  And thunder of irrevocable wheels.

Already in these epigrams we note Mr. Watson's tendency towards a highly Latinised diction and his love of polysyllabic sonorities—a love, as yet, not always controlled by tact.

Between 1880 and 1884, then, Mr. Watson put off the rhapsodist and put on the epigrammatist; and an epigrammatist he has ever since remained. His master quality is impassioned wit; and impassioned wit—of course with thought behind it, for wit is but the edge on the sword of thought—may rank among the very highest of poetic faculties. What Mr. Watson does, in all his more ambitious poems, is to work out a train of reflection in a series of nobly-turned epigrams, each of which, striking, as in a full chord, upon the ear, the imagination, and the intelligence at once, gives us a thrill of rare and complex pleasure. His stanzas, it is true, are charged with a weight of feeling—of pity, indignation, enthusiasm, or what not—which we do not generally associate with the epigram in the narrow modern sense of the word. Rightly considered,

nevertheless, every number of Mr. Watson's most characteristic work—every quatrain of his sonnets, every strophe of
his odes—is an epigram as truly as any couplet of Pope's.
The collocation is not so far-fetched as it may seem. Mr.
Watson resembles the men of the eighteenth century in his
insistence, both theoretical and practical, upon precision
of thought and utterance. He has quoted with approval
Lowell's saying, that the intellectual staple of the best
English poetry is "understanding aerated with imagination"—a definition which Pope or Johnson might have
accepted, though "imagination" would not have meant to
them precisely what it means to us. Mr. Watson employs
a very different vocabulary and metrical system from those
of Pope, and expresses a very different order of thoughts;
but his ideal of poetic style is the same as Pope's in so far
as he aims at beauty only through precision and perspicuity, and forswears all effects which demand the sacrifice of these qualities. Good sense is to him so paramount
a consideration, he has such a laudable abhorrence of the
subordination of meaning to sound, that he now and then
glides over to the opposite extreme of prosaism, and carries
sententiousness to the verge of banality. He is not always
sufficiently mindful of his own golden admonition :

> Forget not, brother singer! that though Prose
> Can never be too truthful or too wise,
> Song is not Truth, not Wisdom, but the rose
> Upon Truth's lips, the light in Wisdom's eyes.

His work marks, in some sense, a reaction against a
dominant tendency of the day, and, like all reactionaries,
he sometimes goes too far. In an essay on Mr. Meredith's
poetry, he says : " An inclination to be distrustful of writing
which the author has been at pains to clarify . . . is rather
the rule nowadays, and it is far more probable that the
twentieth century will see a reaction in favour of eighteenth-
century straightforwardness than an increased lenience

towards opacity of thought and tortuosity of style. These
principles he has condensed in two memorable versicles of
a set headed *Art Maxims :*

> Since Life is rough,
>   Sing smoothly, O Bard.
> Enough, enough,
>   To have *found* Life hard !

> No record Art keeps
>   Of her travail and throes.
> There is toil on the steeps ;
>   On the summits, repose,

Excellent maxims these, and Mr. Watson has acted up to
them with a noble strenuousness. He has given his life to
carving cameos of song, not all of equal value, indeed, but
all marked by high and resolute endeavour after perfection
of utterance. This cameo-like quality in Mr. Watson's
work accounts for its too exiguous quantity. *The Prince's
Quest* apart, his half-dozen books of verse can be read
through in a couple of hours. What is more, they can be
understood in exactly the same time : and critics are not
wanting who write this down to his discredit !

An eclectic Mr. Watson certainly is. His work affords
unmistakable evidence of an assiduous study of the best
models our language affords. This, too, is sometimes set
down to his discredit, by critics who cannot distinguish
between imitation and assimilation. Mr. Watson has
assimilated much, from Milton, from Pope, from Wordsworth, from Keats, from Tennyson, from Arnold ; less, but
still something, from Coleridge, Shelley, Rossetti, Swinburne. He has extracted from these poets whatever
nourishment they could afford to a man of his mental
constitution, whatever he could absorb and make his
own. He has " learned their great language, caught their
clear accents "—none, certainly, that were not clear—but the
voice in which he speaks their language is peculiar to him-

self, and has a beauty of its own. There is all the difference in the world between a mere mocking-bird echo and
a beautiful voice, trained by the greatest masters. On the
question of his eclecticism, Mr. Watson himself, in his
Apologia, has said what might well be the last word:

> Is the Muse
> Fall'n to a thing of Mode, that must each year
> Supplant her derelict self of yester-year?
> Or do the mighty voices of old days
> At last so tedious grow, that one whose lips
> Inherit some far echo of their tones—
> How far, how faint, none better knows than he
> Who hath been nourished on their utterance—can
> But irk the ears of such as care no more
> The accent of dead greatness to recall?
> If, with an ape's ambition, I rehearse
> Their gestures, trick me in their stolen robes,
> The sorry mime of their nobility,
> Dishonouring whom I vainly emulate,
> The poor imposture soon shall shrink revealed
> In the ill grace with which their gems bestar
> An abject brow; but if I be indeed
> Their true descendant, as the veriest hind
> May yet be sprung of kings, their lineaments
> Will out, the signature of ancestry
> Leap unobscured, and somewhat of themselves
> In me, their lowly scion, live once more.
> With grateful, not vainglorious joy, I dreamed
> It did so live; and ev'n such pride was mine
> As is next neighbour to humility.
> For he that claims high lineage yet may feel
> How thinned in the transmission is become
> The ancient blood he boasts; how slight he stands
> In the great shade of his majestic sires.

> *　　　*　　　*　　　*　　　*

> And though I be to these but as a knoll
> About the feet of the high mountains, scarce
> Remarked at all save when a valley cloud
> Holds the high mountains hidden, and the knoll
> Against the cloud shows briefly eminent;
> Yet ev'n as they, I too, with constant heart,

WILLIAM WATSON

And with no light or careless ministry,
Have served what seemed the Voice; and unprofane,
Have dedicated to melodious ends
All of myself that least ignoble was.

Never, perhaps, was there a more purely contemplative poet than Mr. Watson. He has nothing of the dramatist in his composition; even the rush and flush of the true lyrist are generally foreign to him. He is a fine artist in words; but words to him are symbols, not things in themselves of absolute glory and beauty. If he is not a master of metres, still less is he their servant; and "mastery," in this particular, is too often a euphemism for servitude. Within a somewhat limited range, however, he well deserves the name of master. His metres are almost all restrained and, so to speak, short-winded, not impetuous, wide-winged, heaven-storming. No living poet deals less in metrical licences than he. We may almost call him the one upholder of the classical tradition, for whom the accent of an English word does not shift at his own sweet will, and an iambus is still an iambus, and not anything else you please. The critics to whom poetry means a whirlwind of words, a reckless revelry of images, are put out—not to say abashed—by the calm dignity (calm, but far from cold) of Mr. Watson's style. They cannot endure that a poet should think twice before he speaks once, and should resolutely make his words express—not inflate, distort and portentously adumbrate—his thought. Time will show whether the exquisitely-graven cameo or the flagrant phantasmagoria be the more enduring thing of beauty. Meanwhile we may certainly say of Mr. Watson, as Chaucer said of his Clerk of Oxenford:

Of studie took he most cure and most hede,
Noght o word spak he more than was nede,
And that was seyd in forme and reverence,
And short and quik, and ful of hy sentence.

493

Although, putting aside *The Prince's Quest*, we must regard Mr. Watson as a mature artist from the outset of his career, we can trace in his work, from 1884 onwards, a distinct advance both in technical and in intellectual power. His poems may be roughly grouped under four heads: Poems on Literary Subjects; Odes, Epistles and Addresses to Friends; Political Poems; Philosophical Poems. In this order I propose briefly to survey them. A small fifth class—Humorous Poems—ought also to be set apart; but as I hold them almost entirely unworthy of Mr. Watson's talent, I shall pass them over without further mention.

" I have full oft," says Mr. Watson in his *Apologia* :

> In singers' selves found me a theme of song,
> Holding these also to be very part
> Of Nature's greatness, and accounting not
> Their descants least heroical of deeds.

But it is surely a wilfully narrow and wholly untenable conception of poetry to which poetical criticism seems to need any apology. Is it not the one essential function of poetry to say of the glory and beauty of the world things which could not be fitly, adequately, perhaps even decently, said in prose? Our highest exultations, our divinest ecstasies, are instinctively ashamed to go forth in the nakedness of common speech. Verse is not only the robe, but also the veil, of emotion, needful for decency no less than for decoration. But of all beautiful things in the world, poetry is itself the most beautiful; why, then, should it be celebrated only in prose? In the cathedral of Art, the sermon is all very well; it is probably edifying, and possibly not without a beauty of its own; but after the sermon, the anthem; after exposition, adoration. How much of the really great and essential criticism of the world has been done in verse! The first and last word about Shakespeare has been said, not by any of his thousand-and-one prose critics, but the poet who, casting off, in a moment of inspiration, the trammels of his own prosaic intelligence, wrote:

> Triumph, my Britain! Thou hast one to show
> To whom all scenes of Europe homage owe.
> He was not of an age, but for all time!

Virgil, again, has been expounded and eulogised any time these nineteen centuries; but it remained for the Virgil of our own age and tongue to embody the ultimate, unapproachable criticism in one of his noblest, and certainly one of his immortal, numbers. Poets, as a general rule, have been finely inspired in writing about other poets; and Mr. Watson is no exception to the rule.

He has not, indeed, confined himself to panegyric, but has attempted criticism in the narrower sense of the word— that is to say, analysis and definition. Now and again in this attempt, no doubt, he has said a thing in verse that might as well have been said in prose. But of what poem of any length, other than a pure lyric, may not this be alleged? A poet must be allowed a certain proportion of "connective tissue." Mr. Watson's most prosaic passages are redeemed from commonplace by their epigrammatic terseness. If they are versified prose, they are at least good prose, and admirably versified. And they lead up, almost unfailingly, to passages of inherent poetic nobility and beauty, passages in which critical doctrine is touched by emotion into pure poetry.

The first poem that brought Mr. Watson into notice, *Wordsworth's Grave*, was a piece of impassioned criticism. It is marked by a certain youthful petulance which to my mind detracts from its value. It is well to praise Wordsworth, but not well to make his tomb an altar-stone on which to sacrifice more modern singers to his manes. The poet himself, however, checks himself for this churlishness:

> Enough; and wisest who from words forbear.
>   The kindly river * rails not as it glides;
> And suave and charitable, the winning air
>   Chides not at all, or only him who chides.

Apart from its polemical tone, the poem is eminently worthy of its subject. It gives us no new theory of Wordsworth's character or art, but it crystallises the orthodox tenets of the Wordsworthian faith in noble and memorable images. We have, says Mr. Watson:

> Left him for poorer loves, and bowed the knee
>   To misbegotten strange new gods of song.
>
> Yet, led by hollow ghost or beckoning elf
>   Far from her homestead to the desert bourn,
> The vagrant soul returning to herself
>   Wearily wise, must needs to him return.
>
> To him and to the powers that with him dwell:—
>   Inflowings that divulged not whence they came;
> And that secluded spirit unknowable,
>   The mystery we make darker with a name;
>
> The Somewhat which we name but cannot know,
>   Ev'n as we name a star and only see
> His quenchless flashings forth, which ever show
>   And ever hide him, and which are not he.

It is in such a stanza as the last that Mr. Watson's true strength lies. What, again, could be better in its way than this contrast between Coleridge and Wordsworth:

> In elvish speech the *Dreamer* told his tale
>   Of marvellous oceans swept by fateful wings.—
> The *Seer* strayed not from earth's human pale,
>   But the mysterious face of common things
>
> He mirrored as the moon in Rydal Mere
>   Is mirrored, when the breathless night hangs blue:
> Strangely remote she seems and wondrous near,
>   And by some nameless difference born anew.

---

* Rotha.

496

WILLIAM WATSON

In this image, not new, but revivified by sheer charm of expression, Mr. Watson interprets the open secret of all sane art that is not merely decorative. Yet it is not in *Wordsworth's Grave*, I think, that he has written most worthily of Wordsworth, but rather in his epistle to Professor Dowden "on receiving from him a copy of *The Life of Shelley*." After telling how Shelley and Keats were the earliest gods of his idolatry, he continues :

> And then a third voice, long unheeded—held
> Claustral and cold, and dissonant and tame—
> Found me at last with ears to hear. It sang
> Of lowly sorrows and familiar joys,
> Of simple manhood, artless womanhood,
> And childhood fragrant as the limpid morn ;
> And from the homely matter nigh at hand
> Ascending and dilating, it disclosed
> Spaces and avenues, calm heights and breadths
> Of vision, whence I saw each blade of grass
> With roots that groped about eternity,
> And in each drop of dew upon each blade
> The mirror of the inseparable All.
> The first voice, then the second, in their turns
> Had sung me captive. This voice sang me free.
> Therefore, above all vocal sons of men,
> Since him whose sightless eyes saw hell and heaven,
> To Wordsworth be my homage, thanks, and love.

Still more noteworthy are the concluding lines of this poem, to be quoted later.

The least successful of Mr. Watson's poems on poets, in my judgment, are those on Matthew Arnold (*In Laleham Churchyard*) and on *Shelley's Centenary*. Both contain true things and fine things, but neither rises to the poet's best level. This is, perhaps, because he chose to write in the six-line Burns stave, a difficult and thankless stanza for serious poetry. Yet how effectively he can handle it on occasion is proved by his poem on Burns himself, with the following admirable stanzas :—

How could he 'scape the doom of such
As feel the airiest phantom-touch
Keenlier than others feel the clutch
    Of iron powers,—
Who die of having lived so much
    In their large hours ?

He erred, he sinned : and if there be
Who, from his hapless frailties free,
Rich in the poorer virtues, see
    His faults alone,—
To such, O Lord of Charity,
    Be mercy shown !

Singly he faced the bigot brood,
The meanly wise, the feebly good ;
He pelted them with pearl, with mud ;
    He fought them well,—
But ah, the stupid million stood,
    And he—he fell !

Of many other poets Mr. Watson has incidentally said fine and striking things ; but especially has he made great amends to Tennyson for what one cannot but take for a slighting allusion in *Wordsworth's Grave*.* He addressed more than one graceful " copy of verses " to the great Laureate in his lifetime, and he bade him a noble farewell at his death, in *Lacrymæ Musarum*. The poem is, as its title indicates, somewhat conventional in scheme, but in style and feeling it is well worthy of the occasion. Witness this exquisitely-woven strophe :

For lo ! creation's self is one great choir,
And what is nature's order but the rhyme
Whereto the worlds keep time,

---

  * Lo, one with empty music floods the ear,
    And one, the heart refreshing, tires the brain.

I may be wrong in supposing that in the first of these lines Mr. Watson had Tennyson in his mind. There are certainly other poets to whom it would better apply. But as the second line obviously applies to Browning, and as there is no other recognisable allusion to Tennyson in the poem, the identification is at least plausible.

And all things move with all things from their prime?
Who shall expound the mystery of the lyre?
In far retreats of elemental mind
Obscurely comes and goes
The imperative breath of song, that as the wind
Is trackless, and oblivious whence it blows.
Demand of lilies wherefore they are white,
Extort her crimson secret from the rose,
But ask not of the Muse that she disclose
The meaning of the riddle of her might:
Somewhat of all things sealed and recondite,
Save the enigma of herself, she knows.
The master could not tell, with all his lore,
Wherefore he sang, or whence the mandate sped:
Ev'n as the linnet sings, so I, he said;—
Ah, rather as the imperial nightingale,
That held in trance the ancient Attic shore,
And charms the ages with the notes that o'er
All woodland chants immortally prevail!
And now, from our vain plaudits greatly fled,
He with diviner silence dwells instead,
And on no earthly sea with transient roar,
Unto no earthly airs, he trims his sail,
But far beyond our vision and our hail
Is heard for ever and is seen no more.

Familiar epistles and addresses to friends are not without danger for Mr. Watson. They are apt to betray him into that prosaism which is, as we have seen, the main defect of his great qualities. Yet there is scarcely one of his poems of this order which does not imprint itself on the memory in virtue of some fine line, passage, or stanza. Mr. Watson has given us a really beautiful rendering of Horace's ode *To Licinius*, and in his own efforts of the same order there is always present something of the Horatian touch. In spite of its rather constrained metre, there is real grace in his address *To Arthur Christopher Benson*, of which I quote the opening stanzas :—

> In that grave shade august
>   That round your Eton clings,
> To you the centuries must
>   Be visible corporate things,

And the high Past appear
Affably real and near,
For all its grandiose airs, caught from the mien of Kings.

The new age stands as yet
Half built against the sky,
Open to every threat
Of storms that clamour by :
Scaffolding veils the walls,
And dim dust floats and falls,
As, moving to and fro, their tasks the masons ply.

But changeless and complete,
Rise unperturbed and vast,
Above our din and heat,
The turrets of the Past,
Mute as that city asleep,
Lulled with enchantments deep,
Far in Arabian dreamland built where all things last.

Less elaborate, but certainly not less beautiful, is the
following address :—

TO AUSTIN DOBSON.

Yes ! urban is your Muse, and owns
An empire based on London stones ;
Yet flow'rs, as mountain violets sweet,
Spring from the pavement 'neath her feet.

Of wilder birth this Muse of mine,
Hill-cradled, and baptized with brine ;
And 'tis for her a sweet despair
To watch that courtly step and air !

Yet surely she, without reproof,
Greeting may send from realms aloof,
And even claim a tie in blood,
And dare to deem it sisterhood.

For well we know, those Maidens be
All daughters of Mnemosyne ;
And 'neath the unifying sun,
Many the songs—but Song is one.

Mr. Watson shows a just instinct in claiming for his
muse a sisterhood with the dainty Familiar of Mr. Dobson.

WILLIAM WATSON

Though the younger poet goes further afield for his inspiration, and touches his lyre to deeper harmonies, his gracefulness of fancy, and the delicate finish of his rhymes, denote a close kinship to the singer of the Pompadour's Fan. *The Key-Board*, for example, is a copy of society verses (and something more) which Mr. Dobson certainly would not disown.

There are passages of great beauty in the *Epistle* (*To N.A.*) of the 1892 poems, and in the ode *To H. D. Traill*, despite the unfortunate opening stanza, with its allusion to

> hours that flit
> Fledged with the tongues of bard and wit.

Mr. Watson's sonnets to friends are, as a rule, inferior to those inspired by public events, but there are exceptions, such as the sonnet *To Aubrey de Vere* and that *Written in a Copy of Mr. Stevenson's " Catriona."* The following, addressed to Mr. Thomas Bailey Aldrich in answer to his sonnet *On Reading " The Purple East,"* may serve as a point of contact between the personal and the political poems :—

> Idle the churlish leagues 'twixt you and me,
> Singer most rich in charm, most rich in grace !
> What though I cannot see you face to face ?
> Allow my boast, that one in blood are we !
> One by that secret consanguinity
> Which binds the children of melodious race,
> And knows not the fortuities of place
> And cold interposition of the sea :
> You are my noble kinsman in the lyre :
> Forgive the kinsman's freedom that I use,
> Adventuring these imperfect thanks, who late,
> Singing a nation's woe, in wonder and ire,—
> Against me half the wise and all the great—
> Sang not alone, for with me was your muse.

We have here no Rossettian interweaving of languorous sonorities, no lingering, brooding exercise in verbal counterpoint. Such things are good in their way, and we prize them highly; but this thing, too, is good—this clearly and delicately chiselled medallion, a ceremonial offering, indeed, but touched by emotion and style into permanence of beauty.

Mr. Watson's Armenian sonnets were by no means his first political verses. So long ago as March and April 1885, he had written a sequence of fourteen sonnets under the title of *Ver Tenebrosum.* These are for the most part mere 'prentice work, in which a generous and fervid spirit was struggling for command of its instrument. It is interesting, however, to note the progress which the poet makes, even within the limits of this short sequence. By the time he has reached the eleventh and thirteenth sonnets he has acquired that art of concentrating his strength upon a majestic or fulminant conclusion which makes the sonnet so superb a rhetorical instrument in his hands. Ardently combating the wisdom of the " Perish India ! " cry, he thus concludes :—

> It may be that if hands of greed could steal
> From England's grasp the envied Orient prize,
> This tide of gold would flood her still as now:
> But were she the same England made to feel
> A brightness gone from out those starry eyes,
> A splendour from that constellated brow.

Again, he has a nightmare of the downfall of England, dreaming that her greatness has become a legend, and that our children's children are told

> How England once, before the years of bale,
> Throned above trembling, puissant, grandiose, calm,
> Held Asia's richest jewel in her palm;
> And with unnumbered isles barbaric, she
> The broad hem of her glistering robe impearl'd ;
> Then, when she wound her arms about the world,
> And had for vassal the obsequious sea.

In these two sestetts we have a foretaste of the art

which has made the sonnet, in Mr. Watson's hands, a weapon like the sling of David. In the octave he whirls it round and round with ever-gathering momentum, and in the sestett sends his scorn or rebuke singing through the air, arrow-straight to its mark.

Before we reach the Armenian sonnets, however, we find, in the volume of *Odes and other Poems*, published in 1894, that Mr. Watson has been perfecting his mastery of the form. His three sonnets entitled *The World in Armour* are perhaps his strongest sustained effort in this style.

It was, as every one knows, the massacres of 1895 that elicited from Mr. Watson the series of impassioned appeals and scathing invectives which has done more, probably, than any of his other works to bring his name home to the general public. They were first published (for the most part) in the *Westminster Gazette*, then collected under the title of *The Purple East*, and finally re-christened *The Year of Shame*. We are not here concerned with the political justice or injustice, wisdom or unwisdom, of these utterances. It is their literary quality that we have to consider. Wise or unwise, they are generously inspired; they are neither niggling nor time-serving; they must command the moral esteem even of those who hold them hot-headed or wrong-headed. But moral esteem and literary approval do not always go hand in hand. Indignation, as we know, makes verses, but even the most righteous indignation does not guarantee their quality. It may seem paltry to neglect the temper of a sword-blade, and discuss its damascenings; to ignore the message of a clarion-blast, and listen only lest a note here and there should sound a trifle flat. But the sabre belongs to art as well as to war, and ought to survive as a thing of beauty when its hour of utility is over. A poet's trumpet-call, if its tone be pure, may echo down the centuries; and it is only natural that we should ask ourselves, " Will it, or will it not ? "

These sonnets, in my judgment, show both the strength and the weakness of Mr. Watson's endowment; but the strength may be seen on every page, the weakness only here and there. They would stamp him a poet if he had written nothing else. Here, as ever, he is an epigrammatist; but these are white-hot epigrams, searing and branding the cruelty of the East and the apathy of the West. They remind one of the stanzas which Heine addressed, at the close of his *Deutschland* to the King of Prussia of that day (1844) :—

> Kennst du die Hölle des Dante nicht,
> Die schrecklichen Terzetten?
> Wen da der Dichter hineingesperrt,
> Den kann kein Gott mehr retten—
>
> Kein Gott, kein Heiland erlöst ihn je
> Aus diesen singenden Flammen!
> Nimm' dich in Acht, dass wir dich nicht
> Zu solcher Hölle verdammen!

From the sonnets as they now stand in the booklet entitled *The Year of Shame*, Mr. Watson has removed the two "schrecklichen Terzetten" which originally ended the sonnet entitled *Craven England* :

> And the red stream thou might'st have staunched still runs;
> And o'er the earth there sounds no trumpet's tone
> To shake the ignoble torpor of thy sons:
> But with indifferent eyes they watch, and see
> Hell's regent sitting yonder, propped by thee,
> Abdul the Damned, on his infernal throne.

These lines are gone, and a very feeble sestett replaces them; the reason for the change probably being that the title "Abdul" is misused as a proper name. But it may be doubted whether, in deleting the lines, Mr. Watson had any intention of performing a "harrowing of hell" in favour of the Commander of the Faithful. He may have smiled as

he drew his pen through the concluding verses, and murmured to himself

> Kein Gott, kein Heiland erlöst ihn je
> Aus diesen singenden Flammen !

The initial sonnet (after the dedication) is perhaps the
greatest of all :

THE TURK IN ARMENIA.

What profits it, O England, to prevail
In arts and arms, and mighty realms subdue,
And ocean with thine argosies bestrew,
And wrest thy tribute from each golden gale,
If idly thou must hearken to the wail
Of women martyred by the turbaned crew
Whose tenderest mercy was the sword that slew,
And hazard not the dinting of thy mail ?
We deemed of old thou held'st a charge from Him
Who sits companioned by His seraphim,
To smite the wronger with thy destined rod.
Wait'st thou His sign ?   Enough, the unanswered cry
Of virgin souls for vengeance, and on high
The gathering blackness of the frown of God !

This electric and thrilling close is surely a master-stroke
of rhetoric ; and there are several others no less superb in
The Year of Shame.   For example :—

A TRIAL OF ORTHODOXY.

The clinging children at their mother's knee
Slain ; and the sire and kindred one by one
Flayed or hewn piecemeal ; and things nameless done,
Not to be told : while imperturbably
The nations gaze, where Rhine unto the sea,
Where Seine and Danube, Thames and Tiber run,
And where great armies glitter in the sun,
And great kings rule, and man is boasted free !
What wonder if yon torn and naked throng
Should doubt a Heaven that seems to wink and nod,
And having moaned at noontide, " Lord, how long ? "
Should cry, " Where hidest Thou ? " at evenfall,
At midnight, " Is he deaf and blind, our God ? "
And ere day dawn, "Is He indeed at all ? "

If this sestett be not magnificent, I do not know the meaning of the word. These two sonnets, with *The Price of Prestige*, *The Knell of Chivalry*, *A Wondrous Likeness*, and *To the Sultan*, are probably the gems of the sequence; but there is scarcely any which does not contain some memorable passage, some splendid flash of scathing rhetoric. At the same time we are conscious every here and there of a certain laxity of style, marring what ought to be the serried perfection of the sonnet form. Take, for example, *The Tired Lion*, an appeal to a

> Hero withdrawn from senates and their sound
> Unto thy home by Cambria's northern bound.

Apart from the rococo effect of the word " Cambria," this second line has no place within a sonnet's "scanty plot of ground," where everything should be tense with essential significance. The place of Mr. Gladstone's retreat is not germane to the subject. His relation and his duty to Armenia would have been just the same had he lived in Norfolk or in Devonshire. Again, there is no consistency in the images crowded into the following lines :

> . . . but who hath found
> Another man so shod with fire, so crowned
> With thunder, and so armed with wrath divine?

The words here employed are practically interchangeable. Mr. Gladstone might as well—perhaps better—have been represented as crowned with fire and shod with thunder, or shod with wrath and armed with fire divine. In short, there is no inherent fitness and necessity either in the individual images or in their collocation. Further (though this is perhaps hypercriticism) there is a touch of incongruity in the expression, " Alien *paths* of base *repose*." Yet who would not forgive greater blemishes than these for the sake of the haunting beauty of the last two lines :

> Oh, from these alien paths of base repose
> Call back thy England, ere thou too depart—
> *Ere, on some secret mission, thou too start*
> *With silent footsteps, whither no man knows.*

Again, in the sonnet which follows this, aptly entitled *The Bard-in-Waiting*, a superb close redeems a comparatively commonplace poem. Mr. Watson protests his love of England no less fervent than that of the Bard-in-Waiting :

> But for the love I bore her lofty ways,
> What were to me her stumblings and her slips ?
> And lovely is she still, her maiden lips
> Pressed to the lips whose foam around her plays !
> *But on her brow's benignant star whose rays*
> *Lit them that sat in darkness, lo ! the eclipse.*

The image of the "maiden lips pressed to the lips whose foam around her plays" is perhaps a trifle grotesque, though respectable precedent might be pleaded for even more frothy metaphors ; but the transition to the last two lines is singularly telling, and they fall on the ear like a sudden thunderclap.

Not all Mr. Watson's political poems take sonnet form. The last three numbers of *The Year of Shame* are in various measures, and one of them, *How Weary is our Heart*, is very impressive. When Greece, goaded to desperation, broke from the leading-strings of the Concert of Europe and

> Faced the shape whose dragon breath
> Fouled the splendour of the sun,

Mr. Watson was not slow to cheer on the forlorn hope in a spirited ode entitled *Hellas, Hail!* And when the hope was extinct and the brief struggle over, he uttered his indignation in this noble and scathing epigram :

AFTER DEFEAT.

> Pray, what chorus this ? At the tragedy's end, what chorus?
> Surely bewails it the brave, the unhappily starred, the abandoned

Sole unto fate, by yonder invincible kin of the vanquished?
Surely salutes it the fallen, not mocks the protagonist prostrate?

Hark. " Make merry. Ye dreamed that a monster sickened :
   behold him
Rise, new-fanged. Make merry. A hero troubled and shamed
   you.
Jousting in desperate lists, he is trodden of giants in armour.
Mighty is Night. Make merry. The dawn for a season is
   frustrate."

Thus, after all these ages, a pæan, a loud jubilation,
Mounts, from peoples bemused, to a heaven refraining its
   thunder.

Because a poet's politics are seldom translated into practice,
we are apt to assume that they are essentially impracticable.
A policy of inaction and procrastination has always this in
its favour—that it staves off an evil day. But there is
nothing to prove that it has not also staved off a good day,
and made the evil day harder to face when it can be staved
off no longer. This is not an expression of personal
opinion, but a plea for abstract justice of thought. We
must not take it for granted that the ideal policy was
impracticable, and would have been disastrous, merely
because the opposite policy has, so far, proved practicable,
and has not as yet brought disaster to our own doors. At
any rate, it is not the poet's business to sing the wisdom of
acquiescence and the duty of compromise. In whatever
juncture of affairs, the comfortable and convenient course
has always plenty of advocates, with plenty of prose at their
command ; and the poet is merely performing his predestined function who raises his voice, however hopelessly
for the moment, to ask whether " British interests " may not,
in the long run, be identical with the interests of humanity.
That, I take it, is the sum total of Mr. Watson's political
creed. He has eyes only for the ideal aspect of a political
question. In a statesman, no doubt, such a limitation of
view might be dangerous; yet I sometimes wonder why

Bunyan did not give a companion to Mr. Facing-both-ways in the person of his cousin-german, Mr. Seeing-all-sides.

It is really a false classification which provides a separate pigeon-hole for Mr. Watson's Philosophical Poems. All his poems, down to his lightest lyric, one may almost say, are philosophical. Whatever the text he takes, or the form of his utterance, he will still be brooding on the nature and destinies of man. Even in his attitude towards the physical world he is a moralist rather than a painter. He is far more intent on reading Nature's lessons than on portraying her pageantry. When he writes of the skylark, for instance, he does not, like so many other poets, strive to find phrases, similitudes, even metres, that shall present to us the "blithe spirit" in its quiddity, but at once sets about contrasting the lot of the skylark with that of man in general, and the poet in particular. In speaking of Mr. Watson's Philosophical Poems, then, I imply a negative rather than a positive definition : I mean poems which are not on the face of them epigrams ; which are not directly addressed to friends ; and which do not find their text in literature or politics.

Mr. Watson is not one of those poets whose minds remain stationary at a given point : who, having sung their thoughts in youth, sing merely their prejudices in later life. There is a very distinct advance, in range and individuality of intelligence, between *Wordsworth's Grave* and *The Unknown God*. Volume by volume, we see the poet's thought maturing and clarifying. In his *Epigrams* he dwelt with complacency on such ideas as this :

> One music maketh its occult abode
>> In all things scatter'd from great Beauty's hand ;
> And evermore the deepest words of God
>> Are yet the easiest to understand.

In *Wordsworth's Grave*, and several other poems of that early period, he gave not merely literary homage but personal adhesion to a resolute Wordsworthian optimism.

Other poets had "sung him captive"; Wordsworth "sang him free."

> From Shelley's dazzling glow or thunderous haze,
>   From Byron's tempest-anger, tempest-mirth,
> Men turned to thee and found—not blast and blaze,
>   Tumult of tottering heavens, but peace on earth.
>
> Nor peace that grows by Lethe, scentless flower,
>   There in white languors to decline and cease;
> But peace whose names are also rapture, power,
>   Clear sight, and love: for these are parts of peace.

At the close of the Epistle *To Edward Dowden*, Mr. Watson makes still more definite confession of Wordsworthian faith, celebrating the supreme wisdom of the poet

> Who trusted nature, trusted fate, nor found
> An Ogre, sovereign on the throne of things;
> Who felt the incumbence of the unknown, yet bore
> Without resentment the Divine reserve;
> Who suffered not his spirit to dash itself
> Against the crags and wavelike break in spray,
> But 'midst the infinite tranquillities
> Moved tranquil, and henceforth, by Rotha stream
> And Rydal's mountain-mirror, and where flows
> Yarrow thrice sung or Duddon to the sea,
> And wheresoe'er man's heart is thrilled by tones
> Struck from man's lyric heartstrings, shall survive.

But even before the third edition of *Wordsworth's Grave* was published, in the *Poems* of 1892, very un-Wordsworthian moods had begun to creep in. Significant in this sense is the little poem entitled *World-Strangeness*, in which, comparing the world to a "house with starry dome, Floored with gemlike plains and seas," the poet continues:

> On from room to room I stray,
>   Yet my Host can ne'er espy,
> And I know not to this day
>   Whether guest or captive I.

From this doubt there is no such great stride to that vision

of " an Ogre, sovereign on the throne of things," and that
" resentment of the Divine reserve," which Wordsworth is
praised for never having entertained. In his next book,
however, *Odes and Other Poems* (1894) Mr. Watson is still
in a more or less Wordsworthian frame of mind ; for a
passionate meliorism, and discontent with the actual and
transitory conditions of sublunary affairs, are by no means
forbidden in the Sermon of Rydal Mount. Here is a
sonnet which would neither in spirit nor in accomplishment
seem misplaced among the best of Wordsworth's own :

> I think the immortal servants of mankind,
>> Who, from their graves, watch by how slow degrees
>> The World-Soul greatens with the centuries,
> Mourn most Man's barren levity of mind,
> The ear to no grave harmonies inclined,
>> The witless thirst for false wit's worthless lees,
>> The laugh mistimed in tragic presences,
> The eye to all majestic meanings blind.
> O prophets, martyrs, saviours, *ye* were great,
>> All truth being great to you : ye deemed Man more
>> Than a dull jest, God's ennui to amuse :
>> The world, for you, held purport : Life ye wore
> Proudly, as Kings their solemn robes of state ;
>> And humbly, as the mightiest monarchs use.

In the same collection, besides the *World in Armour* sonnets,
occurs the following quite Wordsworthian utterance, which
I quote, not for its form, but for the sake of the profound
truth it embodies :

CHRISTMAS DAY.

> The morn broke bright : the thronging people wore
>> Their best ; but in the general face I saw
>> No touch of veneration or of awe.
> Christ's natal day ?   'Twas merely one day more
> On which the mart agreed to close its door ;
>> A lounging-time by usage and by law
>> Sanctioned ; nor recked they, beyond this, one straw
> Of any meaning which for man it bore !

Fated among time's fallen leaves to stray,
　　We breathe an air that savours of the tomb,
Heavy with dissolution and decay;
　　Waiting till some new world-emotion rise,
And with the shattering might of the simoom
　　Sweep clean this dying Past that never dies.

It is the succeeding volume, *The Father of the Forest*
(1895), that marks Mr. Watson's final exodus from Lakeland.
The *Hymn to the Sea*—not faultless, truly, but a glorious
poem none the less, and one of the summits of recent
poetical achievement—takes a far larger, sterner, more
cosmic view of man and his destinies than we have yet
found in Mr. Watson's verse. I quote the essential portions
of its second and fourth strophes:

Athlete mightily frustrate, who pittest thy thews against legions,
　　Locked with fantastical hosts, bodiless arms of the sky;
Sea that breakest for ever, that breakest and never art broken,
　　Like unto thine, from of old, springeth the spirit of man,—
Nature's wooer and fighter, whose years are a suit and a wrestling,
　　All their hours, from his birth, hot with desire and with fray;
Amorist agonist man, that, immortally pining and striving,
　　Snatches the glory of life only from love and from war;
Man that, rejoicing in conflict, like thee when precipitate tempest,
　　Charge after thundering charge, clangs on thy resonant mail,
Seemeth so easy to shatter, and proveth so hard to be cloven;
　　Man whom the gods, in his pain, curse with a soul that endures;
Man whose deeds, to the doer, come back as thine own exhalations
　　Into thy bosom return, weepings of mountain and vale;
Man with the cosmic fortunes and starry vicissitudes tangled,
　　Chained to the wheel of the world, blind with the dust of its speed,
Even as thou, O giant, whom trailed in the wake of her conquests
　　Night's sweet despot draws, bound to her ivory car;
Man with inviolate caverns, impregnable holds in his nature,
　　Depths no storm can pierce, pierced with a shaft of the sun;
Man that is galled with his confines, and burdened yet more with
　　　　his vastness,
Born too great for his ends, never at peace with his goal.

　　　　*　　　*　　　*　　　*　　　*

Thou, with punctual service, fulfillest thy task, being constant;
　　Thine but to ponder the Law, labour and greatly obey:

Wherefore, with leapings of spirit, thou chantest the chant of the
  faithful,
  Chantest aloud at thy toil, cleansing the Earth of her stain;
Leagued in antiphonal chorus with stars and the populous
  Systems,
  Following these as their feet dance to the rhyme of the Suns;
Thou thyself but a billow, a ripple, a drop of that Ocean,
  Which, labyrinthine of arm, folding us meshed in its coil,
Shall, as now, with elations, august exultations and ardours,
  Pour, in unfaltering tide, all its unanimous waves,
When, from this threshold of being, these steps of the Presence,
  this precinct,
  Into the matrix of Life darkly divinely resumed,
Man and his littleness perish, erased like an error and cancelled,
  Man and his greatness survive, lost in the greatness of God.

If this poem can be called in any sense optimistic, the optimism is certainly stoical rather than serene; and the same may be said of *The Dream of Man* in the *Lachrymæ Musarum* volume (1896), which enforces the old observation that if Death were no more, Life would have lost its savour. Man, in the poet's vision, after æons of struggle, succeeds in storming the fortress of Death and casting Asrael into chains:

And behold, his Soul rejoiced not,
  The breath of whose being was strife,
For life with nothing to vanquish
  Seemed but the shadow of life.
No goal invited and promised
  And divinely provocative shone;
And Fear having fled, her sister,
  Blest Hope, in her train was gone;
And the coping and crown of achievement
  Was hell than defeat more dire—
The torment of all-things-compassed,
  The plague of nought-to-desire;
And Man the invincible queller,
  Man with his foot on his foes,
In boundless satiety hungered,
  Restless from utter repose,

> Victor of nature, victor
> Of the prince of the powers of the air,
> By mighty weariness vanquished.
> And crowned with august despair.

The psychological observation underlying this " Vision " is undoubted, and those may find comfort in it who can. But it is clearly no answer to an arraignment of the nature of things, since it is precisely this inseparable characteristic of the mind of man that an intelligent pessimism most vehemently arraigns. To allege it as a defence of the First Cause is to suppose the First Cause subject to a law exterior to itself: in other words, to commit a contradiction in terms. To prove Zeus the vassal of an elder divinity—Ananké, or what not—is not to quash the indictment, but merely to expunge the name of Zeus and substitute another.

If Mr. Watson was ever deceived by this theological thimble-rigging (for it is nothing else), he quickly detected the imposture. In his last volume, *The Hope of the World*, he takes up a definite attitude, not of dogmatic pessimism, but of not irreverent protest against the mysteries and apparent contradictions in the moral scheme of things. He contemplates with wonder and awe the spectacle of the universe, the enigma of the soul. In his opening poem (the least successful, to my thinking) he confesses that, while he sees Life and Law throned above the heavens, he cannot discern Love completing the trinity. For that he has to look " On earth, in homes of men, In hearts that crave and die."

> Did Heaven vouchsafe some sign
> That through all Nature's frame
> Boundless ascent benign
> Is everywhere her aim,
> Such as man hopes it here,
> Where he from beasts hath risen,—
> Then might I read full clear,
> Ev'n in my sensual prison,
> That Life and Law and Love are one symphonious name.

But, to his perception at least, no such sign is vouchsafed. The ascent of man does not reassure him. It is true that—

> In cave and bosky dene
> Of old there crept and ran
> The gibbering form obscene
> That was and was not man.
> With fairer covering clad
> The desert beasts went by ;
> The couchant lion had
> More speculative eye,
> And goodlier speech the birds, than we when we began.

But this rise seems to have proceeded from " some random throw of heedless Nature's die "—the poet, at any rate, cannot descry in it any design animated by Love. Hope, indeed, lingers unsubdued :

> As some adventurous flower,
> On savage crag-side grown,
> Seems nourished hour by hour
> From its wild self alone,
> So lives inveterate Hope, on her own hardihood.

The poet rehearses the arguments of Hope, but recognises in them the whisperings of an instinct to which reason gives no sanction ; wherefore, in the end, he braces himself

> . . . to endure
> Chance, and victorious Death,
> Life and my doom obscure.

The second poem of the volume, *The Unknown God* (quoted at the end of this article), takes its keynote from that utterance of pure Pantheism among the recently-discovered " Sayings of Jesus " which so potently thrilled the imagination of the world. It contains, too, in the tenth stanza, a clear allusion, not to say retort, to Mr. Kipling's *Recessional*, with its too facile faith (so Mr. Watson would say) in success as a test of harmony with the will of a beneficent deity. *The Lost Eden* (misplaced in the volume) really belongs to this group of poems. It tells how " But yesterday was Man from Eden driven," on finding himself, not, as he had deemed, the centre and meaning of the universe, but an accident in its indifferent immensity. Then

> an imperative world-thirst drave him forth,
> And the gold gates of Eden clanged behind.
>
> Never shall he return : for he hath sent
> His spirit abroad among the infinitudes,
> And may no more to the ancient pales recall
> The travelled feet. But oftentimes he feels
> The intolerable vastness bow him down,
> The awful homeless spaces scare his soul ;
> And half-regretful he remembers then
> His Eden lost, as some grey mariner
> May think of the far fields where he was bred,
> And woody ways unbreathed-on by the sea,
> Though more familiar now the ocean-paths
> Gleam, and the stars his fathers never knew.

Of this group of poems, however, the *Ode in May* is unquestionably the finest. It is a truly magnificent utterance of the religion which views the universe with awe, and man's lot in it, not with complacency, but with a courageous, almost a thankful, acceptance of its glories and its terrors. I quote three of its seven stanzas—

> For of old the Sun, our sire,
> Came wooing the mother of men,
> Earth, that was virginal then,
> Vestal fire to his fire.
> Silent her bosom and coy,
> But the strong god sued and pressed ;
> And born of their starry nuptial joy
> Are all that drink of her breast.
>
> And the triumph of him that begot,
> And the travail of her that bore,
> Behold, they are evermore
> As warp and weft in our lot.

We are children of splendour and flame,
Of shuddering, also, and tears.
Magnificent out of the dust we came,
And abject from the Spheres.

O bright irresistible lord,
We are fruit of Earth's womb, each one,
And fruit of thy loins, O Sun,
Whence first was the seed outpoured.
To thee as our Father we bow,
Forbidden thy Father to see,
Who is older and greater than thou, as thou
Art greater and older than we.

There is a swing in this poem that recalls the great chorus
in *Atalanta in Calydon ;* and Mr. Watson need not shrink
from the comparison. He has invented a beautiful stanza,
and he has used it majestically.

Mr. Watson is a poet of obvious limitations, on which I
have dwelt perhaps more than sufficiently. He is not (to
use an exceedingly peccant word) an impeccable artist ; and
though I have not gone out of my way to seek out flaws in
his workmanship, still less have I attempted to dissemble
them where, as it seemed to me, they came in my way. He
is not an adventurous, innovating spirit either in thought or
in technique; it is his function and his glory to hand on, in
this generation, the great classical tradition of English
poetry. On the threshold of the twentieth century, he
reconciles and brings to a common denominator, as it were,
the best qualities of eighteenth-century and of nineteenth-
century verse. He is the heir no less of Dryden than of
Tennyson ; it is hard to say whether Keats or Pope has
more potently influenced him. There is significance in the
fact that his favourite instrument, which he fingers with the
utmost mastery, is the classic instrument of the English
muse—the iambic pentameter. His poetry is starred with
splendid single lines in this measure. They occur by the

score in the poems I have quoted; from other poems I pick out a few more at random—

> And spurns the gibbering mime into the night.
> And snare him into greatness for an hour.
> With whiteness clothed of dedicated days.
> And where far isles the languid ocean fleck.
> Tremendous silence, older than the world.
> The dire compulsion of infertile days.
> Reveres the reverence which it cannot feel.
> Sire of huge sorrows, yet erect of soul.
> The sense of greatness keeps a nation great.

It is true that the great single line affords no conclusive measure of a poet's greatness. There is profound critical truth in that scornful "Xenie" of Schiller's—

> Weil ein Vers dir gelingt in einer gebildete Sprache
> Die für dich dichtet und denkt, glaubst du ein Dichter zu sein?

But it is not one verse, nor a dozen, that "succeeds to" Mr. Watson. Pregnant, resonant, memorable lines flow inexhaustibly from his pen; and some of them, I venture to predict, will live with the language.

One can well understand that (even putting aside the very greatest names) other poets, both living and dead, may have more potent fascinations for individual readers than this staid, strenuous, self-respecting thinker and artist, who neither dazzles with paradoxes, piques with enigmas, nor lulls with undulant melodies and tintinnabulating rhymes. But while dignity, perspicuity and measure are still recognised among the high qualities of song, Mr. Watson will be accounted a landmark of sense and style in an age too apt to go astray in labyrinths of eccentricity, obscurity and excess.

WILLIAM WATSON

THE UNKNOWN GOD.

When, overarched by gorgeous night,
    I wave my trivial self away;
When all I was to all men's sight
    Shares the erasure of the day;
Then do I cast my cumbering load,
Then do I gain a sense of God.

Not him that with fantastic boasts
    A sombre people dreamed they knew;
The mere barbaric God of Hosts
    That edged their sword and braced their thew:
A God they pitted 'gainst a swarm
Of neighbour Gods less vast of arm;

A God like some imperious king,
    Wroth, were his realm not duly awed;
A God for ever hearkening
    Unto his self-commanded laud;
A God for ever jealous grown
Of carven wood and graven stone;

A God whose ghost, in arch and aisle,
    Yet haunts his temple—and his tomb;
But follows in a little while
    Odin and Zeus to equal doom;
A God of kindred seed and line;
Man's giant shadow, hailed divine.

O streaming worlds, O crowded sky,
    O Life, and mine own soul's abyss,
Myself am scarce so small that I
    Should bow to Deity like this!
This my Begetter? This was what
Man in his violent youth begot.

The God I know of, I shall ne'er
   Know, though he dwells exceeding nigh.
Raise thou the stone and find me there,
   Cleave thou the wood and there am I.
Yea, in my flesh his spirit doth flow,
Too near, too far, for me to know.

Whate'er my deeds, I am not sure
   That I can pleasure him or vex;
I that must use a speech so poor
   It narrows the Supreme with sex.
Notes he the good or ill in man?
To hope he cares is all I can.

I hope—with fear.   For did I trust
   This vision granted me at birth,
The sire of heaven would seem less just
   Than many a faulty son of earth.
And so he seems indeed!   But then,
I trust it not, this bounded ken.

And dreaming much, I never dare
   To dream that in my prisoned soul
The flutter of a trembling prayer
   Can move the Mind that is the Whole.
Though kneeling nations watch and yearn,
Does the primordial purpose turn?

Best by remembering God, say some,
   We keep our high imperial lot.
Fortune, I fear, hath oftenest come
   When we forgot—when we forgot!
A lovelier faith their happier crown,
B.t history laughs and weeps it down!

Know they not well, how seven times seven,
   Wronging our mighty arms with rust,
We dared not do the work of heaven
   Lest heaven should hurl us in the drst
The work of heaven!   'Tis waiting still
The sanction of the heavenly will.

WILLIAM WATSON

Unmeet to be profaned by praise
   Is he whose coils the world enfold;
The God on whom I ever gaze,
   The God I never once behold:
Above the cloud, beneath the clod:
The Unknown God, the Unknown God.

MRS. WOODS

ALTHOUGH all her work is womanly enough; although
is no aping of masculinity about it; yet if Mrs. W
poems had been published anonymously, it would
taken a rather keen critic to declare with confidenc
their author was a woman. This remark has a two-
bearing. It implies a quality and a defect. Discr
reserve, is the quality : a very real and valuable one.
Woods writes from sublimated experience. There
crudity of immediate outcry in her work. On the
hand—and this is the correlative defect—we feel a la
intimacy, almost of individuality, in the utterances o
fastidious spirit. Her poems have sometimes the
literary exercises, evidences of faculty rather than expres
of feeling. We are more conscious of their talent thar
vinced of their inspiration. Even when most succe
they do not strike us as inevitable. In avoiding exc
self-revelation, Mrs. Woods verges towards defect of
expression.

The consequence is that we turn to Mrs. Woods rath
intellectual than for emotional pleasure. There is no
laugh, never a sob, never a pulse-beat of exultation or of
in her work. On the other hand, there is plenty of the
contemplation, imagination, expressed in a style whic
speaks close familiarity with the best models. It neede
her strange and powerful neo-Elizabethan play, *Wild J*

MARGARET · L · WOODS

to prove that Mrs. Woods had come very close in spirit to the seventeenth century. The cool, clear metres and delicate diction of her lyrics had already proclaimed this unmistakably. Of nineteenth-century influence one traces but little in her work ; at any rate, she has not taken any individual poet for her master. Neither in style nor in thought, however, is her work affectedly archaic. It would be fairest to say, perhaps, that it shows a very wide poetic culture, with a special bent towards seventeenth-century methods, and an avoidance of evanescent latter-day fashions of verse-making. Once or twice (notably in a poem entitled *Beside the Door*) one seems to catch an echo from the Roumanian Folk-songs translated by Miss Alma Strettell ; but this can scarcely be called a nineteenth-century influence.

The most living of all Mrs. Woods's lyrics, to my thinking, is *Gaudeamus Igitur*, quoted at the end of this article. Here she in some measure throws off her limitations, and gives us a large, full-throated song ; emboldened, perhaps, by the semi-conventional theme, which leaves undetermined the pressure of personal conviction behind the singing. It may be absolutely sincere, it may be partly dramatic ; for a pessimist may on occasion strike up " Gaudeamus igitur," a teetotaller carol " Nunc est bibendum." More characteristic, inasmuch as it is more staid and reflective, is the following poem :

TO THE FORGOTTEN DEAD.

> To the forgotten dead,
> Come, let us drink in silence ere we part.
> To every fervent yet resolvèd heart
> That brought its tameless passion and its tears,
> Renunciation and laborious years,
> To lay the deep foundations of our race,
> To rear its stately fabric overhead
> And light its pinnacles with golden grace.
> To the unhonoured dead.

> To the forgotten dead,
> Whose dauntless hands were stretched to grasp the rein
> Of Fate and hurl into the void again
> Her thunder-hoofèd horses, rushing blind
> Earthward along the courses of the wind.
> Among the stars, along the wind in vain
> Their souls were scattered and their blood was shed,
> And nothing, nothing of them doth remain.
> To the thrice-perished dead.

In point of high imagination, Mrs. Woods has done nothing finer than the poem entitled *Again I saw Another Angel*, telling how

> An angel cinctured with the gleam
> Of topaz and of chrysoprase
>
> *　　*　　*　　*　　*
>
> Leapt into heaven's deserted ways,
> And cried "The message of the Lord."
>
> Then suddenly the earth was white
> With faces turned towards the light.
> The nations' pale expectancy
> Sobbed far beneath him like the sea,
> But men exulting in their dread,
> And drunken with an awful glee
> Beat at the portals of the dead.
>
> I saw this monstrous grave the earth
> Shake with a spasm as though of birth,
> And shudder with a sullen sound,
> As though the dead stirred in the ground.
> And that great angel girt with flame
> Cried till the heavens were rent around,
> "Come forth, ye dead!"—Yet no man came.
>
> Then there was silence overhead:
> But far below the ancient dead
> Muttered as if in mockery;
> And there was darkness in the sky,
> And rolling through the realm of death
> Laughter and some obscure reply
> With tongues that none interpreteth.

The dead refuse to rise, the "undeluded dead," and the trump of doom is blown in vain. The final stanzas, I think, are scarcely up to the level of those I have quoted ; but the poem, as a whole, is very impressive. *To the Earth* is a strong and memorable ode, and *The Death of Hjörward* a fine ballad ; *Rameses*, though spirited, strikes me as less happily inspired. The sonnet is not a favourite form with Mrs. Woods, and her *Tasso to Leonora* sequence is not one of her chief successes. On the other hand, I find real charm in this sonnet, despite its somewhat weak seventh and eighth lines :-

THE EARTH ANGEL.

Beloved spirit, whom the angels miss,
While those heaven-wandering wings thou foldest here,
Love musing on thee, Love whose shadow is fear,
Divines thee born of fairer worlds than this,
And fain ere long to reassume their bliss.
Stay, wingèd soul! for earth, this human sphere,
Claims thee her own, her light that storms swept clear ;
Her righteousness that love, not peace, shall kiss.
'Twas out of time thou camest to be ours,
And dead men made thee in the darkling years,
Thy tenderness they bought for thee with tears,
Pity with pain that nothing could requite,
And all thy sweetness springs like later flowers
Thick on the field of some forgotten fight.

The poem *On the Death of an Infant* contains many beautiful touches, but at the same time exemplifies the philosophic rather than simply human bent of Mrs. Woods' talent. How exquisite, for instance, are the lines about

. . . The blossom-coloured feet
That in our dusty pathways yet
No print had set,
So that the world will scarcely mark
Their little track into the dark.

And again this verse :

When last she wept—how many years
Ago it seems!—he dried her tears

With wandering touches velvet-sleek
    Upon her cheek.
Now on his fragile breast she bows
Her shaken mouth and heavy brows,
And holds him fast, while he nor fears
    Nor wonders at her tears.

It seems a pity that Babylon and Egypt, Hera and Aphrodite, should enter into a strain which begins so simply. The thought—that the grief of a bereaved mother is one of the "ancient mysteries of Earth," making kin the whole world and all time—might surely have found simpler, briefer and not less poignant expression. Still, it would be unjust to deny the power and nobility of the poem, merely because it might have been cast in a different form.

Mrs. Woods's one experiment in drama is deliberately and emphatically Elizabethan. *Wild Justice* deals with the theme of *The Cenci*, minus its crowning horror. The scene is a remote island off the Welsh coast, where Gryffith Gwyllim, a lighthouse owner (in the days when the lighting of our coasts was largely left to the private enterprise), abominably tyrannises over his wife and his many children. Precisely as in *The Cenci*, they have tried in vain every legal means of restraining his malevolent cruelty; there is nothing that meets the case save the "wild justice" of murder; and the matter of the play consists of the struggles endured by the long-suffering mother and children in arriving at this resolution. The eldest son, Owain, is a cripple, having been thrown downstairs in childhood by his father. Imprisoned in his chair, he has nothing to do but to read Shakespeare and brood on the iniquities of the oppressor. He it is that conceives the scheme of misplacing the light which guides his father home after his nightly visit to the lighthouse, and so luring him into a quicksand. The plan is to be carried out by the eldest daughter, Nelto, a strongly-drawn character: but when Shonnin, the second son, hears of it, his shrinking nature is outraged, and he rushes forth to prevent Nelto from becoming a murderess. There is a powerful, though not very clear scene in which Owain and his mother watch from the window the moving lanterns outside, and divine from them the course of events. If I understand the matter aright, Nelto, having successfully entrapped her father into the quicksand, is seized with remorse, and she and Shonnin both perish in trying to rescue him. This little tragedy in six scenes is very vigorously written, with flashes of true psychological insight. Here is a passage from the scene in which Mrs. Gwyllim and Owain watch, haggard and intent, the lantern whose fallacious gleam is to bring them freedom. They do not know yet that Shonnin has determined to frustrate their plot.

MRS. GWYLLIM.   But tell me, Owain,
What if he does not come?

OWAIN.   Impossible.
He never yet delayed the night there.

MRS. GWYLLIM.   Never!
These will-o'-the-wisps, "never," "impossible,"
Misguide men to their ruin. What if he did?
There's not another boat on the island.

OWAIN.   None.
But, mother, do not with distracted horrors
Flaw the firm texture of resolvèd minds.
Rather we should drug deep imagination,
Leaving a mere mechanic sense to observe
An unmeaning light, nor search the invisible
Behind it, even for facts; to see her yonder,
Alone on the bar, and—Vengeance on all sight
But eyesight! What do we see here that's fearful?
A night much less tempestuous than most
Of this mad season, darkness and two lights.
Ah, but another, as I live! Yes, surely;
'Tis gone now, but I'd swear—quick, mother, quick!
Bring me the telescope.

MRS. GWYLLIM.   His telescope?
It is forbidden, I dare not.

527

OWAIN.   You forget
How much you dare to-night.

MRS. GWYLLIM.
[*Laughing wildly.*]   Oh, I'm a fool,
A very idiot !   I will fetch it.   [*Goes out.*

OWAIN.   Now,
Gwyllim, my devil has yours by the throat ;
They tussle up and down.   Shall's wager on them ?
Hike a good devil !   Yours is a tough grey fellow,
Yet will I back my pup—he bears a name,
A dreadful name, whose echoes roar of blood
Down the black galleries of bottomless Hell
To the unplumbed primal void.

The dialogue throughout is, like this passage, with its
"shall's" and its echoes from *King Lear*, unequivocally
Shakespearean.   The point is driven home, in fact, by
Owain's quotations from Shakespeare ; it is evidently suggested that, in his imprisonment, he has pastured his soul
on the Elizabethans.   Mrs. Woods, in a word, has consciously and not unsuccessfully done what most blank-verse
dramatists feebly and half-unconsciously attempt.   She has
not merely mimicked the limbs and outward flourishes of
Shakespearean diction, but has here and there reproduced
something of its essential quality.

MRS. WOODS

GAUDEAMUS IGITUR.

Come, no more of grief and dying!
Sing the time too swiftly flying.
  Just an hour
  Youth's in flower;
Give me roses to remember
In the shadow of December.

Fie on steeds with leaden paces!
Winds shall bear us on our races:
  Speed, O speed,
  Wind, my steed,
Beat the lightning for your master,
Yet my Fancy shall fly faster.

Give me music, give me rapture,
Youth that's fled can none recapture:
  Not with thought
  Wisdom's bought.
Out on pride and scorn and sadness!
Give me laughter, give me gladness.

Sweetest Earth, I love and love thee,
Seas about thee, skies above thee,
  Sun and storms,
  Hues and forms
Of the clouds with floating shadows
On thy mountains and thy meadows.

Earth, there's none that can enslave thee,
Not thy lords it is that have thee:
  Not for gold
  Art thou sold,
But thy lovers at their pleasure
Take thy beauty and thy treasure.

     2 L

While sweet fancies meet me singing,
While the April blood is springing
    In my breast,
    While a jest,
And my youth thou yet must leave me,
Fortune, 'tis not thou canst grieve me.

When at length the grasses cover
Me, the world's unwearied lover,
    If regret
    Haunt me yet,
It shall be for joys untasted,
Nature lent and folly wasted.

Youth and jests and summer weather,
Goods that kings and clowns together
    Waste or use
    As they choose,
These, the best, we miss pursuing
Sullen shades that mock our wooing.

Feigning Age will not delay it—
When the reckoning comes we'll pay it,
    Own our mirth
    Has been worth
All the forfeit, light or heavy,
Wintry Time and Fortune levy.

Feigning grief will not escape it,
What though ne'er so well you ape it—
    Age and care
    All must share,
All alike must pay hereafter,
Some for sighs and some for laughter.

Know, ye sons of Melancholy,
To be young and wise is folly.
    'Tis the weak
    Fear to wreak
On this clay of life their fancies,
Shaping battles, shaping dances.

While ye scorn our names unspoken,
Roses dead and follies broken,
    O ye wise,
    We arise,
Out of failures, dreams, disasters,
We arise to be your masters,

WILLIAM BUTLER YEATS

It is easy, or so it seems to me, to make too much of the influence of race upon literature. On the one hand, he would be a bold man who should postulate absolute purity of race for any mother's son in this mingle-mangle of a Western world. "It's a wise child who knows his own great-great-great-great-grandfathers." On the other hand, I would engage to take a child of guaranteed Saxon ancestry and make him a Kelt of the Kelts by bringing him up in Keltic country and under exclusively Keltic influences. I know at this moment a boy of ten, born of English parents—his mother of a good Yorkshire stock, his father hailing from the south of England—whom the influence of sheer environment has made a typical Parisian. Were he older, one might suspect a certain affectation in his ultra-Gallicism. As it is, there can be no room for any such suspicion. The race-characteristics (one would say) of the Parisian child have developed in him spontaneously, irrepressibly; and although English influences are not absent from his environment, their effect is absolutely superficial, leaving him fundamentally French. I am not disputing, be it observed, the existence of marked and potent race-characteristics. On the contrary, I assert their existence and their strength, but suggest that they are transmitted rather in the atmosphere than in the blood, and are at least as much a matter of tradition as of heredity.

531

This by way of proviso, lest I should seem to mean too much or too little in describing Mr. W. B. Yeats as the incarnation of the Irish Kelt. Incarnation, indeed, is scarcely the right word; he is rather the quintessentiated spirit of Keltic eld. His name does not imply an exclusively Irish ancestry, and his physique is so ultra-Keltic as almost to suggest a Southern admixture. There has been a good deal of Spanish blood in Ireland since 1588 or earlier; does any of it flow in Mr. Yeats's veins? Or shall we try further back, perhaps, to the Phœnicians? For aught I know, Mr. Yeats's family-tree may disprove all these speculations, and trace his ancestry in a direct line to Brian Borhoime. The matter is really unimportant according to my theory, which is that a Yorkshireman, a Scandinavian, or even a Scot, if caught young enough, might have become equally impregnated with the melancholy, the mystery, the supersensual grace and beauty of the Keltic imagination and its treasure of myth and folk-lore. I know one Scotchman, at any rate, unconscious of any but Sassenach blood in his composition, who feels the beauty of Deirdre and Grania scarcely less intimately than Mr. Yeats himself.

It is with Mr. Yeats that, so far as I know, the genuine spirit of Irish antiquity and Irish folk-lore makes its first entrance into English verse. Irish poets before him have either been absorbed in love, potheen, and politics—as Mr. Yeats himself puts it, they have "sung their loudest when a company of rebels or revellers has been at hand to applaud"—or (like Goldsmith and Moore) they have become to all intents and purposes Anglicised. Even William Allingham's fairies, pleasant little people though they be, are rather Anglo-Saxon Brownies than Keltic Sheogues. In Mr. Yeats we have an astonishing union of primitive imagination and feeling with cultivated and consciously artistic expression. He does not manipulate

· W·B·YEATS ·

from outside a dead and conventionalised mythological machinery. The very spirit of the myth-makers and myth-believers is in him. His imaginative life finds its spontaneous, natural utterance in the language of the " Keltic twilight." This is no literary jargon to him, but his veritable mother-tongue. When he deals with Catholicism, you see in his mental processes a living repetition of what occurred when the first missionaries evangelised Hibernia. You see the primitive pagan assimilating the Catholic mythology to his own spiritual habits and needs, and attaching purely pagan concepts to Christian names and terms. His moral ideas are enlarged, no doubt ; his metaphysics are practically unaffected. Christianity, in Mr. Yeats's poems, is not a creed, but a system of folk-lore. You do not trouble about its historical basis, you neither accept nor reject its dogmas. It is part and parcel of the innumerable host of spiritual entities and influences which beleaguers humanity from the cradle to the grave. Belief in these entities and influences is no more a matter of intellectual determination, of voluntary assent, than belief in the air we breathe. It is part of our constitution : innate, inevitable. Mr. Yeats's religion (I speak, of course, of Mr. Yeats the poet, not of the theoretical mystic and editor of Blake) is not " morality touched with emotion," but rather superstition touched with morality. It is " older than any history that is written in any book."

Mr. Yeats has in some measure simplified the task of criticism by collecting in a single book of *Poems* (1895) all that he " cares to preserve out of his previous volumes of verse." The previous volumes were three : *The Wanderings of Oisin and other Poems* (1889), *The Countess Cathleen, and Various Legends and Lyrics* (1892), and a little play called *The Land of Heart's Desire*, which appeared in 1894. The second of these three books contained the following preface:

" The greater number of the poems in this book, as also in *The Wanderings of Oisin*, are founded on Irish tradition. The chief poem (*The Countess Cathleen*) is an attempt to mingle personal thought and feeling with the beliefs and customs of Christian Ireland ; whereas the longest poem in my earlier book endeavoured to set forth the impress left on my imagination by the Pre-Christian cycle of legends. The Christian cycle, being mainly concerned with contending moods and moral motives, needed, I thought, a dramatic vehicle. The tumultuous and heroic Pagan cycle, on the other hand, having to do with vast and shadowy activities and with the great impersonal emotions, expressed itself naturally — or so I imagined—in epic and epic-lyric measures. No epic method seemed sufficiently minute and subtle for the one, and no dramatic method elastic and all-containing enough for the other.

The distinction thus indicated is just enough ; but in whatever form Mr. Yeats chooses to write, his genius is essentially lyrical. His epic poem, *The Wanderings of Oisin* consists of three long lyrical ballads, as who should say three *Ancient Mariners* bracketed together. The charm of his two dramas lies in the " lyric cry " which runs through them. There are touches of character in them, no doubt, but no character-development or clash of will with will. They show the melancholy race of mortals at the mercy of vague and for the most part malevolent external powers, and their chief beauty lies in single speeches, easily detachable from their context, each of which is a little lyric in itself. From *The Countess Cathleen*, for instance, take these five lines addressed by old Oona to her mistress :

> Dear heart, make a soft cradle of old tales,
> And songs and music : wherefore should you sadden
> For wrongs you cannot hinder ? The great God
> Smiling condemns the lost : be mirthful : He
> Bids you be merry and old age be wise.

This is a little lyric as complete in itself as a quatrain of Omar Khayyam. Here, again, is a speech of the good priest, Father Hart, in *The Land of Heart's Desire* :

> My colleen, I have seen some other girls
> Restless and ill at ease, but years went by

And they grew like their neighbours and were glad
In minding children, working at the churn,
And gossipping of weddings and of wakes ;
For life moves out of a red flare of dreams
Into a common light of common hours,
Until old age bring the red flare again.

To feel the beauty of this you require no knowledge of
either the characters or the situation.   It is as self-explana-
tory as *O' a' the airts the wind can blaw* or *Tears, idle tears*.
The whole play might be called a dialogue in folk-songs.

But before examining the plays more closely, let us
glance at Mr. Yeats's epic, *The Wanderings of Oisin*.*
And here it must be said that the curious crispness,
delicacy, and artful simplicity of his style is the result of
patient effort and slow development.   His verse has now a
peculiar, indefinable distinction, as of one tiptoeing
exquisitely through a fairy minuet ; whereas ten years ago
its movement was often flat-footed and conventional
enough.   *The Wanderings of Oisin*, as it now stands, is
very different from the poem originally published under
that title.   It would be a curious and very profitable
critical exercise to make an exhaustive comparison of
the two texts ; but this is not the place for such
a study.   I content myself with quoting the opening
passage of each version, to show how radical has been the
remodelling to which Mr. Yeats has subjected his early
work, and how remarkably his individuality has accentuated
itself in the interim.   Let us take the cruder form first :

[SAINT] PATRICK.

Oisin, tell me the famous story
Why thou outlivest, blind and hoary,
The bad old days.   Thou wert, men sing,
Trapped of an amorous demon thing.

---

* In the edition of 1895, Mr. Yeats spelt " Oisin " " Usheen,"
but in the edition of 1901 he reverts to the original form.

OISIN.

'Tis sad remembering, sick with years,
The swift, innumerable spears,
The long-haired warriors, the spread feast,
And love, in the hours when youth has ceased;
Yet will I make all plain for thee.
We rode in sorrow, with strong hounds three,
Bran, Sgeolan, and Lomair,
On a morning misty and mild and fair.
The mist-drops hung on the fragrant trees,
And in the blossoms hung the bees.
We rode in sadness above Loch Laen,
For our best were dead on Gavra's green.

*   *   *   *   *

And Bran, Sgeolan, and Lomair
Were lolling their tongues, and the silken hair
Of our strong steeds was dark with sweat,
When ambling down the vale we met
A maiden on a slender steed,
Whose careful pastern pressed the sod
As though he held an earthly mead
Scarce worthy of a hoof gold-shod.
For gold his hoofs and silk his rein,
And 'tween his ears above his mane
A golden crescent lit the plain,
And pearly white his well-groomed hair.
His mistress was more mild and fair
Than doves that moaned round Eman's hall
Among the leaves of the laurel wall,
And feared always the bowstring's twanging.
Her eyes were soft as dew drops hanging
Upon the grass-blade's bending tips,
And like a sunset were her lips,
A stormy sunset o'er doomed ships.
Her hair was of a citron tincture,
And gathered in a silver cincture;
Down to her feet white vesture flowed,
And with the woven crimson glowed,
Of many a figured creature strange,
And birds that on the seven seas range.
For brooch 'twas bound with a bright sea-shell,
And wavered like a summer rill,
As her soft bosom rose and fell.

WILLIAM BUTLER YEATS

PATRICK.

Oisin, thou art half heathen still!

This is pretty, indeed, and fancifully decorative, with unmistakable foretastes of the poet's maturer quality; but it is nerveless, diffuse, and now and then commonplace. Everything of value is retained in the later version; some exquisite touches are added; and the whole passage is compressed into little more than two-thirds of its original length:

S. PATRIC.

You who are bent, and bald, and blind,
With a heavy heart and a wandering mind,
Have known three centuries, poets sing,
Of dalliance with a demon thing.

OISIN.

Sad to remember, sick with years,
The swift innumerable spears,
The horsemen with their floating hair,
The bowls of barley, honey, and wine,
And feet of maidens dancing in tune,
And the white body that lay by mine;
But the tale, though words be lighter than air,
Must live to be old like the wandering moon.

Caolte, and Conan, and Finn were there,
When we followed a deer with our baying hounds,
With Bran, Sgeolan and Lomair,
And passing the Firbolgs' burial mounds,
Came to the cairn-heaped grassy hill
Where passionate Maive is stony still;
And found on the dove-gray edge of the sea
A pearl-pale, high-born lady, who rode
On a horse with bridle of findrinny;
And like a sunset were her lips,
A stormy sunset on doomed ships;
A citron colour gloomed in her hair,
But down to her feet white vesture flowed,
And with the glimmering crimson glowed

Of many a figured embroidery ;
And it was bound with a pearl pale shell
That wavered like the summer streams,
As her soft bosom rose and fell.

S. PATRIC.

You are still wrecked among heathen dreams.

Here everything, to my thinking, is bettered with an unerring touch. The burdensome and irrelevant description of the horse, with its "pearly white well-groomed hair," has altogether disappeared ; so has the laboured image of the doves ; so has the superficially pretty but essentially grotesque comparison of the lady's eyes to dewdrops hanging upon bending grass-blades. On the other hand, the noble audacity of the "stormy sunset on doomed ships," is retained intact, while two of the rejected colour-motives reappear in the beautiful lines

And found on the dove-gray edge of the sea
A pearl-pale, high-born lady, who rode
On a horse with a bridle of findrinny,

—"a kind of red bronze," as the glossary explains. Note, too, how every change tends to heighten the racial colour of the passage (if I may call it so) and make it more characteristically Keltic. The first form might have been the work of an Englishman cleverly applying the method of *Christabel* to an Irish subject ; the second form is Irish to its inmost fibre.

The poem sets forth how Oisin rode away with his faery bride

To shores by the wash of the tremulous tide,
Where men have heaped no burial mounds,
And the days pass by like a wayward tune.

In this Island of the Blest dwells an immortal race who "mock at Time and Fate and Chance." "You slaves of God," they sing,

538

He rules you with an iron rod,
He holds you with an iron bond,
Each one woven to the other,
Each one woven to his brother
Like bubbles in a frozen pond ;
But we in a lonely land abide
Unchainable as the dim tide,
With hearts that know nor law nor rule,
And hands that hold no wearisome tool,
Folded in love that fears no morrow,
Nor the gray wandering osprey Sorrow.

And again :

Joy drowns the twilight in the dew,
And fills with stars night's purple cup
And wakes the sluggard seeds of corn,
And stirs the young kid's budding horn,
And makes the infant ferns unwrap,
And for the peewit paints his cap,
And rolls along the unwieldy sun,
And makes the little planets run :
And if joy were not on the earth,
There were an end of change and birth,
And earth and heaven and hell would die,
And in some gloomy barrow lie
Folded like a frozen fly ;
Then mock at Death and Time with glances
And waving arms and wandering dances.

In this lotus-land Oisin dwells with Niam * for a hundred
years, until "some dead warrior's broken lance" lying
among the jetsam of the beach reawakens in him the desire
for a life of deeds and glory.

Thereon young Niam softly came
And caught my hands, but spake no word
Save only many times my name,
In murmurs, like a frighted bird.

---

* In the earlier editions " Naevë."

This is the picture of their riding away:

> We passed by woods, and lawns of clover,
> And found the horse and bridled him,
> For we knew well the old was over.
> I heard one say " His eyes grow dim
> With all the ancient sorrow of men ; "
> And wrapped in dreams rode out again
> With hoofs of the pale findrinny
> Over the glimmering purple sea:
> Under the golden evening light.
> The immortals moved among the fountains
> By rivers and the woods' old night ;
> Some danced like shadows on the mountains,
> Some wandered ever hand in hand,
> Or sat in dreams on the pale strand
> Each forehead like an obscure star
> Bent down above each hooked knee :
> And sang, and with a dreamy gaze
> Watched where the sun in a saffron blaze
> Was slumbering half in the sea ways ;
> And, as they sang, the painted birds
> Kept time with their bright wings and feet ;
> Like drops of honey came their words,
> But fainter than a young lamb's bleat.

As a mere piece of decoration, how unmistakably Keltic this is ! Magical and mysterious though the subject be, the design is perfectly definite, and is picked out, so to speak, in washes of brilliant, translucent, almost unharmonised colours. The picture is illuminated rather than painted, like the border of an ancient manuscript. It is characteristic of the Keltic imagination, though it may dwell by preference in the mist, to emerge at times into a scintillant blaze of light and colour.

In the second book, Niam carries Oisin from the Isle of Dancing to the Isle of Victories, where he for ever fights and overcomes a deathless demon, who for ever revives again after three days. Finally, they seek the Isle of Forgetfulness ; but even there, as Oisin says, " Remembrance, lifting her leanness, keened in the gates of my heart."

WILLIAM BUTLER YEATS

He leaves Niam, who can no longer follow him, and returns
to Ireland, to find that it has been Christianised during his
three centuries of absence ; and the moment he touches the
soil, the full weight of his years falls upon him.   But still
he resents and contemns the preachings of St. Patrick.

S. PATRIC.

On the flaming stones, without refuge, the limbs of the Fenians are
tost ;
None war on the masters of Hell, who could break up the world in
their rage ;
But kneel and wear out the flags and pray for your soul that is
lost
Through the demon love of its youth and its godless and passionate
age.

OISIN.

Ah, me! to be shaken with coughing and broken with old age and
pain,
Without laughter, a show unto children, alone with remembrance
and fear,
All emptied of purple hours as a beggar's cloak in the rain,
As a grass seed crushed by a pebble, as a wolf sucked under a weir.

It were sad to gaze on the blessed and no man I loved of old there ;
I throw down the chain of small stones! when life in my body has
ceased,
I will go to Caolte, and Conan, and Bran, Sgeolan, Lomair,
And dwell in the house of the Fenians, be they in flames or at feast.

These are the last words of a singularly beautiful and
moving poem, in which the high-hearted bravery and the
wistful beauty of the old Irish myth-cycle find the most
sympathetic of interpreters.

In Mr. Yeats's first book there were several brief dramatic
sketches of no very notable merit.   One of them reappears,
considerably altered, in the *Anashuya and Vijaya* of the
1895 volume.   The scene of another was laid in Spain, of
a third in some Arthurian region ; not one of them was located
in Ireland.   But Mr. Yeats draws his true strength from his
native soil.   In these early experiments the conventionality

of the verse was particularly noticeable. It showed scarcely a trace of individual accent, and was not to be distinguished from the blank verse of the scores of stillborn " poetic dramas " which every year brings forth. No sooner had Mr. Yeats returned to Ireland and chosen a dramatic motive from Irish folk-lore, than his individuality asserted itself not only in the idea and structure of his work but in its rhythms as well. *The Countess Cathleen* has undergone stringent revision since its first appearance ; and here, as in *The Wanderings of Oisin*, the changes—and especially the rounding-off of metrically defective lines—have all been for the better. But even in its original form the poem was full of a weird impressiveness which was then new to dramatic literature.

It is not easy to determine the precise relation between Mr. Yeats and M. Maurice Maeterlinck. Their affinity of spirit is obvious. Both are mystics ; both regard the visible world as little more than a hampering veil between them and the far more real and momentous unseen universe ; both are full of pity for the blindness and helplessness of man, encompassed, in all his goings out and comings in, by capricious, vaguely divined, and generally malevolent powers. M. Maeterlinck, no less than Mr. Yeats, goes to folklore, to nursery legend one might say, for his material ; though his folklore is generalised, not local or even racial. The Flemish poet has, to my thinking, a less melodious, less lyrical, but more specifically dramatic genius, and he is certainly the more penetrating and accomplished psychologist. But the true problem for criticism is not to balance the merits of the two writers, but to determine whether their curious similarity of method is due to independent development along parallel lines, or is partly attributable to the direct influence of the one upon the other. In *The Countess Cathleen* we recognise some of the most original features of M. Maeterlinck's dramatic method : the indeterminate time and place, the almost childlike simplicity of speech, the art of eliminating even the illusion of free-will, and representing human beings as the passive, plaintive puppets of dominions and powers unseen. Now, *The Countess Cathleen* was published in the autumn of 1892, and Maeterlinck's early works, *La Princess Maleine*, *L'Intruse*, and *Les Aveugles*, had been read and discussed in England for at least a year previously.* Thus it is probable enough that Mr. Yeats was acquainted with these plays of Maeterlinck's before his own play was published. But in dedicating it to Miss Maud Gonne, he stated that it was "planned out and begun some three years ago"—that is to say, before any of M. Maeterlinck's works were published, or at all events before the first rumour of them had crossed the Channel. The original conception and plan, then, which are quite as Maeterlinckian as any of the details, cannot owe anything to M. Maeterlinck. Unknown to each other, and almost simultaneously, the two poets must have sought and found a similar vehicle for expression. M. Maeterlinck, possessing, as I have said, the more distinctively dramatic talent, was the first to perfect his vehicle; and his example may very likely have been of assistance to Mr. Yeats. But it may with confidence be said that the similarity between them is much more truly attributable to general sympathy of spirit than to conscious, or even unconscious, imitation on Mr. Yeats's part.

A melancholy theme indeed is that of *The Countess Cathleen*. It can be told in a few words: The land is famine-stricken; Satan sends two demons in the guise of merchants to buy the souls of the starving peasants; the Countess Cathleen will sacrifice all her vast wealth, her

---

* An article by me entitled "A Pessimist Playwright" appeared in the *Fortnightly Review* for September 1891, and I believe Mr. George Moore had published an appreciation of Maeterlinck even earlier.

"gold and green forests," to save the people; but the emissaries of hell (the heavenly powers being apparently asleep) steal her treasure, becalm her ships, delay the passage of her flocks and herds; so that at last there is nothing for her to do but to sell her own soul and feed the people with the proceeds. The absolute impotence, the practical non-existence, of the powers of good, and the perfect ease with which the powers of evil execute their plots, render the play depressing almost to the point of exaspera-tion. It is true that at the end an Angel intervenes, and gives us to understand that Cathleen's soul is safe, because

> The Light of Lights
> Looks always on the motive, not the deed,
> The Shadow of Shadows on the deed alone.

But this is a tardy consolation to the reader, who feels, moreover, that Satan is not quite fairly dealt with, being baulked by a quibble, not openly encountered and van-quished. Oppressive melancholy, however, is the note of the folklore from which Mr. Yeats draws his inspiration; though in his delightful little book of prose, *The Celtic Twilight*, he seems inclined to contest the fact. Be this as it may, *The Countess Cathleen* (especially in its revised form) is as beautiful as it is sad. The blank verse has a monotonous, insinuating melody which is all its own, arising not only from the dainty simplicity of the diction, but from the pre-ponderance of final monosyllables and of what the professors of Shakespearometry call "end-stopped" lines. Mr. Yeats eschews all attempt to get dramatic force and variety into his verse by aid of the well-known tricks of frequent elisions, feminine endings, periodic structure, and all the rest of it. And herein he does well. No rush and tumult of versifi-cation could suit his mournful fantasies so perfectly as this crooning rhythm, this limpid melody, which seems, as Cyrano de Bergerac would say, to have a touch of the brogue in it.

Let me now note a few passages in which the resemblance to Maeterlinck is most apparent. The first scene takes place in the famine-stricken cabin of Shemus Rua, the personages being Shemus, his wife Maire, and their son Teig:

MAIRE.   Why did the house-dog bay?
SHEMUS. He heard me coming and smelt food—what else?
TEIG. We will not starve awhile.
SHEMUS.   What food is within?
TEIG. There is a bag half full of meal, a pan
    Half full of milk.
SHEMUS.   And we have Maive the hen.
TEIG. The pinewood were less hard.
MAIRE.   Before you came
    She made a great noise in the hencoop, Shemus.
    What fluttered in the window?
TEIG.   Two horned owls
    Have blinked and fluttered on the window sill
    From when the dog began to bay.
SHEMUS.   Hush, hush.

Who can fail to be reminded here of M. Maeterlinck's fondness for extracting eerie effects from the (alleged) sensitiveness of the animal kingdom to spritual presences? The baying of the dog and the fluttering of the hen are eminently Maeterlinckian— nly that in Maeterlinck the hen would be a swan. Think, for example, of the part played by the swans in *L'Intruse*, or of the fight of the dogs and the swans in *Pelléas et Mélisande*. The two owls, I should add, are not on the same plane as the dog and the hen, for they are the demons in disguise. They are first-cousins, not of M. Maeterlinck's swans, but of the poodle in *Faust*. Nevertheless, the passage is absolutely Maeterlinckian in effect; and so is the following:

MAIRE. Who knows what evil you have brought to us?
    I fear the wood things, Shemus.
                                [A knock at the door.
                                Do not open.

SHEMUS. A crown and twenty pennies are not enough
    To stop the hole that lets the famine in.

                                    [The little shrine falls.
MAIRE. Look! look!
SHEMUS [*crushing it underfoot*]. The Mother of God has dropped
    asleep,
    And all her household things have gone to wrack.
MAIRE. O Mary, Mother of God, be pitiful

              [SHEMUS *opens the door. Two* MERCHANTS
              stand without. They have bands of gold round
              their foreheads, and each carries a bag upon his
              shoulder.

The two Merchants are the owls of the previous passage,
in another disguise; and the falling of the shrine at their
approach is a piece of pure Maeterlinck. Take, again, the
following:

COUNTESS CATHLEEN. We must find out this castle in the wood
    Before the chill o' the night.

            [The MUSICIANS *begin to tune their instruments.*

                       Do not blame me,
    Good woman, for the tympan and the harp:
    I was bid fly the terror of the times
    And wrap me round with music and sweet song
    Or else pine to my grave. I have lost my way;
    Aleel, the poet who should know these woods,
    Because we met him on their border but now
    Wandering and singing like the foam of the sea,
    Is so wrapped up in dreams of terrors to come
    That he can give no help.
MAIRE [*Going to the door with her*]. Beyond the hazel
    Is a green shadowed pathway, and it goes
    To your great castle in malevolent woods.

Here the style is not at all that of Maeterlinck; but the
concluding phrase—the "great castle in malevolent woods"
depicts in five words the scene of half of M. Maeterlinck's
dramas. The old nurse Oona, too, is entirely in the spirit
of the author of *Les Aveugles* and the creator of so many

weird embodiments of pallid eld.   Take this for an
example :

OONA. Now lay your head once more upon my knees.
　　　I'll sing how Fergus drove his brazen cars.
　　　　　　　　　　　[*She chaunts with the thin voice of age.*
　　　　　Who will go drive with Fergus now,
　　　　　　And pierce the deep wood's woven shade,
　　　　　　　And dance upon the level shore ?
　　　　　Young man, lift up your russet brow,
　　　　　　And lift your tender eyelids, maid,
　　　　　　　And brood on hopes and fears no more.
　　　You have dropped down again into your trouble.
　　　You do not hear me.
CATHLEEN.　　　　　　　Ah, sing on, old Oona,
　　　I hear the horn of Fergus in my heart.
OONA. I do not know the meaning of the song.
　　　I am too old.
CATHLEEN.　　　　　The horn is calling, calling.
OONA.　　*And no more turn aside and brood*
　　　　　Upon Love's bitter mystery ;
　　　　　　For Fergus rules the brazen cars,
　　　　And rules the shadows of the wood,
　　　　And the white breast of the dim sea
　　　　　And all dishevelled wandering stars.

　　　*　　　*　　　*　　　*　　　*

　　　Why, you are weeping—and such tears !   Such tears !
　　　Look, child, how big they are.   Your shadow falls,
　　　O Weeping Willow of the World, O Eri,
　　　On this the loveliest daughter of your race,
　　　Your leaves blow round her.   I give God great thanks
　　　That I am old—lost in the sleep of age.*

Like Oona, " I do not know the meaning of the song," but
I know that it is beautiful ; and I know that Oona speaks
with the tongue of her aged sisters in the dramas of
M. Maeterlinck.

　　And here I am tempted to return for a moment to
the question of race-influence, suggested in the opening
paragraph of this essay.   M. Maeterlinck's swans and Mr.
Yeats's hen may stand in the relation of cause and effect, or

* These six lines do not appear in the 1901 edition of the play.

(as I rather believe) may be co-ordinate effects of similar psychological causes; but in any case there can be no possible doubt of the strong spiritual affinity between the two poets. Now mark the difficulty with which we are brought face to face. M. Maeterlinck, as a Fleming, is presumably of Teutonic race; while Mr. Yeats, as we know, is a Kelt of the Kelts. How do the critics who found their faith (like the lady in Dickens) upon "blood," account for this close brotherhood between men of two races which it is the fashion to regard as diametrically antagonistic to each other in the structure of their souls? Observe, too, that it is precisely in his most Keltic qualities that Mr. Yeats approximates most closely to M. Maeterlinck. The Teuton is, if possible, more Keltic than the Kelt. Are we to assume that some single far-off Keltic ancestor (perhaps one of the Irish soldiers in the army which "swore terribly in Flanders") lives again, by a freak of atavism, in M. Maeterlinck? There is nothing impossible in such a conjecture; but if we admit it in this case, we can scarcely exclude a similar conjecture in any other case.* And thus we strike at the root of all race-theorising by owning it impossible to assert, of any Western European, that the blood of any one of the great races flows untainted in his veins. Wherefore I suggest that, as a foundation for theories of the artistic temperament, blood is very little thicker than water.

Mr. Yeats's second play is less ambitious, but more evenly beautiful and successful, than his first. It is a flawless little poem, concentrating into a single scene the pure essence of Keltic folklore. The spirit of Irish legend may say with Cleopatra:

> I am fire and air ; my other elements
> I give to baser life—

---

* It is suggested that M. Maeterlinck may be a Walloon, and so of Keltic stock.

and this spirit has happily inspired Mr. Yeats in *The Land of Heart's Desire.* We are in the kitchen of a well-to-do peasant's cottage in the county of Sligo, one May-Day Eve at the end of the eighteenth century. Here are gathered old Maurteen Bruin, his shrewish wife Bridget, their son Shawn, his newly-married bride Mairë, and the white-haired priest Father Hart. Bridget scolds Mairë bitterly for poring over a yellow manuscript instead of going about her household tasks. Mairë is reading

> How a Princess Adene,
> A daughter of a King of Ireland, heard
> A voice singing on a May Eve like this,
> And followed, half awake and half asleep,
> Until she came into the land of faery,
> Where nobody gets old and godly and grave.
> Where nobody gets old and crafty and wise,
> Where nobody gets old and bitter of tongue ;
> And she is still there, busied with a dance,
> Deep in the dewy shadow of a wood,
> Or where stars walk upon a mountain-top.

The priest (in a speech the main part of which is quoted above) bids her not dwell on such fantasies, but seek her joys in the workaday world. Mairë strews primroses before the door to propitiate the "good people" who have power on May Eve ; but the wind "cries and hurries them away." Then a little old woman knocks at the door and asks for a basin of milk ; and presently a little old man demands a burning turf to light his pipe. Mairë grants both requests, thus "giving milk and fire" to the "good people," and bringing the house within their power for a whole year. When old Bridget scolds her, she bursts out :

> MAIRË BRUIN. Come, faeries, take me out of this dull house !
> Let me have all the freedom I have lost ;
> Work when I will and idle when I will !
> Faeries, come take me out of this dull world,
> For I would ride with you upon the wind,

> Run on the top of the dishevelled tide.
> And dance upon the mountains like a flame !
>
> FATHER HART. You cannot know the meaning of your words.
>
> MAIRË BRUIN. Father, I am right weary of four tongues:
> A tongue that is too crafty and too wise,
> A tongue that is too godly and too grave,
> A tongue that is more bitter than the tide,
> And a kind tongue too full of drowsy love,
> Of drowsy love and my captivity.

Then there comes to the door a child, dressed in a green jacket and red cap, so pretty and graceful that even the old people, the shrewish Bridget herself, give her tender welcome. She eats a little bite of bread and honey, she drinks a sip of milk; she persuades the old priest in her "wild, pretty prattle" to take down the ugly crucifix which frightens her.

> FATHER HART. Because you are so young and little a child
> I will go take it down.
>
> THE CHILD.   Hide it away,
> And cover it out of sight and out of mind.
>
> FATHER HART [to the others]. We must be tender with all budding
> things.
> Our Maker let no thought of Calvary
> Trouble the morning stars in their first song.

Then the child dances, "swaying about like the reeds," and presently, taking primroses from the great bowl on the table, she strews them in a circle round Mairë, saying :

> No one whose heart is heavy with human tears
> Can cross these little cressets of the wood.

By this time the elders have realised that they have to do with no human visitant, but with one of the "unholy creatures of the Raths."

> FATHER HART. Be not afraid, the Father is with us,
> And all the nine angelic hierarchies,
> The Holy Martyrs and the Innocents,

WILLIAM BUTLER YEATS

The adoring Magi in their coats of mail,
And He who died and rose on the third day,
And Mary with her seven times wounded heart.

[THE CHILD *ceases strewing the primroses, and kneels
upon the settle beside* MAIRË *and puts her arms
about her neck.*

Cry, daughter, to the Angels and the Saints.

THE CHILD. You shall go with me, newly-married bride,
And gaze upon a merrier multitude:
White-armed Nuala and Aengus of the birds,
And Feacra of the hurtling foam, and him
Who is the ruler of the western host,
Finvarra, and their Land of Heart's Desire,
Where beauty has no ebb, decay no flood,
But joy is wisdom, Time an endless song.
I kiss you and the world begins to fade.

The fairy-folk are the stronger, and here is the end of
the story:

MAIRË BRUIN. I will go with you.
FATHER HART.   She is lost, alas!
THE CHILD [*standing by the door*]. Then, follow: but the heavy
        body of clay
And clinging mortal hope must fall from you;
For we who ride the winds, run on the waves,
And dance upon the mountains, are more light
Than dewdrops on the banners of the dawn.
MAIRË BRUIN. Then take my soul.

[SHAWN BRUIN *goes over to her.*

SHAWN BRUIN.   Beloved, do not leave me!
Remember when I met you by the well
And took your hand in mine and spoke of love.
MAIRË BRUIN. Dear face! Dear voice!
THE CHILD.   Come, newly-married bride!
MAIRË BRUIN. I always loved her world—and yet—and yet—

[*Sinks into his arms.*

THE CHILD [*from the door*]. White bird, white bird, come with
        me, little bird!
MAIRË BRUIN, She calls my soul!
THE CHILD.   Come with me, little bird!

MAIRË BRUIN. I can hear songs and dancing!

SHAWN BRUIN. Stay with me!

MAIRË BRUIN. I think that I would stay—and yet—and yet—

THE CHILD. Come, little bird with crest of gold!

MAIRË BRUIN [*very softly*]. And yet—

THE CHILD. Come, little bird with silver feet!

[MAIRË *dies, and* THE CHILD *goes.*

SHAWN BRUIN. She is dead!

    *   *   *   *   *

A VOICE [sings outside]. *The wind blows out of the gates of the day,*
The wind blows over the lonely of heart,
And the lonely of heart is withered away
While the faeries dance in a place apart,
Shaking their milk-white feet in a ring,
Tossing their milk-white arms in the air;
For they hear the wind laugh and murmur and sing
Of a land where even the old are fair,
And even the wise are merry of tongue:
But I heard a reed of Coolaney say,
" When the wind has laughed and murmured and sung,
The lonely of heart is withered away."

No mere quotations, however, can do justice to the tender beauty of the little poem. Every word of it is right and delightful, and every word should be read in its place and re-read. There is a murmuring, cooing melody in the verse that familiarity renders only the more charming.

Talking of melody, however, I cannot but remark that Mr. Yeats is one of the poets who seem to despise accent—who ignore it, at all events, whenever they find it convenient. He is inordinately fond of putting a trochee (or, as Mr. Bridges would call it, inverting the stress) in the second foot in the line—a licence which even in Milton is very rare, and rarer still in other masters. The trochee is apt to be a present participle, as in Mairë Bruin's line

A voice singing on a May Eve like this.

Here the stress is inverted in both the second and the

third foot. The verse of *The Land of Heart's Desire* is much smoother, however, than that of *The Countess Cathleen* (even in its revised form), from which I will cull the following examples of this particular irregularity :

> A wing moving in all the famished woods, . . .
> And saw, sniffing the floor in a bare cow-house. . . .
> The noise wakened the household.   While you spoke.   . .
> Your eyes lighted, and the strange weariness. . . .
> Are not precious to God as your soul is. . . .
> So black, bitter, blinding and sudden a storm. . . .
> Have plucked thunder and lightning on our heads.*

In these lines we should have to read "mov-*ing*," "sniff-*ing*," "wak-*en'd*," "light-*ed*," "pre-*cious*," "bit-*ter*," and "thun-*der*," in order to avoid what is, to my ear, a marked cacophony. In one place Mr. Yeats actually inverts the final stress :

> We do but ask what each man has.   Merchants

thus producing a line of which the effect is, to me, about as pleasant as that of walking against a closed door in the dark. This question of accent in verse is discussed at some length in an earlier essay,† and I need not here repeat my argument.

Mr. Yeats's pure lyrics and ballads, too few in number, are full of beauty and charm.   I can only refer to a few of those which have most impressed me : the dedication *To Some I have Talked with by the Fire*, *To the Rose upon the Rood of Time*, *When You are Old*, *The White Birds*, *To Ireland in the Coming Time*, *The Lake Isle of Innisfree* (praised by Stevenson and quoted by Mr. Lucas), *The*

---

* In other poems we find :
> A king sitting upon a chair of gold. . . .
> And said, casting aside his draggled hair. . . .

Note that the trochee is much less jarring when, as in the last line, and in the second of those quoted above, it immediately follows a pause.

† Pages 315–327.

Stolen Child, and *The Ballad of Father O'Hart*. Other readers may prefer other poems; these are the ones which have taken most hold upon me. But the masterpiece of all, to my mind—an inspiration and a possession for ever—is this

DREAM OF A BLESSED SPIRIT

All the heavy days are over;
 Leave the body's coloured pride
Underneath the grass and clover,
 With the feet laid side by side.

One with her are mirth and duty;
 Bear the gold embroidered dress,
For she needs not her sad beauty,
 To the scented oaken press.

Hers the kiss of Mother Mary,
 The long hair shadows her face;
Still she goes with footsteps wary,
 Full of earth's old timid grace:

With white feet of angels seven
 Her white feet so glimmering;
And above the deep of heaven,
 Flame on flame and wing on wing.

This song originally formed part of *The Countess Cathleen*, being sung as a dirge at Cathleen's death, but with a totally different concluding stanza:

She goes down the floor of heaven
 Shining bright as a new lance,
And her guides are angels seven,
 While young stars about her dance.

Mr. Yeats's alterations, unlike those of most poets, are always amendments, but this is more than an amendment—it is a transfiguration. What a glorious moment it must have been in which the poet conceived that sudden soaring transition from the almost infantile tenderness of

With white feet of angels seven
Her white feet go glimmering,

to the rapturous vision of the close:

> *And above the deep of heaven,*
> *Flame on flame and wing on wing,*

Since the foregoing pages were written, Mr. Yeats has published two books: *The Wind among the Reeds*, a collection of lyrics, and *The Shadowy Waters*, a poem in dramatic form. In these his peculiar gifts of imagination and of utterance are seen at their best. He extracts from a simple and rather limited vocabulary effects of the rarest delicacy and distinction. There is a certain appearance of mannerism, no doubt, in Mr. Yeats's individuality. One can scarcely turn a page of these books without coming upon the epithets "dim," "glimmering," "wandering," "pearl-pale," "dove-grey," "dew-dropping," and the like. His imagery is built up out of a very few simple elements, which he combines and re-combines unweariedly. The materials he employs, in short, are those of primitive folk-poetry; but he touches them to new and often marvellous beauty. What in our haste we take for mannerism may be more justly denominated style, the inevitable accent of his genius.

Is it mere mannerism, for instance, that constitutes the haunting individuality of such "swallow flights of song" as the following?

AEDH TELLS OF THE PERFECT BEAUTY.

> O cloud-pale eyelids, dream-dimmed eyes,
> The poets labouring all their days
> To build a perfect beauty in rhyme
> Are overthrown by a woman's gaze
> And by the unlabouring brood of the skies:
> And therefore my heart will bow, when dew
> Is dropping sleep, until God burn time,
> Before the unlabouring stars and you.

POETS OF THE YOUNGER GENERATION

AEDH THINKS OF THOSE WHO HAVE SPOKEN EVIL OF HIS BELOVED.

Half close your eyelids, loosen your hair,
And dream about the great and their pride;
They have spoken against you everywhere,
But weigh this song with the great and their pride;
I made it out of a mouthful of air,
Their children's children shall say they have lied.

The Shadowy Waters, it seems to me, is in reality a ballad in dialogue rather than a drama; and I am not sure but that it would gain by being cast in ballad form. At the same time, it contains some very beautiful writing, such as this passage from the prologue:

How shall I name you, immortal, mild proud shadows?
I only know that all we know comes from you,
And that you come from Eden on flying feet.
Is Eden far away, or do you hide
From human thought, as hares and mice and coneys
That run before the reaping-hook and lie
In the last ridge of the barley? Do our woods
And winds and ponds cover more quiet woods,
More shining winds, more star-glimmering ponds?

I wish I could feel certain that the last line was corrupt. Unfortunately, it is quite possible that Mr. Yeats wrote it, and thought it was blank verse. But when one finds a halting line in this poet's work, there is always the consolation that he may very likely emend it in the next edition.

One other word, and I have done. It appears from the notes to *The Wind in the Reeds*, rather than from the poems themselves, that Mr Yeats is becoming more and more addicted to a petrified, fossilised symbolism, a system of hieroglyphs which may have had some inherent significance for their inventors, but which have now become matters of research, of speculation, of convention. I cannot but regard this tendency as ominous. His art cannot gain and may very easily lose by it. A conventional symbol may be of the greatest interest to the anthropologist or the antiquary; for the poet it can have no value. If a symbol does not spring spontaneously from his own imagination and express an analogy borne in upon his own spiritual perception, he may treasure it in his mental museum, but he ought not to let such a piece of inert matter cumber the seed-plot of his poetry.

THE LAKE ISLE OF INNISFREE.

I will arise and go now, and go to Innisfree,
And a small cabin build there, of clay and wattles made;
Nine bean rows will I have there, a hive for the honey-bee,
And live alone in the bee-loud glade.

And I shall have some peace there, for peace comes dropping
    slow;
Dropping from the veils of morning to where the cricket
    sings;
There midnight's all a glimmer, and noon a purple glow,
And evening full of the linnet's wings.

I will arise and go now, for always night and day
I hear lake water lapping with low sounds by the shore;
While I stand on the roadway, or on the pavements gray,
I hear it in the deep heart's core.

INTO THE TWILIGHT.

Out-worn heart, in a time out-worn,
Come clear of the nets of wrong and right;
Laugh heart again in the gray twilight,
Sigh, heart, again in the dew of the morn.

Your mother Eire is always young,
Dew ever shining and twilight gray;
Though hope fall from you and love decay,
Burning in fires of a slanderous tongue.

WILLIAM BUTLER YEATS

Come, heart, where hill is heaped upon hill:
For there the mystical brotherhood
Of the sun and moon and hollow and wood
And river and stream work out their will;

And God stands winding His lonely horn,
And time and the world are ever in flight;
And love is less kind than the gray twilight
And hope is less dear than the dew of the morn.

THE FIDDLER OF DOONEY.

When I play on my fiddle in Dooney,
Folk dance like a wave of the sea;
My cousin is priest in Kilvarnet,
My brother in Moharabuiee.

I passed my brother and cousin;
They read in their books of prayer;
I read in my book of songs
I bought at the Sligo fair.

When we come at the end of time
To Peter sitting in state,
He will smile on the three old spirits,
But call me first through the gate;

For the good are always merry,
Save by an evil chance,
And the merry love the fiddle
And the merry love to dance:

And when the folk there spy me,
They will all come up to me,
With " Here is the fiddler of Dooney! "
And dance like a wave of the sea.

BIBLIOGRAPHICAL APPENDIX

[The lists here given do not pretend to be complete bibliographies of the poetical works of the authors in question, but enumerate only the books mentioned in the text.]

BEECHING, HENRY CHARLES.
In a Garden, and other Poems. London, John Lane. 1895.
St. Augustine at Ostia. London, John Lane. 1896.

BENSON, ARTHUR CHRISTOPHER.
Poems. London, John Lane. 1893.
Lyrics. London, John Lane. 1895.
Lord Vyet and other Poems. London, John Lane. 1897.

BINYON, ROBERT LAURENCE.
Persephone. *The Newdigate Poem*, 1890. Oxford, B. H. Blackwell. 1890.
Lyric Poems. London, Mathews & Lane. 1894.
Poems. Oxford, Daniel. 1895.
London Visions ("Shilling Garland"). London, Elkin Mathews. 1896.
The Praise of Life ("Shilling Garland"). London, Elkin Mathews. 1896.
Porphyrion, and other Poems. London, Grant Richards. 1898.

BROWN, ALICE.
The Road to Castaly. Boston, Copeland & Day. 1896.

CARMAN, BLISS.
Low Tide on Grand Pré: a Book of Lyrics, London, D. Nutt; New York, Webster & Co. 1893.
Behind the Arras: a Book of the Unseen. Boston, Lamson & Wolffe. 1895.
Ballads of Lost Haven. Boston, Lamson & Wolffe. 1897.
By the Aurelian Wall, and other Elegies. Boston, Lamson, Wolffe & Co. 1898.

BIBLIOGRAPHICAL APPENDIX

CARMAN, BLISS, and HOVEY, RICHARD.
Songs from Vagabondia. London, Mathews & Lane ; Boston, Copeland & Day. 1894.
More Songs from Vagabondia. Boston, Copeland & Day. 1896.

CAWEIN, MADISON JULIUS.
Days and Dreams. 1891.
Moods and Memories. 1892.
Poems of Nature and Love. 1893.
Red Leaves and Roses. 1893.
Intimations of the Beautiful. 1894.

    All published by G. P. Putnam's Sons, New York and London.

Undertones. Boston, Copeland & Day. 1896.
Idyllic Monologues. Louisville, J. P. Morton & Co. 1898.
Myth and Romance. London and New York, G. P. Putman's Sons, 1899.

COUCH, ARTHUR THOMAS QUILLER.
Athens: a Poem. Bodmin, Liddell & Son. [1881.]
Green Bays: Verses and Parodies. London, Methuen & Co. 1893.
Poems and Ballads. London, Methuen & Co. 1896.

DAVIDSON, JOHN.
Bruce: a Drama in Five Acts. Glasgow, Wilson & McCormick. 1886.
Smith: a Tragedy. Glasgow, F. W. Wilson & Bro. 1888.
Plays: An Unhistorical Pastoral, A Romantic Farce, Scaramouch in Naxos. Greenock, J. Davidson. 1889.
Scaramouch in Naxos, A Pantomime, and other Plays. Second Edition. London, T. Fisher Unwin. 1890.
Plays. [All the above Plays in one volume.] London, Mathews & Lane. 1894.
In a Music-Hall, and other Poems. London, Ward & Downey. 1891.
Fleet Street Eclogues. London, Mathews & Lane. 1893.
Ballads and Songs. London, John Lane. 1894.
A Second Series of Fleet Street Eclogues. London, John Lane. 1896.
New Ballads. London and New York, John Lane. 1897.
Godfrida: a Play. New York and London, John Lane. 1898.
The Last Ballad, and other Poems. London and New York, John Lane. 1899.

POETS OF THE YOUNGER GENERATION

HINKSON, KATHARINE TYNAN.
> *Louise de la Vallière, and other Poems.* London, Kegan Paul & Co. 1885.
> *Shamrocks.* London, Kegan Paul & Co. 1887.
> *Ballads and Lyrics.* London, Kegan Paul & Co. 1891.
> *Cuckoo Songs.* London, Mathews & Lane. 1894.
> *A Lover's Breast-Knot.* London, Elkin Mathews. 1896.
> *The Wind in the Trees : a Book of Country Verse.* London, Grant Richards. 1898.

HOPPER, NORA (Mrs. Chesson).
> *Under Quicken Boughs.* London, John Lane. 1896.
> *Songs of the Morning.* London, Grant Richards. 1900.

HOUSMAN, ALFRED EDWARD.
> *A Shropshire Lad.* London, Kegan Paul & Co. ; New York, John Lane. 1896.
>> Second Edition. London, Grant Richards. 1898.

HOUSMAN, LAURENCE.
> *Green Arras.* London, John Lane. 1896.
> *All Fellows : Seven Legends of Lower Redemption, with insets of Verse.* London, Kegan Paul & Co. 1896.
> *Spikenard : a Book of Devotional Love-Poems.* London, Grant Richards. 1898.

HOVEY, RICHARD.
> *Launcelot and Guinevere : a Poem in Dramas.* New York, United States Book Co. 1891.
> *Along the Trail : a Book of Lyrics.* Boston, Small, Maynard & Co. 1898.
> See also under CARMAN, BLISS.

KIPLING, RUDYARD.
> *Departmental Ditties.* First Edition. Lahore. 1886. Numerous reprints published in England and America.
> *Barrack-Room Ballads and other Verses.* London, Methuen & Co. 1892.
> *The Seven Seas.* London, Methuen & Co. 1896.

LE GALLIENNE, RICHARD.
> *English Poems.* London, Mathews & Lane. 1892.
> *Robert Louis Stevenson : an Elegy, and other Poems, mainly Personal.* London, John Lane. 1895.
> *Rubáiyát of Omar Khayyám : a Paraphrase from several Literal Translations.* London, Grant Richards. 1897.

BIBLIOGRAPHICAL APPENDIX

MEYNELL, ALICE CHRISTIANA.
Poems. London, Mathews & Lane. 1893.

MONEY-COUTTS, FRANCIS BURDETT.
Poems. London, John Lane. 1896.
The Revelation of St. Love the Divine. London, John Lane. 1898.
The Alhambra, and other Poems, London, John Lane. 1898.

NESBIT, EDITH (Mrs. Bland).
Lays and Legends. Two Series. London, Longmans & Co. 1886, 1892.
Leaves of Life. London, Longmans & Co. 1888.
A Pomander of Verse. London, John Lane. 1895.
Songs of Love and Empire. London, A. Constable & Co. 1898.

NEWBOLT, HENRY.
Mordred: a Tragedy. London, T. Fisher Unwin. 1895.
Admirals All, and other Verses ("Shilling Garland"). London, Elkin Mathews. 1897.
The Island Race. London, Elkin Mathews. 1898.

PHILLIPS, STEPHEN.
Primavera: Poems by four Authors (Stephen Phillips, Laurence Binyon, Manmohan Ghose, Arthur S. Cripps). Oxford, B. H. Blackwell. 1890.
Eremus: a Poem. London, Kegan Paul & Co. 1894.
Christ in Hades, and other Poems ("Shilling Garland"). London, Elkin Mathews. 1896.
Poems. London and New York, John Lane. 1898.
Paolo and Francesca; a Tragedy in Four Acts. London and New York, John Lane. 1900.
Herod: a Tragedy. London, John Lane. 1901.

RADFORD, DOLLIE.
A Light Load, London, Elkin Mathews. 1891 and 1897.
Songs and other Verses. London, John Lane. 1895.

ROBERTS, CHARLES GEORGE DOUGLAS.
Orion, and other Poems. Philadelphia, Lippincott & Co. 1880.
In Divers Tones. Boston, D. Lothrop & Co. [1887.]
Songs of the Common Day, and Ave! an Ode for the Shelley Centenary. London, Longmans & Co. 1893.
The Book of the Native. Boston, Lamson, Wolffe & Co. 1896.
New York Nocturnes, and other Poems. Boston, Lamson, Wolffe & Co. 1898.

S<small>ANTAYANA</small>, G<small>EORGE</small>.
> *Sonnets and other Verses.* Cambridge [Mass.] and Chicago, Stone & Kimball. 1874.

S<small>COTT</small>, D<small>UNCAN</small> C<small>AMPBELL</small>.
> *The Magic House, and other Poems.* Ottawa, J. Durie & Sons; London, Methuen & Co. 1893.
> *Labor and the Angel.* Boston, Copeland & Day. 1898.

S<small>IGERSON</small>, D<small>ORA</small> (Mrs. Shorter).
> *The Fairy Changeling, and other Poems.* London and New York, John Lane. 1898.
> *Ballads and Poems.* London, J. Bowden. 1899.

S<small>YMONS</small>, A<small>RTHUR</small>.
> *Days and Nights.* London, Macmillan & Co. 1899.
> *Silhouettes.* London, Mathews & Lane. 1892.
> *London Nights.* London, L. C. Smithers. 1895.
> *Amoris Victima.* London, L. C. Smithers. 1897.

T<small>ABB</small>, J<small>OHN</small> B.
> *Poems.* London, John Lane; Boston, Copeland & Day. 1894.
> *Lyrics.* Boston, Copeland & Day; London, John Lane. 1897.

T<small>HOMPSON</small>, F<small>RANCIS</small>.
> *Poems.* London, Mathews & Lane. 1893.
> *Sister Songs: an Offering to Two Sisters.* London, John Lane. 1895.
> *New Poems.* Westminster, Constable & Co. 1897.

T<small>RENCH</small>, F<small>REDERIC</small> H<small>ERBERT</small>.
> *Deirdre Wed, and other Poems.* London, Methuen & Co. 1901.

W<small>ATSON</small>, R<small>OSAMUND</small> M<small>ARRIOTT</small>.
> *The Bird Bride: a Volume of Ballads and Sonnets.* London, Longmans & Co. 1889.
> *A Summer Night, and other Poems.* London, Methuen & Co. 1891.
> *Vespertilia, and other Verses.* London, John Lane. 1895.

W<small>ATSON</small>, W<small>ILLIAM</small>.
> *The Prince's Quest, and other Poems.* London, Kegan Paul & Co. 1880. New Edition, Mathews & Lane. 1893.
> *Epigrams of Art, Life, and Nature.* Liverpool, G. G. Walmsley. 1884.
> *Wordsworth's Grave, and other Poems* ("Cameo Series"). London, T. Fisher Unwin. 1889.
> *Poems.* London, Macmillan & Co. 1892.

BIBLIOGRAPHICAL APPENDIX

WATSON, WILLIAM—*continued.*

Lachrymæ Musarum, and other Poems.　London, Macmillan & Co.
1893.

The Eloping Angels: a Caprice.　London, Mathews & Lane.
1893.

Odes, and other Poems.　London, John Lane.　1894.

The Father of the Forest, and other Poems.　London, John Lane.
1895.

The Purple East: a Series of Sonnets on England's Desertion of Armenia.　London, John Lane.　1896.

The Year of Shame.　London and New York, John Lane.　1897.

The Hope of the World, and other Poems.　London and New York, John Lane.　1898.

Collected Poems.　London, John Lane.　1899.

WOODS, MARGARET LOUISE.

Lyrics.　Oxford, H. Daniel.　1888.

Lyrics and Ballads.　London, Bentley & Son.　1889.

Songs.　Oxford, H. Daniel.　1896.

Aëromancy, and other Poems ("Shilling Garland").　London, Elkin Mathews.　1896.

Wild Justice: a Dramatic Poem.　London, Smith & Elder.　1896.

YEATS, WILLIAM BUTLER.

The Wanderings of Oisin, and other Poems.　London; Kegan Paul & Co.　1889.

The Countess Kathleen: an Irish Drama; and various Legends and Lyrics ("Cameo Series").　London, T. Fisher Unwin.
1892.

The Land of Heart's Desire.　London, T. Fisher Unwin.　1894.

Poems.　London, T. Fisher Unwin.　1895.

Poems.　London, T. Fisher Unwin.　1899.

The Wind among the Reeds.　London, Elkin Mathews.　1899.

The Shadowy Waters.　London, Hodder & Stoughton.　1900.